Between the Ropes
at Madison Square Garden

ALSO BY MARK ALLEN BAKER

The Fighting Times of Abe Attell (McFarland, 2018)

*Battling Nelson, the Durable Dane:
World Lightweight Champion,
1882–1954* (McFarland, 2017)

Between the Ropes at Madison Square Garden

The History of an Iconic Boxing Ring, 1925–2007

Mark Allen Baker

McFarland & Company, Inc., Publishers
Jefferson, North Carolina

ISBN (print) 978-1-4766-7183-3
ISBN (ebook) 978-1-4766-3722-8

LIBRARY OF CONGRESS AND BRITISH LIBRARY
CATALOGUING DATA ARE AVAILABLE

Library of Congress Control Number: 2019942369

© 2019 Mark Allen Baker. All rights reserved

No part of this book may be reproduced or transmitted in any form or by any means, electronic or mechanical, including photocopying or recording, or by any information storage and retrieval system, without permission in writing from the publisher.

Front cover image © 2019 Shutterstock

Printed in the United States of America

McFarland & Company, Inc., Publishers
Box 611, Jefferson, North Carolina 28640
www.mcfarlandpub.com

To the next generation:
Elliott Mark Baker, Paisley Renee Taylor,
and Elijah Michael Lane.

Live! Live the wonderful life that is in you!
Let nothing be lost upon you.
Be always searching for new sensations.
Be afraid of nothing.
—Oscar Wilde

Table of Contents

Acknowledgments   ix
Preface   1
Introduction   3

1. The Early Years of New York City Boxing, 1871–1889   7
2. Madison Square Garden II, 1890–1919   14
3. Rickard's Roost, 1920–1924   22
4. City Ring, 1925 until January 6, 1929   29
5. Dealing with the Loss, January 7, 1929–1934   41
6. Depression-Era Boxing, 1935–1939   56
7. World War II and a City Ring, 1940–1945   75
8. So, Where Were We? 1946–1949   98
9. The Marciano Era, 1950–1955   111
10. Exercising Control, 1956–1959   132
11. A Cloud of Uncertainty, 1960–1962   145
12. "I Must Be the Greatest," 1963–1967   155
13. In the Eye of the Storm, 1968–1969   169
14. New York City Serenade, 1970–1976   176
15. Fade Away, 1977–1978   193
16. Your Kingdom Come, 1979–1985   201
17. Iron Mike, 1986–1990   220
18. Comfortably Numb, 1991–1996   231
19. Captain Hook, 1997–2002   250

20. The Final Rounds, 2003–2007	264
21. Retirement, September 19, 2007	274
Appendix I: Boxing Lineal Heavyweight Champions	283
Appendix II: Noteworthy Ring Adjustments	285
Chapter Notes	287
Bibliography	305
Index	307

Acknowledgments

Thankfully, I was never in the City Ring alone with this task. I had assistance every step of the way and am grateful to so many for their assistance in this work. Please allow me to sing the praises of a few.

Those who know me know of my proud association with the International Boxing Hall of Fame in Canastota, New York. My service has been particularly rewarding because of some incredible individuals: Edward Brophy, Jeffrey S. Brophy, Chris Bowers, Rachel Shaw, and Mike Delaney. I would like to single out in particular the efforts of Jeffrey S. Brophy for his outstanding research and ongoing friendship.

This book would not have been possible without the assistance of the Library of Congress and their Digital Collections and Services staff. Chronicling America, a Web site providing access to information about historic newspapers and select digitized newspaper pages, was also useful. All the images included in this work are sourced through the Library of Congress or the author's private collection.

I owe a debt of gratitude, as well, to the following boxing promoters, who were kind enough to share information with me: Bob Arum, Top Rank; Jimmy Burchfield, Classic Entertainment & Sports; Joe DeGuardia, Star Boxing; Lou DiBella, DiBella Entertainment; Oscar De La Hoya, Golden Boy Promotions; Cathy Duva of Main Events; Don King, Don King Productions; and Russell Peltz, Peltz Boxing.

My sincere appreciation to everyone associated with the Madison Square Garden Company (MSG). For presenting a global standard for excellence in live experiences and creating indelible connections with diverse and passionate audiences that span generations, there is no better representative.

To the hundreds who appear in the Bibliography, and to all the individuals pictured inside, I am so very grateful to share this work with you.

Living in the historic state of Connecticut, I am fortune to have a great support system. My gratitude to all of the independent bookstores in Connecticut, especially Bank Square Books in Mystic (Annie Philbrick, Elissa Englund), and Book Club Bookstore & More in South Windsor (Cynde Acanto). Also, my appreciation to Larry Dasilva (Nutmeg TV), Larry Rifkin (WATR), Wayne Norman (WILI), Ryan Kristafer and Teresa Dufour (CTSTYLE, on ABC 8), Nathan Grube (The Travelers), Don Trella (*Mohegan Sun*), Glenn Feldman (CT-BHOF), Amanda Brouwer (Douglas Library of Hebron) and Geeta S. Sandberg (*Rivereast News Bulletin*) for their contributions to my work. Also, thanks to my friends Dana Beck and Brian Brinkman, Kelly and Dennis DiGiovanni, Ann and Mark Lepkowski, and Jim Risley.

To my family: Marilyn Allen Baker; Aaron, Sharon and Elliott Baker; Mark, Elizabeth and Paisley Taylor; Brad, Rebecca and Elijah Lane; and especially Debra and Dick Long, thank you for your love and support. To Richard Long, my wonderful father-in-law, who has always been a second in my corner, I extend my sincere appreciation. In memory of Ford William Baker, James Buford Bird, Flavil Q. Van Dyke III, Deborah Jean Long and David Arthur Mumper.

To my wife Alison, "Missing you is my hobby, caring for you is my job, making you happy is my duty and loving you is my life." I could not be more appreciative.

Preface

During the 20th century, Madison Square Garden was to New York City what the Colosseum or Flavian Amphitheatre was to the city of Rome in ancient times. It was renowned for its public spectacles, and none were more vivid than the gladiatorial contests. Similarly, for boxing fans, each of the four iterations of the Garden was a treasure trove of indelible memories.

Generations were raised around its history, as Garden milestones marked key events in a family's history: a grandfather recalling taking his son to see Willie Pep in his final appearance at the Garden in 1955; a father taking his son to witness Cassius Clay in his initial appearance at the venue back in 1962; and a grandson taking his son, which could be any of us, to watch Roberto Durán, on his 32nd birthday in 1983, defeat Davey Moore.

When Madison Square Garden announced on September 19, 2007, that it was retiring one of its most treasured artifacts, a boxing ring, and donating it to the International Boxing Hall of Fame in Canastota, New York, it was nearly beyond belief. Ever since I first saw it, I wanted to tell its story. I wanted to crawl between the ropes, put my ear to the canvas and listen. I just wanted to hear the accelerated heartbeats of the fighters, the screams from their seconds in their corners, the crunching resonance made by the flesh and bones hitting the canvas. Selfishly, I wanted to know every detail.

Looking everywhere for a book about this unforgettable confinement, the City Ring, I found nothing. Not certain anyone had ever written a book about a single boxing artifact, I grew tired of searching. There were good books about Madison Square Garden, but none that put this extraordinary stage into perspective. As the author of many books about the fight game, including *TITLE TOWN, USA: Boxing in Upstate New York*; *Battling Nelson: The Durable Dane*; and *The Fighting Times of Abe Attell*, I pondered my next move. Do I dare write a book about an inanimate object? But as the only person to serve the International Boxing Hall of Fame as a historian, chairperson, sponsor, volunteer and biographer, I believed it was my obligation.

How to structure the book was right in front of me. Even before the fight game was legal, boxing was being presented in the original Garden as "exhibitions" or "illustrated lectures." Although the venue stayed in the same place, pugilism evolved. Contests were being conducted, traditions were being formed, personalities were emerging and history was being written in the second version of the Garden, located at 26th Street and Madison Avenue in Manhattan. In the third iteration of the indoor arena, located on Eighth Avenue between 49th and 50th streets, the fight game was a matter of performance. Every famous boxer of the era fought inside the City Ring. For the current Garden, located in Midtown Manhattan between Seventh and Eighth avenues from 31st to 33rd streets, boxing need only look as far as tradition. The biggest names in boxing wanted to fight in the Garden, because their heroes fought there, and their heroes' heroes fought inside the City Ring. History, performance and tradition, the perfect recipe for success.

Hundreds of days, and over eight thousand hours of reading, produced multiple databases and detailed research that progressed to over a quarter of a million characters of an initial manuscript. Through my fact-finding, I've gained a new perspective on the fight game and unearthed many forgotten battles and gladiators. The results of this work I will share with you. I wrote this book for every boxing fan, from city gentry, dressed to the nines, who saw "The Fight of the Century" on March 8, 1971, to the ring zealot who took the bus from Syracuse to New York to watch hometown favorite Joey DeJohn face Pete Mead inside the Garden on February 25, 1949.

Space alone prohibited me from including every fight or fighter, so I focused on the most memorable, many of which were championship fights. But outstanding fights were not always the main events, so some fabulous undercards were also included. A cursory glance at the bibliography will reveal the wealth of materials I had access to—from film and videotape, to press kits and Security and Exchange Commission filings, resources weren't hard to find.

Although the frequency of Garden fights fell off during the end of the last century, this boxing history will allow you a better understanding of the significance of the Garden fights that were held during the final years of the City Ring.

So, drop into your recliner, hum the theme music to *The Gillette Cavalcade of Sports*, and enjoy the finest moments of the fight game. A boxing ring can't talk, but if it could, this would be its tale.

A Note to the Reader

Commonly known today as the "traditional divisions," the following were the only weight classes for the early 20th century, before the numerous "super," "junior" and "light" classes were added: Flyweight, 112 lbs.; Bantamweight, 118 lbs.; Featherweight, 126 lbs.; Lightweight, 135 lbs.; Welterweight, 147 lbs.; Middleweight, 160 lbs.; Light Heavyweight, 175 lbs. and Heavyweight, unlimited.

In addition, sanctioning organizations are mentioned throughout the text, sometimes in abbreviated form. Each is listed below for convenience, along with the year of its founding.

WBA (World Boxing Association)—1962 (1921 as the National Boxing Association)
WBC (World Boxing Council)—1963
IBF (International Boxing Federation)—1983
NBA (National Boxing Association)—1984
WBF (World Boxing Federation)—1988
WBO (World Boxing Organization)—1988
IBC (International Boxing Council)—1990
IWBF (International Women's Boxing Federation)—1992
IBO (International Boxing Organization)—1993
WIBF (Women's International Boxing Federation)—1995
IFBA (International Female Boxers Association)—1997

Introduction

If you were to choose one item that reflects the entire history of the twentieth century, what would it be?

Selecting a single item, so powerful that its narrative speaks for itself, would not be easy. Ideally it would be a universal object, diverse enough to encompass every aspect of who and what we were. Like some symbols, it may not have been conceived as an iconic representation, but over time evolved into one. Think about it for a minute.

Not immediately obvious would be a boxing ring. And not just any confinement, but the one used inside Madison Square Garden. The (New York) "City Ring," which now rests in Canastota, New York, *was* boxing during this era. But did it represent even more?

What elements were necessary to transform a piece of sports equipment into a metaphor for our culture? How have circumstances enhanced its meaning? How can a symbol communicate an idea?

The history of the (New York) City Ring was important because it allows us to understand our past, which in turn permits us to comprehend our present. Its history answers how and why our world is the way it is today.

Since boxing—composed of numerous divisions segmented by weight—has always looked to the heavyweight division, its oldest weight class, as being its most evocative, it makes the perfect beginning. The Heavyweight Championship of the World has historically been its most coveted title, and as many believe, the most prestigious in all of sport. As such, it is not a surprise to learn that most of those who have held the lineal title have fought inside Madison Square Garden.

There have been four iterations of the historic venue. Each of them has added richly to the history, performance and tradition the name represents. And it was these three ingredients that enabled the City Ring to become an iconic symbol of our culture:

History

Madison Square was constituted by the intersection of Fifth Avenue and Broadway at 23rd Street in Manhattan. The public plaza was named after James Madison, fourth president of the United States. Two venues were located just northeast of the square, the first from 1879 to 1890, and the second from 1890 to 1925. The location, as Commodore Vanderbilt recognized, was perfect. As the original venue had no roof and was inconvenient for use during inclement weather, it was demolished after 11 years.

The second iteration of Madison Square Garden was designed by the noted architect

Stanford White and was far more elegant. Like the original venue, it too outgrew its walls, and the New York Life Insurance Company, which held the mortgage on it, tore it down in 1925. The legacy of Madison Square Garden—or its brand, if you will—was created from these two sites.

Boxing, during this period, resonated with urban ethnicity, yet struggled with a legality issue. But that didn't deter the popularity of the sport. The Walker Law, passed in 1920, was an early New York State law regulating boxing. It reestablished legal boxing in the state following the three-year ban.

Although boxing promotion was in its infancy, Tex Rickard, an early advocate, was instrumental in bringing boxing to a whole new audience. All he lacked was a venue he could call home, and he would find that with the third iteration of Madison Square Garden.

To stay relevant, especially in the area of boxing, traditions evolved. For example, among the game's lineal heavyweight champions who sanctified the venue were the pugilists John L. Sullivan, James J. Corbett, Bob Fitzsimmons, Marvin Hart, Jess Willard and Jack Dempsey.

Performance

A third Madison Square Garden was inaugurated in a different location, on Eighth Avenue between 49th and 50th streets, from 1925 to 1968. Groundbreaking on the third Madison Square Garden took place on January 9, 1925. As its impresario was George Lewis "Tex" Rickard, the arena was appropriately dubbed "The House That Tex Built."

Rickard was a brilliant businessman and founder of the New York Rangers of the National Hockey League (NHL). He had established himself as a boxing promoter, and Madison Square Garden gave him an epicenter to work from, and a brand to work with. His seasonal (marketing) approach to managing a venue created a precedent that was followed for decades. Although his time at this iteration of the Garden was short-lived, Tex Rickard polished his image as the leading impresario of the day, and was often compared to P.T. Barnum.

Associated with the history and the name of Madison Square Garden, the City Ring was born from this location. Built to specifications defined by the sport, the piece of equipment would have been just another roped confinement if it weren't for its home. This was where most of the performances that would to catapult the ring into legendary status took place. Primarily an indoor fixture, the City Ring was on call, be it fully or partially assembled, to its owner.

Memorable, recognizable, and without an equivalent, Jack Dempsey became Rickard's brand equity. Like his predecessor John L. Sullivan, the talented pugilist had an enormous impact on whether the fight game prospered. The pugilist also fits perfectly into the Garden scheme, even though he never fought inside this iteration (Dempsey's star power had outgrown indoor facilities).

Following Rickard's recipe, Mike Jacobs would replace Dempsey with Joe Louis. Of the lineal heavyweight champions who anointed the venue, not to mention the City Ring, were Gene Tunney, Max Schmeling, Jack Sharkey, Primo Carnera, Max Baer, James J. Braddock, Louis, Ezzard Charles, Jersey Joe Walcott, Rocky Marciano, Floyd Patterson and Cassius Clay.

It too exceeded its capacity to meet demand, and its demolition commenced in 1968, after the opening of the current Garden. The structure was among the first of its kind to be built above the platforms of an active railroad station. Irving Mitchell Felt, who purchased the air rights from the Pennsylvania Railroad, tore down the above-ground portions of the original Pennsylvania Station, located at 4 Pennsylvania Plaza in Manhattan. The fourth and current Madison Square Garden opened on February 11, 1968.

Tradition

As Madison Square Garden spanned generations, it created incomparable memories, such as "The Fight." Tradition, a factor that can't be bought but must be earned, remained a key attraction to Madison Square Garden. The lineal heavyweight boxing champions who blessed the venue, not to mention the City Ring, included Joe Frazier, George Foreman, Muhammad Ali, Leon Spinks, Larry Holmes, Mike Tyson, James "Buster" Douglas, Evander Holyfield, Riddick Bowe, Shannon Briggs, Lennox Lewis, Hasim Rahman and Wladimir Klitschko.

As a form of entertainment, boxing has always played into the economics of venues of all types, including casinos, or public rooms or buildings where gambling games are played. This became more apparent during the latter half of the last century, when the revenue generation capacity of gambling justified a casino's paying pugilists more for their services. Institutions that do not have this revenue generating capacity, such as Madison Square Garden, were forced to follow a different business model.[1] And they have successfully done just that.

It's no surprise to learn that many pugilists contributed to the rich history of the City Ring. Of the top fifty fighters, as chosen by boxing historian Bert Randolph Sugar in his epic *Boxing's Greatest Fighters*, forty-two fought inside Madison Square Garden. The names include Sugar Ray Robinson, Henry Armstrong, Willie Pep, Joe Louis, Harry Greb, Benny Leonard, Muhammad Ali, Roberto Durán, Jack Dempsey, Mickey Walker, Tony Canzoneri, Rocky Marciano, Joe Gans, Sam Langford, Julio César Chávez, Barney Ross, Jimmy McLarnin, Archie Moore, Marcel Cerdan, Ezzard Charles, Sugar Ray Leonard, and many more. Of that same top fifty list, Sugar Ray Robinson, George Foreman, Evander Holyfield and Pernell Whitaker fought their very first professional fights inside the City Ring, while Harry Greb, Benny Leonard, Tony Canzoneri, and Jimmy McLarnin hung up the mitts following their last duel inside of it.[2]

City Ring

The altar of pugilism, from 1925 until 2007, was the (New York) City Ring. Within its ropes, and upon its surface, was where the physical prowess of the finest gladiators consecrated the fight game. At times the City Ring typified a new life, a way out of poverty for some. But it could also represent the final landscape, or death. No other single table of humanity offered so much opportunity, or destroyed so many dreams more quickly.

As a tangible symbol, this historic artifact has communicated the intangible (ideas, values, feelings) through the contrasts of its participants. These attributes have included age, gender, physicality, titles, ethnicity, religion, class, desire and even citizenship. The City Ring's 132 assembled pieces represent the most accurate reflection of who we were during the twentieth century. While entire books have been written about the symbolism of a single Madison Square Garden conflict, no book has ever been written about its sacred battleground. There was no better portrait of a sport or our society than the (New York) City Ring, and there never will be.

1

The Early Years of New York City Boxing, 1871–1889

> We do not desire prize fighting in America. It never was admired by the better classes of our citizens; and, although we have had prize fights time and again in the land, they have always been witnessed by the lowest and most depraved classes of society.[1]
> —*New York Herald*, 1871

Six years had passed since the bloody American Civil War had drawn to a conclusion, but on the streets of New York you could still witness the ravages of conflict. Disabled veterans were a common sight and a near constant reminder that real courage was sanctified on a battlefield. To the eyes of most, there had been enough fighting on American soil.

However, a recent migration of English pugilists seeking refuge on our shores did not go unnoticed. The *New York Herald* penned: "These boxers have come here in the hope that they may carry on their trade without molestation and reap rewards by their profession, and it is time that stringent laws were enacted in every State, as in their mother country, to put an end to this brutal practice."[2] It was just an all too familiar scenario—English fighters landing in New York to suppress the will of the people—that had happened over a century earlier during the American Revolution.[3]

By the 1870s, Americans had become far more civilized, or so we hoped. Having forgotten that the British boxed in their encampments during their occupation of the city in the American Revolution, the *New York Herald* remarked: "Boxing was first taught in this country by a man named Fuller, who had been unsuccessful in the English ring. He came to this city about fifty years ago (1820s) and established himself in the Shakespeare Hotel, then at the corner of Fulton and Nassau streets where he was patronized by the young men of the first families of New York—among others the Hones and the Livingstons."[4]

Ironically, the newspaper went on to justify Fuller's instruction on the art of self-defense. They did, however, point out: "Fuller's scholars, unfortunately, were not all gentlemen's sons. Some of them were of the rougher element, who also became boxers, and in a short time prize fighting was inaugurated in the land, and it has continued at intervals ever since. The first fight in the ring in this country was between George Kensett, an Englishman, and Ned Hammond, an Irishman."[5]

So what went wrong, and who was to blame? The *Herald* had the answer: "It was not until the advent of Yankee Sullivan that the villainous classes were enlisted in the business. Since that time, with few exceptions, all the prize fights in this country have been gotten up by gamblers and thieves for the purpose of plunder."[6] This was coming from the very same source that, on February 9, 1849, announced the result of the contest between Tom Hyer and Yankee Sullivan with front-page coverage in their morning edition. The *Herald* published the "New Rules of Fistiana" (London Prize Ring Rules) on the cover page as well.

Rules

Since society was more urbane, so too must be the primordial practice of fighting with the fists. What choice did such a dangerous game have? To advance interest and participation, boxing modified its set of explicit or understood regulations. And, as we will see, some of those alterations included the boxing ring.

It was longshoreman turned pugilist Jack Broughton who stripped some of the barbarism from boxing. He was the first to formulate a set of rules in 1743. For the better part of a century, his seven rules guided the fight game. "Broughton's Rules" were superseded by a new set of guidelines called the "London Prize Rules" in 1838.[7]

The London-based Pugilistic Society decided to advance "Broughton's Rules" with a list of their own. Of the 23 guidelines (see citation), only these mention the ring[8]:

1. That the ring shall be made on turf, and shall be four-and-twenty feet square, formed of eight stakes and ropes, the latter extending in double lines, the uppermost line being four feet from the ground, the lower two feet from the ground. That in the centre of the ring a mark be formed, to be termed a scratch; and that at two opposite corners, as may be selected, spaces be enclosed by other marks sufficiently large for the reception of the seconds and bottle holders, to be entitled "the corners."

2. That each man shall be attended to the ring by a second and a bottle-holder, the former provided with a sponge, and the latter with a bottle of water. That the combatants, on shaking hands, shall retire until the seconds of each have tossed for choice of position; which adjusted, the winner shall choose his corner according to the state of the wind or sun, and conduct his man thereto, the loser taking the opposite corner....

9. That on no consideration whatever shall any person be permitted to enter the ring during the battle, or till it shall have been concluded; and that in the event of such unfair practice, or the ropes and stakes being disturbed or removed, it shall be in the power of the umpires and referee to award the victory to that man who in their honest opinion shall have the best of the contest....

19. That no person on any pretence whatever shall be permitted to approach nearer the ring than ten feet, with the exception of the umpires and referee, and the persons appointed to take charge of the water or other refreshment for the combatants, who shall take their seats close to the corners selected by the seconds.

Additional rules were also attached:

26. That if in a rally at the ropes a man steps outside the ring, to avoid his antagonist or escape punishment, he shall forfeit the battle....

28. That where a man shall have his antagonist across the ropes in such a position as to be helpless, and to endanger his life by strangulation or apoplexy, it shall be in the power of the referee to direct the seconds to take their man away, and thus conclude the round, and that the man or his seconds refusing to obey the direction of the referee, shall be deemed the loser.

As the nature of rules has always been modification via simplification, another round was inevitable. John Graham Chambers, a member of the British Amateur Athletic Club, first authored and published by the Marquess of Queensberry rules in 1867. The goal was to make the game better and cleaner. Of these twelve guidelines (see citation), only these mention the ring[9]:

1. To be a fair stand-up boxing match in a 24-foot ring, or as near that size as practicable....

5. A man hanging on the ropes in a helpless state, with his toes off the ground, shall be considered down.

6. No seconds or any other person to be allowed in the ring during the rounds.

Like any set of rules, they were subject to interpretation—much of it left in the hands of the arbiter. And while rules certainly added civility to boxing, they couldn't suppress all the public discourse regarding the game's legalization. (A list of Noteworthy Ring Adjustments appears at the end of this work.)

Fighters don't like rules, and when possible will do everything they can to get around them, but they are part of the sport. As an individual activity, boxing has always been self-reliant, and unlike bowling, golf and tennis, it does not use a ball. Those athletes who excel in individual sport seem to have a better understanding of the rules than your average participant; therefore, they understand how to use them to their advantage.

1870s

To close out the century, America entered the Gilded Age (1870s until about 1900). It was a term coined by Hartford humorist and author Samuel Langhorne Clemens, whose moniker was Mark Twain. Twain and his friend and neighbor Charles Dudley Warner had coauthored a novel they titled *The Gilded Age: A Tale of Today*. The work, published in 1873, satirized an era of profound social problems (greed and political corruption) masked by gilding—the glittering golden surface masking the corruption beneath. Consequently, the title quickly became synonymous with graft, materialism, and unscrupulousness in public life.

Rapid economic growth fueled the Gilded Age, as higher American wages spurred European immigration. However, the balance was difficult to maintain, causing abject poverty, wage discrimination and a conspicuous level of economic disparity. A key component to this commercial expansion was the railroads. Interwoven with so many sectors of our economy, America's reliance on this form of transportation had never been greater. Naturally, it didn't take a ship's captain to see the economic opportunities that lay before him, but one did.

American businessman and philanthropist, Cornelius Vanderbilt (1794–1877) amassed a fortune from shipping and railroads. His grandson was William Kissam Vanderbilt (1849–1920) (*Library of Congress, LC-DIG-ggbain-50402* [*digital file from original negative*]).

Commodore Vanderbilt

Born on May 27, 1794, Cornelius Vanderbilt, or "Commodore Vanderbilt" as his friends would call him, was a business magnate and visionary who amassed a tremendous fortune thanks to the rapidly growing railroad industry. As a youth he worked on his father's ferry in New York Harbor and quickly learned that the art of transportation could pay dividends. Before his fourteenth birthday Vanderbilt owned and operated a successful steamboat operation on Long Island Sound.

Witnessing the growth in New England textile mills during the 1830s, not to mention their need for both steamboat and rail transportation, Commodore Vanderbilt began to take over management of the connecting railroads. His first strategic target was the attractive New York, Providence and Boston Railroad, popularly known as the Stonington. Utilizing his sound business acumen, Vanderbilt tookover the presidency of the company by 1847. Later, he would relinquish the premier office of the Stonington in favor of a more discreet participation on the board of directors of a number of lines including the New York and Harlem (popularly known as the Harlem).

In a bold stock market corner, Vanderbilt took control of the Harlem in 1863. The beauty of the line, as he saw it, was that it was the only steam railroad to enter the center of Manhattan, running down Fourth Avenue (later Park Avenue) to a station on 26th Street, where it connected with a horse-drawn streetcar line—a connection mandated by a city ordinance. It was all about location. And it just happened to have a passenger depot adjacent to an attractive piece of property called Madison Square.

Madison Square

Located in Manhattan, Madison Square was framed by two well-known New York City routes, Fifth Avenue (west) and Madison Avenue (east), along with East 26th Street (north) and East 23rd Street (south). Named for James Madison, the fourth president of the United States, it was intersected by Broadway in the southwestern corner opposite where the Flatiron Building would be completed in 1902. Madison Square Park, a landscaped communal garden that exceeded six acres, was opened on May 10, 1847; however, it was not completed until some months later.

The square became a center of public activity ranging from riots (the New York City draft riot of 1863) to rallies (for 1864 presidential candidate General George B. McClellan). The unstoppable wave of residential development, which had steadily shifted uptown, finally reached the area in the 1870s. City gentry flocked to the brownstone row houses and mansions that soon dotted an aristocratic landscape. If you wished to be noticed, Madison Square was the place.

Madison Square Garden I, 1874–1889

Located at East 26th Street and Madison Avenue in Manhattan, Madison Square Garden I (also spelled Madison-Square Garden) was originally the passenger depot for the New York and Harlem Railroad. When the company opted for a move uptown in 1871, many took notice of the abandoned property, including the aging impresario Phineas T. Barnum. Similar to Vanderbilt, he understood the value of location.

Having entered the circus business at the age of sixty, Barnum leased the roofless building and called it the Great Roman Hippodrome. He quickly converted it into an oval arena 270 feet long, with seats and benches in banks, to cater to the needs of his circus clientele. The grand opening of the vast amphitheatre took place on the evening of April 27, 1874, and included chariot races, steeplechases, and gymnastics. The impresario presented a number of circuses and other performances, before giving up his lease on February 27, 1875.

Bandleader Patrick Sarsfield Gilmore leased the Hippodrome on April 11, 1875.[10] He understood the value of the location and was more than happy to follow in Barnum's entertainment footsteps, even if it meant a different form. Gilmore's Concert Garden was formally opened on May 29, 1875. An estimated crowd of 5,000 persons witnessed the maestro conducting his band of 100 talented musicians. From all accounts, Gilmore did a marvelous job of transforming the unattractive Hippodrome into an outdoor paradise.

But Gilmore, similar to Barnum, could not curtail the chill of a New York City winter and the decreased attendance that resulted. All options needed to be considered, including fisticuffs. Since competitive boxing matches were illegal, Gilmore creatively catered to fans of the sport with benefits, illustrated lectures and exhibitions.

In a January 1, 1879, article subtitled "Jimmy Elliott's Benefit at Gilmore's Garden—His Set-To With Paddy Ryan," the *New York Herald* reported: "Between six and eight hundred patrons of pugilism mustered last night at Gilmore's Garden to witness the sparring announced to come off, but particularly to see the beneficiary (Jimmy Elliott) 'put up his hands' with Paddy Ryan, so that they might form some idea of his capabilities as a fighter and the chances he will have with John Dwyer when he meets the latter in the 'roped arena' in their coming fight."[11]

However, demands of the Garden detracted from Gilmore's first love, music. After making the decision to leave Gilmore's Garden, he took his band on acclaimed tours of Europe. While preparing an 1892 musical celebration of the quadricentennial anniversary of Christopher Columbus's voyage of discovery, Gilmore collapsed and died in St. Louis.[12]

Anticipating Gilmore's decision not to renew his $40,000 lease, building owner William K. Vanderbilt, Cornelius Vanderbilt's grandson, had begun exploring his options. When no viable alternatives were presented, he opted to purchase the building's fixtures from Gilmore and appointed Mr. William M. Tilston to manage the property. Having been involved in the

John Lawrence Sullivan (1858–1918). His bare-knuckle conflicts garnered him the title of world heavyweight champion in 1882. In 1892, when boxing rules changed and padded gloves were used, he fought James J. Corbett for the heavyweight championship and lost (*Library of Congress, LC-USZ62-119896 [film copy negative]*).

New York Bench Shows, Tilston was no stranger to the venue known as Madison-Square Garden.

Madison-Square Garden, formerly "Gilmore's Garden," opened for business under its new name on June 1, 1879. While the Hahnemann Hospital Fair was in progress inside Madison-Square Garden, on April 21, 1880, one hundred feet of the second story fronting on Madison Avenue, and including the tower at the northwestern corner, came crashing into the street.

On May 14, 1880, the Department of Buildings served on the Messrs. Vanderbilt a formal notice condemning the Madison-Square Garden, and ordering the entire structure to be razed to the ground. To some the action appeared harsh, especially since Vanderbilt had seen to some corrections, but to others the notice was more than appropriate.

Enter the "Boston Strong Boy"

If there were four Gospels to the "sweet science," one would certainly have been penned by John Lawrence Sullivan. Tipping the scales at 190 pounds, Sullivan was by most accounts a marvel of man, or the perfect combination of muscle and bone. And if his physique didn't intimidate a challenger, his trademark "glare" certainly would. On February 7, 1882, Sullivan got his wish and met Paddy Ryan for the American title at Mississippi City. As the *Tribune* noted: "The Boston boy won that fight, knocking Ryan out in the ninth round with a terrific blow from his right across the back of Paddy's neck. The champion went down under the blow like a log and it was ten minutes before he recovered consciousness. Ryan always maintained afterward that Sullivan did not knock him out, but that a telegraph pole had fallen across his neck."[13]

The Garden continued to lease the facility based on the safety derived from its own improvements. On June 29, 1882, it was announced that articles of agreement had been drawn up and signed for an exhibition between Bare Knuckle World Heavyweight Champion John L. Sullivan of Boston, and Mr. Joseph Collins, otherwise known as Mr. Tug Wilson, the renowned English pugilist.[14] The fight would consist of four three-minute rounds, with one minute's rest after each round, inside Madison-Square Garden on the evening of July 17. The match was to be fought under the Marquess of Queensberry's rules using ordinary size soft boxing gloves. Should Wilson fight for the duration, Sullivan would be engaged to pay him $1,000. This was deposited into the hands of Harry Hill, the final stakeholder and referee.

The excitement engendered by the thought of a glove-fight inside Madison-Square Garden attracted an enormous congregation of fight followers. A twenty-four-foot ring had been erected, five feet above the floor, in the center of the great auditorium. Surrounded by about two thousand seats, it looked like it was meant to be there. Order, and there would be order, would be overseen by a couple of hundred New York City police officers, including Inspector Thorne and Captain Williams. A crowd estimated at 15,000 spectators gathered outside the venue while the exhibition was being conducted.

Harry Hill began the preliminaries at about 8:15. The first three-rounder was an exhibition between Harry Evans and Tommy Cook, a pair of English boxers who had fought for three hours and twenty minutes in England. The crowd loved it. Next, Jimmy Kelly tangled with Jerry Murphy for three rounds. The confrontation, for the most part, was a brilliant display; however, the crowd was growing impatient for the main event.[15] An unsuccessful attempt at two additional exhibitions followed before the crowd had seen enough—they demanded that Hill produce the featured champions.

At 9:40, Referee Hill, watch in hand, called time. As the *National Republican* observed:

> When both men were in full view, Sullivan seemed to tower above his adversary. Wilson's face is the perfect one of a fighter. His body is stout, his legs good, and his arms powerful, although his physique is nothing compared with the magnificent one of Sullivan. Sullivan weighed about 190 pounds and Wilson 160. Notwithstanding the difference, the Englishman, though manifestly no match for his powerful opponent, showed himself full of pluck, and made a game fight. He stood the punishment inflicted on him by Sullivan bravely, and though knocked down twenty-seven times, fought against the ropes, and pummeled and hammered in every conceivable manner, managed to stand out for four rounds and won the $1,000.[16]

Wilson hit the canvas nine times in the first round, eight times in the second, five in the third and five times in the final three minutes. By the final round, Sullivan was angry, but there was just nothing he could do to keep the little man down. At the conclusion of the spectacle, both adversaries shook hands. Sullivan left the ring as Wilson, surrounded by fans, was being sponged down.

During the preceding twelve months, sparked by the John L. Sullivan v. Paddy Ryan title fight, a remarkable revival of pugilism seemed to be taking place. Many, including the press, believed it was time to repeal the law against prizefighting. Not to mention, as comprehensive as the statute was against the manly art, it wasn't being enforced. Neither fine nor imprisonment was being handed out to those engaging in or witnessing the act.

Other noteworthy battles inside Madison-Square Garden: John L. Sullivan met Englishman Charles Mitchell on May 14, 1883. The encounter with soft gloves lasted until the third round, when Captain Williams stopped the fight. Sullivan knocked out Herbert Slade in the third round of their battle on August 6, 1883. On May 12, 1884, Charlie Mitchell, the English pugilist, disposed of William Edwards in the third round. Sullivan flattened Professor John M. Laflin in the third round of their bout on November 10, 1884; then on November 17, Sullivan jettisoned Englishman Alfred Greenfield in two rounds before the fight was stopped and both pugilists arrested.[17] The following year, on January 19, Sullivan stopped Paddy Ryan in the first round—the police stopped the affair on orders from Mayor William Grace.[18]

On June 23, 1887, the City of New York's registrar's office recorded that Madison-Square Garden had become the property of the Madison Square Garden Company. The new owners planned on tearing down the structure on the 425-feet-by-197-feet-6-inches lot in order to construct a new building.

Architectural firm McKim, Mead & White announced their plans for the new Madison-Square Garden on March 22, 1889. They intended to build an impressive Italian Renaissance quadrangular structure that would be highlighted by multicolored masonry, iron and glass. It would be constructed in two sections and include an observation tower. The amphitheatre, which would include a running track, would have a seating capacity of 5,060, or double the capacity of the present structure. In the summer, the amphitheatre could expand to a capacity of 12,000. And a large section of the roof would be able to open in favorable conditions. A 3,046-seat grand concert hall would also be included. Additional features mentioned included unobstructed-view seating, a restaurant and cafe, and an exhibition hall. The work of tearing down the old Madison-Square Garden began on August 7, 1889.

2

Madison Square Garden II, 1890–1919

The *Evening World* would declare: "It is extremely immense. The men and women look like dolls. The vast building is certainly far from handsome, but it is light and decidedly cheerful. The rafters are positively scintillant, while the galleries, that seem to dwindle away into nothingness, are rings of brilliancy. The floor is very bare, the chairs are circusy and somehow or other Barnum creeps into your imagination and won't be ousted.... The boxes are very obtrusive, and are undoubtedly made to be stared at."[1] This was only one of the mixed reviews received when the new Madison Square Garden amphitheatre debuted on June 16, 1890.

Madison Square Garden II, 1890

A capacity crowd was greeted by the music of Austrian composer Eduard Strauss, with his Imperial Vienna Orchestra and two grand corps de ballet imported from London. Like any new venue, it would take time and fine-tuning to alter the experience.

The systematic unveiling of each segment of the new Madison Square Garden proved to be far more efficient than a grand launch of the complete facility. The Garden Theatre's opening followed on September 27, 1890, and was described in this manner by the *Sun*: "The Garden Theatre, in which the play, 'Dr. Bill,' is to have the run of the season, differs from the amphitheatre in that in it a strong endeavor has been made to aplly rich decoration. If the characteristic of the amphitheatre is its simplicity the characteristic of the theatre, on the other hand, will be its gorgeousness. The theatre is a serious study in architecture, and with in its walls Mr. [Stanford] White has demonstrated what may be accomplished—in the construction and ornamentation of a playhouse—by an architect of artistic impulse."[2]

So, what about boxing?

A Gentleman's Journal

Finally, on August 29, 1892, fans of pugilism were treated to a special event. They could pay a small admission and view a first-class prizefighter, James J. Corbett. Gentleman Jim" was utilizing the venue to train for his September 7 New Orleans battle against John

2. Madison Square Garden II, 1890–1919

This version of Madison Square Garden—the second of that name and the second to be located at 26th Street and Madison Avenue in Manhattan—opened in 1890. It was closed in 1925, and was replaced by the third Madison Square Garden at Eighth Avenue and 50th Street (*Library of Congress, LC-DIG-det-4a17562* [*digital file from original*]).

L. Sullivan. Corbett and his manager William A. Brady had arrived the previous day to oversee the transformation of the Garden amphitheatre into a training complex. A platform was erected in the center of the venue and a ring constructed upon it. Exercise equipment found a home in virtually every available space.[3]

The machismo that had become characteristic for heavyweight champions, thanks to John L. Sullivan, was undetectable in Corbett. To many it was confirmation that they were going to lay their money down on Sullivan—in their eyes, it was a sure thing. Despite the casual analysis, on September 7, 1892, James J. Corbett would capture the Queensberry World Heavyweight title with a twenty-first-round knockout of "The Boston Strong Boy."

Less than a week after capturing the crown, Corbett was back in New York City and inside the new Garden. A most sincere crowd, estimated at 3,000 boxing fans, greeted him on this occasion and viewed a four-round exhibition prior to a short speech given by the new champion. The highlight of the evening appeared to be Corbett's announcement that he would attend Sullivan's Madison Square Garden benefit scheduled for Saturday, September 17, 1892.

The thought of the former champion in the ring with the present champion was sufficient to arouse the interest of virtually everyone in New York City, including the police. A perceptive John L., having been locked up about a year and a half earlier following his battle with Kilrain, drove his coupe to police headquarters on the morning of September 16. Sullivan, accompanied by a throng of his fans, wanted to be certain that the superintendent did not interfere with his event. In his convincing verbal manner, Big John pled his case to the constable. The result was recognition of the event and the well wishes of authorities; however, it came with a warning not to violate the law.

With enormous mitts, John L. Sullivan sparred three unimpressive rounds with champion James J. Corbett inside Madison Square Garden. In front of a crowd estimated as high as 7,000 people—those who paid as much as $6 for their reserve seats seemed to have as good a time as everyone else—two of the greatest champions the ring would ever know put on a three-act performance. Genuine sparring was nowhere to be found, but it didn't seem to matter to those in attendance, who just wanted to see their idols in person. In addition to the featured exhibition of the evening, middleweight champion Jack McAuliffe also sparred three rounds.[4]

The State of New York had legislatively criminalized "prizefighting" in 1859—it was a misdemeanor to engage in a "prizefight," to arrange a "prizefight," or help a fighter train for a "prizefight." On April 17, 1896, the governor signed the Horton Law, which legalized boxing in the state of New York until August 31, 1900, when it was repealed.

From 1896 until 1900, there would be

A British boxer who made history as the sport's first three-division world champion, Robert James Fitzsimmons (1863–1917) achieved fame by beating Gentleman Jim Corbett, the man who beat John L. Sullivan (*Library of Congress, LC-USZ62-78720* [*film copy negative*]).

far more paws, whiskers and walkers in Madison Square Garden than pugilists. No longer a participant, Sullivan could only sit and watch as the list of lineal heavyweight champions grew longer. On March 17, 1897, in Carson City, Nevada, Robert Fitzsimmons knocked out James J. Corbett in the fourteenth round. The duel was a rather serious affair. Wyatt Earp and four other men with revolvers were in Corbett's corner, and an equal number of gunmen were in Fitzsimmons's corner to ensure "fair play." "Ruby Robert" would hold the title until June 9, 1899, when James J. Jeffries would knock him out in the eleventh round of their battle at Coney Island.

New York City

In 1898, the five boroughs—Manhattan, Brooklyn, the Bronx, Queens and Staten Island—were consolidated into a single city. The populous City of New York, which had exerted a significant impact on commerce, diplomacy, education, entertainment and finance during the last one hundred years, was expected to do the same in the twentieth century. As the premier gateway for legal immigration to the United States, its population rose from 3.4 million people in 1900 to over 8 million by the end of the century. The presence of the world's largest foreign-born population of any city had contributed greatly to the hundreds of distinct neighborhoods throughout the boroughs.

The most densely populated borough, not to mention geographically smallest, was Manhattan. Home to all four iterations of Madison Square Garden, along with Central Park and most of the city's skyscrapers, it has often been described as the financial and cultural center of the world. Situated primarily on Manhattan Island, at the mouth of the Hudson River, it also includes a number of islands (Governors, Liberty, Randall's, Roosevelt and Wards) and is informally segmented into Lower, Midtown and Uptown regions.

With the advent of transportation links such as the Brighton Beach Line (1878) and the Brooklyn Bridge (1883), Brooklyn had witnessed enormous growth. Located on the western tip of Long Island, and including a long beachfront shoreline highlighted by the seaside resort of Coney Island, Brooklyn had only begun to explore its sport potential. The borough would soon be home to Ebbets Field at Bedford Avenue and Sullivan Place, Broadway Arena at 944 Halsey Street, and Coney Island Stadium on Surf Avenue near West 6th Street.

Most of the northernmost borough, or the Bronx, rests on the mainland. A haven for housing complexes, the borough is also home to a large zoo that opened in 1899 (Bronx Zoo) and the largest public park in New York City, Pelham Bay Park. Twentieth-century pugilists found work at the Fairmont Athletic Club at 251 East 137th Street, the Bronx Velodrome at Broadway and 225th Street (1920 until 1930), and the Bronx Coliseum at 1100 East 177th Street (1929–1997). Built in 1923, Yankee Stadium at River Avenue and East 157th Street would later host ring battles. Over at 434 Westchester Avenue, Gleason's Gym would begin its champion incubation in 1935.

Geographically the largest borough, Queens, on Long Island north and east of Brooklyn, was often viewed as the most ethnically diverse urban area in the world. Such demographics, as any successful twentieth-century boxing promoter could tell you, only needed an accommodating venue and a strong boxing card to lure spectators. Queens would soon host the Queensboro Arena at 29–49 Northern Boulevard (1920s until late 1940s), the

Ridgewood Grove Arena at St. Nicholas Avenue and Palmetto Street on the Brooklyn-Queens border (1926 until 1956), and later the Madison Square Garden Bowl (Long Island City Bowl) at Northern Boulevard and 45th Street (1932 until late 1930s).

Staten Island completed the list and was considered the most suburban in character of all five boroughs. It would be served by a ferry system, most notably the Staten Island Ferry for most of the twentieth century, until the completion of the Verrazano-Narrows Bridge (1960s) that connected it to Brooklyn.

A Reading of the Pugilistic Gospel According to John L.

As boxing entered the twentieth century, the first real champion wasn't shy about expressing his feelings to the *Tribune*: "I made boxing popular in this country, but the dubs they have had for champions of late years have done their best to kill it. There is not a champion in any class. My idea of a champion is one who fights with his fists and not with a typewriter. In my time all a man had to do to get a fight with me was to show some color of championship form and a bit of change to back his opinion of himself."[5]

An American boxing promoter, founder of the New York Rangers of the National Hockey League (NHL), and builder of the third incarnation of Madison Square Garden in New York City, George Lewis "Tex" Rickard (1870–1929) is pictured here in 1924. As the leading promoter of the day, he was often compared to P.T. Barnum (*Library of Congress, LC-DIG-hec-43808* [*digital file from original negative*]).

As for the current champions, Sullivan continued: "I am, I guess, about the only one of the ex-champions that has in any way held his own with the crowds. The others as soon as they lost their titles dropped out of sight. Who cares a continental about Jeffries to-day? Nobody. Why, in order to get his name in the papers he has to make some bluff about enlisting. You could not get him to enlist if you pulled a Gatling gun on him."[6]

Calling the latest participants "tango champions," Sullivan blamed their greed—in the form of large purses and moving picture rights—as being responsible for the anti-boxing laws. On February 2, 1918, Sullivan died at his Abington, Massachusetts, home from heart failure.

While nobody can be certain just how much money passed through the hands of John L. Sullivan, there have been estimates of his ring earnings topping $1.2 million, or $31.1 million in today's economy.[7] From 1878 until 1915, Sullivan boxed, sparred and toured from New York to Australia, often laying down cash as fast as he picked it up. Sullivan's New York City earnings alone topped $75,000, and that did not include presentations, tours and vaudeville work.[8] And it was the latter that netted the most significant earnings. For example, Sullivan's tour with Al Smith from September 28, 1883, until May 23, 1884, was said to have earned the pugilist $195,000.[9] Whether or not that included the Sullivan standing challenge of $250 to anybody who survived four rounds against him was uncertain. Was there money in dem mitts? You betcha.

As the century drew to a close, James J. Jeffries was atop the heavyweight division, Tommy Ryan held the middleweight crown, the dynamic welter division finished with William "Matty" Matthews holding the belt, Frank Erne was over the lightweights, and Terry McGovern held both the featherweight and the bantam titles—with the latter crown subject to interpretation.

A New Century

From 1901 to 1911, excluding only a few battles, the New York market catered primarily to undercard boxers and club fighters. Meanwhile, Fort Erie, Ontario, Canada, followed by San Francisco, Colma, and Vernon, California, along with Reno, Nevada, dominated top-shelf boxing with a handful of one-off exceptions.

Driven by demand, not to mention the legality of the sport, a few significant encounters are worth noting:

The boomtown of Goldfield, Nevada, decided to promote its community, or place it on the map if you will, by using the sport of boxing as a marketing vehicle. To do so, a small group of community leaders led by George Lewis "Tex" Rickard was able to match Joe Gans with Oscar "Battling" Nelson in a lightweight championship fight on September 3, 1906. Gans, a black champion born in the United States, would face Nelson, a white fearless champion who had relocated as a child from Copenhagen, Denmark. A weakened Gans, who harbored a broken right hand in the thirty-third round, dominated his opponent until Nelson was disqualified for dropping Gans with a punch to the groin in the forty-second round.

In Colma, California, on July 4, 1908, Gans, then a 3–1 favorite, put his championship on the line in a rematch with Nelson. Having unified the title, Gans had nothing to prove. Yet he allowed his white opponent an opportunity to take it from him. Nelson, after six warmup rounds, woke up and floored Gans nine times to win the lightweight title. Returning the favor, Nelson offered Gans a rematch on September 9, 1908. Although exhibiting physical signs that all was not well, Gans took the fight anyway.[10] Nelson defeated him in the twenty-first round.

In a one-off event held in Sydney, Australia, Canadian-born World Heavyweight Boxing Champion Tommy Burns, a.k.a. Noah Brusso, agreed to a bout with Jack Johnson, becoming the first white fighter to agree to a heavyweight championship bout with an African American. The battle, dominated by the Texas-born Galveston Giant, took place on December 26, 1908. After dropping Burns in the opening seconds of the fight, Johnson simply toyed with his much smaller opponent—honestly speaking, fearing for his life should he decide to destroy his white adversary—until knocking him out in the fourteenth round. After witnessing the first black man to win the heavyweight title, novelist Jack London, then covering the bout for the *New York Herald*, called for James J. Jeffries to emerge from retirement and defeat Johnson.

In the first "Fight of the Century," held on July 4, 1910, in Reno, Nevada, and promoted by Tex Rickard, Jack Johnson knocked out the "Great White Hope," James J. Jeffries, in round fifteen to retain his world heavyweight championship title. Lured out of retirement and enduring an excruciating training regiment, a courageous Jeffries simply had nothing to offer. Johnson, exhibiting more entertainer than boxer—a display of unmerciful taunting took place between the corners of both fighters and the audience—played with the former champion before dropping him three times in the fifteenth round.

The decade had challenged the boundaries of the fight game and even introduced new concepts: cognitive conflict, the "color line," and the art of promotion.[11] Both the legality and the safety of the sport continued to undermine its existence. And despite the title transfers in all seven weight classes that would exist by 1911, the decade really belonged to Jack Johnson, James J. Jeffries, Joe Gans, Battling Nelson, and Abe Attell.[12]

Perhaps the most notable Garden show of the period happened on May 3, 1906. The Twentieth Century Club presented at least four, four-round preliminaries before a four-round main event between Marvin Hart and Mike Schreck. The *Evening World* provided the details: "The ring will be pitched in the Concert Hall of the big garden, but the succeeding shows will be held in the main amphitheatre. Twelve hundred persons (members) can be seated at to-night's performance and already half that number have made application."[13] Ironically, the first two pugilists on the docket were arrested in order to ensure immunity from police interference with the featured prizefighters. As for the fight, it entered the record books with the mandatory conclusion of "ND," which stands for no decision. Ringside experts called the fight "the worst they had ever seen."[14]

Madison Square Garden was a reflection of the time and as such provided a plethora of amusements. If city gentry sought entertainment, they need go no further than their own backyard as everything from plays and balls to animal shows and autos could be found during the decade.

The Roof Garden Murder

Fifty-three days later, on Monday, June 25, 1906, the bold headlines in the *New York Tribune* shocked the world:

THAW KILLS STANFORD WHITE, Shoots Him at Madison Square Roof Garden Opening—Architect Dies Instantly.[15]

Following two more subtitles, the newspaper detailed the event: "Stanford White, well known architect, a member of the firm of McKim, Mead & White, was murdered last night by Harry K. Shaw, of Pittsburg [sic], member of the well known family of that name. White died almost instantly. The shooting took place on the roof of Madison Square Garden, while the opening performance of 'Mam'zelle Champagne' was being given. There was [sic] fully one thousand persons present, and a panic followed the shooting, women fainting and screaming and men cursing and chasing Thaw."[16] The event added a mystique to the venue and captivated New York City like none before.

When Mrs. Thaw, or Evelyn Nesbit, testified that at the age of sixteen she was drugged and seduced by the architect in an apartment on 24th Street, that was like pouring gasoline on a fire. Residents clamored for every detail surrounding the event and became so involved that the combined circulation of the dailies rose by 100,000 copies. When the first trial ended in a deadlocked jury, everyone in the publishing industry celebrated. A second trial commenced in 1908 and Thaw was found guilty by reason of insanity.

Despite its established traditions and service to the community, the Garden was struggling for its survival by 1908. Its real estate was simply far too valuable and alternatives were being considered, including the sale of the entire operation. On December 8, 1916, Madison Square Garden went on the auction block to satisfy a $2,300,000 mortgage being held by the New York Life Insurance Company. And, as fate may have it, the plaintiff in the foreclosure proceedings was the only bidder. Word also hit the streets that one Tex Rickard, promoter of boxing bouts, was negotiating with the New York Life Insurance Company, to lease the Garden on behalf of a group he was affiliated with. Rickard would state, "I have made an offer to the new owners of the Garden to take over the whole building for a period of either 5 or 10 years."[17] But boxing would soon take a back seat to World War I.

In 1911, the Frawley Act, which permitted fights of up to ten rounds, but prohibited decisions, gave boxing a slight rebirth, even if it was bit confusing. Gamblers, never far from a contest, had to rely on an agreed-upon newspaper source to obtain a verdict. The problem was finding an objective source. Since newspaper writers are people too, and subject to subjectivity, the law once again was under scrutiny.[18]

As World War I drew to a conclusion, boxing was witnessing the meteoric rise of two figures, promoter George Lewis "Tex" Rickard, and fighter William Harrison "Jack" Dempsey, both of whom would rewrite the history of the sport.

3

Rickard's Roost, 1920–1924

> When the five-foot bookshelf of biography containing the life records of America's great showmen is complete the names of Phineas T. Barnum and George L. Rickard will stand forth supreme.[1]
> —*New York Tribune*

Just three notable fights into his career as a promoter, George Lewis "Tex" Rickard was chomping at the bit to control Madison Square Garden. The talented impresario was not just the topic of conversation along Madison Square, but routinely found himself adorning sections of newspapers all across the country.

George Lewis "Tex" Rickard

According to legal documents, Rickard was born on January 2, 1873, in Kansas City, Missouri, to Robert R. Rickard and Lacricia Adams. (Both census data and his gravestone conflict with this date.)[2] His family moved to Sherman, Texas, when George was only four. Brought up on a cattle ranch suited the youth just fine, until his father passed in 1881. George was then forced to mature quickly while supporting his family (a mother, two brothers and three sisters). Driving cattle at age ten, Rickard soon established himself as a point or lead rider. And it was these skills—determining direction, controlling speed, and guidance—that he applied to other aspects of his life.

At age twenty-three, Rickard was elected city marshal of Henrietta, the Clay County seat. According to the *Bridgeport Evening Farmer*: "In '95 Tex pulled freight for Alaska. He dragged a sleigh over 300 miles of snow to reach Dawson City, the journey lasting two months. He made several lucky strikes, but lost out by opening a gambling house (The Northern), and, flat broke, went to Nome for a new start."[3] Rickard's stories, and he had many, could get a bit cloudy at times, with some of the facts lost in translation or contradicted by the passing of time. This would lead more than one reporter back to his notes trying to determine just when, and if, Tex actually found gold during the 1890s.

The *Farmer* continued: "There [Nome] he started another palace of chance, and cleaned up $100,000 a year for four annums. With a fortune in his pockets he returned to the States [Alaska was a territory at the time], and in 1904 landed in Goldfield, Nevada, where he opened a gambling resort. There he made more money than he knew what to do with, and he decided to promote boxing bouts as a means of getting rid of the surplus. The first real fight Tex ever saw was between Terry McGovern and Jimmy Britt in New York (May 28, 1906), and from that time he became a red hot fight fan."[4]

A novice at the fight game during the Gans-Nelson lightweight affair (1906) that put Goldfield on the map, Rickard was snake-bitten by Nelson's crafty manager Billy Nolan and determined to end his affiliation with the sport. However, Rickard couldn't resist the chance to "bring the championship back to the White race," so he stole the Jeffries-Johnson affair (1910) from right underneath the noses of more experienced promoters. After Rickard built an arena in San Francisco, the governor nearly executed a knockout punch when he announced that the fight could not be legally held in California. But Rickard took the blow

An American boxer who competed from 1914 to 1927, William Harrison "Jack" Dempsey (1895–1983)—nicknamed "Kid Blackie" and "The Manassa Mauler"—was the greatest boxer of the first half of the twentieth century (*Library of Congress, LC-USZ62-60707* [*film copy negative*]).

before shifting his interest to Reno, Nevada. And it was there that the gambler laid his cards down and made a small fortune.

Rickard's third fight was his New York debut and it was inside Madison Square Garden on March 25, 1916. There, heavyweight champion Jess Willard, in his first title defense, would get the best of his challenger Frank Moran. Willard had captured the crown by knocking out Jack Johnson in the twenty-sixth round of an exhausting fight held in Havana, Cuba, back on April 5, 1915. Sensing the demand, Rickard felt the Willard-Moran match would be a winner and he was right. It was $7,500 to rent the Garden, the Boxing Commission grabbed $11,344.05, and additional expenses were estimated at about $10,000. The no decision bout drew a crowd paid $151,254; accordingly, Willard received $47,500 and Moran took home $23,750.[5] It was a hefty take and did not go unnoticed.

Rickard, with an eye for talent, a nose for opportunity, a taste for the mighty dollar, and a touch for promotion, only heard what he wanted to hear. And that was precisely why he was such a great promoter, selective hearing having benefited more than one successful impresario. It was the public that created the demand for a match, Rickard believed, not the promoter. This conclusion led to his successful handling of the media—support, he understood, that had a price.

Detailed Promotion

In January 1919, Rickard confirmed that Jack Dempsey would meet heavyweight champion Jess Willard. The choice made sense from every perspective: it had to be a white opponent, as the controversy surrounding Jack Johnson was still fresh in people's minds; and Willard's adversary had to look and act the part with a boxing provenance that was unquestionable. Since Rickard had promoted two fights with black boxers, everyone around the fight game understood that the decision was motivated by economics and not bigotry. And the date made sense too: July 4, 1919.[6]

With a population under 150,000, Toledo, Ohio, wasn't the first city that came to mind when Rickard was thinking about staging a boxing match, but it would be his last. It was serviced by ten railroads and six steamship companies, so transportation to the city—a key consideration of any promotion—wouldn't be an issue. And Toledo had the liberal edge—free-flowing bootleg whiskey, affordable dance halls and a hearty supply of promiscuous women—capable of keeping Rickard's potential audience occupied. The promoter would tell the *Topeka State Journal*, "I'd rather promote ten or twelve rounds in the east than to go for the twenty-round stuff in the west."[7]

At the expense of $150,000, Bay View Park was built with 180,000,000 feet of lumber in Toledo. The immense arena seated 80,000 spectators and was held together by two traincar loads of nails. Long runways led to each section and an elaborate system of external fencing to prevent "rushing the gates." Rickard had worked with contractor James P. McLaughlin to ensure every level of detail. For example, the night before the fight, seats were flooded with water to reduce the possibility of fire from half-burned cigarettes or cigars. An emergency hospital had been constructed in the bowels of the plant with a nurse in attendance. Rickard and McLaughlin had calculated that all 80,000 spectators could exit the arena in ten minutes, through sixteen exits, if they moved at three miles per hour. While it didn't take a cattleman to promote a boxing match, it certainly didn't hurt.[8]

The Golden Age

Boxing's "Golden Age" was ushered in with a knockout by its next apostle, William Harrison "Jack" Dempsey. Flooring Willard seven times in the first round, Dempsey was indefatigable. He even broke bones—jaw, ribs and cheek—at a record pace. The impressive third-round victory garnered him the heavyweight championship.

When speculation regarding a possible Carpentier-Dempsey match hit the press in early 1920, it was tough for Rickard to ignore. He quietly went to work. A battle between heavyweight champion Jack Dempsey and Georges Carpentier, he believed, could be the fight of the century, but only if the terms and conditions were favorable.

On May 24, 1920, legislation in the form of the (James J.) Walker Law dried some of the tears following Prohibition. It transformed the sport of boxing in New York State. Bouts up to fifteen rounds were allowed with decisions given by a referee or judges. The law also mandated the licensing of boxers, managers, physicians, promoters, and trainers. Overseeing the fight game would be a state boxing commission. The legislation cast a new light on boxing, leaving many to believe as New York goes, so to the rest of the sport.

Under the Walker Law umbrella, Rickard felt confident enough to conduct the first lightweight title bout at New York City in twenty years. Inside Madison Square Garden, Benny Leonard, who had taken Freddie Welsh's lightweight crown in 1917, would meet Joe Welling on November 26. The battle, at 135 pounds or less, pledged to be interesting even if Welling was far from Rickard's first choice. Leonard took the battle with a fourteenth-round knockout.[9]

Soon, Rickard was being compared to Barnum—it was like contrasting a magician to Harry Houdini, the ultimate compliment. On July 2, 1921, heavyweight champion Jack Dempsey knocked out light heavyweight champion Georges Carpentier in the fourth round of the sport's first million-dollar gate.[10] In the second round, a right to the chin dazed Dempsey. However, it would not be enough to slow the much stronger "Manassa Mauler." Dempsey, a favorite (2–1) who outweighed his opponent by 16 pounds, dropped "The Orchid Man" twice in the fourth. The ring was twenty feet square and the fighters wore eight-ounce gloves.

Standing five feet eight inches, Tex Rickard had a long face, brown eyes and high cheekbones. His smooth-skinned face was typically painted with little emotion. Rickard's raised eyebrows and thin-lined mouth could transform his stern poker face, but those instances were rare. As he got older his hair thinned, requiring a brushover to cover a large bald spot. For the most part, Rickard was all business. Seldom without his trademark gold-headed malacca cane and a fine cigar, he topped off his look with a straw hat or a light-colored fedora. Rickard always looked more city than country, even if he had an aura of the West about him. Of slow speech and keen mind, he kept his cards close to the vest— whether he had a royal flush, or simply a pair of deuces, you could never tell by looking at him.

By age 50, Tex Rickard was the most sought-after man in New York. From his office in the tower of Madison Square Garden, he sat behind barred doors and dreamed of his next big venture. While some gamblers disregarded an even bet, Rickard always saw even in his favor. He was that self-confident. Through a little door in the back of his office, Rickard could step onto a balcony high among the rafters of the great complex, look across the horizon and envision his dreams. He was the genie, and the Garden his lamp.

William Harrison "Jack" Dempsey

From ex-hobo, fortune hunter and spendthrift, to world champion, would not be an easy task for any man, but William Harrison Dempsey was not just any man. Born on June 24, 1895, in Manassa, Colorado, young William would grow to the imposing height of seventy-two inches. He was the sixth child of an Irish-Scottish and Indian family of eight—his claim to the source of his combative qualities. As a fighter, he assumed the then logical Christian name of "Jack" in tribute to Brooklyn's famous "Nonpariel," who was a middleweight champion.

Although the records are incomplete, the youngster was tackling his fair share of pugs by 1914, primarily in and around Salt Lake City. Dempsey triumphed over the bulk of his challengers. Like many fighters, he liked the thrill and hit the road picking up fights to supplement his farming and mining work. It was after 1916 that his record began to take shape.

Following nine fights in Nevada and Utah, Dempsey headed for New York City.[11] There he was greeted by a situation he had yet to adapt to: three uninspiring ten-round battles during what would be known as "The No Decision Era." Convinced that New York club boxing wasn't for him, Dempsey returned home.

The following year opened in the fashion every boxer tries to avoid: a first-round knockout loss. It's one thing to be humiliated by a knockout, but it's just plain embarrassing if it happens in the very first round. Dempsey lasted only twenty seconds against his first real opponent. It was veteran "Pueblo Fireman" Jim Flynn who did the damage. Looking back, it might have been the wake-up call Dempsey needed. (Jack's versions, and there were countless, differed just a tad.) Battling at least eleven more times during the year, the Colorado fighter was gaining valuable experience against gladiators like Willie Meehan, Gunboat Smith and Carl Morris.

In 1918, Dempsey had a banner year and turned more heads than Pola Negri. In 21 ring bat-

An American boxer who competed from 1915 to 1928, James Joseph "Gene" Tunney (1897–1978) knocked out Georges Carpentier and defeated Jack Dempsey twice, first in 1926 and again in 1927. His five-fight rivalry with Harry Greb—three of which took place in Madison Square Garden—was one of the finest of the era (*Library of Congress, LC-DIG-hec-21490* [*digital file from original negative*]).

tles, Dempsey lost only one fight. Twelve of his victories were first-round knockouts. He scored 17 knockouts in 21 ring battles, and people took notice. He avenged his loss to Jim Flynn by putting out the fireman in the very first round. Among those hitting the canvas: Bill Brennan, Arthur Pelkey, Battling Levinsky, Bob Devere, Dan "Porky" Flynn, Carl Morris and Ed "Gunboat" Smith.

In preparation for his July encounter with Willard, Dempsey fought at least five times, against five different opponents and disposed of each one of them in the very first round.[12] He also jettisoned numerous sparring partners during multiple exhibitions culminating in the duel. In his mind, he had earned the right to face Willard, and had every intention of disposing him in an equally impressive manner.

New York City, 1922–1925

Some Garden battles appeared routine, such as the one in which Gene Tunney, the Pride of Greenwich Village, captured the lightweight crown from Battling Levinsky on January 13, 1922—a twelve-round decision that was entertaining but not sensational.

Rickard wisely used his Garden cards to leverage his larger promotions. He was controlling fighters like chess pieces, and every city boxing manager knew the promoter had a lease on Boyle's Thirty Acres over in Jersey City. He was keeping a sharp eye on his competition, or the club fights. During a typical week, fight fans could look to the Broadway E.A., Star Sporting Club or Freeport S.C. on Monday, Pioneer Athletic Club on Tuesday, and Rink Sporting Club on Thursday, and Madison Square Garden on Wednesday, Thursday and Friday, and perhaps the weekend. Armory fights, a politically motivated alternative to Rickard's perceived monopoly over the fight game, were also scattered among weekend events.

Described as a keen-eyed, nimble-brained Irishman, among other things, Leo P. Flynn wasn't officially the matchmaker at the Garden; however, unofficially, he was. Having his own stable of fighters—under Flynn's guidance were Dave Shade, Jack Renault, and Bill Brennan—prohibited Flynn from officially being a matchmaker of the same venue frequented by his boxers. Ever since Rickard had taken over the Garden, Flynn stood as a buffer between the promoter's bankroll and many money-hungry managers and fighters.

On May 31, 1923, papers were filed for the incorporation of the new Madison Square Garden Corporation. Rickard confirmed on June 14 he planned to build a new arena, complete with a bicycle track and artificial ice plant for skating. He also stated that he believed the city was ready for a professional hockey team. Rickard would serve as president of the corporation for twenty years.

On July 12, at Boyle's Thirty Acres in Jersey City, the former heavyweight champion Jess Willard met Luis Ángel Firpo. Although Willard, the "Pottawatomie Giant," outweighed his opponent by 28 pounds, he was knocked out at the 1:55 mark in round eight—the fight was scheduled for 12 rounds. The Rickard promotion, which did not sell out, still established a new paid attendance record for a boxing event conducted in this country. More importantly, at least to Firpo, it positioned him for Dempsey, or one enormous payday.

That day came on September 14, 1923, at the Polo Grounds. The event, conducted by Rickard, saw Firpo, nicknamed "El Toro de las Pampas" ("The Bull of the Pampas") challenging *the* established heavyweight champion of the world. Having knocked out eleven of his last twelve opponents, many in record time, the fierce Argentinian had paid his dues. In the ring, he was a commanding figure, standing six feet three inches and weighing over 200 pounds. He was as tenacious as one might expect from a boxer who carried such a moniker, so Dempsey had his hands full.[13]

In what some historians would consider the most dramatic event in twentieth-century sport history, Jack Dempsey bolted from his corner when the opening bell sounded. Immediately dropped to his knees, Dempsey got up to floor Firpo seven times. Enraged, Firpo used his anger to catapult Dempsey out of the ring—all this in round one. Dempsey recovered, and after dropping Firpo again, he finally ended the battle with a knockout combination in the second term. The crowd of more than 80,000, which had produced a staggering $1.2 million gate, cheered as Dempsey came out of his corner after the count to pick up Firpo from the canvas. Reinvigorating boxing, the fight placed William Harrison "Jack" Dempsey into the pantheon of all-time greats.

Filed with the Bureau of Buildings on Friday, May 16, 1924, tentative plans called for a twenty-eight-story building to replace the current Madison Square Garden. The company served notice to Rickard to vacate the current location by August 1, 1925. Just over a month later, on June 17, Rickard announced the purchase of the car barns located on Eighth Avenue from 49th to 50th streets. It was hoped that work on the new structure could begin in less than 100 days.

The last gasp at the old Garden took place on Tuesday, May 5, 1925. A crowd of 13,000 spectators witnessed East Sider Sid Terris take a decision over the veteran Johnny Dundee. Once the decision had been given, silence overcame the venue. "Taps," a bugle call for the lights to be put out in army quarters (so named because the signal was originally sounded on a drum), was played by a member of the "Fighting Sixty-Ninth." Boxing history had been written in the name of Madison Square Garden and will endure.[14]

4

City Ring, 1925 until January 6, 1929

> I can only note that the past is beautiful because one never realises an emotion at the time. It expands later, and thus we don't have complete emotions about the present, only about the past.
> —Virginia Woolf

Foundation firmly in place, Rickard was ready to carry the Madison Square Garden banner into a new home located on Eighth Avenue between 49th and 50th streets in Manhattan. The name came with an unparalleled history, especially with regard to boxing. And that past would yield to unrivaled prizefighting, with the christening of a modern venue. To think that the fight game's premier impresario had at his disposal the foremost venue and participant (Jack Dempsey) was compelling to every boxing fan.

In celebration, a modern ring was built. It was set on a raised square platform, with a post at each corner, and a set of parallel ropes secured its borders. Its use would be dependent on the needs of its owner. Like a Broadway stage, it would rely on its participants to sanctify it in the name of its art. Thousands would perform within the ropes, but only a small number would leave behind a lasting impression.

Madison Square Garden III, 1925

With the completion of his new surroundings and restructuring of his staff, Rickard began concentrating on his outdoor events, the linchpin to his success. On July 16, he managed to get Dempsey to commit to two battles, likely Gene Tunney and possibly Harry Wills. The bouts, of course, would proceed if the state commission (NYSAC) agreed, and if Dempsey could settle his own management affairs: he was battling with Kearns over control of his enterprises.

Rickard also drove the last rivet into the steel frame of his new facility on August 24. It was then that he hinted at some of the possible opening events (such as a six-day bicycle race). Seating 18,496, the new structure permitted smoking—an issue with many boxing fans—thanks to a modern air-cooling system. Every detail seemed to excite his potential audience. But what about boxing?

That announcement finally came on October 9: Light heavyweight champion Paul Berlenbach and contender Jack Delaney had agreed to meet in the new Madison Square

Garden on December 11. The contentious rivalry was perfect and it promised to be a real barnburner. Perhaps even more important, at least to Berlenbach, was the opportunity for him to vindicate his previous loss to Delaney—an event that saw the fighter knocked out.[1]

Naturally, a new facility needed a new ring, and oh, what a ring! It was like no other with its shining metal posts, topped with reflective spheres the size of grapefruits. The thick ropes were plush, lined with the finest available fabric. A new electronic timing system, complete with a ringside clock, would record the seconds being ticked off by the timekeeper with a lit red bulb. One more note about the City Ring: it would be tested during the amateur boxing tournament held inside the Garden on December 7 and 8. If it passed the test, then it was on to the light heavyweight championship of the world.

Boxing fans also delighted at the sight of two additional four-foot clocks installed conveniently on the front of the mezzanine seating sections. The four-minute clocks ticked off the seconds of the round plus the one-minute intermission; to guarantee accuracy, the timekeeper was responsible for the operation of the equipment.

Since the new facility was composed only of steel, stone, concrete and brick, fans weren't going to miss that musty smell of old lumber. And the dull gray haze of tobacco smoke over the squared ring was now a memory. A modern ventilation system, complete with filtered air, would see to that. Summer boxing was also more comfortable as the pipes used for ice hockey could drop the interior temperature by a good ten to fifteen degrees.

Electricity was everywhere in the establishment, from the latest modern public address system to an interior telephone communication network. Power was at an employee's fingertips. The facility was well-lit—a large cluster of lights dropped from the rafters for ring events—and included a state-of-the-art security and fire alarm system. Electricity also powered restaurants adjacent to the exhibition halls and rooms on the 50th Street side.

Seven entrances—three for each street, plus a main entrance—and five box offices were provided for spectator convenience. Even though boxing was a key consideration in the construction of the venue, it wasn't the only one. Hockey, along with other amusements, also garnered attention. For example, a solid ice surface could be created in eight hours and removed in three.

City Ring

The City Ring made its public debut on December 7, 1925, when thirty-two preliminary bouts were staged as part of an amateur tournament that was conducted by the Metropolitan AAU. The crowd, estimated at 10,000, was the largest to ever witness amateur boxing in New York City. The very first boxer to win a bout inside the ring was Johnny Erickson, of St. Lucy's Catholic Club, who surprised a few by defeating a seasoned Jack McDermott. But McDermott, as the holder of the Metropolitan AAU title, could be viewed as the first titleholder to battle inside the ring. The quickest knockout of the evening was Charlie Duffin's one-punch blast to William J. Jaegelo.

With the ring—minus some minor alterations, such as perfecting the tension of the bull ropes—proving its worthiness, it was high time for its professional debut on Friday, December 11, 1925.

The First Professional Card—A World Lightweight Championship

It was a spectacular evening that saw a talented Paul Berlenbach, the "Astoria Assassin," retain his world light heavyweight crown over Jack Delaney after fifteen hard-fought rounds. From every account, it was a convincing demonstration of Berlenbach's strength and improving ring skills. Delaney's devastating right, the punch that kayoed the "Astoria Assassin" back in the old Garden in 1924, was still there, but less effective. It surfaced in the fourth round and sent Berlenbach down for a count of three. Yet the champion recovered and slowly regained his strength. Berlenbach did, however, have to close strong in order to negate Delaney's earlier rounds.[2]

It ws the largest indoor gallery ever to witness a fight, and it was perfectly orchestrated inside the new Garden arena by the maestro himself, Tex Rickard. Everyone who was anyone, or so it appeared, turned out, including George M. Cohan, Mr. and Mrs. James J. Farley, Jersey City Mayor Frank Hague, John J. McGraw, Magistrate Francis X. McQuade, Justice Jeremiah Mahoney, Colonel Jacob Ruppert, Warner F. Russell, A.G. Southworth, Charles A. Stoneham, Mayor-elect James J. Walker and Florenz Ziegfeld.

With regard to the ring's professional details: George Jackson became the first professional fighter to win a fight inside the ring, and a four-round one at that, when he defeated Mike Reilly. Harold Mays took a four-round decision over Andy "Kid" Palmer to become the second professional boxer to win inside the ring. Pat McCarthy became the third with a victory over Alex Relys. George Cook was the fourth by taking a decision over King Solomon. New York City—born Paul Berlenbach became the first elite boxer (member of the International Boxing Hall of Fame) to win in the ring, and did so by defeating another elite pugilist in Jack Delaney (French-Canadian born member of the International Boxing Hall of Fame). Also, Berlenbach, a former AAU national wrestling champion, could add the two-sport distinction to the ring's provenance.[3]

On December 23, Mike McTigue, former world's light heavyweight champion, took a very close and controversial decision over Tiger Flowers in the ten-round feature event. So enraged was the Garden crowd that they stood for ten minutes yelling after the announcement of the verdict by Joe Humphreys. By all unofficial accounts, Flowers had won the fight, making this the first contentious decision in the history of the City Ring. The initial battle of the evening also made history when Tony Canzoneri, the future lightweight champion, in only his eleventh professional fight, knocked out Danny Terris. The four-round bout was Canzoneri's fourth win by knockout and the first ever by a pro inside the new Garden.[4]

The City Ring's First Full Year, 1926

Reigning over the sport during the first half of the decade, Jack Dempsey would remain one of America's preeminent celebrities for the next five years. In the seven years and two months that followed World War I, he held the greatest title in the world. And as Dempsey's popularity grew, so too did that of boxing. But the boxing legend would never fight in the new Madison Square Garden. In fact, he would only fight three more times, all of which were stadium bouts; the fighter's popularity had outgrown indoor facilities. Rickard would utilize the fighter's services as a key driver for his large-scale outdoor promotions, which in turn would leverage his smaller indoor cards.

Tunney v. Dempsey I

Dempsey's fight on September 23, 1926, was his first meeting against contender Gene Tunney and as it would turn out, his sixth and final title defense. Battling "The Fighting Marine" for ten rounds inside Philadelphia's Sesquicentennial Stadium, the world's heavyweight champion faced a unanimous decision against his performance. The heavyweight championship had changed hands on points for the very first time.

If spectator tears were shed, few noticed, as the rain began just in time for the main event. Rickard, who had the promotion, initially wanted it in Yankee Stadium, but NYSAC would not grant Dempsey a boxing license until he complied with their order to defend the title against Harry Wills. So Rickard turned to Philadelphia.

A crowd of more than 120,000, the largest paid attendance to ever watch a boxing match, turned out to witness the production.[5] Dempsey, who was heavily favored, found himself dominated by Tunney. Naturally this generated all sorts of speculation regarding the fight. From questions about Dempsey's health to the image of racketeer Arnold Rothstein sitting ringside, there was a sense of discomfort hanging over the event; moreover, it was rumored that the gambler dropped over $100,000 (at 4 to 1 odds) that Tunney would win. The fight, seen as the "Upset of the Decade" by many historians including those working at *The Ring* magazine, bewildered the fight world.

About 4,000 New York City fight fans listened to the championship inside the new Madison Square Garden thanks to a radio broadcast. According to a *New York Times* assessment of the broadcast, those in attendance could only hear "half the words."[6] Nevertheless, it was enough to understand that the champion was being dismantled. The crown that once fit Dempsey perfectly would have a new owner.

As strange as it may sound, the loss only served to enhance Dempsey's popularity. While he had always resonated with boxing fans, the defeat seemed to humanize the great fighter. Most loved the outlaw in Dempsey and just didn't understand the literary avocations of a pugilist such as Tunney. Regardless, Gene Tunney was clearly the most distinguished fighter of the year with his victory.

Tiger Flowers v. Harry Greb

Conspicuous among all the fights undertaken inside the City Ring during its inaugural season were a pair fights between two elite fighters, Tiger Flowers and Harry Greb. Having fought Flowers at Freemont, Ohio, back in August of 1924 to a ten-round no-decision, Greb put his middleweight title on the line at Madison Square Garden on February 26. And it wasn't a simple negotiation. Rickard had worked hard with his matchmaker Jess McMahon to bring the deal to fruition.[7]

Appearing much stronger, Greb did not disappoint fight fans. With his wild swings and relentless charges, he worked Flowers over but could not put him away. Seen as equally aggressive, Flowers mounted a robust body assault. In the end many, including Frank Getty of the United Press, believed the champion deserved at least a draw. Nonetheless, judges

Charles F. Mathison and Tom Flynn, along with referee Ed Smith, split their decision, giving the fifteen-round decision to Flowers.

With the victory, Theodore Flowers, a southpaw from Camille, Georgia, became the first African-American middleweight champion. Flowers had begun his career back in 1918 and paid his dues by fighting many outstanding boxers including Jack Delaney, Jamaica Kid and Kid Norfolk.

Their final meeting, and Greb's last professional fight, came on August 19. When it was over, both fighters had given every ounce of energy they possessed, used all their tricks, and mixed it up in just about every form imaginable. James P. Dawson of the *New York Times* summarized it as a "no holds barred" contest.[8] The verdict, which was not a popular one with the masses, was a split decision that again favored Flowers; consequently, a large collection of debris, including straw hats, found its way into the City Ring.

Forgotten Rounds

It's impossible to note every outstanding fight inside the City Ring, but some simply have to be mentioned.[9] Local favorite Joe Glick took a points decision over Johnny Dundee on January 26. Granted, Dundee was nearing the end of his career, but Glick, a tailor from the Williamsburg section of Brooklyn, also had nearly a hundred fights under his belt. Undefeated Tony Canzoneri battled to a draw with Stamford, Connecticut, featherweight Mike Esposito on March 25. Esposito was the brother of Andrea E. Esposito, a.k.a. KO Morgan. And Brooklyn's own Anthony Andrew DiVodi, an undefeated welterweight, took a points decision over an undefeated Vince Dundee on October 15. Less than thirty fights into his pro career, DiVodi already held victories over Phil Richards, Mickey Travers and Dundee.

For boxing, the fighter of the year was likely Gene Tunney. However, inside the City Ring you would have to hand the honor to both Tiger Flowers and Harry Greb.[10]

In its first year of operation, November 29, 1925, until December 1, 1926, the Madison Square Garden Corporation reported a net profit of about $975,000, or earnings of $3 per share of 325,000 outstanding shares of stock.[11]

1927

In 1927, Charles Augustus Lindbergh completed the first solo transatlantic flight in a single-engine monoplane, *Spirit of St. Louis*; the Holland Tunnel opened to connect Canal Street in Manhattan with Jersey City, New Jersey; transatlantic telephone service began; and the first Golden Gloves boxing tournament for amateur fighters started. When city pugilists found out that the finals of this amateur boxing contest were going to be held inside the new Madison Square Garden, participation, not to mention public interest, soared.

Tex Rickard signed Gene Tunney, the heavyweight champion, to an exclusive one-year agreement on January 6. Sensing discontent between the champion and his manager Billy Gibson, the business-savvy promoter seized the moment and executed the pact as an insurance mechanism. Other than noting that the fighter would defend his title by July 1, everything else regarding the agreement was rather vague.[12]

In May, Jack Sharkey knocked out Jim Maloney fifty-two seconds into the fifth round of their Yankee Stadium clash. Sharkey's decisive victory placed him in line for a battle with Jack Dempsey; moreover, the winner of that contest would meet Gene Tunney for the heavyweight championship of the world. Sharkey, the son of Lithuanian immigrants, was clever, quicker, and far more accurate than Maloney. And when the crowd on hand wasn't chatting about Sharkey, Maloney, or Dempsey, their thoughts drifted to aviator Lindbergh. Ring announcer Joe Humphreys, no stranger to a fight crowd and their demands, even provided an update on Lindbergh's progress.[13]

Like Lindbergh, Rickard was also flying high. Two outdoor promotions, along with one inside Madison Square Garden, would highlight his year.

Jacks of All Trades

Tex Rickard confirmed the news that everyone had been waiting for: Jack Dempsey would meet Jack Sharkey inside Yankee Stadium on July 21. The winner would meet Gene Tunney for the world heavyweight championship.

In the heat of the summer sun, inside "The House that Ruth Built," Jack Dempsey emerged to face Jack Sharkey. "The Manassa Mauler," who hadn't fought since his battle with Tunney back in September of the previous year, was a box office darling, ring rust or not. But it was Sharkey who was the odds-on favorite (7–5). It was the "Boston Gob's" swiftness, clever combinations, high waistband and, should we say, poor vision that tilted the bar in his direction. Sharkey was a dirty fighter: there, I said it. Since money talks—and it spoke volumes as Dempsey pocketed over $250,000 and Sharkey over $200,000—and, well, you know the rest of the line, it was "game on" in front of a crowd of more than 80,000.

Sharkey came out strong, and by the fourth round had Dempsey wondering why he hadn't trained harder. Whether it was out of frustration or simply his corners edict, Dempsey dropped his punches and went to the body following the fifth—a Sharkey foible. When a couple of Dempsey shots appeared to land low in the seventh round, Sharkey turned to referee Jack O'Sullivan to protest. It was then that he dropped his guard, and Dempsey couldn't resist landing a left hook to the chin. However, when the Gob dropped, he appeared impacted by a shot to the groin instead of one to the kisser. Nobody bought the act. Now on to Tunney.[14]

Tunney v. Dempsey II

In what could arguably be referred to as the most familiar boxing event of all time, Gene Tunney retained his heavyweight title in a ten-round unanimous decision over Jack Dempsey on September 22 at Soldier Field in Chicago. It became known as the "Long Count" due to an incident that took place less than a minute into the seventh round. Taking a vicious Dempsey left hook, Gene Tunney collapsed to the floor. Illinois State Athletic Commission rules stated that in the event of a knockdown, the fighter scoring the knockdown must go to the farthest neutral corner before the referee begins his count. However, Dempsey did not retreat, but simply hovered over his prey. Finally, after precious seconds had already ticked off the clock, Dempsey's ultimate compliance led to a count by Referee Dave Barry. Tunney, who wisely stayed down until the count of nine by Barry, survived the round. But was the count honest? Wasn't Tunney down much longer than the count of nine?

Nevertheless, Barry's response time exhibited remarkable improvement. When a rejuvenated Tunney dropped Dempsey briefly in the eighth round, Referee Barry was over him like a hunting dog and counting before Tunney left the neighborhood. The fight went ten rounds before entering the record books as a Tunney victory, or "W10."

It was Tunney's first title defense, the second time the fighters had met, and the second time Dempsey had lost twice to the same fighter (the other was Willie Meehan). It was also financial bonanza—the first nearly $3-million gate and Tunney's first $1-million check (even if Rickard also provided a check for $9,555 to add to his purse to reach the figure). It may have been Dempsey's last call, but nobody was certain. Or, as some believed, it was proof that despite every effort, boxing was prone to conspiracy. Every sportswriter seemed to have a unique interpretation of the incident. For example, *Washington Post* columnist Shirley L. Povich buried Dempsey, while syndicated wordsmith Damon Runyon praised Tunney. As though looking at a child's first finger-painting, nobody was certain just how to elucidate the event. The only thing certain about the affair was that George Lewis "Tex" Rickard was the greatest impresario of his time. Barnum had rolled over.

Back at the Garden, it was the final week of July and time for the summer boxing shows to open. Ticket prices for these shows ranged from $1 to $5. To get a sense of how boxing related to other Garden events, you could pick a month, say November. During this month, according to a Garden press release, there were four professional boxing cards that drew an average 11,750, with the largest crowd (15,500) being that of the Johnny Risko versus Paulino Uzcudon bout, which took place on November 25. There were likewise two amateur boxing nights held on November 16 and 23, which drew 8,000 fans. So boxing occupied six evenings inside the facility. In comparison, there were seven hockey nights that drew on average about 10,900 fans, and two professional basketball games that drew an average of 6,000 spectators per game. Additionally, a six-day horse show drew a crowd of 75,000. All other days were idle.

Tommy Loughran picked up the NYSAC light heavyweight championship by defeating the National Boxing Association (NBA) designated champion Jimmy Slattery in fifteen very tough rounds inside the Garden on December 12; the light heavyweight picture had been a bit clouded until this battle. While Loughran was the odds-on favorite, Slattery, a fierce Buffalo boxer, didn't miss by much, according to accounts. It was just an impressive display of skill by both fighters who were not overwhelming power punchers. Although Slattery showed more explosive bursts, Loughran took control of the fight.

Forgotten Rounds

Mike McTigue, having fought professionally since 1915, proved at age thirty-four that his only nemesis was Father Time. On January 28, the Irishman battered Paul Berlenbach into submission, and it took only four rounds. After Berlenbach had been dropped for two nine-counts in the fourth round, referee Kid McPartland had seen enough and stepped in to halt the fight. Noteworthy as one of the preliminaries: James J. Braddock, in his Madison Square Garden debut, knocked out George LaRocco in the very first round of a scheduled four-term affair.

Weeks later, on March 3, Mike McTigue made a gallant effort for ten rounds against the Binghamton-born Jack Sharkey on March 3. The only problem was it was a fifteen-round contest. Sharkey impressed many with his first appearance inside the new Garden. From the tenth round onward, he battered a bloodied McTigue like a defenseless midshipman. Referee Billy McPartland finally intervened at the halfway mark of the twelfth to hand the knockout victory to Sharkey. The much younger pugilist, who was also nearly twenty pounds heavier, had proved too much for "Irish" Mike.

Albert Morgan Pilkingon, a.k.a. "Tod Morgan," retained his junior lightweight championship on December 16 when he won by foul over Williamsburg's Joe Glick in the fourteenth round. Glick, a local favorite, pounded Morgan relentlessly for ten rounds—Morgan hit the canvas three times as a result of punches he claimed were foul. Finally, Glick became so frustrated with Morgan that he fired low and his rival sank to the canvas. It was so obvious the punch that referee Eddie Forbes didn't even bother with a count and immediately disqualified Glick.

If you had to choose a fighter who impressed the most during the year, it was clearly Tommy Loughran. The Philadelphia-born light heavy posted an undefeated record of 10-0, while picking up victories over Tony Marullo, Johnny Risko, Young Stribling, Mike McTigue and Jimmy Slattery; he took both his Garden contests. Having defeated Johnny Dundee in a unanimous decision to capture the vacant NYSAC world featherweight title, Tony Canzoneri finished the year with four Garden victories, including two solid back-to-back triumphs.

1928

Five outstanding fights—three indoor shows and two outdoor—highlighted the year for Tex Rickard and company:

A Handful of Highlights

Tommy Loughran v. Leo Lomski

The season started off in grand fashion at the Garden on January 6. The main event witnessed light-heavy champion Tommy Loughran battle his way to a challenging victory over Leo Lomski in fifteen rounds. Loughran was dropped twice for the count of nine in the very first round. The champion, who hadn't lost a battle since 1925, looked overwhelmed at the start but slowly regained his composure.[15]

The beginning of February brought word from Tex Rickard that Jack Dempsey had decided to retire. Naturally, all boxing retirements are greeted with incredulity, so why should Dempsey's be any different? The reason was simple: to blow out the Dempsey candle was to say goodbye to an era. It was just an acknowledgment that Rickard couldn't afford to accept, or elaborate upon.

It appeared like business as usual inside the Garden; however, summer planning inside big venues takes time. Under an agreement with the heavyweight champion, Rickard needed to find the perfect rival for Gene Tunney, if there was such a thing. (There was, but he had retired.) Having already chosen June 14 (later moved to July 26) as the date for Tunney's battle meant the promoter likely had to choose between Jack Delaney, Tom Heeney, Tommy

Loughran, Paulino Uzcudun, Risko, or perhaps British heavy Phil Scott or Sharkey. It was going to be a difficult as well as risky choice.

Jack Sharkey v. Jack Delaney

Garden gatherings, such as meeting with a fighter or his manager, were "hot" news items—not capable of filling an entire column, but a large portion of one was certainly feasible. For Rickard and matchmaker McMahon, they were chess moves, or leverage for negotiation. If they wanted Sharkey or Delaney to lower their demands, they would just grab some headlines that they were meeting with Risko's team. You get the picture, and one painted by a master.[16] Later, Rickard announced that Heeney would meet Tunney on July 26 in Yankee Stadium. It was also believed, and later confirmed, that the Garden would not conduct summer boxing.

Wasting little time, 73 seconds to be exact, Jack Sharkey knocked out ex-light heavyweight champion Jack Delaney in the first round of their April 30 confrontation inside Madison Square Garden. The Gob didn't waste time because he didn't have it—to perform in any other manner would not guarantee that he would remain in the heavyweight or "Big Money" mix. As for Delaney, well, it appeared as if the sun had set on the Bridgeport light heavyweight. Having won the world light heavyweight title against Paul Berlenbach back in June 1926, he relinquished his crown a year later. His next pursuit: a career at heavyweight.[17]

Sammy Mandell v. Jimmy McLarnin

In what many consider his finest hour, Sammy Mandell, the "Rockford Sheik," captured a fifteen-round unanimous decision over future welterweight champion Jimmy McLarnin on May 21 at the Polo Grounds. Trained by the legendary Jack Blackburn, Mandell was outstanding; his fast hands and superb defensive skills proved too much for McLarnin. "The Sheik" had slipped out of the limelight since capturing the lightweight title from Rocky Kansas two years earlier. Much of the disappearance was blamed on injuries and sickness. As for McLarnin, he would score an impressive first-round knockout of Phil McGraw on June 21 inside the Garden. McGraw had been dropped four times before the referee stopped the fight at the 2:45 mark. The win would keep the Ireland-born fighter in the mix.

Gene Tunney v. Tom Heeney

In typical Tunney manner, the undefeated heavyweight champion knocked out sturdy New Zealander Tom Heeney in the eleventh round of their July 26 battle inside Yankee Stadium. But, contrary to Rickard's reputation, the promotion was a financial failure, the promoter blaming his error on timing. While the hope of the British Empire may have been dashed, it may have only been for a short period of time: Tunney had been rumored to be retiring. For the world's heavyweight champion, who had never left Dempsey's shadow, he considered it his turn to shine. Yet, having defeated his rival not once, but twice, the Greenwich Village boxer seemed only to have been tolerated as titleholder. Much of that had been attributed to Tunney's quiet and humble style; he was a fighter who was far happier out of the limelight than in it. Whereas Dempsey was a rough-edged cowboy you could ride the rails with, Tunney's air of aristocracy sent shivers of uneasiness up your spine.

Sure enough, heavyweight champion Gene Tunney formally announced his retirement on July 31, 1928. Which invited the question: Now what? Talk of an elimination tournament made sense from Rickard's perspective, but he was not the only promoter capable of such an event. Adding to the complexity, at least for Rickard, was the departure of matchmaker Jess McMahon, who would take over the direction of boxing at Starlight Park Arena, located at 177th Street and Tremont Avenue. Succeeding McMahon was Tom McArdle, a matchmaker at the Queensboro A.C.

James J. Braddock v. Tuffy Griffiths

Surprising everyone, Jersey City's James J. Braddock, who filled in for Jack Delaney, found a hole in the defenses of a 38-1-1 fighter named Gerald "Tuffy" Griffiths and knocked him out in the second round of their November 30 bout inside Madison Square Garden. Griffiths was originally matched with Pete Latzo, who was replaced by Delaney before Braddock entered the picture. Braddock, himself on the short end of the betting odds, overcame every perceived weakness to drop his adversary four times in the second round before referee Kid McPartland had seen enough. Hailed by many as the West Coast's Jack Dempsey, Griffiths had won fifty-five consecutive bouts before meeting the Jersey City fighter. It was Braddock's straight right during the first knockdown that appeared to do the damage, as Griffiths never regained his composure.

Forgotten Rounds

Two challengers were vying for a shot at Sammy Mandell's lightweight title, Sid Terris and Jimmy McLarnin. And as fate might have it, both were matched against each other on February 24. In the opening round, before Sid Terris could mount an offensive, a lightning bolt of a right struck his chin. Terris dropped like an anvil from the roof of the Flatiron Building. Counted out, Terris never moved a muscle and had to be carried to his corner. Not enough time had ticked off the clock to even a light a cigarette (which was just fine, as management had initiated a "No Smoking" policy). Sid's 107 seconds of fame had been vanquished with a single knockout punch.

Panama Al Brown picked up two back-to-back victories when he knocked out Billy Shaw on June 21, and took a tough points victory over Kid Francis on September 13. Maxie Rosenbloom picked up three Garden victories: Phil Kaplan on February 3, Jack McVey on February 17, and Jack Payne on October 11. Max Schmeling made his Garden debut by knocking out Joe Monte on November 23. Kid Chocolate debuted a week later with a draw against Joey Scalfaro. Finally, a record crowd poured into the Garden on December 14 to witness a boxing card perfectly gauged to the New York fight scene. In the main event, Bronx youngster Al Singer drew Brooklyn's Tony Canzoneri, the former feather champion, over ten rounds.

If 1928 belonged to any single fighter, it was Young Stribling, or William Lawrence Stribling, Jr., alias "King of the Canebrakes." The boxer went 38–0 with 33 knockouts. Hailing from Macon, Georgia, he defeated Johnny Squires in his only Garden battle of the year.

While Jack Sharkey's three consecutive Garden battles (1-1-1) were notable, so too were the performances of Tony Canzoneri. He defeated Benny Bass on February 10, lost to André Routis on September 28, and drew Al Singer on December 14. The Staten Island pugilist fought his heart out against Routis, and while the Frenchman took the split decision, "Canzi," a local Italian favorite, won over the hearts of many.

Rickard's Passing

For Rickard, it was off to Miami Beach for a bit of rest and relaxation. He had not felt well for a period of time, suffering from abdominal pain, and pressure in the lower-right abdomen along with temperature fluctuations. Rickard, on the advice of Dr. E.H. Adkins, opted for an appendectomy on the evening of January 1, 1929. The Rickards, Tex along with his wife Maxine, were at their Miami Beach home at 2983 North Bay Road. Following the operation, and while exhibiting a normal recovery, Rickard suffered a relapse and infection developed.[18] Gallantly trying to fight his infection, he eventually slipped into a coma. He passed away inside Allison Hospital at 8:37 A.M. on January 6. Tex Rickard was fifty-six years and four days old.[19] According to reports, Dr. Adkins, Jack Dempsey, Mr. and Mrs. Walter Field (the promoter's assistant), Mrs. Maxine Hodges Rickard, and two nurses were at his bedside.[20]

Transforming a sport, especially one as shunned as boxing, into an industry was no easy task, yet George Lewis "Tex" Rickard seemed to revel in the challenge. It was through his vision and dogged determination that the fight game grew from local athletic clubs, featuring neighborhood pugs, to the country's largest venues, presenting the finest national and international talent. When "Tex" dreamed, he dreamed big, and when it was time to convert those visions into reality, he did so with precision.

Having a knack for promotion and an eye for opportunity, Rickard understood the instant credibility associated with large-scale promotions. However, he also acknowledged that a larger venue needed a star attraction, and he found it with Jack Dempsey. The young fighter was everything a big-eyed boxing promoter needed—the treasure at the end of the boxing rainbow and much more. So did Rickard make Dempsey? Or did Dempsey make Rickard? Or was it the quintessential relationship for both?

The bout between Dempsey and Carpentier at Boyle's Thirty Acres would result in Rickard's being compared to Barnum, and Dempsey to Sullivan. As the promoter spun his fighters, especially Dempsey, into fascinating characters, the press took the bait, hook, line and sinker. As a result, people knew more about "The Manassa Mauler" than they knew about the president of the United States. And for the very first time, city gentry could be found ringside to see just what all the fuss was about, and some of them happened to be women.

Tex Rickard was also the first boxing promoter to pay a boxer what he was worth. You could keep a fighter if you paid him, and you could motivate him if he had a stake in the gate. The guarantees were incomprehensible to the average man, but so too was facing Jess Willard.

With the passing of the Walker boxing bill, Rickard turned to his next treasure, Madison Square Garden. There he cultivated relationships, nurtured the lower weight classes, and used his position to leverage his larger promotions. If you shined for Rickard, return engagements were a given.

Although Rickard wasn't afraid of a racially mixed bout—he proved that by his promotions, including Nelson-Gans and Johnson-Jeffries—he understood its sensitivity. Under enormous pressure to take a Dempsey-Wills bout, he chose to turn away.

Seeing promise in a new Garden, he enlisted the financial assistance of some friends, including John Ringling. Madison Square Garden Corporation was destined to become a success with Tex at the helm. Like any strong leader, he surrounded himself with capable individuals, especially his matchmakers. From his two-ton bronze desk inside the Garden, he ruled boxing. If you were lucky enough to get an audience with him, it could mean a career-changing opportunity, and everyone associated with the fight game knew it.

So gifted a promoter was Rickard, that he had a symbiotic relationship with NYSAC. The promoter was breaking new ground with his promotions, leaving the commission almost no choice but to accept many of his recommendations. For example, when Rickard made a request to charge the maximum of $27.50 a ticket for his July 21, 1927, promotion (Dempsey v. Sharkey) inside Yankee Stadium, it was accepted. Nevertheless, NYSAC also asked the promoter to scale tickets at the championship level, so that they could get a sense of the market for such a title fight. Underlying this effort, which was certainly obvious to a fox like Rickard, was that NYSAC wanted the bout between the winner and Tunney to stay in New York.[21]

Rickard changed the public's opinion of boxing through many communication vehicles including newspapers, magazines and radio. His strategic marketing included clubs—he organized a club called "Six Hundred Millionaires," or a group of selected individuals who received the first call for tickets—and even railroads where he offered ticket discounts. The promoter built facilities for fights, lined up substitute fighters as a precautionary measure, and assisted in drawing more women to watch boxing shows (primarily following the Milk Fund shows held after 1923). All of these were accomplishments many felt were unachievable or simply far from cost-effective.

Five great fights will forever shadow Rickard, and they all had Dempsey as the common numerator: Dempsey-Carpentier (1921), Dempsey-Firpo (1923), Dempsey-Tunney (1926), Dempsey-Tunney (1927), and Dempsey-Sharkey (1927). Guess who was the common denominator? And while he rode Dempsey, he understood the value of smaller promotions. Most champions, he believed, were like ice cubes in a summer drink, so he enjoyed his cold lemonade while he still could.

Draped in mourning for the first time since opening, the new Madison Square had the flag atop the building flying at half-staff. Inside rested an unassembled City Ring, and if it were ever possible for an inanimate object to shed a tear, this would have been the time.

5

Dealing with the Loss, January 7, 1929–1934

> Poverty is apt to strike suddenly like influenza, it is well to have a few memories of extravagance in store for bad times.
> —Graham Greene, *Travels with My Aunt*

1929

Flamboyant New York City Mayor Jimmy Walker won reelection during a year that would witness the improbable. "Wall Street laid an egg," or least *Variety* thought so, as they reported on the beginning of the longest, deepest, and most widespread depression of the 20th century.

Understanding that there's no replacing a visionary such as Tex Rickard, boxing could only hope that at some point someone would come along to embellish his genius. He was dominant in so many aspects of business, it was tough to imagine anyone tackling his agenda with precision. Some believed a boxing promoter, such as Humbert J. Fugazy, could take over where Rickard left off with his large promotions, but that was only one aspect of the profession. It was the promoter's keen overall insights that needed to be restored, and that required more than just anyone sitting behind the impresario's desk inside Madison Square Garden. (Rickard's bronze bureau, emblematic of many qualities including leadership, was originally owned by President William McKinley.) Yet, with agreements on the books, such as Jack Sharkey meeting Young Stribling at Miami Beach on February 27, 1929, the issue needed to be resolved as soon as possible.

Immediately, Madison Square Garden Corporation took action. William F. Carey, who was first vice president and treasurer, met with Colonel John S. Hammond, a vice president and assistant general manager, along with matchmaker Tom McArdle, to consider their options. Each of the three men was quickly rumored to be Rickard's successor, but nobody was certain. As a public company, the corporation's primary concern was stabilizing its stock after the impact of Rickard's passing. This would be achieved through comprehensive press statements acknowledging the loss yet reaffirming the group's goals and visions.

The Garden's acting general manager, John S. Hammond, did his best to create the impression that it was business as usual with the corporation. Exercising park options for both Yankee Stadium and the Polo Grounds confirmed the corporation's commitment to large-venue promotions. It was a notable first step before picking up the other pieces Rickard had left behind.

Schmeling Salts

A capacity crowd watched as German Max Schmeling destroyed "The Cleveland Rubber Man," a.k.a. Johnny Risko, on February 1 inside the City Ring.[1] Floored in the 1st, 7th, 8th and 9th rounds, Risko had no place to go to avoid his opponent's devastating punishment. Finally, referee Art Donovan had seen enough and stopped the fight in the ninth round. Elated, the crowd gave Schmeling an enormous ovation. It was the German's powerful right that carried him to victory and the first genuine knockout of heavyweight contender Risko. In only his third Garden battle, Schmeling confirmed that he was a force in his division.[2]

Arriving in New York for the first time in 1928, Schmeling went virtually unnoticed. It wasn't until he hooked up with American manager Joe Jacobs that everything changed. The quintessential boxing manager of his era, Jacobs was an audacious, pugnacious, cigar-chomping, and fedora-wearing salesman who knew a deal when he saw it, and *it* was Schmeling. Under the cogent manager the German made his debut in America at Madison Square Garden with an eighth-round knockout of Joe Monte on November 23, 1928. In January of 1929, a couple of victories—Joe Sekyra and Pietro Corri—led to his fight with Risko.

Rickard's Last Dance

The first contest aimed at producing a successor to Gene Tunney, and the last fight arranged by Tex Rickard before his death, took place inside Flamingo Park in Miami Beach, Florida, on Wednesday, February 27, 1929. Unfortunately, at least for the 35,000 spectators in attendance, both heavyweights danced a lackluster ten rounds before Sharkey took the unanimous verdict. The large crowd had turned out in support of the city's vision of becoming a boxing hub.[3] The numbers were good even if the fight wasn't: the gate take was $400,000; Sharkey's cut was a guaranteed $100,000; Stribling's slice, a gate percentage, was $60,000; and the Madison Square Garden Corporation dealt with the rest.[4]

In one of the earliest signs that life at the Garden was going to be different without Rickard, William F. Carey issued a statement that the corporation would no longer provide fighters with forfeits or guarantees. The practice, as far as Carey was concerned, was backward and unnecessary. On Monday, March 18, 1929, William F. Carey was formally named as president of the Madison Square Garden Corporation.[5]

On the undercard of the Al Singer versus Ignacio Fernandez bout on May 17, 1929, was a bout between William "Gorilla" Jones and Bronx boxer Izzy Grove. Both 153-pound fighters valued their Garden exposure and were hellbent on a victory. Jones, a black American, began his professional career in 1924 fighting out of Memphis. Grove, a white slugger whose real name was Eddie Poplick, started his pro career in 1926 boxing out of the Walker Athletic Club. In front of a partisan crowd, Grove, who gained a bit of a following thanks to his appearances on some large cards, was continually being "thumbed" in the eye by Jones. But when the fighter complained, referee Jack Dorfman simply ignored the allegations. Finally, in the sixth round, Grove could no longer see and the fight was awarded to

Jones. Grove's handlers were incensed, but their complaints to the NYSAC ringside physician were ignored. Following an examination, it was proven that there was an irritant in Grove's left eye, and that the fighter's claims were indeed valid. Team Jones, having been behind in points, may have initiated the move out of frustration.[6] The incident, only one of many, endorsed the importance of NYSAC to the sport of boxing.

On September 26, Jack Sharkey, whose proposed bout with Max Schmeling was nixed by NYSAC, met Tommy Loughran inside Yankee Stadium.[7] In the eyes of the Madison Square Garden Corporation, the choice of Loughran to meet the "Boston Gob" in the event's feature was the better option. Sharkey, who wasted no time proving he was Tunney's logical successor, knocked out Loughran in the third round. Sharkey was always a dollar-per-minute pugilist.

Irish Eyes

Like an unexpected overhand right to the head—similar to what Sharkey delivered to Loughran but far more devastating—the stock market crash of 1929 began on Thursday, October 24, and was the most devastating stock market collapse in the history of the United States. Wall Street's desolation, which followed the London Stock Exchange's crash in September, signaled the beginning of a long Great Depression that affected all Western industrialized countries.

Nevertheless, despite Wall Street's downfall, or because of it, over 18,000 paid spectators couldn't resist the opportunity to witness Irish-Canadian Jimmy McLarnin battle the East Side's Ruby Goldstein on Friday, December 13, inside Madison Square Garden.

In Round One, McLarnin found an angle and connected with a powerful right to the jaw, followed by a left hook to the head. Goldstein collapsed. Slow to regain his composure, he arose at nine. McLarnin tried to finish him, but Goldstein was resilient and made it to the bell.

When the gong sounded for Round Two, the "Baby Faced Assassin" took command. Pushing Goldstein about the ring, McLarnin finally boxed him and landed a destructive right to the jaw. Goldstein dropped like a log onto the lower ring rope, before slipping through. As the count began, the East Sider succeeded at slowly pulling himself back into the ring, then standing, at nine. Hopelessly erect, Goldstein could only await the inevitable. McLarnin, unable to resist the opportunity, lunged forward with a ruinous right that dropped his adversary for the final time. With six straight victories during the year, McLarnin was undeniable.

As the decade closed, the fighter of the year could easily be recognized as Jack Sharkey, who fought in only one Garden battle but proved himself as the premier heavyweight.

Inside the City Ring: Max Schmeling battled twice in the ring and never lost. The German also battered Paulino Uzcudon unmercifully for fifteen rounds to take a decisive victory on June 27 at Yankee Stadium. Lost in the shuffle was "Slapsie" Maxi Rosenbloom, an outstanding defensive boxer, who fought brilliantly in the light heavyweight sector. He took four wins inside the Garden, including a decision over James J. Braddock on November 15. However, fighting four times at the Garden, Jimmy McLarnin never lost. He fought in three consecutive battles, including back-to-back confrontations against Joe Glick.

The Thirties: 1930

More than 13,000 banks closed during the first year of the decade. Just making ends meet, at least for most, was a daily challenge. The freelance world of the boxing ring continued to be an extension of the crucible of street existence, as matchmakers wisely used ethnic pride to drive promotions.

FOUL PLAY

The earliest notable corporate show of the outdoor season was a heavyweight fight between Jack Sharkey and Phil Scott on Thursday, February 27, inside Miami Stadium. As both fighters were no strangers to foul play, everyone expected a controversy.

Wasting little time, which was his hallmark, Jack Sharkey grabbed a third-round knockout victory from the Englishman. A disappointing crowd of only 30,000 witnessed the unusual affair. Referee Lou Magnolia disqualified Scott in the third round: the Englishman, who had been floored three times, fell to the canvas following a clean left hook, and then claimed a low blow. The disqualification confused everyone, including Sharkey; it was the punch prior to the clean blow to Scott that was questionable. Perhaps it was a delayed reaction. Regardless, Scott's seconds carried him to his corner, where the fighter was warned to continue in one minute or face disqualification. At first it looked as if Scott was continuing, but he slowly sank to the floor.

A delegation of baseball stars also attended—which created much of the event's early excitement—including slugger Babe Ruth, umpire Bill Klem, former umpire Billy Evans and Giants infielder Freddy Lindstrom. Overall the event, despite the presence of "The Bambino," was a disappointment.

What the Garden didn't need after their Miami event was more controversial endings. However, on Monday, March 10, inside the City Ring, that was precisely what they received in the form of a trio of fouls. Light heavyweight contender Maxie Rosenbloom won on a foul over Chicagoan Larry Johnson in the sixth round of a scheduled ten-round duel. It was the main event and unfortunately it was preceded by two additional disqualifications in the preliminaries: Binghamton's Joe Banovic won on a first-round foul from Henry Lamar, and Westchester's Bruno Salo won on a third-round foul by Italian Armadeo Grillo.

THUNDERSTRUCK

Moving outside, on June 12 in Yankee Stadium, German Max Schmeling captured the heavyweight title (vacated by Gene Tunney's retirement) as a result of a foul by his opponent Jack Sharkey in the fourth round. "The Gob," having put on a steadfast display for three rounds, reached into his bag of tricks, pulled out a conspicuously low left hook, and sent it special delivery to a paralyzing area of the German's body. Schmeling was so incapacitated that he had to be carried to his corner. It wasn't pretty. Nor was it an action taken by someone vying for the most coveted title in the world. The fight, attended by an estimated 80,000 fight fans, was a joint promotion between the Free Milk Fund for Babies, Inc., and the Madison Square Garden Corporation. In the face of the main event, the evening proved an enormous financial success.[8]

Back inside Yankee Stadium on July 17, Al Singer shocked the boxing world with a first-round knockout of lightweight champion Sammy Mandell. For four years, Mandell had proven himself invincible among the lightweights. Yet he could last less than two minutes against Singer. The "Rockford Sheik" was dropped four times in front of 35,000 spectators. Singer, the new world's lightweight champion, and his sizable fan contingent were elated. Surprisingly, Singer was a favorite (3–1) at fight time.

During the fall schedule, on November 3, a bout between Fidel La Barba, the former flyweight champion, and Kid Chocolate attracted considerable attention. A partisan Garden crowd estimated at 17,000 watched as the New York—born La Barba fought brilliantly to collect the ten-round unanimous decision. For Chocolate, it was just his second loss in over 160 (amateur and professional) ring battles. It was La Barba's consistent body assault that gradually wore down his adversary.

In proof of the old adage "what goes around comes around," Al Singer, having stunned the world back in July with his knockout of Sammy Mandell, found himself introduced to the canvas 66 seconds into the first round of his face-off against Tony Canzoneri. The devastation took place inside the Garden on November 14. Brooklyn's Canzoneri, who formerly ruled the featherweight division, had trained hard for the encounter and it showed.[9]

Forgotten Rounds

Pennsylvania's Pete Latzo upset Chicago's Larry Johnson in a ten-round decision on February 21. Also fighting on the card was Newark's Vince Dundee, who took a ten-rounder from Bucky Lawless of Auburn, New York. Both Latzo and Dundee, who began boxing in the early 1920s, had seen more rings than P.T. Barnum.

NBA (National Boxing Association, not recognized by New York State) junior welterweight champion Jack Berg waged a ten-round bitter battle against Williamsburg (Brooklyn) lightweight Joe Glick on Friday, April 4.[10] In taking the unanimous decision, Berg confirmed what a dogged fighter he had become, and for his part, Glick impressed many with his power and perseverance.

On October 10, Berg took a hard-fought a ten-round decision over Billy Petrolle, a.k.a. "Fargo Express." In typical fashion, Berg, who had been knocked out two years earlier by his opponent, was relentless and indefatigable. He swarmed Petrolle like bees to honey.

On November 21, Billy Petrolle took a ten-round points decision over Jimmy McLarnin in a superb welterweight battle. Flooring McLarnin twice, Petrolle hammered the Baby Faced Assassin's countenance into a bloodied mess (a rare occurrence).

Appearing on the undercard of the LaBarba versus Taylor match on November 28 was a ten-round conflict between Brownsville's Lew Feldman and Long Island's Pete DeGrasse.[11] Fought to a vicious draw, it led to the predictable discontent via boos and hisses.[12]

Ageless Hartford wonder Christopher "Bat" Battalino, who also happened to be the world's featherweight champion, took a tough decision over Kid Chocolate on December 12. Chocolate, who managed to floor the champion in the very first round, was shocked by the verdict. However, in order to beat a champion, a victory must be decisive, and some felt Chocolate was not.

California heavyweight Max Baer made his first Garden appearance on Friday, December 19, when he met Boston's Ernie Schaff. The Californian's impressive knockout record had brought him into the heavyweight picture, so all he had to do was stay there. But Schaff thought otherwise and took a close but unanimous ten-round decision from the "Livermore Larupper."[13]

Fighter of the Year

While some would choose Max Schmeling as the fighter or the year, for Garden followers it was a unanimous decision for Maxie Rosenbloom. How many arms did he have? Winning all of his Garden appearances, the fighter had captured the world lightweight crown with his split decision over tough Buffalo boxer Jimmy Slattery. Yet for all his success inside the City Ring, he would not be back until 1933.[14]

1931

Unlike previous years, the City Ring would not feature a preeminent ring battle in 1931. However, it would present numerous outstanding engagements. And during these difficult financial times, that was hard enough.

Rather than beginning on a high note, the sweet science turned to some housekeeping. On January 7, 1931, Max Schmeling was stripped of his heavyweight crown by NYSAC for his refusal to accept Jack Sharkey as the outstanding challenger for the title. Additionally, the commission indefinitely suspended the boxer and his manager, Joe Jacobs. In a similar move, NYSAC withdrew Mickey Walker's middleweight title for rules violations.

Floored twice in the first round—a nine count followed by an eight count—Vince Dundee roared back to take a decision over English middleweight Len Harvey on Friday, January 9. It was Harvey's American debut, and Dundee's determination provided him with a memory he wouldn't soon forget, as the American delivered a fierce body assault. The two would battle again, inside Madison Square Garden on February 13, to the same result.

The confrontation between heavyweights Max Baer of California and Tom Heeney of New Zealand was scheduled for ten rounds, but it would end much sooner. A mere sixteen days into the new year, Jack Dempsey, who was serving as arbiter inside the City Ring, would pick up a count incorrectly to mark the ring's first gaffe of the annum. It happened in the third round, when Baer sent Heeney to the canvas and referee Dempsey found himself two counts behind timekeeper Arthur Donovan. As Dempsey hit eight, Donovan awarded the fight to Baer—this as both Dempsey and Heeney were looking straight into the eyes of the timekeeper. Heeney, who had been shipped through the ropes by Baer and then pushed back into the ring, was waiting on one knee to arise at the count of nine. When both the crowd and Heeney learned of the verdict, they went crazy. Dempsey had not only overlooked the elapsed time that Heeney spent outside the ring, but should have disqualified the fighter for being assisted back into it. NYSAC would later state that they would have supported Dempsey's position to resume fighting had he chosen such an option. The commission also ordered that a two-foot extension be added to all ring floors, meaning from the ropes to the edge of the ring would measure three and one-half feet. As for Dempsey, he would redeem himself as a referee during Tommy Loughran's unanimous ten-round decision over Max Baer on February 6.

In Cleveland on July 3, Max Schmeling knocked out Young Stribling in the fifteenth round. As "kayo" was an unheard-of word in the Stribling vernacular, it was hard for him to stomach. The veteran of hundreds of bouts needed only 14 more seconds to go the distance. Nonetheless, he could not. It would be the sole knockout loss suffered by "King of the Canebrakes" during his brilliant career. Referee George Blake made the correct choice by stepping in and awarding the knockout of the "Black Uhlan of the Rhine." Stribling had been floored by a powerful Schmeling right earlier in the round and it had taken its toll. Madison Square Garden Corporation of Ohio was delighted—the German was under contract to defend his title with the company, which meant more opportunities—despite the fact that the event was deemed a financial failure.

On Friday, November 20, Tony Canzoneri battled Kid Chocolate for fifteen brisk rounds to take the decision. Canzoneri dominated the fight with his offensive prowess, but the verdict was divided. The pronouncement was so unpopular with the large Garden crowd that they decided to catapult everything within arm's distance into the ring. For Canzoneri, it was his last battle for the year.[15]

Forgotten Rounds

On February 13, in a warm-up to the Dundee-Harvey bout, Yorkville welterweight Vincent Serici, a bit behind in points, delivered an incredible right to the jaw of San Francisco's Madison Dix that sent the Californian flat on his back in the sixth round of their contest.

Polish welterweight Eddie Ran, who had taken a horrible beating for eight rounds, stunned everyone by knocking out St. Paul boxer Billy Light in the ninth round of their February 27 contest. Light was floored three times in the final round. Speaking of Eddie, during the semifinal of the Canzoneri versus Chocolate bout held on November 20, the welterweight knocked out Louis "Kid" Kaplan in the first round of a scheduled eight-rounder.

If any boxer seemed to defy his critics, it was Christopher "Bat" Battalino. Demonstrating yet again why he was the featherweight champion of New York State, the Hartford boxer pounded Fidel La Barba through most of their fifteen-round Garden contest on May 22. Retaining the 126-pound crown, Bat kept La Barba constantly on the defensive. This was only LaBarba's third fight of the year and it showed. Following his June loss to Claude Varner, LaBarba would win his next ten fights to finish the year at 12-2-1.

Jimmy McLarnin avenged his loss to Billy Petrolle the previous November by taking a May 27 decision over the fighter. McLarnin repeated his performance in August to complete the pair's trilogy.

Solly Krieger dropped German Hans Muller nine times on his way to a win in a brutal eight-round battle on Thursday, August 27, and Battling Levinsky dropped Tommy Loughran three times on December 18 to take a ten-round decision. The upset was a major setback for Loughran, who had hoped to find himself in the heavyweight mix.

Again, Hartford's "Bat" Battalino, the featherweight titleholder, stepped forward and destroyed a contender. This time it was former lightweight champion Al "The Bronx Beauty" Singer on December 11 inside the City Ring. After Singer had hit the canvas four times, the NYSAC physician signaled the referee to stop the fight in the second round. Battalino, who was fighting at just over 135 pounds, was even more convincing at the heavier weight than he had been at 126 pounds.

Fighter of the Year

As the sport's fighter of the year, you would have to turn to Mickey Walker. Despite relinquishing his middleweight championship, the "Toy Bulldog" drew Jack Sharkey and took four other bouts by knockout—three of which were in the first round. But Walker didn't fight inside Madison Square Garden during the year. Of those who did, a pair of fighters stick out as the most notable: Middleweight Vince Dundee won all four of his Garden appearances, two of which were back-to-back wins over Len Harvey. Yet, if you subtract Tommy Loughran's final ring appearance against Battling Levinsky, his victories over Max Baer, Ernie Schaaf, Victorio Campolo and Paulino Uzcudun can be viewed as equally as impressive.

1932

The Great Depression seemed to hit the hardest in 1932. Every economic indicator was down, from industrial production to wholesale prices. Soup kitchen lines seemed longer and there were simply no jobs. Everybody and everything seemed to take a beating.

Matter what it may, the maximum admission charge to a championship ring battle at Madison Square Garden was still reasonable at $5.74. Not everybody, or so it was believed by James J. Johnston, the Garden's boxing director, could resist an opportunity to see ageless feather champion Christopher "Bat" Battalino defend his title against Brownsville's Lew Feldman in January. But just when Johnston thought he had a winning ticket to open the year, the situation changed.[16]

Hartford's master craftsman and titleholder failed to reach the required 126 pounds and had to forfeit his title. The situation would become the first abandonment of a boxing match on the day of the show in Madison Square Garden history. When Battalino tipped higher than 135, nobody could believe the scale. As a result of the fiasco, NYSAC initiated a rule requiring out-of-town boxers to be in the city five days prior to their scheduled match.

On Petrolle

On March 24, "Bat" Battalino, former feather champion after relinquishing the title, met Fargo's Billy Petrolle for twelve rounds inside Madison Square Garden.[17] Battalino was 116–22 with one no contest—Petrolle entered the ring 40–12. Both boxers were ceaseless in their assaults, and the large crowd of New York fight fans reveled in the action. In the twelfth and final round, Petrolle accomplished what no other Battalino opponent had managed: he stopped the Hartford fighter from going the distance. Referee Gunboat Smith had to stop the fight at the midway point in the round to protect Battalino from further damage—the exhausted Connecticut fighter was simply powerless to defend himself. The victory advanced Petrolle, a ferocious body puncher, into the forefront of challenges for either the light or welterweight title. As for Battalino, he would lose five of his next seven contests.[18]

WE WUZ ROBBED!

Max Schmeling and Jack Sharkey were finally scheduled to meet on Tuesday, June 21. Schmeling arrived via the Hamburg-American liner *New York* on April 8 to begin preparation. Sharkey, who was training out of his hometown of Boston and conducting entertaining exhibitions, also planned to arrive soon. Unable to find a suitable existing facility for the fight, the Garden turned to constructing a venue—no simple task considering the time restraints. On Monday, April 11, ground was broken for the Madison Square Garden Bowl, an over 90,000-seat facility to be constructed on an 18-acre plot on Northern Boulevard, from 48th to 43rd streets in Queens.[19] Tickets for the event were approved at the $3.45, $5.75, $11.50, $17.25 and $23 pricing levels, with distribution slated for numerous large cities.

As a heavyweight championship, the event played out just as it should. Each round was an enhancement of the excitement generated by its predecessor. Punching distances were measured during the early rounds, before being applied with greater force and accuracy with each passing term. The champion was the aggressor, far more truculent than his cautious challenger. For a moment, in the seventh round, Schmeling took Sharkey out of his

An American boxer who held both the world welterweight and world middleweight championships at different points in his career, Edward Patrick "Mickey" Walker (1903 [some sources indicate 1901]–1981) was as versatile as he was prolific. He is pictured here while visiting the White House in 1925 (*Library of Congress, LC-DIG-npcc-12970* [*digital file from original*]).

game plan with a solid right to the jaw. This caused the Bostonian to briefly drop his conservative approach in order to fire a roundhouse right at the German.

Both fighters rode their left hands for the first ten rounds, systematically, or so it appeared, conserving their rights. After the tenth round, Sharkey's left eye began to close. Still the aggressor into the fourteenth round, Schmeling was engaging but finding it difficult to connect with his retreating antagonist. When the split decision favoring Sharkey was announced—the most dramatic moment in the entire fight—few could believe it. Even Mayor Jimmy Walker of New York believed Schmeling had won. The incident caused Schmeling's manager Joe Jacobs to cry out in disbelief, "We wuz robbed!"[20]

Forgotten Rounds

Boston's Sammy "Little Dynamite" Fuller, during twelve rounds, managed to hold off the ever-aggressive Jack "Kid" Berg to take a May 20 decision. The former lightweight champion of New England then claimed the junior welterweight's crown.

Heavyweight hopeful Mickey Walker took a unanimous ten-round decision over Paulino Uzcudon on May 26. He would finish the year 6–2.

On July 18, back inside the Madison Square Garden Bowl, Jack "Kid" Berg took a controversial fifteen-round decision over Kid Chocolate during a non-title bout. About 15,000 fans witnessed the exciting and savage affair that unfortunately ended in controversy—virtually every expert felt the Cuban deserved the award. The fight's poor attendance was an indication that holding regular boxing bouts at the Bowl might not be a wise economic decision.

Kid Chocolate solidified his position as world's featherweight champion on October 13 by knocking out Lew Feldman in the twelfth round. The "Cuban Bon Bon," who also held the junior lightweight title, finished the year with four straight victories.

Jimmy McLarnin knocked out Sammy Fuller in the eighth round of a scheduled ten-round battle on December 16.

The deteriorating fiscal conditions saw Garden management taking more chances with amateur intercity tournaments. On a much brighter note, the General Electric Corporation answered the Garden's call for improved lighting and installed a system making it over three times brighter. Atop the ring, an area that had been prone to obscure illumination, the company installed thirty-six lighting fixtures.

The year reflected the difficult fiscal times facing the country. Add to it the lack of a strong box office draw—there were no Jack Dempseys in the mix—and it didn't bode well for the fight game. An economic indicator of just how low the industry had sunk was that tax revenue, as reported by NYSAC's annual report, was a quarter of what it had been the previous year.

Fighter of the Year

Choosing a single fighter who added the most to the legacy of the City Ring in 1932 would be difficult, but choosing two would not. Featherweight Eligio Sardinias Montalvo, a.k.a. Kid Chocolate, fought twenty times, including two title fights inside Madison Square Garden, suffering only one loss (to Jack "Kid" Berg). For the "Cuban Bon Bon," it was an outstanding year. Jimmy McLarnin fought in only three bouts in 1932, but despite the split

An American world heavyweight boxing champion, Jack Sharkey—real name Joseph Paul Zukauskas—(1902–1994) was born in Binghamton, New York, but moved to Boston, Massachusetts, as a young man. He turned pro in 1924 (*Library of Congress, LC-DIG-npcc-12970 [digital file from original]*).

decision loss to Lou Brouillard at Yankee Stadium, his two Garden victories—the first against the aging Benny Leonard and the second over Sammy Fuller—were solid displays of just how truly brilliant he was as a boxer.[21]

1933

"The only thing we have to fear is fear itself," proclaimed President Roosevelt. Some of those fighting in the City Ring thought otherwise.

On Friday, February 10, a large Garden crowd—estimated at 20,000 fans—watched as Italian giant Primo Carnera altered the heavyweight horizon by knocking out Ernie Schaaf, who was managed by Jack Sharkey, in the thirteenth round. The fight had meandered along until 51 seconds into the thirteenth round, when Carnera's judicious left hand landed flush to the face of Schaaf. Although it didn't look powerful, it was. Schaaf collapsed and was carried to his dressing room. Twenty minutes of respiratory work was needed to restore the fighter's consciousness.[22] Stunned by the knockout and its lack of perceived power, the crowd booed in dissatisfaction over the result.

On Monday, February 13, *New York Times* boxing beat writer James P. Dawson penned the headline "Garden Planning Drastic Policy Change; To End Regular Boxing, Wrestling Dates." Other Garden events, such as bike races and track meets, didn't involve intense negotiations, integrity issues or as significant a financial risk—nor were they nearly as dangerous. Like boxing matches, sometimes these issues were just thrown to the public to clarify sentiment, or in this case to defuse a potential concern: Dawson had been tipped off that Schaaf's situation was grave.

Ernie Schaaf died on Tuesday, February 14, 1933, in Polyclinic Hospital at the age of 24. It was nothing short of an enormous tragedy. NYSAC issued a statement initially barring the proposed Sharkey versus Carnera match and also announced plans to resurrect the "dreadnaught" class of 1931, to service the needs of boxers of Carnera's size.[23]

Lights Out

There was a time when nobody thought the Sharkey versus Carnera bout would ever take place, and understandably so. But Madison Square Garden Corporation met the safety obligations placed before them and pressed onward. The heavyweight champion met the colossus on June 29, inside the Bowl for a scheduled fifteen rounds. Sharkey, as anticipated (based on the pair's history), was favored (8–5).

In the sixth round, Carnera saw an opportunity and nearly decapitated Sharkey with a right uppercut to the chin. The impact was so powerful that it lifted the champion slightly upward prior to sending his limp body starboard. Sharkey then rolled face-first into the canvas. As referee Donovan's count began, Sharkey was motionless and stayed that way until it was concluded. His seconds leaped into the ring at the conclusion of the count and carried the former champion to his corner. Over 40,000 fans, who were given round-by-round judging over the loudspeakers, were shocked by the action, as up to that point there had been no display of Carnera's tremendous power.

Division Driven

Barney Ross, who took Tony Canzoneri's lightweight and junior welterweight titles in Chicago on June 23, defeated the Brooklyn Italian again on September 12—only this time it was during a fifteen-round decision affair instead of ten. A crowd estimated at 35,000 witnessed the exciting display inside the Polo Grounds. Canzoneri, who resorted to many of his old tricks, was warned numerous times about low blows. When the two judges disagreed on their ballots, it left the decision solely to referee Donovan, who chose Ross. Beryl David Rosofsky, a.k.a. Barney Ross, hadn't lost a fight since March 27, 1931, and frankly speaking, looked unstoppable.

Canzoneri, the former world's lightweight champion, made a statement on November 24 by knocking out Kid Chocolate in spectacular fashion in the second round of their scheduled ten-term affair. In over 200 ring battles, Chocolate had never been knocked out—even grazing the canvas was a rarity for him. To many the action-packed lightweight event was as memorable as some of the old-style contests held in the former Garden. Canzoneri caught Chocolate coming out of a clinch and unloaded a vicious right to the jaw that dropped the Cuban. Face forward he plunged to the canvas.

As if this fight were not proof enough that Canzoneri was a force to contend with, he knocked out Cecil Payne in Cleveland on December 4 and was back in the Garden to take a ten-round decision from Cleto Locatelli on December 15. "Canzi" finished the year at 7–3.

Forgotten Rounds

On January 20, the Friday night Garden show—in this case, it featured a substitute battle between heavyweights James J. Braddock and Hans Birkie—drew only about 3,500 fans. Slipping attendance needed to be halted and quickly. By the way, Braddock lost the decision.

Bringing the lightweight champion, Tony Canzoneri, back into the Garden for a main event pledged to be exciting, and it was. A crowd of 10,000 watched as the Louisiana-born boxer knocked out Canadian welterweight Billy Townsend a mere sixty-five seconds into their ten-round feature on February 3. It was four machine-gun rights that did the damage. Since Townsend was signed at catchweight, Canzoneri's title was never at risk.

When Maxie Rosenbloom valued a championship, he typically made it a priority. Understanding that Mickey Walker was out for blood in their Garden meeting on November 3, Rosenbloom was up to the challenge. In front of a crowd of 9,000 fans, the light-heavyweight champion successfully defended over fifteen rounds. Behaving as expected, Rosenbloom, with his trademark open-glove style, was warned repeatedly for his legerdemain (discreet holding, hitting on the break, etc.).

Fighter of the Year

It was a great year for boxer Barney Ross, who went 8–0 in 1933. Still, he never fought inside the Garden during the year. Tony Canzoneri knocked out Kid Chocolate, which was nothing short of sensational for the City Ring. Nevertheless, Maxie Rosenbloom fought his heart out in 1933 while compiling a record of 20–5–4. Three of his 29 fights were in the City Ring and all were victories.[24]

1934

As only Dempsey could do, he shook the heavyweight tree in January by informing the press that he had no intention of allowing Max Baer, on whom he held a service contract, to fight heavyweight champion Primo Carnera for the Madison Square Garden Corporation. Naturally, this aroused the interest of Carnera's American representative, who confirmed that unless his fighter received a championship by June, he would simply let his Garden contract expire.[25]

Just when boxing fans thought they had seen everything during a boxing match—a phrase I will overuse—inside Madison Square Garden, they were wrong. During the conclusion of the February 2 bout between former champion Tony Canzoneri and Cleto Locatelli, presenter Joe Humphreys announced a draw. Be that as it may, Humphreys had misread the ballots. The mistake wasn't discovered until after the fighters had left the ring. A routine ballot inspection by NYSAC Chairman Brig. Gen. John J. Phelan uncovered the flaw and the verdict was corrected. It was a win for Canzoneri, and the first time that two different decisions had been rendered under the Garden banner.

The sport of boxing struggled in February: a Garden card had to be postponed due to lack of public interest; outside influences continued to stir the heavyweight pot; NYSAC stripped Kid Chocolate of his world's featherweight championship for failing to honor a challenge; and the Garden's willingness to arrange elimination tournaments just didn't have the appeal it once had. Perhaps it was confirmation that a multipurpose facility really was necessary to sustain a corporation's desired profitability. Hey, if boxing doesn't bring them in, try an ice show.

On a positive note, New York's Golden Gloves boxing team outperformed their Chicago rivals in front of a capacity crowd on March 28. The seventh annual tournament conducted by the *Daily News* AA had grown increasingly popular over the years and was drawing some very impressive talent, including New York University's Bob Pastor, New York's Melio Bettina, Chicago's Anthony Zale, and New York's Gus Lesnevich,

Seeing that the box office was struggling a bit, the Garden boxing staff, headed up by James J. Johnston and matchmaker Sam McQuade, worked very hard to generate interest in their May 28 welterweight championship inside the Madison Square Garden Bowl. And it appeared to work. Boxing fans came from downtown, many aboard the Eighth Avenue subway—a line that ran from 42nd Street and Eighth, to the 46th Street station in Long Island City—the others by just about every mode of transportation conceivable.

An estimated crowd of 60,000 was there to witness the main event: Champion Jimmy McLarnin putting his 147-pound crown on the line against New York—born Barney Ross, the world's lightweight champion. Packing a powerful knockout punch, McLarnin was favored over the younger Ross, but not by much. The pair fought hard, from start to finish, and at the end of the fifteen rounds not a single spectator was confident of the outcome. It was announcer Joe Humphreys who revealed the disagreement between the two judges, leaving it to referee Eddie Forbes to make the call: It was Ross. Everyone had witnessed a terrific night of boxing and the birth of a rivalry.[26]

A Heavyweight Overture

Having little time to take a breath, the Garden boxing staff turned their attention back to the Bowl on June 14, and a heavyweight extravaganza. It featured champion Primo Carnera against Max Baer. Obviously, the Garden met Dempsey's concerns. If you were to examine how the rivals compared, you would have noted that Max Baer had only an inch reach advantage, backed by inch larger biceps, behind twelve months more of youth and vitality. Oh yeah, almost forgot: he also had a hammer-wielding right hand similar to that of the Norse mythological figure of Thor.

Contrary to virtually every prognosis, it happened. After Carnera had been floored for the twelfth time in the eleventh round, referee Arthur Donovan had seen enough damage inflicted on the champion. He stepped in and stopped the fight. The world's heavyweight crown had returned to America and into the hands of Max Baer. Not a soul could have predicted the outcome, and likely not a soul other than Carnera could have endured the most knockdowns ever in a championship contest. Granted Baer wasn't Dempsey, but he was the closest thing boxing had seen in many years—and he came at the perfect time.[27]

Lost in all the excitement was the last preliminary of the evening. Jersey City's James

J. Braddock, weighing 180 pounds and considered washed up as a fighter, managed to knock out Fort Benning's Corn Griffin in the third round of a scheduled six-round confrontation.

On September 17, Jimmy McLarnin took his title back from Barney Ross inside the Madison Square Garden Bowl. The match took place in front of a disappointing crowd of 25,000; the weather, which had not cooperated and had led to postponements, was certainly a factor. The pair again put on a spectacular display of boxing, and once again had to turn to the referee—Arthur Donovan, in this instance—to make the final decision. After fifteen rounds, the decision went to McLarnin. The series stood at 1–1. Was a rubber match in order?

Forgotten Rounds

In the first battle of the Garden's indoor season, heavyweight Steve Hamas defeated Art Laskey in a strenuous ten-round decision. Both fighters really mixed it up and impressed the crowd estimated at 12,000 boxing fans. It appeared that some of the excitement generated by the outdoor season had thankfully carried over and into the Garden.

German Walter Neusel, floored in the second round by Chicago's battler King Levinsky, rallied back to take a ten-round decision on March 9. It was a close fight that required Neusel to come on strong in the closing sessions or risk defeat.

On November 16, East Side battler Bob Olin took the light heavyweight championship from Maxie Rosenbloom by a fifteen-round decision inside the City Ring. It wasn't an exciting championship affair, but the undercard was: James J. Braddock upset favorite John Henry Lewis in the ten-round semifinal.

Former welter and middle champion Lou Brouillard took a well-fought decision over New Haven's hard-hitting Al Gainer on November 23. Finally, Panama's Carlos Quintana defeated Korean Joe Tei Ken in eight brutal rounds fought on November 30 after the Fuller-Jadick Garden feature.

Fighter of the Year

In what was far from a prolific year for the Garden, a boxer who seemed to slip between the ropes of the City Ring was John Henry Lewis, who went 2–1 in three consecutive Garden appearances. The impressive light heavyweight had only lost two fights in his career—both, coincidentally, on the same date, November 16, but separated by two years—and they were to Maxie Rosenbloom in 1932, and James J. Braddock in 1934.[28]

6

Depression-Era Boxing, 1935–1939

Talent hits a target no one else can hit. Genius hits a target no one else can see.
—Arthur Schopenhauer

An improving economy brought an increased use of the City Ring, not to mention three large-scale promotions that would prove remarkably symbolic: James J. Braddock v. Max Baer, and Max Schmeling v. Joe Louis, I and II.

1935

The first fistic event of every year was always invigorating, and this year would be no different as the Garden arranged for a ten-round battle between Chicago welterweight Harry Dublinsky and Lou Ambers, the No. 1 challenger for the 135-pound championship held by Barney Ross.[1] The fight, scheduled for January 11, marked the first appearance by Ambers, a.k.a. the "Herkimer Hurricane," in the City Ring. He did not disappoint. Dublinsky, who had won only two of his last six bouts, was given a lesson by Ambers, who had won his six most recent battles.

Impressed by the youngster's performance, Garden management scheduled Ambers for another battle on March 1, this time against a very tough Sammy Fuller. The Boston lightweight Sabino Ferullo, a.k.a. Sammy Fuller, had won five of his last six battles. From the onset, it appeared like a distance duel could be expected, and fifteen rounds it indeed went. In the end, however, Ambers took the unanimous decision. Jack Dempsey was the third man in the ring.[2]

In what appeared to be a back-room deal, Barney Ross relinquished his lightweight championship and immediately entered negotiations with promoter Mike Jacobs to fight Jimmy McLarnin for the welterweight crown. No sooner had the telegram proclaiming his intentions reached the boxing commission than James J. Johnston announced he had closed an Ambers versus Canzoneri contest, or what would prove to be viewed as a lightweight championship contest. NYSAC amazingly agreed.

On May 10, Tony Canzoneri regained his world's lightweight championship—he had won it back in 1930 inside the same City Ring—by outpointing Lou Ambers in a tremendous fifteen-round Garden affair. A crafty, yet flat-footed veteran, Canzoneri watched and waited for the perfect angle to unleash his power on his mobile opponent. And when he found it, he delivered with pinpoint accuracy—Ambers hit the canvas twice in the third round and was close to a knockout. However, Canzoneri, who picked up the decision, was unable to finish the job. Ambers fought eight times in 1935, losing only his Garden battle against Canzoneri. The "Herkimer Hurricane" took an impressive record of 49-2-5 into the following year and would not face defeat until October 1936.

Good news! Garden events were drawing more spectators. This according to a statement released by the Madison Square Garden Corporation. Attendance rose by over 175,000 from June 1, 1934, until January 15, 1935, when compared to the same period the previous year. The figure was based on the 99 events conducted during the period, 8 of which were professional boxing.[3] So the Garden held four fewer events than the year before, but drew more spectators. The bulk of the increase was attributed to hockey, college basketball, the 6-day bicycle race, and animal attractions (rodeo, horse show, etc.).[4]

On February 5, NYSAC decided that they would assist the heavyweight class by allowing its champion to protect his title in bouts of fewer than fifteen rounds. A non-championship affair could be designated in advance to protect the titleholder. So, if Max Baer wanted to pick up some extra cash, he could do some boxing without risking his crown—if, of course, it was conducted as specified.

Speaking of heavyweights, Dempsey opened his restaurant on the evening of February 17 in the two-story brick building across from the Garden. Whatever fight decisions couldn't be made inside the famous venue, could now be made accordingly across the street—who's gonna argue with Dempsey?

The New York State Athletic Commission might have been in a position to turn back decisions, but they couldn't turn back time. It appeared that only James J. Braddock could do that. A crowd of more than 10,000 Garden boxing fans watched as the New Jersey boxer nullified his favored adversary, Minneapolis fighter Art Lasky, in a fifteen-round decision. It happened on March 22. Were Braddock's stars beginning to align in favor of a heavyweight battle against Primo Carnera?

On May 28, Barney Ross, having relinquished his lightweight title, regained the welterweight crown from Jimmy McLarnin in a tough but unanimous fifteen-round decision. It was officiated by Jack Dempsey inside the Polo Grounds, and there was little opposition to the verdict. The fight completed an outstanding trilogy that favored Ross, and continued the jinx of the welterweight crown: it was the 12th consecutive time that a champion (in this case McLarnin) had lost in his first defense.

WHEN IMPROBABLE TURNS TO POSSIBLE

James J. Braddock entered into a contract to meet heavyweight champion Max Baer inside the Madison Square Garden Bowl in Long Island City on June 13. Having once retired from the ring to work on the docks at $5 a day to feed his wife and three children, Braddock's re-emergence was astounding. Obtaining recognition and success after a period of obscurity and neglect, Braddock was dubbed the "Cinderella Man." Nearly every newspaper in the country documented a life that had been filled with hardship. The boxer had to hit the relief rolls in New Jersey only to overcome impecuniousness through sheer determination.

As if destined, James J. Braddock weathered fifteen rounds to take the heavyweight championship from Max Baer. The cheers of 30,000 euphoric fans inside the Madison Square

Garden Bowl resonated in the hearts of virtually everyone present. There were no dissenting views when the result was announced. According to most, it was the greatest fistic upset since the defeat of John L. Sullivan by Jim Corbett. For nine of the fifteen rounds, Braddock fought like a champion, and that was the difference. Warned a couple of times for his low blows, Baer clowned and appeared preoccupied with anything but the fight. For his improbable comeback, Braddock became the people's champion, and his devotion to providing for his family elevated him to the status of national legend in the eyes of his hopeful fans.[5]

It had ever been believed, and it would later be proved, that the brain relates to symbolic objects in the same way it relates to social beings. Though no two individuals had the same understanding of the Depression, everyone felt challenged and changed by the experience. By 1932, three years after the initial stock market crash, nearly thirty million Americans had lost their source of income, be it from unemployment or loss of a family breadwinner. People of all ages, religions and ethnic backgrounds could relate to the story of James J. Braddock. Boxing was the fighter's way out of poverty; therefore, the inanimate objects associated with him, which can prompt social cognition and emotion, were his tools. As a clock represented time to most, or a wedding ring equated to marriage or never-ending love, a boxing ring represented opportunity or conviction. To many, if James J. Braddock (a common man with typical talent, who was determined, hopeful, and impoverished) could triumph over Max Baer (a rare individual with extraordinary talent, who was irresolute, cocky and affluent), then perhaps they too could overcome adversity.

By the Pound

On June 25, promoter Mike Jacobs, who had signed an exclusive contract with Joseph Louis Barrow, walked into Yankee Stadium with his fighter. Joe Louis, who had knocked out 18 opponents in his last 22 professional fights, was about to face perhaps his greatest challenge, Primo Carnera. And Louis would not disappoint. The Detroit slasher took nearly every round on the way to a sixth-round knockout. Over 50,000 fans watched in awe as Louis floored the Italian giant three times.

It was far more confident Mike Jacobs, billed as the "new Tex Rickard," who next presented his case to NYSAC for a heavyweight match between Joe Louis and Max Baer inside Yankee Stadium on September 24. Following a physical examination of Baer, who had injured his hands against Braddock, NYSAC agreed. The match lasted only four rounds as Joe Louis soundly defeated "The Livermore Larruper"; it was Baer's first loss by knockout. For all intents and purposes, it was over by the third round—a term that saw Baer, who was on the canvas, rescued by the bell. A crowd of 90,000 watched in disbelief as Baer hit the canvas three times—nothing short of a rare occurrence. With his lower lip cut and his face swelled, an exhausted Baer sought only a beer and cigarette after the conflict. As his handlers cleaned him up, Baer, also a part-time actor, pondered his future. As for the victor, and newlywed, Louis had not a scratch.[6]

In an attempt to manage a proxy battle for control of Madison Square Garden Corporation, management considered an offer from Mike Jacobs of the Twentieth Century Sports Club for boxing jurisdiction over the venue and its related outdoor facilities, for the next five years. Jacobs, having known Rickard, understood his recipe for success and was more than willing to carry it forward.

In a trial run, Madison Square Garden Corporation, along with Mike Jacobs, agreed to promote a fifteen-round battle between Paulino Uzcudun, a.k.a. the "Basque Woodchopper," and Joe Louis, a.k.a. the "Brown Bomber," on December 13. For the latter, in his twenty-third career fight, this would be his first appearance inside the venue. Jacobs, heavily connected in the city, pulled out all the stops on the way to the Garden sell-out.

A capacity crowd witnessed Joe Louis batter Paulino Uzcudun to a fourth-round technical knockout. Not only had the granite-jawed Uzcudun never been knocked out, he had never even been knocked down. Louis, who later believed it was the hardest punch he ever threw, hit Paulino with a right to the jaw that tore open the left side of the boxer's face, slicing his lip and lacerating the inside of his mouth; the blow was so powerful it drove Uzcudun's mouthpiece through his upper lip. When the pride of the Pyrenees struck the canvas, he was a sign of helplessness. To his credit, Uzcudun somehow managed to use the ring ropes to pull himself up. Following two more rights by Louis, referee Art Donovan stepped in to stop the fight.[7]

THE BLACK DIAMOND GLOVE TOURNAMENT

Tough times were nothing new for black Americans living during the Thirties. For many it was simply life as usual. Granted the Great Depression, which was a slap in the face to many, added to the consternation, but this was a segment of society that was only generations removed from Southern slavery. Intolerance, be it via living conditions or employment opportunities, had become a way of life. Violence rose against blacks, and for the first time in decades painted a true picture of the intolerance they faced. Destiny shed no mercy on black Americans, and without mincing one's words, their plight was a disgrace. Those resilient to the infection of racism persevered—thank God, from so many perspectives—and turned to what few opportunities they had, including inside a boxing ring.

It was ten bouts of four rounds each, inside the Garden on Friday, December 27. It was considered a novelty at the time, a boxing program in which all the participants were black Americans. Garden executive James J. Johnston gave it the name the Black Diamond Glove Tournament and even arranged five additional fights should they be needed. Each boxer who scored a knockout victory took home an additional $25, while the boxer making the best showing took home a stickpin. Multicolored robes, which the fighters could keep, were used, as were white boxing gloves.[8] And because it was a lucky chance, some good boxers were on the bill, including Long Island's Eddie Blunt, Syracuse fighter Eddie Saxon, Cuba's Joe Pimental, Florida's Dewey Anderson and New York's Howard Clark.[9] View it as an opportunity, a racist event, or both, it was inside the City Ring and part of its history.

FORGOTTEN ROUNDS

Baltimore's Vince Dundee, a former middleweight champ, managed a controversial decision, in a lackluster fight, over Syracuse scrapper Eddie "Babe" Risko on January 25. Having said that, the absurdity of the verdict must be noted: Over 8,000 confused fans witnessed the improbable as a decision was made and announced, only to have it overturned and corrected fifteen minutes later.

In one of those fights that most thought would never amount to much, but did, Risko (without putting his middleweight title on the line) agreed to meet Great Britain's champion

Jock McAvoy for ten rounds on December 20. The elapsed time, from the second Risko left his corner, to the time he hit the canvas for the sixth time and was counted out, was 2 minutes and 48 seconds. Risko never threw a punch.

Similarly, in the semifinal, Brooklyn's middleweight Solly Krieger dropped Asbury Park's Jack Ennis in 2 minutes and 53 seconds of the first round.

Fighter of the Year

It was a peculiar year both inside and outside the ropes: judges couldn't make decisions; executives couldn't make decisions (see proxy battle); giants fought giants; giants like James J. Braddock and Joe Louis emerged, as did Mike Jacobs; Eddie "Babe" Risko took a loss and never threw a punch; and an all-black American boxing tournament was held inside Madison Square Garden. Primo Carnera and Tony Canzoneri both won a pair of Garden bouts and polished the roped confinement, but Lou Ambers went 2–1, with back-to-back Garden victories.

1936

Not since the days of Tex Rickard had boxing seen one individual, in this case Mike Jacobs of The Twentieth Century Sporting Club, ignite so much interest in the sport. And

A German boxer who was heavyweight champion of the world between 1930 and 1932, Maximillian Adolph Otto Siegfried "Max" Schmeling (1905–2005) was perhaps best known for his two fights with Joe Louis in 1936 and 1938. His first fight inside the City Ring took place in 1928 and his last in 1937 (*Library of Congress, LC-USZ62-125851* [*film copy negative*]).

Jacobs might have owned the dynamite, but Joe Louis, the best boxer to emerge since Jack Dempsey, lit the fuse. A black fighter without a single weakness, Louis seemed destined to become the latest heavyweight sensation. Hailing from Detroit, the big man was turning heads with an impressive string of knockouts that included two in Yankee Stadium and one in Madison Square Garden. His meteoric rise through the nonprofessional ranks culminated with the 1934 national AAU light heavyweight crown.[10] A triumvirate of supporting individuals—John Roxborough, Julian Black and Jack Blackburn—nurtured Louis along a path that saw him turn pro in 1934. Compiling a record of 23–0 entering 1936, he was a smooth fighter who possessed an arsenal of quick punches—a fabulous right cross and a commanding left jab—and deadly combinations. He also seemed to harness every ounce of power from his perfect physique.

HOLD THE *HINDENBURG*

It happened inside Yankee Stadium on June 19, and was one of boxing's greatest upsets. German Max Schmeling stunned an audience of more than 40,000 by not only flooring Joe Louis, who was heavily favored, but knocking him out in the twelfth round. The former heavyweight champion was in top form and delivered an arsenal highlighted by his trademark right hand. As for Louis, he was simply overwhelmed by Schmeling's offensive display. When he shifted to the body with hopes of slowing Schmeling, it didn't work. Louis became noticeably frustrated—twice he hit low, was warned, and lost the rounds.

Dropped in the fourth term by a right to the temple, Louis appeared dazed, and he never appeared to regain his equilibrium. He was counted out at 2 minutes and 29 seconds into the twelfth round. On Tuesday, June 23, Max Schmeling boarded the airship *Hindenburg* at Lakehurst, New Jersey, bound for his home country.

After the death of the German President Hindenburg on August 2, 1934, Adolf Hitler merged the offices of party leader, head of state and chief of government into one, taking the title of Führer und Reichskanzler. The Chancellery of the Führer, officially an organization of the Nazi Party, took over the functions of the Office of the President (a government agency), blurring the distinction between structures of party and state even further. The Nazi propaganda machine, understanding that every conquest was important to the mission, clung to Schmeling's victory like rust to a tailpipe—it was, as they saw the victory over Joe Louis, the perfect example of German supremacy over the rest of the world. Hitler sent flowers to Schmeling's wife, had him greeted upon his arrival in Germany, and brought him to the (old) Reich Chancellery. The government also ordered parades and rallies in his honor.[11]

BABY FACED ASSASSIN

James Archibald McLarnin, a.k.a. the "Baby Faced Assassin," was born on December 19, 1907, in Hillsborough, County Down, Ireland. His family immigrated to Saskatchewan, Canada, when he was age three, then moved on to Vancouver. Displaying terrific athleticism as a child, McLarnin took up boxing at the age of ten. He turned pro in 1923, but finding limited competition, not to mention poor pay, he drifted south to fight out of the Bay Area. A hotbed for boxing, San Francisco, Oakland and Vernon provided all a fighter the caliber of McLarnin needed to garner some attention. Handsome, with a thick head of hair that he combed back, the five-foot six-inch boxer had a youthful appearance that required him to occasionally lie about his age to obtain a payday. By 1927, McLarnin had already tangled with Fidel LaBarba, Bud Taylor, Pancho Villa, Jackie Fields, Joe Glick and Louis "Kid" Kaplan. By 1936, his two trilogies, the first with Billy Petrolle (he was 2–1) and the second with Barney Ross (he was 1–2), catapulted him into legendary status as a welterweight.

In a grand New York exit, McLarnin would finish his career with back-to-back winning battles inside the City Ring:

> Canzoneri and McLarnin, having fought in May, returned to the Garden on October 5. But on this day, the ring belonged to the "Baby Faced Assassin." After ten rounds, the verdict went in his favor. It was a far more scientific battle—perhaps McLarnin had finally learned to conserve energy rather than displace it during the early rounds—both fighters saved their heavy artillery for the right moment and both were floored once during the affair.
>
> On November 20, a confident Jimmy McLarnin, 1–1 on the year, entered his non-title bout against Lou Ambers, the lightweight champion. Seven years older and nine pounds heavier than his adversary, the Irish-born boxer was favored in the bout. Sure enough, McLarnin overcame his three-inch shorter reach, and effectively utilized his right to outpunch Ambers. After capturing the victory over ten rounds in his systematic manner, he calmly exited the City Ring. Then, without fanfare, he retired.[12]

Forgotten Rounds

The best fight of the evening, on January 3, was not the main event (Lou Ambers v. Frankie Klick), but an undercard battle between Los Angeles lightweight Bobby Pacho and Harlem's Leonard Del Genio. Both lightweights just tore into each other, with Pacho eventually taking the ten-round bout. Del Genio was staggered numerous times in the early rounds and even floored in the second, before attempting an unsuccessful fight-ending rally. Pacho's impressive performance brought him main event honors inside the City Ring on January 17.

It was during the aforementioned battle that a thirty-one-year-old boxing manager, by the name of Frankie Carbo, was arrested on a charge that he was a fugitive from justice in Union County, New Jersey. Carbo, a resident of Maspeth, Long Island, denied having any knowledge of the 1933 murder of Max Greenberg and Max Hassel at the Elizabeth-Carteret Hotel in Elizabeth, New Jersey. Unfortunately for boxing, it wouldn't be the last fight Carbo ever witnessed.

Chicago lightweight Leo "The Chicago Flash" Rodak, nearly knocked out on his feet, rallied back to draw Utica veteran Angelo Geraci, a.k.a. Bushy Graham, on February 7. It was no simple task as Graham was working his way toward the bantam title.

Friday night's attendance had been off at the Garden, and a record low was hit for the arena's boxing on February 21. Just over 2,300 spectators viewed a ten-round victory by welterweight Cleto Locatelli over Izzy Jannazzo. Also on February 21, Rodak slugged his way to victory over Italian Aldo Spoldi.

In other action, NYU's big Robert E. Pasternak, a.k.a. Bob Pastor, defeated Edgewater's Steve Dudas in a six-round savage ring battle on March 13.[13] East Sider Izzy Jannazzo, who struggled a bit early, fought to an impressive fifteen-round draw with Filipino Ceferino Garcia on October 30. Jannazzo was fighting well and would battle Barney Ross in less than a month. One punch—a perfect right to the jaw of Carlos "Indian" Quintana in the very first round on November 13—was all Sixto Escobar needed to knock out his adversary. With the victory, Escobar became the first Puerto Rican to win a title fight in the first

6. Depression-Era Boxing, 1935–1939

An American boxer, James Walter "Cinderella Man" Braddock (1905–1974) was the world heavyweight champion from 1935 to 1937. Known for his spoiling, counterpunching style, powerful right hand and iron chin, Braddock was undeniable in his quest for a crown (*Library of Congress, LC-USZC2-5862* [color film copy slide]).

round. Finally, heavyweight Bob Pastor, from the Washington Heights neighborhood of Manhattan, scored an impressive seventh-round knockout of giant (6-feet 7-inch) Ray "Skyscraper" Impellittiere on December 18.

Fighter of the Year

Braddock may have had the heavyweight title, but Max Schmeling had the ratings as pugilism's premier glove man. For the City Ring, it was hard to say goodbye to Jimmy McLarnin.[14]

1937

Mike Jacobs finally allowed Joe Louis to meet contender Bob Pastor inside Madison Square Garden on January 29. However, it wasn't an easy negotiation, nor was it particularly enjoyable for Garden matchmaker James J. Johnston. Jacobs held an exclusive option on Louis's services and wouldn't agree to the date without being certain that they had first call on Pastor's services should he defeat Louis. The savvy boxing manager wasn't taking any chances with his meal ticket. Since his loss to Schmeling, the "Brown Bomber" had knocked out four opponents—Jack Sharkey, Al Ettore, Jorge Brescia and Eddie Sims—in twelve rounds of boxing.

As for Schmeling, on January 8, an anti–Nazi League made it very clear that they objected to a boxing bout between the German and an American opponent—in this case it was the heavyweight champion James J. Braddock. The world's most sought-after title should not have an opportunity to return to Nazi Germany. Nor should American-generated dollars from such an instance fall into the hands of the Third Reich. This appeal was made to the Madison Square Garden Corporation, then later to NYSAC. In an attempt to quell the uprising, Schmeling's manager Joe Jacobs planned a five-week exhibition tour across America; unfortunately, the fighter had become the poster child for the Third Reich.[15]

It began on June 22 in Chicago, and would become one of the longest and most prestigious heavyweight boxing reigns in history. Joe Louis, floored by James J. Braddock in the very first round, managed to recover, regain his composure, and go on to knock out the "Cinderella Man" in the eighth round of their scheduled fifteen-round heavyweight championship.

With all the politics that revolved around the battle—primarily between Mike Jacobs and the Madison Square Garden Corporation (MSGC)—it was amazing that the event ever took place. The MSGC was protecting a proposed, and later canceled, championship fight between Braddock and Max Schmeling scheduled for June 3 over in Long Island City. By the middle of June, the MSGC had lost two pleas for an injunction to stop the Braddock v. Louis bout. After the fight, Louis signed a contract with promoter Jacobs, giving exclusive call on all his services for five years. The catbird seat was now occupied.

On Wednesday, August 4, Mike Jacobs took over control of New York City boxing by leasing both Madison Square Garden and the Garden Bowl for two full seasons. So, in addition to having the services of the sport's premier talent, he also had its foremost venues. The MSGC reluctantly, but perhaps wisely, threw up the sponge. Jacobs also promoted at Yankee Stadium and the Polo Grounds, and his sporting club conducted bouts at the Hippodrome.[16] As for the Garden, Tom McArdle handed over his resignation in September, and Jacobs wasted no time by bringing Armand "Al" Weill to take over the matchmaking duties. Many knew Weill as the manager of Lou Ambers, but he had also handled matchmaking duties at numerous facilities including Ebbets Field and the Boston Garden.[17] Well-connected, to put it mildly, Weill had more City tentacles than a New York Bay jellyfish.

Taking It Too Farr

In his very first title defense, Joe Louis was caught somewhat by surprise when Welshman Tommy Farr managed to go the distance with the champion on August 30 at Yankee Stadium. Farr, or the "Tonypandy Terror," not only made the fifteen rounds, but he made it still standing on his feet. People forgot that Louis had only gone ten rounds or longer on six occasions. Although Louis received the decision, it was a razor-thin victory.

Play Me a Melody

Henry Melody Jackson, Jr., was born on December 12, 1912, in Columbus, Mississippi. As the eleventh child in a large sharecropper's family, he learned quickly that if you wanted something, even at the kitchen table, you had to fight for it.

Borrowing a name from a friend, he became Henry Armstrong. After turning pro in 1931, he went 4–2 in 1932, 10–1–5 in 1933, and 12–1 in 1934. Armstrong crossed into Mexico to battle Baby Arizmendi for the vacant California-Mexico world featherweight title in January 1935, but lost in a twelve-round decision. He finished the year with a record of 8–2–1.

By chance, Armstrong's contract was bought out by his manager Eddie Meade—thanks to the financing by, of all people, some Hollywood royalty (Ruby Keeler, Al Jolson and George Raft) who just happened to take a liking to the boxer—and it was then that Armstrong's career blossomed. In 1936, the fighter compiled a record of 11–3 while picking up wins over Baby Arizmendi (a fight that vindicated his loss), Juan Zurita and Mike Belloise. And a year later, Armstrong, or "Homocide Hank," compiled a record of 27–0, which included 26 knockouts and the world featherweight title.

He had been as indefatigable as he was undeniable. And, was the best pound-for-pound fighter on the planet.

Forgotten Rounds

Looking at some of the overlooked Garden engagements: Camden's Frank Blair fought in a gallant losing effort against Bobby Pacho during eight rounds. With his extensive New Jersey following present, Blair was embarrassed that he did not receive the fight's verdict. So he hooted and hollered through the main event between Ambers and Venturi on January 8.

North Carolina's Eddie Blunt dropped Jack Trammell five times in his first-round victory on January 29. Known for his short rabbit punches, Blunt would not relent.

Italian heavyweight Italo Colonello took an eight-round decision over Charlotte's Dewey Kimery in a savagely fought crusade on July 15. Both fighters were relentless with their offensive attacks.

On August 6, in a preliminary on the undercard of the Del Genio versus Pacho fight, referee Jack Goodman stopped a contest between Corona's Eddie Blunt and Brooklyn's Yustin Sirutis in the third round and declared the altercation a no contest. The fighters would not engage and simply went from one clinch into another.

Brooklyn's Solly Krieger knocked out East Sider Walter Woods in spectacular fashion in the eighth round of their August 12 clash. Krieger caught his adversary with a crushing right cross perfectly to the chin that Woods never saw.

Finally, Kid Chocolate, on the comeback path, took a well-fought ten-round decision over West Sider Johnny De Foe on August 19.

Fighter of the Year

With all the rousing things that happened in and around the fight game, it's hard to select a defining moment. But taking everything into consideration, the year inside the City Ring belonged to only one man, Henry Armstrong. Compiling a 1937 record of 27-0, with 26 knockouts, the fighter won all six of his City Ring appearances.[18]

1938

The world's featherweight champion, Henry Armstrong, dropped opponent Enrico Venturi in the sixth round of their scheduled ten-round Garden feature on January 12. Upon doing so, Venturi's face grimaced with pain as the Italian claimed foul. Referee Art Donovan rushed between the pair and proceeded to issue a warning to Armstrong; this unfortunately stripped the champion of a round he had clearly won.

Returning to his corner, Venturi, instead of sitting on his stool, sank to the floor, then onto his back. Witnessing the descent, Donovan motioned to the knockdown timekeeper to start a count. Standing over a prostrate Venturi, Donovan proceeded to count him out; consequently, over 12,000 fight fans in attendance had no idea what had just happened. In an evaluation by NYSAC, Venturi was declared the loser by knockout and suspended. He was the first boxer to take the count under a purported foul blow since a regulation stating that a foul in the form of a low blow cannot terminate a fight in favor of the stricken boxer.

Baer On

Former heavyweight champion Max Baer upset Tommy Farr in a fifteen-round unanimous decision inside the City Ring on March 11. Farr, the British Empire titleholder, was floored twice in front of a near capacity crowd. Not even Louis could drop the iron-jawed Farr, but "Madcap Max" proved he still had a tremendous left hook and dynamite in his right hand. Baer was not without punishment, however, as his left eye was completely closed by the seventh round.

By late April, the rematch between Joe Louis and Max Schmeling was on everyone's minds; just how much the current state of global affairs played into the symbolism of the battle was subject to interpretation. Systematically revealing his plans for the event to the media, Jacobs was cautious to approach every element of the promotion with care—he did not want to detract from the significance of the event in any manner. The venue of choice was Yankee Stadium, with the date set for June 22. This allowed the promoter greater control and kept the jurisdiction under the NYSAC umbrella.[19] The tickets would range from $3.50 for general admission to $30 for ringside.[20] By June, Mike Jacobs was thinking that a million-dollar gate was feasible.

A crowd of 30,000 turned out to watch Los Angeles fighter Henry Armstrong, with his powerful overhand right and thrusting left jab, become the first boxer to hold both the welter and featherweight crowns at the same time. It happened on May 31. For fifteen rounds, Barney Ross, the welterweight champion, took a horrible beating on the way to losing the title in a decision. No titleholder had ever successfully defended his crown inside the Madison Square Garden Bowl, so why should things be any different? A courageous Ross, with neither the stamina nor the defense to mount the resistance necessary to slow Armstrong, refused to relent. When it was over, Armstrong turned his attention to his next quest, which was the lightweight crown owned by Lou Ambers.

Foreshadowing: Louis v. Schmeling II

Promoted by Mike Jacobs on behalf of the Twentieth Century Sporting Club, it was *the* fight, Joe Louis versus Max Schmeling, and it was for the heavyweight championship of the world. Fifteen rounds inside Yankee Stadium, at 161st Street and River Avenue in the Bronx, with the main event beginning at 10:00 P.M. For his night's work, Joe Louis would take home 40 percent of the net receipts and Max Schmeling twenty percent. Both fighters were required to weighed in at noon on the day of the battle. Schmeling tipped at 193, while Louis weighed 198¾ pounds. The gates opened at 6:00 P.M., with the first preliminary beginning at 8:20 P.M. The betting was very heavy with Louis favored (1–2). All the specifics are out of the way, so let's get started.[21]

As they left their corners, Joe Louis was taller with a one-inch reach advantage. His hands looked bigger, and were, and his waist was one inch larger, as were his biceps, forearm, and thighs. Max Schmeling was eight years older, with a larger chest, neck and thighs. Both fighters appeared primed for their encounter: the American had trained at Pompton Lakes, New Jersey, while the German worked at Speculator, New York, in the Adirondacks.

A minute into the battle, Louis took command. Delivering a solid body attack before moving to the face, Louis was firing at will and doing considerable damage. A crashing right then struck Schmeling's jaw. Hanging on the ropes, the German began to drop. Referee

Donovan then stepped in, as if to stop the fight, but instead motioned Louis back before starting a standing count. That count appeared to end at two.

Since Schmeling was back on his feet, Donovan signaled to continue. Finally letting go of the rope, Schmeling stood before Louis almost begging for the crushing right that floored him. Schmeling arose swiftly (some say at a count of two, if that), a bit dazed, before encountering a vicious series of combinations by Louis that sent him gloves down.

An American boxer, Luigi Giuseppe d'Ambrosio (1913–1995), a.k.a. Lou Ambers, was a world lightweight boxing champion who fought from 1932 to 1941 (*Library of Congress, LC-USZ62-128436* [*film copy negative*]).

After Schmeling recovered again, it was a repeat performance by Louis that once more delivered a flooring right hand to the jaw. Schmeling was down, and while he scrambled to make all fours, his corner tossed in the towel at a count of three—a futile effort, as in New York rules, only the referee could stop the fight. Donovan finally waved it off at the count of five and it was over. All 124 seconds of it were officially recorded. By then, Schmeling's trainer Max Machon had entered the ring confirming the conclusion. Later, it was discovered that Schmeling sustained a fracture of the third lumbar vertebra.

The fight had ended before many of the celebrities sitting ringside ever knew what happened. Even the millions listening over the airwaves had difficulty interpreting what had taken place. From an international perspective, the fight had symbolized the silencing of Nazi jackboots—the enemy had exhibited its vulnerability. For Americans the victory was sweet, and Joe Louis was the people's champion—a belief shared by blacks and whites, along with Jews and Gentiles. For black Americans, who celebrated every Joe Louis's victory, it was indeed special, if not overly entertaining. They got to witness, if only temporarily, a colorblind white American press try to explain how a black man defeated a member of the Aryan race.

Great promoters know how and when to seize a moment, and that's what Mike Jacobs did on July 19 when he bought the rained-out bout between Al "Bummy" Davis and Bernie "Schoolboy" Friedkin. Both lightweights were neighborhood rivals from the Brownsville section of Brooklyn and dead set on destroying each other. Originally planned for Dexter Park, the match was postponed twice before Jacobs brought it inside for a Thursday night Garden show. In twenty-three professional fights, Davis was undefeated, while Friedkin had only one loss to his name. Although only a six-round fight, it attracted 6,000 fans. Davis immediately ripped into Friedkin, who was a 6–5 favorite, like a wild animal. In the fourth round, Friedkin collapsed in his own corner and was unable to recover.

The Inexorable Armstrong

Lou Ambers, world lightweight champion, put his crown on the line against the unstoppable Henry Armstrong, who held both the feather and welterweight titles, on August 17, inside the City Ring. Despite all three titles' being represented, it was agreed upon that only the lightweight crown was at stake. The bout, twice postponed due to rain, was wisely moved indoors.

In fifteen rounds of fast-paced action, both fighters refused to capitulate—Ambers hit the canvas multiple times. When it was over, the split decision—which should have been a majority verdict, considering Ambers was dominated by his antagonist—went to Armstrong. The gifted pugilist had his title. The capacity Garden crowd appeared to enjoy every minute while watching Henry Armstrong become the first fighter in history to hold three titles simultaneously.

The only knockout of the evening came in the semifinal, when Los Angeles featherweight Chalky Wright stopped Bronx boxer Al Reid in the fourth round of a scheduled six-round contest.

Jacobs's Beach

Sitting ringside dressed in his three-piece suit and overcoat, his fedora placed squarely and never tilted on his head, instinct identified the man, as did those around him. The hat that covered his bald round head also shrouded his forehead and eyebrows that seldom, if ever, clarified an emotion. His open ears, large nose and facial gestures also confirmed his identity. While seated, he always looked impatient, right hand placed slightly backward on his right thigh, with pinky extended, and his left hand draped over his left knee. He always pushed his jacket cuffs up, revealing his shirt cuffs along with the watch he wore on his left hand. The appearance gave you the impression that his tailored suits didn't fit. When he didn't have a cigarette in his mouth, which was seldom, he locked his lips and pushed his chin out in a manner that would make you believe that you were about to be fired even if you didn't work for him. He was Michael Strauss Jacobs. And from the mid–1930s until his retirement in 1946, he was the most influential man in boxing and one of the most powerful individuals in all of sport.

Born in New York City in March of 1880, he was a city boy through and through—always rugged, enterprising, and unafraid. Legend has it that a young Jacobs was peddling newspapers around Tammany Hall, over on East 14th Street (everything else was being transacted there, so why not tabloids?) when he bumped into Joe Bannon, a Hearst circulation manager. The executive, who had been given two complimentary tickets to the January 9, 1900, bout between Terry McGovern and George Dixon at the Broadway Athletic Club in New York, couldn't use them, so he gave them to Jacobs. The enterprising youth then sold the $1 priced tickets for twice their face value. It would be the transaction of a lifetime for Jacobs, who had just found his calling.

In 1907, he expanded his ticket offering to include music, theater and other athletic endeavors, while running a small ticket agency in the lobby of the Hotel Normandie at Broadway and 38th Street.

Jacobs's association with Tex Rickard stemmed either from contact during his 1906 promotion of the Joe Gans versus Battling Nelson fight held in Goldfield, Nevada, or through a 1915 introduction made by Walter St. Denis, the sports editor of the old *Globe* newspaper. Even if Jacobs had met Rickard earlier, it was the latter association, during the time of his Jess Willard-Frank Moran promotion, that Rickard recalled. Jacobs, understanding that the promoter was a conduit for both fighters and city gentry, was said to have advanced to Rickard some money for a piece of the action.

It was through the ticket agency that Jacobs learned to gauge the popularity of a promotion and if possible, grab a stake in it. He became a barometer for everything from theater productions to musical tours.

In 1933, Jacobs teamed with Wilton "Bill" Farnsworth, Ed Frayne and Damon Runyon, to assist in the charitable promotions of the distinguished Mrs. William Randolph Hearst, many of which were associated with boxing. When the group had a falling-out with Madison Square Garden, they organized the Twentieth Century Sporting Club and planted Jacobs at the helm.

The group began their boxing promotions at the Coliseum in the Bronx, but grew quickly to include other venues such as the Hippodrome. Jacobs, sensing his need for greater command, not to mention real estate, gradually bought out his partners in the enterprise. With Joe Louis in his pocket, Jacobs called the shots. When Louis took the championship from Braddock, the MSGC couldn't establish their ground. Mike Jacobs took it and moved into the forefront.

On Friday, August 26, whatever bad blood existed between Jacobs and the MSGC was set aside by an agreement signed by both parties to promote jointly for a period of four years.[22]

The sidewalk along the North side of 49th Street, between Eighth and Broadway, would soon become known as Jacobs's Beach. Everyone connected with the fight game idled on this strip of ground, from the fighters, managers, and even promoters down on their luck, to mobsters looking for a hot tip. Beat writers used to flock there to catch a story, and while waiting might plant a foot against a wall, lift their face upward while tilting their hat back, and try to catch some rays. If you were anybody in the fight game, you were on the beach or over at Stillman's (Gym), on the West side of Eighth Avenue 'tween 54th and 55th streets.

Forgotten Rounds

In the first heavyweight championship contest held indoors in eighteen years—that's true, going back to the days when Dempsey dropped Brennan in 1920—Joe Louis knocked out New Haven's Nathan Mann in the third round of a scheduled fifteen-round battle. The fight was held on February 23, and the designation was more memorable than the fight.

On September 16, Jack Sharkey, Jr. (Joseph Cervati), who was dropped for a nine count in the first round, managed to hang on and draw the very tough and undefeated Al Davis of Brownsville in a six-round contest.

On October 3, Lou Nova defeated Finland's favored Gunnar Barlund by a seventh-round technical knockout (TKO), or stoppage, declared when the referee or official ring physician decides that a fighter cannot safely continue the match.

Finally, Henry Armstrong, in a welter crown defense, eliminated a dangerous contender in Ceferino Garcia by taking a unanimous fifteen-round decision on November 25.

Fighter of the Year

As for boxing, 1938 belonged to Joe Louis, who defended his crown—against Nathan Mann, Harry Thomas and Max Schmeling—in what would total nine rounds of heavyweight championship boxing. Of greater importance, however, was the symbolism Louis created by defeating Schmeling, and the nationalism his victory brought to America. It was a year that saw the City Ring take on a whole new level of significance thanks to Mike Jacobs. Not since Tex Rickard had someone emerged as such a dynamic figure in the sport of boxing.

1939

The Pittsburgh Kid

In 1936, William David "Billy" Conn, hailing from Pittsburgh's East End, ran his record to 19-0 with wins over Ralph Chong, Jimmy Brown and Fritzie Zivic. Having gradually introduced the youngster to better and better talent, not to mention more and more rounds, Conn's trainer Johnny Ray leaped the fighter in 1937. Still fighting out of Pittsburgh, Conn picked up six wins against only two losses. With victories over Babe Risko, Vince Dundee, Teddy Yarosz and Young Corbett III, the light heavyweight was clearly in the division mix.

Back-to-back unanimous decision victories, both against Freddie Apostoli inside the City Ring, positioned the "Pittsburgh Kid" for one of the most memorable years of his life.

The world light heavyweight champion was Beacon, New York's Melio Bettina. A knockout artist who seemed to thrive on being the underdog, Bettina was a talented southpaw. Billy Conn, favored against the Golden Gloves veteran, met him inside the City Ring on July 13. In a "Tale of the Tape," the only thing the "Pittsburgh Kid" had going for him was a three-and-a-half-inch height advantage. But boxing bouts are fought on canvas and not paper—at least not during this era. When it was over, Billy Conn was the new king of the 175-pound fighters.

It wasn't thrilling, nor was it dull; it was simply a systematic fifteen-round points victory. Bettina was in fact ahead during the first half of the fight, but Conn slowly found a rhythm to overcome his rival's approach. He kept Bettina at bay with his left for most of the remainder of the battle and gradually accumulated a majority of rounds to take the united verdict.

UNPRECEDENTED—LOUIS V. LEWIS

It took only 89 seconds for champion Joe Louis to knock out his challenger, John Henry Lewis, on January 25 inside Madison Square Garden. Referee Art Donovan halted the City Ring battle in the first round, having witnessed Lewis drop to the canvas for the third time. Considered the (NBA) light heavyweight champion outside New York State, Lewis was hammered about the ring at will and was clearly no match for his adversary. Louis was a betting favorite (8–1), and for all intents and purposes, was matching himself against a good friend who was, as it proved, at the very end of his career. Lewis retired after this defeat. It was the only knockout he suffered in 117 fights.

John Henry Lewis was a well-rounded boxer with superlative skills who was essentially born to box; his great-great-uncle was Tom Molineaux, an early bare-knuckle heavyweight. If that were not enough proof, his father owned a gym in Phoenix. Lewis was the first black American to win the light heavyweight championship, a title he retained for four years. And as with many light heavyweights, Lewis often fought larger heavyweights in a quest for a bigger paycheck. In 1932, he received considerable attention when he took a decision victory over future heavyweight champion James J. Braddock in San Francisco. He posted a record of 6–1 in 1933, 9–1–2 in 1934, and 13–2 in 1935. Lewis won the world light heavyweight title by taking a decision from Bob Olin on October 31, 1935. He defended it five times before meeting Louis.[23] By 1939, it was widely known that Lewis was blind in one eye and facing a possible retirement, thus the match with his good friend, Joe Louis.

This fight, Louis v. Lewis, was the first world heavyweight championship fought between two black boxers in the United States, and the second ever between fighters of the same or similar last names. (Jack Johnson defended the title with a ten-round draw against Battling Jim Johnson on December 19, 1913, in Paris, France.) It was likewise the first world heavyweight championship fought between two elite (both eventually members of the International Boxing Hall of Fame) black boxers in the United States. To think that there was a time not long before, that if you told boxing fans that such a fight would be conducted in Madison Square Garden, they wouldn't have believed you.

On Monday, March 6, the *New York Times*, on page 20, previewed the final-round bouts of the *New York Daily News* Golden Gloves boxing tournament being staged inside Madison Square Garden that evening. The contest that began with almost 6,000 entries had been reduced to a very qualified thirty-six fighters. Even if you followed boxing, many of the names were unfamiliar, but most understood that would change for some. In the open-division, a fighter at the 126-pound class named Ray Robinson was scheduled to battle Louis Valentine. The youngster, fighting out of the Salem-Crescent Athletic club, would take the decision while being noted for "his defensive skills as well as a punishing long right uppercut."[24]

A Garden Trio in Yankee Stadium

Lou Nova v. Max Baer

On June 1, Max Baer, badly cut on his lower lip, took a heartbreaking eleventh-round loss to Alameda's Lou Nova inside Yankee Stadium. It took referee Frank Fullam to step between the fighters to relieve Baer of the butchering he was receiving; he was covered with blood and gasping for air, so it was a logical call. It was just the second time in his career that Baer had been knocked out.

An American heavyweight boxer, Domenico "Two Ton" Antonio Galento (1910–1979) was a brawler who was noted for his dirty tricks and enormous left hook. Born in Orange, New Jersey, Galento also became known as much for his gluttony as his boxing prowess (*Library of Congress, LC-DIG-hec-25347* [*film copy negative*]).

Joe Louis v. Tony Galento

Nobody expected "Two-Ton Tony" to send the heavyweight champion of the world to the canvas, but that's exactly what Tony Galento did to Joe Louis in their June 28 battle inside the Yankee ballpark. A left hook to the jaw hit its mark in the third round and stunned the crowd of more than 34,000 spectators. But Louis was up at the count of one, looking more embarrassed than injured, and finished the round. Composure intact, Louis came out like the champion he was in the fourth term and unmercifully pounded his opponent. Dazed, Galento clinched for a single moment of repose before the artillery continued. When he was forced into an additional life-saving clinch, it was over. Referee Art Donovan wisely stepped in and stopped the fight.

Lou Ambers v. Henry Armstrong

Lou Ambers, on August 22 inside Yankee Stadium, became the first boxer in ring history to regain the lightweight crown from the very man who took it from him. He defeated Henry Armstrong in a unanimous fifteen round decision. The "Herkimer Hurricane" also became only the second boxer (the first was Tony Canzoneri) to regain the 135-pound designation. Nevertheless, it was not without controversy. Invincible Henry Armstrong was penalized in five rounds—second, fifth, seventh, ninth and eleventh—for low blows. Armstrong lost the fight on fouls. While it was close, damn close, many ringside eyes saw it as Armstrong's fight. However, the judges—including the third man in the ring (referee Arthur Donovan)—saw it for Ambers. Regardless of how you viewed the outcome, both gladiators fought a courageous and savage battle.

END OF AN ERA

The end of a brilliant career was marked on Wednesday, November 1, when Tony Canzoneri, with a record of 137–20–10, stepped between the ropes of the City Ring for the very last time.[25] On this day, Canzoneri would face an undefeated pug from Brooklyn, Al Davis. Born Albert Abraham Davidoff, Davis, or "Bummy" as his friends called him, possessed one of the finest left hooks in the business. And he admired Tony Canzoneri.

During the fight, the first two rounds went as planned. Canzoneri worked the ring like a craftsman. But in the third round he walked into a left hook without forgiveness, and down he went to a count of four. Arising a bit dazed, Canzoneri tried to regain his faculties. Sensing the kill, Davis unloaded two lefts to the jaw and Canzoneri slumped to the floor. Struggling to all fours, he forced himself up at four, but it was over. Referee Donovan stepped in at the 2:13 mark.

THRILLING—DAVIS V. LARKIN

There are people who believe that the Madison Square Garden boxing card, on Friday, December 15, 1939, was one of the most thrilling boxing events ever held inside the City Ring. And it was tough to argue differently, as over 17,000 fans watched an incredible evening of action. In the main event, Brooklyn's Al Davis, an undefeated welterweight, stayed that way by knocking out Tippy Larkin, of Garfield, New Jersey, in the fifth round of their scheduled ten-round duel. Davis, who was struggling a bit in the early rounds, appeared to reach the pinnacle of his frustration in the fifth term. It was then that he landed two powerful left hooks to the body that floored his adversary. For Davis, Larkin was his twenty-second knockout victim.

As for the preliminaries: Edgewater, New Jersey's Steve Dudas took an eight-round decision from the hard-hitting Patrick Edward Comiskey. Lew Jenkins, a Texas lightweight who packed a heavyweight punch, kayoed Winnipeg's Billy Marquart in the third round of a scheduled eight-rounder. And Puerto Rican Wilce Rivera knocked out Long Island's Lou Barbetta in the very first round.

Forgotten Rounds

Talk about determination: East Side lightweight Gene Molnar, who was floored in the first round to a count of nine, managed an astonishing six-round comeback to take a decision from Marty Marino on February 24.

On Friday, March 17, undefeated lightweight Al "Bummy" Davis opposed East Sider Mickey Farber. Yep, two Jewish pugs battling in a St. Patrick's Day event—guaranteed, as Jacobs saw it, to draw an enormous crowd. Only a month earlier, the pair had met at the St. Nicholas Palace, and Davis took the close eight-round conflict. Sharp-eyed Mike Jacobs bought the rematch and brought it to the Garden. Davis did it again: he outpointed Farber to take the decision.

Los Angeles fighter Ceferino Garcia finally stopped the East Side's Walter "Popeye" Woods in the fourth round of their June 15 battle inside the City Ring. The scheduled ten-round clash saw Garcia dominate his opponent while putting him to the canvas five times.

Winnipeg's Billy Marquart made an impressive New York debut on November 1, when he stopped Jersey City's Billy Beauhuld in the fifth round. Marquart dropped Beauhuld in the opening round, only to be himself dropped moments later. Marquart ultimately floored his opponent to a nine count, which was basically the end of the evening for both.

Leave it to the West Side's Petey Scalzo to hand his rival Allie Stolz of Newark his first knockout defeat on December 1. In the fourth, Scalzo sent Stolz to the mat for a count of seven thanks to a sharp left hook to the chin. Upon arising he was knocked to the mat again with a straight right, after which the referee ended the bout.

Finally, Bronx lightweight Al Reid handed East Sider Max Shapiro his first defeat in a bizarre encounter—the original decision was recalled and revised by NYSAC. It was initially announced as a draw, but the crowd became so unruly that it forced an alternate decision.

Fighter of the Year

What a year for boxing, as Ceferino Garcia took the middleweight crown while posting a record of 11–0 with 9 knockouts, and Joe Louis fought 17 rounds and retained his heavyweight championship during four title defenses.

For the City Ring, two names come immediately to mind in 1939: Al "Bummy" Davis and Billy Conn. The undefeated Davis posted an 8–0 record during the year with four of those victories being held inside the Garden. But Billy Conn fought fives times inside the City Ring, winning all five, while posting a record of 7–0 for the year. While some boxing historians might give the year to "Bummy," especially those from the city, a better reflection might be Conn.[26]

7

World War II and a City Ring, 1940–1945

> Joe, we need muscles like yours to beat Germany.
> —President Franklin D. Roosevelt, while feeling the champ's biceps

The first peacetime military draft in United States history began on October 29, a Madison Square Garden basketball game was telecast for the first time on February 28, and Toots Shor's restaurant opened at 51 West 51st Street. Of all three things that took place in 1940, the first was the most significant. However, overhearing a conversation with Toots, Joe (DiMaggio) and Billy (Conn) could be memorable as well.

1940

A young kid fighting out of the Salem-Crescent Gym and Athletic Club named Ray Robinson was generating considerable interest. The youngster drew comparisons to Joe Louis for his lighter version of the champion's skills. Robinson, a Golden Gloves winner only a year earlier, dominated the 135-pound class of the amateur tournament. City fans delighted when the Harlemite's early victories brought him to the Garden on February 19, for the finals. A crowd of more than 17,000 watched Robinson defeat Andy Nonella to win the 135-pound open (tournament experienced fighters only) class. The kid had promise written all over him.

Stepping inside, Lew Jenkins surprised many by defeating Lou Ambers on May 10 to capture the world lightweight championship. Scheduled for fifteen championship rounds, the duel made it only until the third term. That's when the kid from Sweetwater, Texas, Lew Jenkins, an underdog (16–5), did the improbable: he kayoed the iron-chinned Lou Ambers at the 1:29 mark of the term. A Garden crowd estimated at about 15,000 was stunned that Jenkins achieved what Armstrong, Canzoneri, and McLarnin, to name just a few, could not. But Ambers's manager Al Weill claimed his fighter had been hit by two rights after the bell for the second round had sounded. Later, as a way to confirm the round had ended, post lights were installed on the City Ring.[1]

Moving Outside

As the decade opened, the two greatest drawing cards for Mike Jacobs were Joe Louis and Henry Armstrong; therefore, the sagacious promoter executed his marketing strategy for the boxing world with the utmost care so as not to hinder the future of either fighter, or his bottom line.

With the outdoor season at hand, it was time to take advantage of the weather. Three events highlighted the period:

Joe Louis v. Arturo Godoy

Over 27,000 spectators filled Yankee Stadium to witness Joe Louis defend the most coveted title in all of sports in a rematch with Chilean Arturo Godoy on June 20. The latter, having taken the champion the distance to a split decision back in February, was extremely confident. In a match scheduled for fifteen rounds, Louis systematically disposed of Godoy in the eighth term. Knocked down three times, Godoy appeared defenseless when the referee wisely intervened; the Chilean, whose countenance resembled charbroiled beef, had been thrashed unmercifully. However, that was not the way some at ringside saw it, nor Godoy's handlers, who protested to referee Billy Cavanagh. Thankfully, time and reality slowly quelled the dissent over the fighter's condition.

Max Baer v. Tony Galento

Big Max Baer scored an upset victory over "Two-Ton Tony" Galento at Jersey City, New Jersey, on July 2. Over 27,000 fans gathered inside Roosevelt Stadium to watch an exhausted Baer, the former heavyweight champion, pound Galento's bloodied body into capitulation. The barrel-shaped giant was unable to answer the gong for the eighth round. Galento's cheek and lips were bleeding so badly that even the great cornerman Whitey Bimstein couldn't swab quickly enough to stop the gore.

Henry Armstrong v. Lew Jenkins

A crowd of more than 23,000 packed into the Polo Grounds on July 17 to watch the indomitable "Hammering Henry" Armstrong pummel Lew Jenkins. Armstrong, who began slowly and suffered an early cut to his right eye, dropped Jenkins seven times, before knocking him out in the sixth round of the scheduled twelve-round affair. Jenkins had expended most of his energy in the first round, as Armstrong endured the punishment. Waiting patiently for the proper moment, Armstrong knew his time would come. When he unleashed a deadly left hook that dropped Jenkins for a nine count in the fifth term, the fight was essentially over. Unable to maintain his equilibrium, Jenkins slid off the stool in his corner and was in no condition to continue the battle. Referee Donovan, no stranger to precipitous endings, stopped the non-title fight. Two days later, Jacobs signed the pair to a non-title rematch.

Considering all the events happening in Europe, or the prelude to World War II, the outdoor season was successful.

ARMSTRONG RETURNS IN THE RING

The champion was favored (1–3) before the fifteen-round fight, scheduled inside the City Ring on the evening of October 4.[2] When it was over, which was too soon for many, a crowd of just over 12,000 had witnessed a spectacular upset. Fritzie Zivic battered Henry

Armstrong over the later rounds—from the seventh round until the end of the fight—to capture the decision and the welterweight championship. (Yes, you read that correctly.) The Pittsburgh pugilist was masterful and fought to a game plan that sought to conserve energy, maintain a strong defense, avoid close quarters, and when he sensed it was all clear, to reach into his bag of tricks. Armstrong, who was knocked down in the fourteenth just before the bell, was blinded—thanks to Zivic's thumb and laces tactics—and was exhausted by the end of the fight. It was close by every account entering the final round, but the edge belonged to Zivic.[3]

Making his professional debut on the undercard of the Armstrong-Zivic championship fight was Ray Robinson, the 134½-pound Golden Gloves lightweight champion, who stopped Puerto Rican Joe Echevarria in the second frame of their scheduled four-round contest.

Depth Perception

Those who saw it never forgot it. It happened on November 15, inside Madison Square Garden, and was one of the worst displays of pugilism ever conducted at Eighth Avenue and 50th Street. All 17,101 spectators watched in disgust as Fritzie Zivic was declared victorious because his opponent, Al "Bummy" Davis, was disqualified for low blows in the second round. No fewer than ten blows were hurled by the Brownsville boxer, who clearly suffered from depth perception, as his illegal left hooks found their way south of the border, or below the waistband. As Zivic cringed and contorted, a chorus of boos could be heard across the arena. Only once, however, did the arbiter warn Davis to keep his punches up.

So why did it take ten foul blows before referee Billy Cavanagh agreed to intervene? Was it a matter of weighted pockets or simply an oversight?[4] Nobody was certain, perhaps it was his perspective—it was clearly obvious to everyone ringside that Davis was fouling. Upon calling the fight at the 2:34 mark of the second round, then separating Davis from his opponent, the referee tried to take control of the battle but failed. The Brownsville fighter became uncontrollable. Davis tore himself free of Cavanagh before pursuing Zivic. It was during this outburst that the arbiter was struck in the thigh. A riot ensued, as hats, papers, programs and anything that wasn't nailed down rained over the City Ring and the future of Al "Bummy" Davis.

On November 19, Al Davis had his boxer's licensed revoked—the intent being "for life"—by NYSAC, and a penalty of $2,500 was imposed, the amount to be subtracted from his purse being held by Jacobs.

Forgotten Rounds

Lou Ambers, the "Herkimer Hurricane," thrilled the Garden crowd with his boxing prowess on February 23. Al "Bummy" Davis, normally a power puncher, was simply lethargic, his trademark left hook suppressed effectively by his antagonist. Ambers danced circles around the "Brownsville Terror," even when the latter turned southpaw in the later rounds in an attempt to slow the pace. For Davis it was a wake-up call, and his first loss.

A crowd of more than 11,000 went home early on March 8, as lightweight Lew Jenkins sent Tippy Larkin to Neverland at the end of the first round of a scheduled fifteen-round affair. An unconscious Larkin had to be carried to his corner and then worked on for several minutes in order to regain his senses.

At times fights can be dull until they hit a turning point. Such was the case on May 3, when big Jacob "Buddy" Baer, Max's younger brother, met New Haven's Nathan Mann inside the City Ring for twelve scheduled rounds of boxing. But there was little real boxing until the seventh round, when Baer decided to pound his adversary into the canvas; twice Mann was dropped for a count of nine. Mann finally capitulated and told referee Art Donovan that he had enough. Baer was awarded the kayo at 1:36 of the seventh round.

On May 23, Washington's Ken Overlin, in an upset fifteen-round unanimous decision, powered past the heavily favored Ceferino Garcia inside Madison Square Garden. Surprisingly, the Thursday evening boxing show was poorly attended—the arena wasn't even half full.

St. Louis light heavyweight Jimmy Webb managed his way to a decision over East Rockaway's Tommy Tucker on September 6; the semifinal was part of the Conn versus Pastor undercard. Despite the loss, a badly cut Tucker fought valiantly, making Webb work extremely hard for the victory. In the eighth and final round, the fighter even dropped Webb for a nine count.

Michigan's Hank Postaway fought courageously to overcome two first-term knockdowns by tough West Sider Charley Harvey to gain a four-round draw as part of the (Steve) Belloise versus Garcia undercard on September 12. Washington's Ken Overlin successfully defended his (NYSAC) middleweight crown for the very first time, in a highly contested battle against Steve Belloise of the Bronx. Overlin, who was knocked down in the sixth term, gave a spectacular performance in the rounds that followed and took the split decision.

Fighter of the Year

It was a prolific, yet peculiar year for New York City boxing. The "Pittsburgh Kid" fought three times in the City Ring, winning all three battles. To those who followed boxing, and city sluggers, the year belonged to Billy Conn.

1941

The United States entered World War II, which had begun in 1939, after the Japanese attack on the U.S. fleet at Pearl Harbor in December 1941. In conflict, society often turns to the powerful for a sense of nationalism. Thankfully, President Franklin D. Roosevelt understood the importance of recreation and providing entertainment, such as boxing, as both a distraction and security blanket. So, that's precisely what the sweet science did.

Heart of a Champion

The world's heavyweight champion, Joe Louis, appeared in seven professional fights during the year. He successfully defended his title seven times, six by knockout and another with a win through disqualification of his opponent. The "Brown Bomber" engaged for 56 rounds—his longest bout being 13 rounds, his shortest only 2. Three of his battles took place in New York, two outdoors at the Polo Grounds, and one inside at Madison Square Garden.[5]

Three of the heavyweight champion's ring battles, all in large venues, were considered among the year's highlights:

Joe Louis v. Buddy Baer

Joe Louis engaged Buddy Baer in an outdoor show inside Griffith Stadium on May 23. It was the first world heavyweight championship ever held in Washington, D.C., and the most controversial since Jack Dempsey met Luis Ángel Firpo back in 1923. Referee Arthur Donovan awarded Louis the battle on a foul (disqualification) in the seventh round.[6]

Joe Louis v. Billy Conn

On June 18, the world's heavyweight champion met Billy Conn at the Polo Grounds. A crowd of more than 50,000 watched as Conn held his ground for twelve rounds. But when the Pittsburgh fighter staggered Louis in the twelfth, vision of a knockout danced in his head. Meanwhile, Jack Blackburn, Louis's trainer, was concerned that his fighter had fallen behind and needed a knockout to win the bout. When the gong struck for the thirteenth round, both fighters were hellbent on finishing the fight. Louis spotted an angle and delivered a solid right that hurt Conn. Sensing the kill, and nobody was better at it than Louis, the champion finished Conn with a series of uppercuts and an explosive right. Conn was knocked out at the 2:58 mark of the thirteenth round.

Joe Louis v. Lou Nova

Over 50,000 fans turned out at the Polo Grounds on September 29 to watch Louis defend his heavyweight title against Alameda's Lou Nova. Scheduled for the usual fifteen championship rounds, the match would not go the duration. A solid left to the jaw sent Nova quivering to the ring floor for a nine count in the sixth round. Once he got up, he was nothing more than a target. Louis unloaded the artillery, sending Nova backward and eventually into a neutral corner. Witnessing the helplessness, Donovan stepped in to end the fight with only one second left in the round. It was the champion's nineteenth title defense.

Back in the Garden

On Friday, January 3, middleweight Billy Soose met a very determined foe in Tami Mauriello. A Garden crowd of more than 13,000 watched, some in disbelief, as Mauriello took the first defeat of his ring career, a ten-round split decision, following twenty-four consecutive victories. Soose conducted a clinic as he feinted, punched, and parried assaults, while refining his already impressive defensive skills. The most effective punch for the fighter was his straight left that he used to keep Mauriello at bay. Jacobs loved what he saw in Soose, and believed the Pennsylvania youngster was his answer to organizing the middleweight division. If he could pit Soose against Overlin, then the winner could tackle Zale, the NBA crown holder.

Two Rivals

It was an SRO (standing room only) night inside Madison Square Garden on January 17, and for good reason. It was a rematch between Henry Armstrong, who once held three titles simultaneously, and the current world's welterweight champion, Fritzie Zivic. Following the eleventh round, the physician ringside nearly stopped the fight. Armstrong had valiantly attempted to end the bout in the eleventh round by engaging his rival with a crushing assault, but it failed when the fighter ran out of gas. Sensing his rival's fatigue, Zivic pitilessly sliced him up with combinations to the face. When Armstrong came out for the twelfth term, he had nothing left. When he missed and slipped with a wild right, Referee Art Donovan wisely stepped in and waved it off.

THE BUSINESS OF BOXING

On January 21, a *New York Times* piece, picked up and printed from the Associated Press, spoke volumes: "Sharp Rise Is Noted In Boxing Interest, Garden has drawn 185,895 to 13 shows this season."[7] Boxing, as well as the Garden, wasn't placing its entire future in Joe Louis alone. It had become increasingly clear that some of the smaller weight classes could attract fans and that the more familiarity a spectator had with a fighter, the better he would draw. The strategy, as it would prove, was extraordinarily insightful.[8]

Billy Conn surrendered his light-heavyweight title on February 11, under NYSAC's terms and conditions, for an opportunity—a capitulation for compensation, as they used to say—to meet Joe Louis for the heavyweight title.[9] Was there a pot of gold at the end of the heavyweight rainbow? Conn thought so.

FIRST TELEVISED BOXING
FROM MADISON SQUARE GARDEN, APRIL 4, 1941

It was called television, or a new system for transmitting visual images. These moving images were reproduced on screens that even included sound. If the providers of the new technology needed the perfect test bed, they found it in Madison Square Garden. Those who had seen the technology demonstrated at the 1939 New York World's Fair on Long Island just raved about it. And RCA, General Electric, and Dumont were selling television sets in the New York City faster than they could be made. Obviously, watching a fight on a screen size that often ranged from five to twelve inches certainly wasn't as good as being there, but it was gradually becoming an option.[10]

Just a couple of years earlier, the first boxing match had been televised from Yankee Stadium in the Bronx. It was between heavyweights Max Baer and Lou Nova, and took place on June 1, 1939. And the previous year, the Garden participated in two televised events: The first televised ice hockey game between the New York Rangers and Montreal Canadiens was broadcast in the United States on W2XBS-TV; and the first televised basketball game between Fordham University and the University of Pittsburgh was also transmitted. So, why not boxing inside the Garden?

Ironically, the combatants in the first boxing match ever televised, Lou Nova v. Max Baer, christened the City Ring as well. When Lou Nova, having hit the canvas in the fourth round, regained his senses and knocked out Max Baer in the eighth, nobody could believe it. But it happened on April 4, inside Madison Square Garden, in front of a capacity crowd, not to mention those who witnessed it on one of those magic tubes. However, television, like virtually everything else, would be put on hold until after the war.[11]

7. World War II and a City Ring, 1940–1945

Ray Robinson's First Garden Feature, September 19, 1941

There he was, Ray Robinson, in the *New York Times* on page 30, with the headline reading "Robinson Choice In Fight Tonight." His photograph was alongside that of his next opponent, East Sider Maxie Shapiro, as both fighters were part of Madison Square Garden's main event on September 19. The undefeated Harlem fighter, who had already thrilled thousands in the City Ring, both as an amateur and professional, was now feature material. That's what winning 23 consecutive professional battles could do for a fighter.

From the opening bell, the crowd of more than 11,000 expected Robinson to take charge. Instead it was Shapiro. However, early in the second, a sharp left hook landed solidly on Robinson and appeared to wake him up. The Harlem fighter then dropped his antagonist numerous times before being awarded a third-round knockout.

After he had defeated Marty Servo in Philadelphia, Robinson's next fight was an indication of just how fast he was being thrust into the forefront of the sport. He was matched against veteran Fritzie Zivic on October 31, inside the Garden. (I know what you're thinking. Zivic already?) Granted he had won twenty-five consecutive battles, but the Harlem fighter was only 21 years old and a devastating loss to a seasoned pugilist like Zivic could have major consequences. Remember, it was only a year earlier that Zivic won the title from Henry Armstrong. But Robinson's popularity could plant backsides ringside. To the amazement of some, Ray Robinson soundly defeated Fritzie Zivic, the former 147-pound champion, inside the City Ring.

To campaign for the light heavyweight crown, Billy Soose gave up his middleweight title thst same day, on October 31. Accepting the resignation, NYSAC stated that they would recognize the winner of the Zale versus Abrams match, scheduled for November 28 inside the City Ring, as the new titleholder.[12] Tony Zale already held the NBA

The power of persuasion during World War II seemed to rest in the form of words, films and posters. The government launched an aggressive propaganda campaign to galvanize public support, and when it needed a hero they found him in Joe Louis (*Library of Congress, LC-USZC4-1334 [color film copy transparency]*).

crown. Zale hailed from Gary, Indiana, and polished his skills by way of the Golden Gloves tournament in Chicago.

Dropped to the canvas in the first round by Georgie Abrams, Zale regained his composure and fought magnificently to take the fifteen-round unanimous verdict. Mike Jacobs, who could see a dime on a roof in a snowstorm, convinced Zale that he had no suitable challengers at the 160-pound mark. So why not move up, say to the 175-pound class? Zale took the bait and signed to meet Billy Conn in the Garden on February 13.

World War II

A sudden and unanticipated attack on Pearl Harbor in Honolulu, Hawaii, on December 7, by the Japanese air force and navy thrust the United States of America into war with Japan. Soon a world at war would alter the lives of virtually every living creature on the planet. There was now a bigger ring, more worthy opponents, more important battles, and the risk of an enormous knockout punch. World War II was a fight nobody wanted to lose.

Boxers, not to mention many of those around the sport, were proud to serve, and many did, including Billy Conn, Joe Louis and Bob Montgomery, to name only a few. Their participation was welcome, especially that of Joe Louis, whose familiar image adorned

Pictured here is a Madison Square Garden poster featuring Billy Soose vs. Georgie Abrams, along with the corresponding program. The smiling portrait of Billy Soose was during the boxer's first visit to Canastota, New York.

numerous recruitment posters. For many it was hard to comprehend that a fighter they could have met in a ring with gloves only months earlier could now be faced on a battlefield holding a rifle. Almost overnight, German boxer Max Schmeling became German enemy Max Schmeling. And although Schmeling was a lifelong Nazi opponent, he ended up wearing their uniform.

Boxing had become so popular that its metaphors became part of the routine coverage of the war. An enemy could be beaten to the punch, hit below the belt, or boxed into a corner. Our allies could deliver a decisive blow, be in our corner, or deliver a killer assault. And we didn't want to let our guard down, lead with our chin, or be on the ropes. But boxing, like baseball, needed to go on during the war.

Forgotten Rounds

On January 3, as part of the Mauriello versus Soose undercard, Brooklyn's Marty Marino took a decision over Charlottesville, Virginia's Mutt Womer, in an outstanding six-rounder. Hitting the canvas for a count of two in the third, Marino regrouped and went on to outbox his opponent.

Harlem's Ray Robinson took a decision over West Sider George Zengaras in a six-rounder as part of the Louis versus Burman undercard on January 31. Robinson fought at 135 pounds.

Lew Jenkins defeated Lou Ambers for the second time on February 2. Ambers was knocked out in the seventh round of their scheduled ten-round non-title clash.

The "Bronx Barkeep," Tami Mauriello stunned the Garden crowd on March 14 by knocking out his borough rival Steve Belloise in the very first round. With just one second remaining, Belloise, who had hit the canvas five times, collapsed over the bottom rope and onto the ring apron.

On May 9, inside the Garden, Billy Soose met NYSAC world middleweight champion Ken Overlin in a fifteen-round affair. Well, when the observations of the 11,000-plus fight fans didn't match the unanimous decision given by the judges, more boos rose from the Garden than in a graveyard on Halloween. Despite the concordant verdict, some of the newspapers hinted of mystical underpinnings. Overlin's corner was furious, especially his manager Chris Dundee, who lodged a protest against the award. Soose, the new champion, then headed west.

Bob Montgomery, who scored the only knockdown of the fight, outpointed lightweight champion Lew Jenkins in a ten-round non-title bout in Madison Square Garden on May 16.

Brownsville welterweight Al "Bummy" Davis, who had fouled himself out of the sport of boxing, was approved for a return match with Fritzie Zivic on June 25 (later postponed until July 2) inside the Polo Grounds. It took Mike Jacobs to land the deal with a plea for the Army Relief Fund, and it worked. Zivic defeated Davis by TKO in the tenth round of a scheduled twelve-rounder.

On October 6, on the undercard of the Cochrane versus Jenkins fight, Newark lightweight Allie Stolz took an exciting six-round decision over Frankie Martin, a.k.a. "Chief Crazy Horse." The two battled like cats and dogs in nonstop action. Martin, who could take a punch but not curtail his temper, had a tendency to hit south of the border, and in the end it cost him the fight.

Finally, the four-round opener of the Zivic versus McCoy battle on December 12 saw Hartford's Willie Pep take the decision over Puerto Rican Ruby Garcia.

Fighter of the Year

Clearly, Joe Louis was the fighter of the year—although a case could also be made for Tony Zale.

Ray Robinson fought four times in the Garden, and won all four battles, while Billy Soose fought four consecutive fights and won all four. But Gus Lesnevich fought three consecutive times, all title fights, and won all three. Not to mention that he was also NYSAC's world light heavyweight champion. His two distance victories against Tami Mauriello established an outstanding rivalry—the pair would eventually fight four times—and really polished the City Ring in 1941.[13]

1942

Gasoline rationing began on the East Coast to preserve fuel and rubber, crooner Frank Sinatra accepted an eight-week engagement at the Paramount Theater on Times Square, and Katz's Delicatessen on the Lower East Side hung a signing proclaiming, "Send a salami to your boy in the Army." All three, believe it or not, would have an impact on Garden attendance. It wasn't long before black market takes hold. Petrol, or even seasoned sausage for that matter, could be traded for Garden or Paramount tickets. So what's your preference, a four-rounder or "Stardust"?[14]

Ray Robinson

Walker Smith, Jr., was born on May 3, 1921, in Ailey, Georgia, to Walker Smith, Sr., and Leila Hurst. Junior's first major hurdle occurred at the age of fifteen when he was rejected from his first boxing tournament because he didn't possess an AAU membership card. The truth was, he didn't have one because it required him to be eighteen years of age. Circumventing the process, Smith countered by borrowing a birth certificate from his friend Ray Robinson. The name stuck, and Robinson stuck around.

Robinson's next hurdle was maturity. The streets of New York, similar to those of the Midwest, were tough, and like the ring, the youngster needed to prove himself. Hanging with the wrong crowd got him in trouble and challenged his levelheadedness. By the age of 19, he had already been married, divorced and had a son. There was light at the end of the tunnel, however, and it came in the form of a brilliant amateur boxing career: he compiled a record of 85–0 record with 69 knockouts.[15] After winning the Golden Gloves featherweight championship in 1939, and the organization's lightweight championship the following year, he had reached that light. Robinson made his professional debut on October 4, 1940, winning via a second-round stoppage over Joe Echevarria. Entering 1942, the undefeated Ray Robinson was 26–0, a wealthy Harlemite, good-looking, and enormously talented—a meal ticket for any promoter willing to take a bite, and many were hungry.

Baer Down

Buddy Baer got his second shot at Joe Louis on January 9, inside Madison Square Garden. Promoter Mike Jacobs, eager to do his part for the war effort, conducted the bout for the Navy Relief Society. It was scheduled for fifteen championship rounds inside the City Ring, but few thought it would go the distance. And they were right.

A capacity crowd turned out to watch the heavyweight champion pummel Buddy Baer, dropping him twice for a count of nine, before finally delivering the Californian at the 2:56 mark of the very first round. Louis did it with pure talent, as Baer was taller, heavier and possessed a greater reach. Twenty successful title defenses put Louis in a league of his own, destined for immortality. But three days later, citizenship put him in the Army.

Also in the Garden, on January 16, and in a rematch, Harlem phenom Ray Robinson knocked out Fritzie Zivic in the tenth round of a scheduled twelve-round conflict. Robinson not only painted Zivic with punches, he dominated the seasoned veteran before putting him away with a vicious right to the jaw.

As more and more fighters were requested for duty, matchmakers had their hands full trying to build attractive cards. In a splendid display of patriotism, Private Joe Louis donated his entire purse to Army Emergency Relief when he met Abe Simon inside Madison Square Garden on March 27.[16] In his twenty-first title defense, Joe Louis dropped Abe Simon three times to pick up a knockout victory over the Richmond Hill (Queens) giant at the 0:16 mark of the sixth round.[17]

The Garden, blacked out for two months, returned with a vengeance on July 23. Baltimore heavyweight Clarence "Red" Burman brawled Bronx contender Tami Mauriello in one of the better "pendulum," or momentum-shifting, fights held in many a season. Burman finally capitulated at the 2:58 mark in the ninth round when he surrendered to referee Frank Fullam. Upon witnessing the acquiescence, Mauriello, tired and bleeding from his left eye, dropped his gloves to his sides in an more appearance of relief than of victory.

A Rivalry Begins—Robinson v. LaMotta

It was the beginning of what would be one of the greatest sextets in boxing history, Ray Robinson versus Jake LaMotta. And it began with an undefeated Harlem welterweight stepping up to tackle a hard-wearing Bronx shock absorber. Both fighters were extraordinarily dangerous and capable of delivering a fight-ending blow. Robinson's untarnished record made him a natural favorite. LaMotta had a record of 25–4–2 entering the hostilities, with his only losses to Jose Basora, Nate Bolden and a pair to Jimmy Reeves.

Jake LaMotta was born Giacobbe LaMotta on July 10, 1922, in the Bronx. The youngster was a city boy through and through-a dust-eating scrapper who would settle arguments with his fists. Fighting for loose change in the backyard or on neighborhood streets suited him just fine, besides he was good at it. Spending time in reform school, however, did not serve him well-behavior modification was still in its infancy, and besides, Ivan Pavlov never fought in a ring-so he turned to the sweet science as a professional in 1941. He was 19 years of age.

While in the city, LaMotta fought out of the usual venues: St. Nicholas Arena, Ridgewood Grove (Brooklyn), New York Coliseum (Bronx), Queensboro Arena (Queens), and Starlight Park (Bronx); however, he also took some fights up at the Westchester County

Center in White Plains, New York. The first time he ever fought outside the city, he lost, as did he the second time, and the third time; the fight game was an education and he hadn't graduated yet. The New York Coliseum would host most of his battles in 1942, minus, of course, his chances to step into the City Ring. Being matched against Robinson, especially at this time, was like hitting pay dirt.

In preparation for their first battle against one another, LaMotta trained over at Gleason's Gymnasium, while Robinson trained at his camp in Greenwood Lake, New York. Aware that Robinson's distance artillery was delivered with an unprecedented degree of precision and power, LaMotta believed his only chance was to lure him into close quarters. This was like trying to lure a polar bear into a trap baited with ice; Robinson was far too smart.

An American boxer, Guglielmo Papaleo (1922–2006), better known as Willie Pep, held the world featherweight championship twice between the years of 1942 and 1950. His final record was 230-11-1 with 65 KOs.

From the opening bell on October 2, Robinson took command of the City Ring and, for the most part, never looked back. LaMotta's incursions were met with his antagonist's slips to the safety of the perimeter. Once there, Robinson scored points from his effective combinations and long-range rights. Despite being outweighed by 12¾ pounds, Robinson took the unanimous ten-round decision in front of a Garden crowd estimated at over 12,000.

A Quartet of Excitement-Pep v. Wright

Guglielmo Papaleo was born in Middletown, a beautiful city located along the Connecticut River, on September 19, 1922. The metropolitan area was undergoing a demographic transformation at the time as a large number of Irish, Italian, Polish and German immigrants arrived to fulfill the employment needs of Connecticut factories; Guglielmo's parents were from Siracusa in Sicily.[18] Although Middletown was not Brooklyn or the Bronx, times could be tough and a kid had to learn to defend himself. Since Guglielmo stood a mere 5'5" tall, his size wasn't likely to intimidate. Picking up loose change by shining shoes and other odd jobs, the youngster grew bored. So he, along with fellow Hartford bootblack Johnny Duke, decided to join a gym.[19] Honing his skills quickly, Papaleo, having altered his surname to Pep, became a Connecticut state amateur champion (1938–39) before turning pro in 1940. He fought around the Hartford area during his first year, then added Holyoke, Massachusetts, to his growing list of fight centers—by 1941; there were also some occasional one-off bouts in other cities.

The undefeated Pep held victories over Joey Archibald, Bobby Ivy, Bobby McIntire and George Zengaras before entering his November 20 title fight (NYSAC world featherweight championship) with Chalky Wright.

Albert "Chalky" Wright's family history was also fascinating. Born on February 1, 1912, in Wilcox, Arizona, Albert was the youngest of seven children. He was also the grandson of a runaway slave from Natchez, Mississippi, who fled to the Arizona Territory just before the Civil War. His maternal grandfather then served in the Union Army as a Buffalo Soldier, a term given to the "Negro Cavalry" by Native American tribes. Following a split between his parents, Chalky and his siblings ended up in Colton, California. And it was there that the youth took an interest in boxing.

The lanky five-foot-seven-and-a-half-inch fighter possessed a long reach that he could use it to his advantage, if he could hone his skills. And that he did, inside the walls of the Orange Belt Athletic Club in San Bernadino, California. Turning pro in 1928, his early career was an arduous grind, partly because of where he was fighting; it wasn't until about his one-hundredth fight that he really starting tackling some of the better competition. By the time Chalky Wright met Willie Pep, he had already participated in over 180 professional fights.[20]

Only in America could you find a second-generation Italian immigrant, not to mention talented pugilist, battling the grandson of a former slave, who just happened to hold the world's featherweight championship. But such was the case on November 20, 1942, when both collided inside the City Ring.

A near-capacity house watched in amazement as a resolute Willie Pep captured the world featherweight title from "Chalky" Wright. The fluid Pep danced and pranced for fifteen rounds, even poked and prodded his opponent as if her were he were standing still. For the new champion it was his fifty-fourth consecutive victory-a unanimous verdict. As for the house, they broke the previous indoor record for a featherweight championship gate that dated back to the Canzoneri-Bass fight of 1928.

Twentieth Century Sporting Club promoter Mike Jacobs released some fascinating statistics to the public on December 12. The company's press release stated that the twenty-eight boxing shows, all held indoors due to war restrictions, grossed over $1.1 million, while attracting over 300,000 fans. This amounted to a higher average than the previous year and was evidence of the popularity of the sport. Considering the number of boxing champions who were serving in the military, one has to hand it to matchmaker Nat Rogers for a job well done.

Forgotten Rounds

On the Zale versus Conn undercard of February 13, Pittsburgh's Johnny Cregan, having hit the canvas three times, managed to rally back to draw Ohio's George Koch in a six-rounder.

In an unrelenting display of pugilism, heavyweight contenders Bob Pastor and Tami Mauriello fought hammer and tongs for ten rounds on May 22. In front of a Garden crowd estimated at 12,000 fans, the two gave every ounce of effort to conclude at a draw-the judges split and the referee had it a draw.

Marty Servo, a Coast Guard welterweight, was Robinson's thirty-second consecutive victim on May 28; he had also been his twenty-fifth. However, in this ten-round bout, which ended in a split decision, it was far closer than it looked on paper. Early mistakes had cost Servo. He was penalized in the second for a low blow, and in retrospect it may have cost him the fight.

Hartford's undefeated featherweight Willie Pep stopped Bayonne's Frank Franconeri, who had been floored three times, in the first round on September 10. It was on the Zivic versus Cochrane undercard.

Beau Jack upset lightweight contender Allie Stolz with a seventh-round technical knockout during a scheduled ten-rounder on November 13.

Floored for a count of nine in the opening minutes of his Garden battle, Tami Mauriello overcame adversity to knock out Lou Nova in the sixth round of their contest. Over 15,000 spectators attended the December 11 slugfest, as the winner hoped to become a candidate for the prestigious title held by Joe Louis.

Finally, Beau Jack knocked out Tippy Larkin in the third round of a scheduled fifteen-round affair to essentially claim the lightweight championship on December 18.[21]

Fighter of the Year

Whether you followed the sport, or just the bouts inside Madison Square Garden, the year belonged to Ray Robinson. The sensational Harlem pugilist won fourteen bouts in 1942, while pushing his unbeaten streak to forty. Madison Square Garden hosted eight, or over half of Robinson's ring encounters, and couldn't have been prouder to do so.[22]

One of the fight game's most notable rivalries was Ray Robinson (left) versus Jacob La Motta (right). Pictured are two relics from their February 23, 1945, duel inside Madison Square Garden. La Motta fought Robinson six times—twice in a three-week span in 1943—winning only once.

1943

In stark contrast to the previous year, when many key matches were held in New York, 1943 would see relatively few. For example, Robinson v. La Motta II was held in Robinson's former hometown of Detroit. Did it make any difference? We'll see. The war, with its complex economic environment, had made it difficult to gauge demand. Promoting a boxing card, if you could find the talent, became an expensive gamble.

Underdog Jacob LaMotta, a.k.a. the "Raging Bull," took a ten-round unanimous decision over Ray Robinson inside Olympia Stadium on February 5. The triumph put an end to Robinson's victory streak that lasted through 129 bouts, forty of which were professional. In the eighth round, LaMotta hit Robinson so hard with his left that it sent him through the ropes for a nine count. The fight evened the score between the fighters at one win apiece.[23]

Titles on Hold

In the absence of the boxing champions serving their country in the armed forces, NYSAC unanimously voted against recognizing what has been called "duration champions" at a meeting on February 26. The organization also announced the end of their title elimination tournament for the lightweight honor and deemed Philadelphia's Bob Montgomery a more than worthy opponent for Beau Jack to confirm the lightweight crown. In the eyes of many, Jack was the current champion.[24]

The longest winning streak in the history of modern boxing came to an end on March 19, when Sammy Angott, the former lightweight king, took a ten-round unanimous decision over Hartford's Willie Pep. Fortunately for Pep, it was a non-title bout. Angott, who was the underdog, just waltzed around his adversary. The historic, yet lackluster, event drew over 16,000 Garden fans and benefited the Boxing Service Athletic Fund.

Beau Jack

The Black Belt was a term originally used to describe the prairies and dark fertile soil of central Alabama and northeast Mississippi, but it evolved into a phrase associated with a much larger agricultural region in the Southern United States-an area characterized by a history of cotton plantation agriculture in the nineteenth century. This area also was based on enslaved African-American labor that worked tirelessly until they gained their freedom after the American Civil War. Augusta, Georgia, was a market town that benefited from the Black Belt, and by the 1920s its population had grown to over 50,000.

Sidney Walker was born in Augusta on April 1, 1921, and raised by his grandmother on a small farm not far from the city's epicenter. When assisting his grandmother became more important than school, which was in the second grade, Sidney's priorities changed. By the age of eight, he dropped his farming tools in favor of those of a bootblack. The youngster would walk miles to the city in order to set up shop shining shoes-earning money with a shine, he believed, was better than hard labor.

So the story goes: There was a day in which the youth returned home in tears as a result of a confrontation with another boy who had stolen Sidney's "shine" money, along with his polish. That's when his grandmother, Evie Mixom, told him he had to learn to defend himself. Heeding her advice, Sidney "put a whoppin'" on the guilty party a week later. From that point, Evie called him "Beau Jack." The moniker stuck.

Discovering that he had a knack for the sweet science, Jack participated in street contests and battle royals. These were slugfests among multiple blindfolded youth, many African-American, where the last boy standing took the money donated by spectators. It was during one of these street spectacles that a steward at the Augusta National Golf Club noted Jack and hired him as a locker room attendant and bootblack.

The famous writer Ralph Waldo Emerson once quipped, "Once you make a decision, the universe conspires to make it happen." Well, it didn't take long before one of the club's founding members, Bobby Jones, took note of Jack's pugilistic skills. Yep, it was that Robert Tyre "Bobby" Jones, Jr. Convinced he had found something special, the golfing legend decided he would assist on underwriting the boxer's career. Jones put up $500 and persuaded fifty other golfers to ante up $50 each.

Beau Jack turned professional in 1940 at the age of 19, and began fighting around Augusta before heading to Aiken, South Carolina. Sensing that he couldn't find the talent to expand his skills, he headed to New England. Honing his expertise, primarily in Holyoke, Massachusetts, allowed Jack to add over fifteen fights to his resume before the conclusion of the annum.

Jack's breakout year was 1941. Following a string of victories, including defeats of Tommy Speigal and George Zengaras, the fighter headed to New York. There he landed on some nice undercards, fighting at Ebbets Field, Broadway Arena, St. Nicholas Arena, and even at Madison Square Garden. Jack went 13-0 in 1942, and would finish 1943 at 6-2, having lost, then regained the lightweight title.[25]

Pound-for-Pound, Round-by-Round, Not a Sound

The fight between Henry Armstrong and Ray Robinson, originally scheduled for ten rounds inside the Polo Grounds on August 27, was moved inside to the City Ring.[26] Army Corporal Ray Robinson was favored to outpoint his well-known antagonist in front of a large crowd, and he did in fact. In more of a sparring session than a fight, Robinson toyed with "Hammerin' Henry" almost in an expression of commiseration more than conflict. Critics ringside were quick to note the inactivity, not to mention redundancy, of each term. Whether or not that was the plan all along-a final good-bye with some nice pocket change for the road-was just too hard to say. After the fight, and for the second time (but not the last), "Hurricane Hank" retired.

The pair had over two hundred professional fights between them: Armstrong entered the fight 134-17-7, while Robinson posted a record of 44-1-0. As Armstrong shuffled to the center of the ring, in that notable crouch of his-the fighter's right just below the chin, while his left hovered above his left thigh—you could sense the curtain dropping on a fabulous career, and Robinson, more interested in the best seat in the house than battling an adversary, saw it too. It was a sad display. Nevertheless, not a single serious boxing fan would have passed the opportunity to witness such an event. Combined, the pair had graced the Garden on over 35 occasions.

Forgotten Rounds

Canadian Johnny Greco grabbed a ten-round unanimous decision over Californian lightweight Cleo Shans in a slugfest from beginning to end on February 26. Fighting in his very first major bout inside the Garden, Greco traded punches at a furious rate and captivated many of the fans. A month later he also took the rematch with Shans.

For Beau Jack, he started his year with a pair of fights, a month apart, against Fritzie Zivic inside the City Ring. At ten rounds, the first was two rounds shorter than the second held on March 5, but the results were identical: a pair of decision losses for Zivic. It wasn't a battle that emphasized the diminishing skills of the "Croat Comet," a former champion, but quite the contrary. It was a contest that underlined the proficiency of the current lightweight titleholder Beau Jack.

Tami Mauriello, dropped in the second round and outpunched in the early rounds of a ten-round battle, mounted a gallant comeback to take a united verdict over Des Moines' Lee Savold on November 5.

As if God had spoken to him directly, an energy-conscious Beau Jack took a spectacular unanimous decision over Bob Montgomery on November 19. The victory allowed Jack to regain the world lightweight title he lost to his nemesis back in May.

To conclude the year, Sammy Angott, the NBA lightweight champion, conquered Bobby Ruffin in a ten-round split decision on December 17. Angott, who took command of the bout from the beginning, was far more aggressive and polished than his Long Island opponent.

Fighter of the Year

Outside of New York, if boxing belonged to any fighter, it was bantam champion Manuel Ortiz. The talented Californian went 13–0 on the year with seven kayos, defending his title eight times. As fate saw to it, the boxer would never fight inside the City Ring.[27]

The fighter who shined the City Ring with his presence in 1943 was Beau Jack. In six Garden bouts, Jack attracted over 100,000 fans. His gates drew nearly a half a million dollars. Along with Henry Armstrong, he shared the largest gate of the year, over $100,000.[28]

1944

D-Day, or June 6, 1944, saw 176,000 Allied troops storm ashore the beaches of Normandy in France. As the largest seaborne invasion in history, the operation began the liberation of German-occupied territories. Simply put, it was very difficult for anybody to think beyond this event. To borrow the G.K. Chesterton quip, "The true soldier fights not because he hates what is in front of him, but because he loves what is behind him." By 1944, the ramifications of World War II were being felt by everyone.

Even the game's premier impresario, Mike Jacobs, was unsure of the road ahead. Conducting twenty or more shows inside the Garden was going to be a challenge and a question of available talent. Five ring titles were frozen as Louis, Lesnevich, Zale, Cochrane and Pep were serving their Uncle Sam instead of themselves. Over 4,000 boxers, active and retired, came to the aid of their country.[29] If there was a promising sign, it was the potential for outdoor shows. Thanks to the lifting of dimout restrictions, which had limited the use of lights at night especially during the threat of an air raid, it wasn't business as usual, but it was better than the alternative. Jacobs was keeping an open mind; the question was, how late would he stay open?

A Left Hook from the Gods

Al "Bummy" Davis hadn't appeared in Madison Square Garden since November 1940, but that was about to change. The scrappy fighter would meet Bob Montgomery on February 18 for ten rounds inside the City Ring, both fighters weighing 144 pounds or under. Montgomery, as anticipated, was a huge favorite over the Brownsville welterweight. Most recall, vividly in some cases, that Davis was suspended for life following his fight with Fritzie Zivic. It was shortly after that fiasco that the fighter entered the Army. Under the umbrella of the Army Emergency Relief Fund, his suspension was lifted in order for the soldier to fight Zivic once again.

Upon exiting the Army, Davis found that the times were tough and he had few alternatives. So he resorted to the one thing he knew: boxing. Far from oblivious to the road that lay ahead, Davis trained hard and kept his nose clean. Dropping twenty pounds and scraping off the ring rust, he gradually fought his way back to the satisfaction of the commission.

Jacobs watched Davis closely, and when the fighter packed the Broadway Arena in Brooklyn during his last handful of bouts, he bit at an opportunity to match him with Montgomery. And, boy, did the spectators turn out, some 17,000 plus to watch the fight. The preliminaries were nothing to write home about, but the atmosphere was intoxicating. Everybody grabbed a drink or a smoke before the main bout as the venue auctioned off some war bonds. Davis, five pounds heavier than his opposition, entered confidently, and why not? He had performed brilliantly since returning to the ring, and in his last seven fights had gone 5–0–2.[30] Montgomery, the former lightweight champion, also entered the ring with a swagger of optimism that was uncontested. In a career that included nearly seventy ring confrontations, he had posted a record of 57–7–3, and had never been knocked out.

At the opening bell of the ten-rounder, people were still settling into their seats. Both fighters emerged from their corners, claiming their ground and stalking their opponent. As they measured each other a bit with early jabs, the fight had all the appearances of an extended battle. At precisely one minute and 3 seconds into the first round, Davis unleashed a left hook that was fired with such power and precision that when it hit Montgomery, it sent him sprawling to the floor. Nobody could believe their eyes as Montgomery struggled to regain his senses—which, for all intents and purposes, he never did. He was somewhat erect at the count of four, but it was just a matter of time.

Moving in for the kill, Davis was over "Bobcat" like vultures over road kill. The Brownsville boxer then discharged a barrage of lefts that finally sank Montgomery forward and toward his adversary. Davis, with all the graciousness of a vindictive warrior, stepped aside to watch Monty fall-face first to the canvas. Referee Frank Fullam picked up the knockout at the count of four; Benny Leonard was the knockout timekeeper. Montgomery tried desperately, and to his credit, stood at the count of ten. Just the same, he was clearly incapable of defending himself. Fullam threw up his arms and it was over.

Win Some, Lose Some

In what had become a popular rivalry, Bob Montgomery met Beau Jack inside the City Ring on March 3. And the former took the rubber match. For Montgomery, the fifteen-round split decision was particularly noteworthy as it allowed him to regain the NYSAC lightweight championship that he had lost to Jack.

It was a record Garden gate for a non-heavyweight fight and it was the ten-round feature on March 17: Beau Jack versus Al Davis. Although the hard-punching Davis outweighed Jack, he was simply no match on this day. Jack easily took the united ruling on the scorecard of every judge.

Just One of Those Nights

On December 22, Harold Green recovered from an eight count in the eighth round, to take a split decision over Rocky Graziano. It was a rematch of their November 3 battle. Dropped for a three count in the second, Graziano never relented. He was resolved to turn the tide, and he did. However, Green, cut from the same mold, let his antagonist know he was none too happy about hitting the canvas himself. Seconds before the final bell, he cold-cocked Graziano. The Garden crowd of just over 10,000 enjoyed every minute of the battle between these two local pugs. But would they fill out the trilogy?

Forgotten Rounds

As many of those pugilists serving in the military returned, they learned that promoters were as anxious as themselves to see what toll, if any, the war had taken on their ring skills. The City Ring would witness a plethora of sensational rounds. Here is just a sample:

Perseverance was a quality that seemed to come natural to a thirty-one-year-old fighter named Jerry D'Ambrosio. When the Long Island father of five appeared at the eighteenth annual Golden Gloves tournament, held in the Garden in February, it didn't surprise anyone. D'Ambrosio had been a participant at the annual event since 1928. While he had yet to win a title, he certainly won over the many hearts he had impressed over the years with his dogged determination.

Shaking up the heavyweights, a well-traveled Joe Baksi of Kulpmont, Pennsylvania, floored Tami Mauriello for a nine count in the very first round before going on to take the ten-round unanimous Garden decision on February 25.

On March 23, Tippy Larkin sent Allie Stolz to the canvas three times in the third term, during a scheduled ten-round Garden feature. After the third round, however, referee Art Donovan determined that Larkin was in no shape to continue and ended the fight.

For all that, it was a semifinal battle between Aaron Perry of Washington and Joey Manfro of the Bronx that proved the most exciting on the evening's card. At the opening bell of the scheduled six-rounder, Manfro let loose a flying right that nailed Perry's jaw and sent him to the canvas. Managing to arise fully at the count of nine, Perry stood and awaited Manfro's follow-up. But the Bronx fighter missed with his right, allowing Perry to counter with a solid right that dropped Manfro to the floor. It was his turn to take a nine count, but he was in far worse condition than realized. Perry then dropped him again to another nine count. It was here that referee George Walsh stopped the fight. Perry was awarded a knockout at the 1:49 mark of the first round.

Henry Armstrong coldcocked Al Davis in the second round of their June 15 battle. Davis, who was floored three times before the final devastating blow, had to be lifted from the floor and carried to his Garden corner.

On Friday, August 4, Private Beau Jack, stationed at Fort Benning, Georgia, took a decision over Army solider Bob Montgomery, stationed at Keesler Field, Mississippi, in a non-title bout. This was the fourth and final time the elite pair would meet inside a boxing ring.

On September 22, heavyweight Tami Mauriello knocked out Lee Oma, who had substituted for Joe Baksi, in the eighth round of an action-packed contest. In the semifinal on the same card, Bronx lightweight Al Guido handed Tony Janiro his first defeat in twenty-four professional ring contests.

Welterweight Johnny Greco floored Bobby Ruffin twice to take a unanimous ten-round decision on November 17. It was a far more exciting fight than the decision indicated, as both fighters went toe-to-toe into the final seconds. Greco also endured some significant damage in the ninth round. The pair would do battle again on December 15, in what some including James P. Dawson of the *New York Times*, would view, as one of the finest draws ever staged in the Garden. Ruffin, having been floored twice, recomposed himself to deliver a beating to Greco.[31]

Fighter of the Year

In retrospect, it's hard to deny that Willie Pep, who went 16–0 in 1944, was "Fighter of the Year." The "Will o' the Wisp" was simply magnificent. However, inside the City Ring, not one fighter really polished the enclosure. Instead, there were some great moments and rivalries. From the left hook from heaven thrown by Al Davis to the Green v. Graziano rivalry—and you can throw in the Greco v. Ruffin series as well—it was a year composed of moments more than rounds.

1945

Not universally agreed upon, the UK saw the conclusion of World War II with the armistice of August 14, 1945 (V-J Day), rather than the formal surrender of Japan on September 2, 1945, which is the US observation. As peace, according to Albert Einstein, could only be achieved through understanding, it was on whatever day that actually took place.

Nothing Left

Willie Joyce was a lightweight fighter from Gary, Indiana, and he was scheduled to meet Ike Williams for the third time on March 2. Joyce won their first battle in Philadelphia, a ten-rounder, and Williams took the second, a twelve-rounder in New York. Their next bout was another scheduled twelve-rounder, and Joyce had trained particularly hard. Over 14,000 found their way to the Garden and were far from disappointed—in fact, it would prove to be one of the best fights of the year—as two tenacious gladiators fought their hearts out.

In the end, and nobody wanted to see it end, it was a unanimous decision for Joyce. Figuring Williams was going to pour it on during the final rounds, Joyce was prepared to answer. A terrific right caught the jaw of Williams in the final minute of the fight and his knees buckled. Going for the kill, Joyce backed his adversary into the ropes and let loose a volley of punches. But miraculously, Williams was able to dodge the blows and stay on his feet. At that point, Joyce was so fatigued that he fell forward into the ropes following the closing bell. The pace was just relentless.

Thomas Rocco Barbella, a.k.a. Rocky Graziano

Born Thomas Rocco Barbella on January 1, 1919, in Brooklyn, New York, he was the son of Ida Scinto and Nicola Barbella. As a youth his mother filled him with wisdom, such as, "Aiutati che Dio t'aiuta" or help yourself and God will help you. While his father, a streetwise pug who fought under the moniker "Fighting Nick Bob," agreed; the Elder had a good sense of just how far the apple fell from the tree. The family later moved to an Italian enclave centered on East 10th Street, between First Avenue and Avenue A in Manhattan's East Village. It was there that Thomas honed his skills on the street and it cost him: he spent time in reform school—with Jake LaMotta, of all people, as fate would have it—and jail.

Any way you cut it, Thomas Rocco Barbella was a juvenile delinquent. Finally, in 1939, he found Stillman's Gym and the sweet science. It appeared like his calling, at least for now. When a pro boxer by the name of Antonio Fernandez beat Thomas to a pulp, he swore off the game. But like any pug with the bug, he was before long back inside the ring.

The youngster was drafted into the Army in 1942, but soon went AWOL after punching an officer. After fighting eight times as a professional under the name Rocco Graziano, he was caught and served prison time before being given a dishonorable discharge—even the Army understood they couldn't control him. Legend has it that when the investigating officers discovered the fighter, they told him to identify himself. Rocky looked in a mirror and stated, "Yep, it's me." Authority figures never appreciated Graziano's wise-ass humor. Standing five feet seven inches and weighing 154 pounds, Rocky had movie-star looks, but no movie to go with it. That would come later.

Entering 1945, Rocky Graziano had an official record of 35-6-5. His only losses came to Charles Ferguson (1942), Joe Agosta (1943), along with a pair to Steve Riggio (1943, 1944) and the tough Harold Green (1944-twice).[32]

On Friday, March 9, in front of Harry S. Truman, the first vice-president of the United States to attend a boxing program in Madison Square Garden, Rocky Graziano, an enormous underdog, knocked out Billy Arnold in the third round of an eight-round scheduled feature. Arnold decided to come out strong and tame the cocky East Sider right from the start. And he damn near did. Rocky absorbed considerable punishment in the first two rounds and looked to be on the verge of collapse in the second. However, Arnold ran out of gas, and Graziano hammered him inside out during the following term. Three times Arnold hit the canvas in the third round, twice finding himself outside the ropes and clinging to the apron of the City Ring. Referee Frank Fullam, a former boxer himself, sensed that Graziano was about to catapult Arnold again to the canvas, so he intervened. Waving off the East Sider, Fullam stepped in to protect the Philadelphia pug from further damage.

The crowd of more than 14,000, many of whom appeared to have had some money down on Arnold, just couldn't believe it. The Philadelphia fighter had never been knocked out before and had only lost one previous fight.

On Friday, June 29, inside the Garden, Rocky Graziano, trailing on points, dropped Freddie "Red" Cochrane with a convincing right at the end of the ninth round. The welter champion had taken a count of five when the bell sounded. Assisted on his stool, Cochrane did his best, which wasn't much, to gather his senses. Observing that Cochrane's elevator wasn't stopping on all floors, Graziano launched a perfect right to the head that downed his antagonist for the final time. Referee Johnny Burns counted Cochrane out at the 0:16 mark of the tenth and final round.

Then, on Friday, August 24, in a rematch, Graziano repeated the performance.[33]

Forgotten Rounds

Still sorting through the impact of the war, the boxing show frequency seemed to increase in proportion to the boxing staff's comfort level with matches. On January 5, over 16,000 Garden fans watched Fritzie Zivic take an eight-round split decision and hand Billy Arnold his first defeat. While experts ringside were divided in their opinion of the verdict, one thing was certain: had the United States Army understood how much guerrilla warfare was in Zivic's mitts, they would have made him a general.

There was an old line that went something like this: When you dance with a woman for the fourth time, you usually know just how far your right hand can travel. Robinson v. LaMotta IV took place on February 23 inside Madison Square Garden. The Harlem welterweight, who was up two to one in the series, would add a ten-round unanimous victory to his total. While LaMotta didn't disgrace himself, he looked lethargic.

On May 25, Graziano turned his attention to Al Davis, while a Garden crowd of more than 16,000 turned its attention toward two of the scrappiest fighters New York had to offer. It vowed to be a brutal affair. And it was just that, as "Bummy" was floored multiple times, while Rocky only once. Graziano's commanding right overshadowed anything Davis could muster. Having seen enough of Davis's struggles, referee Young Otto halted the bout at the 0:44 mark of the fourth round. It was Graziano by a knockout.

Harlem boxer Joe "Sandy" Saddler turned heads with his quick knockout of Leo Methot at the 0:59 mark of the first round of their scheduled six-round battle on June 29.

Joey LaMotta, Jake's younger brother, took a well-fought six-round decision over North Carolina's Billy Johnson on August 10. People often forget that Joey boxed too.

On September 28, Brooklyn middle Larry Fontana, floored for a nine count in the second, managed to regain control of his senses to take a six-round decision over Connecticut's Billy Walker.

Finally, Brooklyn's Patsy Giovanelli suffered his first career knockout from Greenwich Village rival Tony Pellone in a bitter slugfest. The conflict, held on December 17, was an attempt by the Brooklyn boxer to fight his way back into ring prominence after four years in the Army. On the same card, Newark's Charley Fusari recorded his thirty-first consecutive knockout.[34]

Fighter of the Year

Willie Pep, who went 8–0 during the year with one title defense, was easily the fighter of the year. Defending his title brilliantly against Phil Terranova, Pep confirmed his skills as a champion. Speaking of skills, hats off to Madison Square Garden staff, who managed to conduct 42 shows in 1945, many for the benefit of our troops, and at a time when we needed it most. Nonetheless, the fighter of the year to those who frequented Madison Square Garden was easily Thomas "Rocky" Graziano, who fought five times, four of which were consecutive ring battles, and never lost a contest.

Instrument of Surrender

"Sure, we want to go home. We want this war over with. The quickest way to get it over with is to go get the bastards who started it. The quicker they are whipped, the quicker we can go home. The shortest way home is through Berlin and Tokyo. And when we get to Berlin, I am personally going to shoot that paper-hanging son-of-a-bitch Hitler. Just like I'd shoot a snake!"—General George S. Patton, Jr. (addressing to his troops before Operation Overlord, June 5, 1944)

It was on August 6, 1945, at 8:15 A.M. local time, that the United States detonated an atomic bomb over the Japanese city of Hiroshima. Sixteen hours later, American President Harry S. Truman called again for Japan's surrender. Then, on August 9, 1945, the United States dropped a second atomic bomb, this time on the Japanese city of Nagasaki. Following these events, Emperor Hirohito ordered the Supreme Council for the Direction of the War to accept the terms the Allies had set down in the Potsdam Declaration for ending the war. On September 2, 1945, the Japanese Instrument of Surrender was formally signed on the deck of the USS *Missouri* in Tokyo Bay, bringing the hostilities of World War II to a close.

It was time for our boys and girls to return home. Time to return back to our cities, back to our neighborhoods, back to our girls or our guys. Time to turn back to what we love, to a venue we left behind, to a ring where we left our dreams. Time to take a deep breath, a very deep breath, and thank the Almighty for a chance to fight another day. Welcome home!

8

So, Where Were We?
1946–1949

> It is not titles that honour men, but men that honour titles.
> —Niccolò Machiavelli

With an enormous sense of optimism, reinforced by a degree of liberalism, the attitudes of Americans changed following World War II. The world became a much smaller place and a greater value rested on our individual rights and freedoms. Proven more than willing to fight or work for the common good, it was our turn, or so many of us believed.

1946

So, where were we? With many champions idle due to their military service duties, to say nothing of a number of new faces, it was easy to forget just how the boxing picture looked (bear in mind the multiple organizations). The heavyweight champion was Joe Louis, and in his shadow were Tami Mauriello, Jimmy Bivins and Lee Oma. The light heavyweight champion was Gus Lesnevich, with Archie Moore, Lloyd Marshall and Phil Muscato watching his every move. The middleweights had Tony Zale above them, with Jake LaMotta, Holman Williams, Charley Burley and Rocky Graziano a punch away. The welters looked up to Freddy, or Freddie, "Red" Cochrane, with Ray Robinson, Tippy Larkin and Jimmy Doyle a whisper behind. The lightweight title was open and ready to be filled by Chalky Wright, Allie Stolz, Willie Joyce, or Bob Montgomery. Willie Pep was over the feathers, and Sal Bartolo, Phil Terranova and Jackie Graves were watching him. The bantamweights had Manuel Ortiz atop the division, with Benny Goldberg and Tony Olivera looking up. Finally, the flyweights had a number of outstanding international boxers, like Jackie Patterson, only a punch away.[1]

The Garden was again charged on Friday, January 4, and seeing so many familiar faces back home was encouraging. Boy, it felt good. Even veteran referee Arthur Donovan, back from a tour in the South Pacific, was delighted by the response he received. As Miss Gladys Gooding filled the air with organ music, smiles were as common as beer and hot dogs. The scheduled ten-round feature would need only four, as Beau Jack would knock out Morris Reif at the 2:01 mark of the term with a solid right uppercut. Both fighters provided a tremendous display of pugilism, Reif even rocking Jack a few times with his piercing body punches. As for Jack, he thrilled the crowd when he opted to use his trademark "bolo" punch.

Also on hand was Mike Jacobs. His current three-year Garden contract finished in

June, and he had just signed a fresh five-year agreement. The impresario, along with everybody associated with him, had performed magnificently during the war years. No simple task by any means.

AFTERGLOW

Over 1,800 days, or nearly five years, had passed since the names of Louis and Conn had been jointly recalled. If we needed to put the war years into perspective, or what athletic prowess was lost in the pursuit of freedom, then this conflict could provide the answer. Joe Louis would defend his heavyweight crown against Pittsburgh's Billy Conn on June 19—a rematch of the pair's battle back on June 18, 1941. In the eyes of many boxing fans, the conflict was long overdue, but everyone was mindful of the circumstances. The fight would take place inside Yankee Stadium, where promoter Mike Jacobs believed he could park in excess of 100,000 backsides in the ballpark with tickets at a ceiling price of $100 ringside.[2]

Louis had last fought March 27, 1942, when he knocked out Buddy Baer in the first round of their Garden contest. Granted there had been a multitude of exhibitions, and even his granting of a fifty-three-second audience for Johnny Davis in Buffalo, but that wasn't reality. This was reality, so Louis headed back to Pompton Lakes in New Jersey for some serious training. Conn had last fought on February 13, 1942, when he took a twelve-round decision over Tony Zale. He was rusty and he knew it, so the Pittsburgh fighter trained hard over at Greenwood Lakes, also in New Jersey. Both fighters, having served in the Army, were recently discharged.

Joe Louis, who tipped at 207 pounds, took Conn, who scaled at 182, as far as the eighth round. That's when a combination found the Pittsburgh Kid's chin. The champion followed it with a right that opened a cut over Conn's left eye. Another hard right to the chin buckled the legs of Conn. Smelling blood, the champion stepped in and delivered a robust mixture of punches to his challenger's face that sent him backwards. Conn was counted out at the 2:19 mark of the eighth round. With defeat, William David "Billy" Conn packed away his ring resume and announced his retirement.

ANTHONY FLORIAN ZALESKI—A.K.A. TONY ZALE

He was born Anthony Florian Zaleski, on May 29, 1913, in Gary, Indiana. The city, founded a mere seven years earlier, was for all intents and purposes the home of the United Steel Corporation and its new plant, Gary Works; the city and the facility were both named after the corporation's founder, Elbert Henry Gary. For Gary families, if you weren't working at the steel mill, then you were working in a business that supported it. Life was that simple.

For the young Zaleski, like many of his friends, he knew no other lifestyle. There were times when every part of his body reeked of the mill or was painted with a scar from it. Granted it was a job, but the youth wanted more. For a diversion, Zaleski turned to a gymnasium and the sport of boxing. As an amateur, Zaleski, a.k.a. "The Man of Steel," was impressive, winning 87 of his 95 bouts. Fighting out of Chicago, Zale went 6-2 in 1937, 8-2-1 in 1938, and 7-1 in 1939. By 1940, he had created a name for himself and was looking across the ring at top-shelf talent. Zale posted a record of 6-1 that year, with two victories over Al Hostak, one of which was for the NBA middleweight title. His only loss was to the adept Billy Soose.

Zale's breakout year was 1941. He posted a record of 7–0, defended his (NBA) title twice and picked up the vacant world middleweight title. In 1942, with the war waging in Europe, he signed to fight Billy Conn at the Garden on February 13—there was no title at stake, but the money was good. A good thing, as Zale lost the twelve-round bout. But the *Gillette Sports Cavalcade* broadcast garnered him some good exposure. Anyhow, this would be his last fight until he was discharged from the armed services. Returning to the ring in 1946, Zale compiled a record of 6–0 before facing Rocky Graziano in a title defense.

ZALE V. GRAZIANO I

It's still hard for many to believe that Zale, who had been world champion since November 1941, had yet to defend his title. A crowd of nearly 40,000 packed Yankee Stadium to witness what many believed would be one of the finest battles in years. At a time when pre-fight hype was as common as old ration books, the Tony Zale versus Rocky Graziano fight on the evening of September 27 exceeded every expectation. Champions weren't supposed to work this hard to defend their titles, or at least that's what Zale believed. But few, as he was reminded, faced the likes of an East Side pug like Graziano.

Floored early in the first to a five-count, Rocky fought back and landed a few solid rights before the first gong. When Zale was dropped and saved by the bell in the second, everyone in the audience knew they were in for a barnburner. Zale began going to the body in the second round, but broke his right thumb; the trick then became to mask the injury from his opponent.

The momentum seemed to shift with each barrage of punches. In the sixth, a vicious body assault was capped with a right to Graziano's chin. At the 1:43 mark in the sixth round, Graziano finally took the count. Not a surprise, Rocky was standing a second after referee Ruby Goldstein had spread his arms verifying the knockout.[3] It was only the beginning of one of the greatest trilogies in ring history. A rematch was inked for March 21 inside Madison Square Garden.[4]

With a record of 15–0 on the year, Ray Robinson had only fought once in New York. On December 20, he returned to battle Tommy Bell. The winner of the fifteen-round Garden contest would be recognized as both the NYSAC and NBA welterweight titleholder. Since NYSAC rules didn't allow a fighter to move into a championship without taking part of in a ring battle, and the contenders as viewed by the commission didn't want to fight Robinson, Bell became the sacrificial lamb. Although the Georgian fought extremely well, by the later rounds he had expended most of his energy; consequently, Bell was outboxed and lost the decision.[5]

FORGOTTEN ROUNDS

Schenectady fighter Marty Servo knocked out Freddie "Red" Cochrane in the fourth round of a scheduled fifteen-round contest on February 1. With the victory, Servo became world welterweight champion. It was Cochrane's first defense of the title he won on July 29, 1941.

Beau Jack fought Johnny Greco to a draw inside the City Ring on February 8. It was a verdict NYSAC was trying avoid, but more proof that the new scoring system, which had been scrutinized for months and enacted a year earlier, needed to be overhauled.

Quick to quell concerns over his knockout prowess, Graziano dropped welterweight champion Marty Servo in the second round of a non-title fight on March 29. A sold-out Garden (19,088) watched the popular East Side middleweight work his magic before using that thunderous right hand of his to obliterate his aggressor.

Willie Pep recorded his one hundredth career victory on June 7, when he knocked out Boston fighter Sal Bartolo in the twelfth round of the pair's scheduled fifteen-round match. In front of a half-filled Garden, Pep glided across the ring with all the grace of a champion, and one who had yet to face the agony of defeat.

"Bobcat" Bob Montgomery retained his title by putting on a spectacular display on Friday, June 28. The fight resulted in a knockout of antagonist Allie Stolz in the thirteenth round of their scheduled fifteen-round Garden duel. Montgomery laid out Stolz with a pulverizing right to the jaw that sent the Newark boxer down for the tally.

Marching along the comeback trail, Jersey Joe Walcott dropped Tampa's Tommy Gómez twice before gaining a third-round knockout on August 16.

On September 18, Joe Louis, in his second and last fight of the year, knocked out Tami Mauriello at the 2:09 mark of the very first round.

Finally, Marcel Cerdan, an exciting French import, picked up the unanimous ten-round decision over Washington veteran Georgie Abrams. As a pure slugger, Cerdan was an exciting fighter in the same mold as Tony Zale.

Bad News, Good News

Mike Jacobs, president of the Twentieth Century Sporting Club, suffered a cerebral hemorrhage and was hospitalized on December 3. He was pronounced gravely ill by the attending physician that evening. At sixty-six years of age and intermittently plagued with health problems, Jacobs had been told to eliminate some of the stress in his life, but Uncle Mike had always suffered from selective hearing. Fortunately, his condition exhibited a gradual improvement in the days that followed.

It was just an incredible year for the prolific team at the Twentieth Century Sporting Club. Not only did they manage to promote 83 shows in three venues, they accomplished gross receipts of about $5.5 million. Fewer than half of their boxing shows took place in Madison Square Garden. Thirty-four boxing cards, held inside the City Ring, attracted an average attendance of 12,640 spectators. As anticipated, three Yankee Stadium shows provided the greatest portion of the club's gross receipts.[6]

Fighter of the Year

Jimmy Carter, Paddy DeMarco, Kid Gavilan, and Jersey Joe Walcott debuted in the City Ring, while Bob Montgomery would battle inside the ropes for the final time. With six knockouts in non-championship bouts before he met Rocky Graziano in a spectacular title defense, the year belonged to Tony Zale.[7]

1947

The year started full of promise for the Twentieth Century Sporting Club. Matchmaker Nat Rogers had inked both Louis and Robinson to title matches, along with Gus Lesnevich—

the latter to protect his light heavyweight title. Middleweight Tony Zale also planned to defend his crown against Rocky Graziano in a rematch. Charismatic Marcel Cerdan, the former French Marine from Casablanca, Morocco, indicated that he planned to return to the States. Directing affairs during the illness of promoter Mike Jacobs was Sol Strauss, attorney for the TCSC. Unbeknownst to the barrister was the myriad of issues he would soon face.[8]

In one of those say-it-ain't-so moments in the Garden, Rocky Graziano was questioned about the circumstances surrounding his cancellation of his December 27, 1946, bout with "Cowboy" Ruben Shank.[9] The inquiry centered on reported attempts by a gambling syndicate to "fix" the bout. Not only were there reports of massive amounts of money flooding out of town to bet on Shank against the lack of local betting being accepted on his rival, but the fight was called off due to a suspicious Graziano medical condition.

On January 27, "The Rock" admitted receiving an offer of $100,000 to fix a fight. Since Graziano did not report the incident, NYSAC was expected to block the fighter's hope of a Zale rematch, and they did so.[10] NYSAC also revoked his boxing license. When the fighter opted for court action in an endeavor to block NYSAC, let's just say it didn't sit well. NYSAC denied Graziano's application for a new license on April 11. Confronted with few options for his rematch with Zale, the fighter soon looked to venues unassociated with the governing board; Chicago and Cleveland were mentioned as possible host cities.[11]

By spring, it appeared like boxing, at least in New York State, was sanitizing itself. Ray Robinson was suspended by NYSAC for thirty days and fined $500 for failure to identify a would-be briber. He was none too happy. It was becoming increasingly clear that Robinson wasn't satisfied with the New York City fight scene.[12]

Just as Robinson was trying to leave his troubles behind, disaster struck: Jimmy Doyle, whose real name was James J. Delaney, died on June 25 from injuries he suffered during his fight the previous evening against the Harlem boxer.[13] The event, held inside the Arena in Cleveland, saw Robinson deliver a devastating left hook in the 8th round that resulted in a TKO (the bell rang at the count of 9). As Doyle's helpless body dropped backward to the canvas, he never regained consciousness and had to be carried from the ring on a stretcher. Upon learning of the seriousness of the situation, Robinson rushed to the hospital to offer his assistance.[14] Seventeen hours after being put on the canvas, the boxer died of a cerebral hemorrhage.

Graziano v. Zale II

In Chicago, on July 16, Rocky Graziano knocked out Tony Zale in the sixth round to capture a version of the world middleweight title. In a reversal of roles from their first battle, Graziano endured an early beating, even hitting the canvas in the third, only to rebound and leave Zale clutching on the ropes.

Madison Square Garden Corporation released their fiscal year information to the public on July 28. A new attendance mark (nearly 5.5 million spectators) was recorded for the venue for the fiscal year ending May 31, 1947. As for boxing, it drew over 950,000 spectators during forty-nine events—this included four championship fights, with the largest being the Lesnevich-Fox contest.

Later, on September 26, the Twentieth Century Sporting Club was fined $2,500 by

NYSAC for their known dealings with individuals with criminal records. While the cat's away (Jacobs), the mice will play.[15]

Speaking of foul play: It took eight years for Jake LaMotta to get knocked out, but it happened to the twenty-six-year-old in the fourth round of his fight with Billy Fox on November 14. Referee Frank Fullum, having seen enough of LaMotta pinned against the ropes, finally stepped between the fighters at the 2:26 mark. Right from the start, those in the audience—come on, it's a fight crowd, and everybody knows everybody ringside, especially in the Garden on Friday night—sensed "somethin' ain't right." The betting odds soared from even money to 12 to 5 in favor of Fox. Rumors had spread so dramatically that they reached the newspaper and even the State Athletic Commission before the opening bell. LaMotta's fighting style was unmistakable, and when he wasn't engaged, it was as noticeable as the sun not rising in the morning sky. Not to mention, Jake ain't no actor. To NYSAC's credit, they had visited LaMotta's dressing room before the fight to apprise him of the reports.[16] LaMotta was suspended indefinitely on November 21.

Louis v. Walcott I

Standing between Joe Louis and his twenty-fourth successful title defense, to say nothing of a bid for his fifteenth straight knockout, was a challenging obstacle in the form of Jersey Joe Walcott.[17] The two would meet inside the City Ring on December 5. Arnold Raymond Cream, a.k.a. Jersey Joe Walcott, was a six-foot heavyweight from Camden, New Jersey, who entered the fight with a record of 44–11–2.[18] Granted, both boxers were experienced and the same age (33), but Louis was eighteen pounds heavier and two inches taller. The champion also had a two-inch reach advantage that could not be overlooked or underestimated by his opponent.

Floored twice in the first round, both for two counts, and in the fourth round to a count of seven, Joe Louis managed to take a split decision. For fifteen rounds, Walcott, a 10–1 underdog, pummeled Louis, closed his left eye, and appeared, at least to many, the dominant fighter. However, Louis did do most of the leading, and landed more punches. It was as close as a fight gets—even referee Ruby Goldstein, a friend of the "Brown Bomber," voted for Walcott. But opportunities are few and far between in a battle like this. When Walcott had his rival groggy in the fourth, he couldn't put him away, and it cost him.

Forgotten Rounds

In another one of those rare Garden moments: On January 20, during the main event between Boston's Al "Red" Priest and Cowboy Ruben Shank, the ten-round engagement became so stale that the audience broke out into song. After all, it was Victor Hugo, a New York heavyweight of the literary sort, who remarked, "Music expresses that which cannot be put into words and that which cannot remain silent." Befuddled by the audience reaction, the pugilists weren't certain as to what to do, so they continued doing nothing. As the fighters began the sixth round, the fans on the Eighth Avenue side of the arena broke into "Let Me Call You Sweetheart." Not to be outdone, the Ninth Avenue side followed with their version of the song in the seventh round, followed by "Home On the Range" in the eighth and "Roll Out the Barrel" in the ninth. Meanwhile, Priest took the ten-round split decision, and thankfully there was no encore.[19]

Charley Fusari, the skillful and undefeated New Jersey welter, had not been given the credit he deserved for holding victories over Joey Peralta, Maxie Berger and Freddie Archer. That changed on February 14, when he dropped Tippy Larkin four times on the road to a ninth-round knockout victory in the City Ring.

Jake LaMotta concluded his one-sided trilogy with Tommy Bell on March 14 by earning the united verdict. Like any LaMotta fight, it was grueling in the opening and closing rounds, but smoke 'em if you got 'em, boys, in the third and fourth terms.

Newly crowned light heavyweight champion Gus Lesnevich used three vicious rights to destroy his heavier opponent, Melio Bettina, in 59 seconds in the feature event on May 23. It was the quickest ending to a Garden feature ever, topping the old mark of 63 seconds held by Al Davis, who kayoed Bob Montgomery back on February 18, 1944. The incident was not without a cost, however, as Lesnevich chipped two bones in his right hand.

On June 27, in a semifinal against New Jersey's Jack Kenny, fighter Danny Martin was disqualified for not trying by referee Jack Watson. Think about that for a second: here you are fighting in the most prestigious venue ever and you don't engage. Martin must have had a case of stage fright.

On July 11, in a savage battle scheduled for ten rounds, Steve Belloise knocked out Georgie Abrams in the fifth. Although nobody who witnessed the affair was quite certain what had happened, referee Johnny Burns called the fight with three seconds remaining in the round. Abrams was on the canvas, but clearly not out—the timekeeper, who could have assisted, lacked official clock figures. It was also the second blunder by the arbiter, who had also stepped between the fighters in the second round, as Abrams was against the ropes, but did not stop the fight.

Youngstown, Ohio, fighter Tony "Baby Face" Janiro took a ten-round unanimous decision from Greenwich Village rival Tony Pellone on September 19. Both fighters fought hard and quick, much to the delight of more than 13,000 spectators. The contention between the two, who had met before, was clearly evident by all the heeling and head-butting; Pellone caught a penalty for the latter.

Fighter of the Year

As for the sweet science, the year belonged to Ray Robinson, who went 10–0 on the year with 9 knockouts, despite all his issues with NYSAC. While Madison Square Garden would see Ezzard Charles and Roland LaStarza make their debut, it said "Good-bye" to Tami Mauriello.[20] As for the City Ring, Gus Lesnevich, who went 3–0 inside the ropes, shined its patina the most in 1947.[21]

1948

As the Twentieth Century Sporting Club pondered its strategic direction, it received word on January 22 that an ailing Michael Strauss Jacobs planned to retire following the Joe Louis v. Jersey Joe Walcott rematch planned for the spring.[22] Jacobs, at sixty-seven years of age, had owned Louis's contract since 1935, and would be willing to see it through until the end, the heavyweight champion having announced his plans to retire following the rematch. So as the patron saint of promotion faded into the Florida sunset, where did this leave New York City boxing? Nobody was certain.

On February 13, Jake LaMotta received word from NYSAC that he had been suspended for seven months and fined $1,000. This was for "conduct detrimental to the best interests of boxing," according to the organization in their announcement.[23] The action followed NYSAC's investigation into the bout between LaMotta and Billy Fox back on November 14, 1947.

Louis v. Walcott II

Everybody in the city appeared to be heading to Yankee Stadium for the big fight on June 25. The contest started out in the usual manner, with each fighter marking and measuring his ground while testing his arsenal. In the third round, Walcott fired a solid right to the cheekbone of Louis that dropped the champion for a count of one. The action, as brief as it was, served to awaken the fighter, not to mention the over 40,000 spectators, as Louis seemed far more determined to catch his prey than ever before.

Stepping up his footwork, Louis stalked his antagonist. Walcott stuck to his strategy, believing he could simply wear down his opposition. And such was the case, as for ten laborious rounds the crowd sat yawning, I mean wondering, if Louis would ever capture his adversary. Then, in the eleventh term, Louis caught Walcott, delivering a right to the jaw that drove him into the ropes and leaving him vulnerable. Both fighters traded punches, with Louis sneaking in some solid body blows. It was then that a punishing right from the champion caught the jaw of Walcott and sent him down. As Walcott struggled to his feet at nine, he fell back to the canvas at ten. The Louis knockout came at the 2:56 mark of the eleventh round. For many, including the heavyweight king, it was the end of an era, and one he concluded on his own terms.

Diminishing Returns

Are we open? Garden boxing shows were struggling. For example, the August 26 show that featured elite boxer Billy Graham's decision over Terry Young attracted about 7,000 fans, and the show on September 2, highlighted by welterweight Tommy Bell's outpointing Brooklyn's Doug Ratford, drew fewer than 4,000 spectators. Even Willie Pep's ten-round decision victory over Paddy DeMarco on September 10 pulled in fewer than 10,000 fans. It was time for a change.

On October 12, Harry Markson, who had been the director of publicity for the Twentieth Century Sporting Club, was promoted to managing director of the organization. In addition to the excitement brought by Markson, there had been an announcement the previous month: Joe Louis was returning to the ring the following June to face the winner of the fight between Ezzard Charles and Joe Baksi, scheduled for November 12 inside Madison Square Garden.

Willie Pep v. Sandy Saddler I

It was a crusade for the world featherweight crown and it would be held in the City Ring on October 29. Champion Willie Pep, who had won all fifteen of his fights in 1948 and hadn't lost a bout since 1943, would meet New York's Joseph "Sandy" Saddler, who had won 12 of his 13 fights in 1948. As Willie would later claim, nobody had heard much about Sandy, then all of sudden he was the number-one contender. Since he had already defeated Jock Leslie, who had whooped Saddler, Pep didn't lose any sleep over the pairing.

The battle was scheduled for fifteen rounds. In a tale of the tape: Both fighters would duel at 126 pounds; Pep was four years older; Saddler was taller, by two and one-quarter inches; Pep had a bigger neck, waist and ankles and Saddler had a larger chest and a bigger fist.

Charley Johnston, one of the many Johnston brothers engaged in the fight game, managed Saddler. Lou Viscusi, who managed Pep, knew the Johnston boys. So that's how the Pep camp first heard about Saddler, but that had been years earlier, when Saddler was still paying his dues. Johnston had promised he would give Saddler a shot at Pep when the right time came along. Well, October 29, 1948, was the right time.

Saddler had recorded 63 knockouts in 93 professional fights. While Pep wasn't impressed by statistics, his camp understood the numbers. At the opening bell, Pep bounced out in the usual fashion. Yet before he knew what hit him, Saddler was wielding imposing combinations. It wasn't a good sign. Jumping to the third, Pep caught a left to the face and dropped to a count of nine. After he arose, two punches sent him down again for another nine tally. But the bell sounded before Saddler could finish the job.

The lanky fighter bolted from his corner at the sound of the bell for the fourth round, and sent Pep some solid right hands that he couldn't answer. Boxed into a neutral corner, Pep caught a vicious left hook to the jaw that sent him to the floor for good. Sandy Saddler was the new featherweight champion of the world. It was the first knockout Pep had ever suffered.[24] Another great rivalry was born during a year that was sorely in need of one.

KID GAVILAN

Gerardo Gonzalez, a.k.a. Kid Gavilan, was born on January 6, 1926, in Camaguey, Cuba. By the age of seventeen, he already had over 60 amateur bouts under his belt and was catching the eyes of many. Reaching the height of five feet ten inches, Gerardo had a

A Cuban boxer, Gerardo González (1926–2003), better known as Kid Gavilan, was a former world welterweight champion. From late 1950 until mid–1953, Gavilan dominated the ring with his outstanding skills, speed and trademark "Bolo" punch.

solid welterweight frame and an outstanding reach of seventy-one inches. Turning pro in 1943, and fighting primarily out of Havana, Gavilan made his Garden debut on November 1, 1946. It was also his first pro battle on American soil. Easily defeating tomato can Johnny Ryan, he fought back-to-back contests against Johnny Williams, first at St. Nick's, then back in the Garden. Gavilan won both. With a record of 17-1-1 at the end of 1945, he went 11-1 in 1946, and finished 1947 at 11-1-1. It was obvious by this point that Gavilan could be a factor in the fight game, the questions being just where and when?

Forgotten Rounds

Ike Williams received a unanimous (stretching the term as far as it can go) ten-round decision over Kid Gavilan in a non-title bout on February 27. Having sent Gavilan down for an eight count with a remorseless left hook to the jaw in the eighth, Williams believed he silenced his rival. He did not. He merely motivated the Cuban to pick up the pace, and to deliver twice the number of left hooks to the head of his antagonist and even more combinations to his body.

In the nineteenth annual tournament of champions (Northeast and Puerto Rican Golden Gloves victors) held at Madison Square Garden on March 3, two boxers emerged: Coley Wallace, a twenty-year-old freshman at New York University, who possessed a striking resemblance to Joe Louis, and John Saxton, a seventeen-year-old Brooklyn fighter. Both boxers showed considerable promise.

Gus Lesnevich, who may have been the most expensive fighter if you were to tally his dollar-per-round take, destroyed Billy Fox at the 1:58 mark of the very first round of their March 5 fray. The thirty-two-year-old light heavyweight champion also confirmed that he had no intention of moving up in weight.

Lee Savold, also thirty-two, knocked out Italian Gino Buonvino in a record 54 seconds of the very first round of their scheduled ten-rounder. The incident shaved five seconds off the previous record held by Gus Lesnevich.

Paddy DeMarco, in a rematch with Terry Young, took a ten-round split decision on April 2. The free-swinging confrontation was considered an upset despite the fact that DeMarco had also won the previous encounter.

At last, Kid Gavilan grabbed a unanimous ten-round decision over Tony Pellone on November 12. The encounter was brutally fought and a lot closer than the verdict indicated.

Fighter of the Year

It would be a year remembered by boxing fans for the stark number of quick knockouts. As for the fighters: Roland LaStarza went in the Garden, as did Sandy Saddler. Kid Gavilan, who was becoming a regular in the City Ring, fought there six times and lost only one battle (Ike Williams). Speaking of Williams, 10–0 on the year, the world lightweight champion only fought once in the City Ring. While Williams was clearly the game's boxer of the year, Gavilan's prolific appearances inside Madison Square Garden shined the City Ring's luster the most in 1948.[25]

1949

The minimum wage was raised from forty cents to seventy-five cents an hour in 1949, and since we're on the topic of wages, the average high-school teacher took home less than $5,000 a year, which was about three thousand less than a car salesman. Just for comparison: Jack Dempsey received $5,000 to referee the Chavez versus Escobar fight on April 7, 1940, in Caracas, Venezuela, along with $5,000 for expenses.[26]

WILLIE PEP V. SANDY SADDLER II

Unlike the first time they met, Willie Pep wasn't taking anything for granted stepping into a boxing ring with Sandy Saddler. The pair's highly anticipated rematch was scheduled for February 11 inside Madison Square Garden. Pep had trained hard, real hard. In front of a capacity crowd, Hartford's favorite featherweight took the fifteen-round unanimous decision from Saddler, and more importantly, got his belt back. He became the first boxer in the history of the 126-pound class to reclaim a lost world championship.

By the eleventh round and leading in points, Pep knew Saddler needed a knockout to win, so he acted accordingly: the former champion kept his adversary at a distance with his jabs, and when Saddler ventured too close, he utilized his right. Even then, however, Saddler managed to rock the fighter in both the tenth and fourteenth rounds. Later, Pep admitted that keeping Saddler off balance was essential to limit his power. Judging from the appearance of Pep's slashed eyes after the fight, that was probably a wise choice.[27]

OVERLOOKED

On February 25, 1949, in what some considered to be one of the better fights ever held at Madison Square Garden, Grand Rapids middle Pete Mead knocked out rugged Syracuse fighter Joey DeJohn in the seventh round of a battle scheduled for ten rounds. Having dropped to a count of eight in the third, a nine count in the fifth, and barely surviving the sixth round, Mead was lucky to be alive. Joey DeJohn had butchered Mead's face so badly that he was nearly unrecognizable; his eyes were bleeding profusely and his nose had been bashed into his skull.

Miraculously able to come out of his corner for the seventh, Mead was livid over the beating he had endured. He became transfixed at returning it to DeJohn and he did just that. The third time he dropped DeJohn to the canvas, referee Johnny Burns stopped the fight. One of "the bloodiest" ever in the City Ring, it was also Mead's last victory. *The Ring* magazine recognized it as one of the ten greatest fights of the 20th century.

Joe Louis officially relinquished his heavyweight crown, which he had held since June 22, 1937, on Tuesday, March 1, 1949. He had defended the title twenty-five times over the course of the eleven years, eight months and one week he had it, and decided to turn his attention to fight promotion.

For thirty-five years, Al Weill had been an integral part of boxing as a manager (Lou Ambers, Joey Archibald, and Marty Servo), matchmaker and promoter. But on May 18, he was offered a new role as matchmaker for Madison Square Garden; some recalled that he was Jacobs's first matchmaker back in 1933. He replaced Nat Rogers, who resigned after sixteen years in the position. The Garden was undergoing a facelift. Uncle Mike Jacobs quietly sold his interest in the Twentieth Century Sporting Club, which became effective on May 20. His final promotion was Robert Villemain's victory over Pete Mead. Jacobs's contribution to the sport of boxing was nothing short of monumental.[28]

The Garden also continued to have a strong association with the International Boxing Club, or the successor to the Twentieth Century Sporting Club. James D. Norris was installed as president of the organization (IBC) on July 9. The IBCN had exclusive rights to not only the Garden, but also to St. Nicholas Arena, Yankee Stadium and the Polo Grounds, not to mention some other prominent city venues. The tactical move placed the fight game firmly in the hands of the Madison Square Garden Corporation.

FORGOTTEN ROUNDS

Nebraska fighter Vince Foster knocked out Village boxer Tony Pellone in the seventh round of their scheduled ten-round clash on January 14. Pellone, floored four times during the conflict, was just beaten senseless by Foster. And when he dared to go toe-to-toe with his aggressor, which he did a few times, Pellone was just ripped apart by the machine-gun spray of his opponent. The undercard of the battle saw Roland La Starza capture his twenty-ninth straight victory. Also, Arthur King, the British Empire lightweight champion, put his opponent Willie Beltram to the canvas six times on the way to an eight-round points victory.

It wasn't a title fight, but it had the appearance of one, as welter Kid Gavilan took a fierce ten-round split decision from lightweight champion Ike Williams. It took place on Friday, January 28, in front of more than 15,000 Garden fans who stood for a large portion of the rematch. For Williams, it was his first mishap in two years or 21 bouts.

Irvington, New Jersey's Charley Fusari, having been dropped to a three count in the opening round, fought back in miraculous fashion to defeat Luzerne, Pennsylvania's Rocky Castellani on February 18. A Garden crowd of just over 10,000 witnessed the display, as Fusari's impressive performance garnered him a united verdict.

Charley Fusari began his career in 1944 with a string of impressive victories and didn't take a loss until 1947, a split decision to Tony Pellone. He then lost to Eddie Giosa, Johnny Cesario and Al Priest in less than a year. But Fusari got back on track and was able to grab a date with Rocky Graziano in the Polo Grounds. While his September 14, 1949, loss to "The Rock" impacted the fighter's record, the exposure was well worth it. On November 11, Fusari dropped East Sider Terry Young three times on his way to an eighth-round knockout victory. It was exciting because despite the setbacks, Young never quit.

Finally, on December 2, on the undercard of the Roland LaStarza versus Cesar Brion clash, an undefeated kid from Brockton, Massachusetts, named Rocky Marciano (a.k.a. Rocco Francis Marchegiano) knocked out Columbus, Ohio, fighter Pat Richards. Outweighed by seven pounds, Marciano took out Richards at the 0:39 mark of the second round of a scheduled eight-round semifinal.

FIGHTER OF THE YEAR

It was clear by December of 1949 that boxing had entered a new phase of its existence. How could it not? The sport had lost two giants, Joe Louis and Mike Jacobs. The vacuum that needed to be filled was enormous. Old organizations swallowed new ones and the boxing ship changed captains (James D. Norris and Arthur Wirtz were in command). The question now was navigation, or just where was boxing's port of call?

In the City Ring, Kid Gavilan went 3–0, Roland LaStarza went 3–0, and Willie Pep got his title back. While it's tough to pick a single fighter who shined the ring the most during the year, it was also hard to say good-bye to one particular fighter who never seemed to garner the recognition he deserved: Gus Lesnevich.[29]

9

The Marciano Era, 1950–1955

>Why waltz with a guy for ten rounds when you can knock him out in one?
>—Rocky Marciano

With the war behind us, the "American Dream" was at our fingertips, so all we had to do was grab it and not let go. The economy flourished, as did the suburbs. Middle-class Americans had more money to spend than ever—and, boy, did they spend. Throw away your ration books; it's time to splurge. Short hair, cotton skirts, and saddle shoes were all the rage, as a new style of music filled our heads. If life could get any better, we didn't know how.

1950

The highlight of the spring was an outstanding heavyweight battle that set the stage for an impressive year of New York City boxing.

Undefeated

Heavyweight Roland LaStarza was a vicious warrior from the Van Nest section of the Bronx, but perhaps more intimidating, at least to his competitors, was that he hadn't lost a contest. And the city warrior was scheduled to meet an undefeated youngster from Brockton, Massachusetts, on March 24, for ten rounds inside the City Ring. Frankly speaking, LaStarza didn't give it much thought. Heavily favored, the Bronx boxer had the reputation of being a knockout artist, but surprisingly, so did the youngster. The previous December, the Brockton fighter had knocked out Carmine Vingo, and he was so badly hurt that he had to be admitted to the hospital, where he spent days on the critical list. Everybody understood that La Starza was a gladiator and had the ability to endure a wealth of punches, while the kid from Brockton was less familiar, and was painted as a patient counterpuncher who could turn the lights out on an opponent at any moment. The match sounded like one hell of a crusade, and it was.

Over 13,000 turned out to watch Roland LaStarza battle against Rocky Marciano. And when the ten rounds were over, you could have heard a pin drop. Despite seeing LaStarza dropped in the fourth round to an eight count, nobody had any idea who had won, but they understood that they had just witnessed one of the finest heavyweight confrontations in many a year.

As announcer Johnny Addie approached the microphone, he confirmed the score sheets: Judge Arthur Schwartz judged it 5 rounds to 4 for Marciano, with one even; Judge Arthur Aidala saw it 5 rounds for LaStarza, 4 for Marciano, and one even; and finally, referee Jack Watson scored it 5 rounds for Marciano and 5 rounds for LaStarza, with the points 6 for La Starza and 9 for Marciano. The winner: Marciano![1] It was a hairline-thin victory during a superb confrontation. And as it would turn out, the decision would be one of the most controversial verdicts in boxing history.

Another Rocky Returns

His last fight in the Garden was back on March 29, 1946, sparking many to ask: what happened to Rocky Graziano? You know, the fighter who stopped Marty Servo in two rounds. Where did he go? The answer was simple. Graziano hadn't fought in New York because he couldn't. He had been suspended for almost two years.

Graziano's suspension was lifted the previous summer so that he could fight Charley Fusari inside Yankee Stadium. Many viewed it as a positive sign and hoped for a Garden date. Finally, on March 31, inside the City Ring, Rocky Graziano, the former middleweight champion, tangled for ten rounds with a very tough Tony Janiro. And the verdict was a draw—a rare occurrence under the Eagan scoring system.[2] It was quite a contrast, matching Graziano's wild swings and awkward slips to the floor against the graceful moves of Janiro. The event drew the largest audience since the International Boxing Club (IBC) took over the Garden.

A September to Remember

Not all Septembers are created equal, at least not in the world of boxing. Leave it to some elite fighters to make the ninth month of a new decade memorable.

Sandy Saddler v. Willie Pep III

If ever there was a Cheshire cat of boxing, it was Willie Pep. He was lightning-fast on his feet, so most punches never found him. Having already had an amazing life, one he almost lost back in 1946 when he was involved in a plane crash in New Jersey, Pep was a survivor. As one of the few who escaped the tragedy, he suffered multiple internal injuries, two cracked vertebrae and a broken leg. For three long months, he was hospitalized in a body cast and told he would never fight again. Nor would he walk out of the infirmary. When given the diagnosis, Pep just grinned. As soon as he could stand, he began working with his hands. Five months and twelve days after the accident, he returned to a Hartford ring to fight Victor Flores. You read that correctly. If you knew Willie, you understood that you never told him he couldn't do something, because he would. Pep defied the odds, and occasionally took them in his favor.

On September 8, inside Yankee Stadium, Willie Pep put his coveted crown on the line against the one man many believed could beat him, Sandy Saddler. Since winning that title from the slender and adroit featherweight back on February 11, 1949, Pep had defended it three times, twice in 1950. He had not lost a fight since October 29, 1948, and his opponent then was Sandy Saddler.

Willie Pep went eight hard-fought rounds with his nemesis, Sandy Saddler, before a dislocated shoulder ended his campaign. He was ahead in points when the doctor halted the fight. It was Saddler by a knockout in the eighth round—under NBA jurisdiction, a fight's ending was recorded in the round the affected boxer failed to start. Saddler had his world featherweight championship back.

Ezzard Charles v. Joe Louis

When he retired in March of the previous year, Joe Louis was the "Brown Bomber," the undisputed heavyweight champion of the world and the greatest fighter to enter a boxing ring since Jack Dempsey. He was a pugilist who set his personal goals aside to become a patriot; meeting the needs of his country during World War II was far more important than lining his own pockets.

On September 27, a Yankee Stadium crowd of more than 22,000 watched as Ezzard Charles turned Joe Louis into a punching bag. For fifteen rounds, Charles got the best of Louis, or was it the worst? This before the "Cincinnati Cobra" took a unanimous decision and the heavyweight crown. At thirty-six years of age, Joe Louis was a shadow of himself and incapable of delivering a spirited performance. Good? Yes. Competitive? No. Although he had outpointed his idol to become the recognized lineal champion, many weren't convinced Charles was the heir to the throne. Some viewed him as nothing more than a corpulent light heavyweight and an opportunist, rather than the talented fighter that he was.

FORGOTTEN ROUNDS

Bridgeport, Connecticut, feather Jimmy Rooney fought a grueling battle against Cleveland's Eddie Marotta on January 27. It appeared on the Castellani versus Durando undercard. Rooney, who had been floored in the first round to a nine count, fought back hard and knocked out Eddie Marotta in the fourth round.

Speaking of Rooney, he put on another fabulous display on February 17, when he dropped Bronx lightweight George LaFalgio with a left hook at the 1:16 mark of the opening round of a scheduled eight-rounder. But all great things come to an end, and Rooney's streak of good fortune came on March 3 when he was upset by a stunning knockout handed him by New Jersey fighter Johnny Breeze.

Laurent Dauthuille, in his Garden debut on November 10, took a very close ten-round unanimous decision from Greenwich Village fighter Paddy Young. It was so close, the Garden crowd jeered the announcement when it was made by Johnny Addie. It was one of those fights where you didn't want any of the rounds to end, both gladiators having given their all.

On November 24, the Garden experienced an enormous upset when twenty-year-old heavyweight Rex Layne, of Lewiston, Utah, managed to grab a unanimous ten-round decision over Jersey Joe Walcott. Despite being a favorite (1–5), Walcott failed to impress the judges or the audience.

On December 8, in what was viewed as one of the better slugfests in some time, West Coast fighter Bob Murphy knocked out light heavyweight Jimmy Beau, of Connecticut, at the 1:56 mark of the seventh round. Murphy packed such a devastating punch that he twice took Beau off his feet. Beau, who delivered a solid body attack to Murphy during most of the fight, just didn't have the resilience or power to defeat his opposition.

On December 15, Madison Square Garden held a twenty-fifth anniversary celebration. However, fewer than 5,000 fans attended, partly due to the rain and a coincidental presidential address. The event also suffered due to a rushed program and general lack of interest. Even though boxer Paul Berlenbach, a participant in the City Ring's first feature, was on hand, it failed to ignite the flame of nostalgia with most. The main event didn't help, either, as it saw French feather Ray Famechon take a lackluster ten-round judgment over Glen Flanagan. Buried on the undercard, Hartford's Vic Cardell took a ten-round decision over Syracuse welter Carmen Basilio.

Undefeated Stamford, Connecticut, fighter Chico Vejar continued to turn heads with his second-round knockout victory over Andy Viserto on December 22. It was the twentieth consecutive victory for the exciting 144-pound fighter.

Fighter of the Year

For boxing, the year clearly belonged to Ezzard Charles, who went 3–0, and had become, at least to most, a recognized heavyweight champion.

Looking at the records inside Madison Square Garden: Kid Gavilan went 3–1, as did Joe Miceli, and newcomer Johnny Saxton went 3–0. Two City Ring debuts impressed, those of Carmen Basilio and Saxton, and the Garden said good-bye to Rocky Graziano and Jake LaMotta. Although no one fighter shined the City Ring in 1950, the trio of Gavilan, Miceli and Saxton added much to the lure of the confinement.[3]

1951

As NYSAC continued to experiment with ways of making the ring safer, they turned to the Garden on January 5, where they tested a new floor covering for the City Ring. The padding was composed of three-quarters of an inch of foam rubber and an inch and a quarter of felt. If deemed safer, the material would replace the current flooring.[4]

In a clear sign that something just wasn't right at the Garden, the venue recorded its smallest-ever attendance for a professional boxing match, just under 3,600 spectators, on May 25.[5] Adding insult to the mark was that it occurred during a world lightweight title fight. Bronx scrapper James Carter stopped titleholder Ike Williams in the fourteenth round of a scheduled fifteen-round contest. The fight was stopped by referee Pete Scalzo at the 2:49 mark. Williams had been floored to a count of six and appeared noticeably indisposed. After the fight, Blinky Palermo, who handled Williams, cited his interest in a rematch.[6]

In a surprise move, the heavyweight fight between Joe Louis and Lee Savold was shifted from the Polo Grounds to Madison Square Garden—a second successive rainout can force a promoter to consider alternatives. Also, when you conduct fights inside ballparks, especially during baseball season, logistics aren't always easy.[7] On June 15, Joe Louis entered the City Ring and disposed of his adversary. It was just like the "Brown Bomber" of old— the method was by way of knockout in the sixth round of a scheduled fifteen-round Garden battle.[8]

It was the third meeting between rivals Kid Gavilan, the world welterweight titleholder, and East Sider Billy Graham, and it was scheduled for Wednesday, August 29, inside Madison Square Garden.[9] After fifteen intense rounds of battling, the decision went to the score sheets. Judge Arthur Schwartz had it 9–6, Gavilan, while Judge Frank Forbes had it 7–7, with one round even, as did referee Mark Conn. So it was Conn's three points favoring Gavilan that gave him the fight, and the champion managed to retain his crown by a paper-thin margin. A Garden crowd of more than 8,000 fans was absolutely livid, as most clearly viewed the fight as being won by Graham. As the judge's scores were read, debris in all forms rained into the ring. Then, when Conn's vote was announced, people went crazy, many going as far as entering the ring. Security did what they could to quell the uprising, but it wasn't easy—a couple of fans were even physically removed from the ring. Conn, who expressed concern for his safety, needed a police escort to leave the area.[10]

Ray Robinson v. Randy Turpin II

Ray Robinson, having lost his middleweight title in London back on July 10 to Randy Turpin, managed to overcome a badly cut left eye to regain the crown on September 12, in front of a massive crowd over 60,000 inside the Polo Grounds. Beaten and battered, Turpin was so helpless in the tenth round that referee Ruby Goldstein stepped in at the 2:52 mark to stop the fight. The British champion, floored early in the tenth term to a count of nine, rose to take one of the most merciless beatings a fighter had ever endured. Robinson delivered a machine-gun assault, spraying punches to both the head and jaw before heading south and just hammering Turpin's body. The Harlemite just emptied the arsenal, with every ounce of energy he could muster. On this day, there was no man who could beat Ray Robinson.[11]

The Finale—Saddler v. Pep, IV

It was the fourth, and as it would turn out, the final installment of one of the greatest featherweight rivalries in boxing history, Sandy Saddler versus Willie Pep. So popular, in fact, that the battle had to be conducted in a large venue, in this case the Polo Grounds. To recap: Saddler took their first (1948) and third fights (1950), while Pep took the second (1949).

It was rumored that both fighters would likely pull out their bag of tricks for this fight on September 26, and they certainly did. It was a down-home brawl and about as far from a boxing exhibition as both these talented fighters had ever delivered. However, in the ninth round of a scheduled fifteen-round contest, Willie Pep had seen enough—with only one good eye, mind you. Saddler's exceptional bodywork and targeted jabs had taken such a toll on the fighter, that he couldn't go on, and he told referee Ray Miller this at the end of the ninth term.

The exhibition, or periodic wrestling if you will, saw Saddler wrangled to the canvas twice, while both went at it on the floor during one altercation. Speaking of the floor, a new covering, developed by the Cornell Aeronautical Laboratory, was used for the fight with hopes of minimizing the danger a fighter faces during a knock-down. Both fighters, as anticipated, blamed each other for the lack of fighting etiquette. Nearly everyone ringside felt Pep was winning the fight before it was stopped, but the judges differed in their opinions.

On a different note, Robert K. Christenberry, a former Marine, boxer, writer and hotel executive, was selected by NYSAC to replace Chairman Edward P.F. Eagan, who resigned. In one of his first moves as chairman, he had all the licensed boxing clubs in New York State install the new safety pad that was tested during the Saddler v. Pep fight.[12] In another move, which was his first disciplinary action, he suspended fighter Sandy Saddler for sixty days and revoked the boxing license of Willie Pep. This was a result of the fighters' disregard of ring rules in their recent contest.

Acquiescence

Joe Louis had been an idol to many youngsters, including Rocky Marciano. To stare across the City Ring at the "Brown Bomber" on October 26 must have been a surreal experience for the Brockton boxer. Initially scheduled for the Polo Grounds, the ten-round heavyweight bout was transferred to Madison Square Garden.

In the eighth round, Louis opened with a right to the body. Marciano took the punch, then moved in for a short-range assault to the face. Louis covered while attempting to counter. It was then that Marciano uncorked a left that dropped his rival for the first time. It was an unfamiliar circumstance, to say the least, but Louis knew enough to take the seconds he needed in order to recover. Arising at the count of eight, the former champion was prepared for the inevitable.

Marciano, perhaps a bit anxious, missed with a few punches before zeroing in on his target. Two rigid lefts had Louis back into the ropes, and sensing his opponent's vulnerability, Marciano delivered a destructive right to the jaw that catapulted the former champion through the ropes and onto the ring apron. Referee Ruby Goldstein, understanding that there was no need for a count, signaled that the fight was over by knockout at the 2:36 mark of the eighth round. Forever a gentleman, when Louis finally regained his senses, he climbed back through the ropes to seek out Marciano and congratulate him.

Forgotten Rounds

The heavyweight title returned to the Garden on Friday, January 12. Having successfully defended his title against Syracuse boxer Nick Barone, Ezzard Charles was back inside the City Ring to tackle Buffalo heavy Lee Oma. A successful Charles assault in the tenth round gave the champion a TKO victory.

On February 16, Greenwich Village fighter Paddy Young hit the canvas multiple times on his way to a second-round knockout loss to Harlem's Gene Hairston. When it was determined that Young suffered from no apparent damage and that Hairston had become a peculiar favorite (1–4) entering the fight, let's just say it raised a lot of questions.

On March 2, Seattle light heavy Harry Matthews took a unanimous ten-round decision over southpaw Bob Murphy. Both fighters performed admirably, and most fans never left the edge of their seats.

Utah's Rex Layne, the 1949 National AAU heavyweight champion, surprised nearly all the Garden spectators in attendance on March 9, when he knocked out Chicago heavyweight Bob Satterfield. The fight was halted at the 2:56 mark of the eighth round. Satterfield, who was moving through the rounds at a productive pace, caught a precision right to the jaw that dropped him to the canvas.

Bob Murphy knocked out Philadelphia's Dan Bucceroni in the fifth round of a scheduled ten-round conflict on March 16. Referee Ruby Goldstein halted the fight at the 0:51 mark of the fifth term when it was apparent that the fighter could no longer continue. Murphy, a pure slugger, dropped Bucceroni in the first round to a count of three. However, the Philly fighter managed to recover, and even open cuts around Murphy's eyes. It was inevitable that the far from graceful Murphy would eventually land a big punch, and he did.

On July 12, undefeated Rocky Marciano knocked out Rex Layne in the sixth frame of a scheduled ten-round Garden affair. Catching a dynamite-packed right to the jaw, a mere thirty-five seconds into round six, sent the Utah heavyweight down and then out; since Layne had been sent to the canvas briefly in the fourth round by the same wallop, you would have thought he knew better.

Finally, on December 7, Brooklyn lightweight Paddy DeMarco boxed Sandy Saddler, world featherweight champion, to a ten-round split decision victory in a non-title bout. It was the second time DeMarco beat Saddler, and it completed the pair's boxing trilogy. Saddler was furious over the decision and even threatened to no longer fight in New York State.

Fighter of the Year

From the beginning of an investigation into the IBC for violation of the Sherman antitrust law, to continued concerns regarding television's effect on attendance at boxing events, the year was a challenge for the sport.[13] That said, it had its fair share of upsets, not to mention great rematches. It also witnessed the conclusion of a couple of great rivalries in Saddler versus Pep and Sugar Ray Robinson versus Jake LaMotta. Nonetheless, boxing belonged to "Sugar" Ray Robinson. The graceful pugilist won nine of the eleven fights he entered.

Sadly, the City Ring said good-bye to Joe Louis, Joey Maxim, and even Rocky Marciano. Chico Vejar fought four times in the City Ring, posting a record of 3–1, and Kid Gavilan went 5–0. While Gavilan had a tremendous year, for sentimental reasons it's hard not to recognize Rocky Marciano's City Ring swan song.[14]

1952

By spring, Robert K. Christenberry took three actions in an attempt to gain control of the sport. He threatened to strip Jersey Joe Walcott of his heavyweight title if he didn't defend it by February 5, reprimanded light heavyweight contender Harry Matthews for evading Archie Moore, and on February 22, he intervened to give Frenchman Robert Villemain a unanimous decision over Tampa light heavy Danny Nardico in the pair's ten-round Garden feature. But was it enough?

Francis Vejar, a.k.a. Chico Vejar, was born on September 5, 1931, in Stamford, Connecticut. He called himself a wise guy—part of it was his good looks and underlying charm—and dropped out of school at age 16. Like most his age, Vejar took the jobs he could to make a buck, even if his heart wasn't in it. His ring career didn't begin by sparring in a gym, but with a cheap shot at a police officer. It cost him a fine, but found him a career. Hooking up with the Holy Name Athletic Club, Vejar soon found solace between the ropes. With a bit of advice and training, he began a semi-pro career, his debut taking place inside the New Haven Arena.

Turning pro in 1950, he fought in the usual city haunts: Ridgewood Grove and Broadway Arena in Brooklyn, Sunnyside Gardens and Dexter Park Arena in Queens, and Braybrooks Stadium on Staten Island. And Vejar did so while commuting to New York to study drama at New York University. It wasn't long before the media pegged him as "Stamford's Socking Schoolboy." Vejar, like many boxers, also managed his way north to White Plains to fight at the Westchester County Center. In his first trip to Madison Square Garden, he defeated Andy Viserto on December 22, 1950. Exhilarated by the battle inside the prestigious venue, Vejar found himself far more determined than ever before. He tallied an impressive string of thirty-two consecutive wins before Eddie Compo, with a record of 66–3–4, put an end to his glory on September 21, 1951.

Vejar entered 1952 with a record of 36–1–0, having defeated some impressive names including Terry Young and Carmine Fiore. He would finish the year at 45–3–0, having stepped up to the middleweight ranks. His two losses on the year were courtesy of Chuck Davey.

There were times when Garden boxing matches never should have been made. But television, with its lucrative contracts, changed everything except the value of the mighty dollar. On March 14, Johnny Saxton was scheduled to meet Chicago boxer Johnny Bratton in a Garden feature. On paper it sounded like a good match, but a hand injury forced Bratton to withdraw. A scramble ensued and Detroit's Lester Felton was given the nod— which, in retrospect, was as much as he deserved—as his replacement.[15]

Undefeated Johnny Saxton entered the ring and essentially sparred for five and a half rounds, before being named the winner by disqualification at the 1:31 mark of the sixth term. And of all things, it took place during a Friday evening Garden feature. Referee Harry Kessler, himself bored by the lack of action and disobedience, finally stepped between the fighters and signaled the end. Kessler had warned Felton repeatedly not to hold and to engage, but the fighter disregarded his orders. Ring announcer Johnny Addie first informed the crowd that Saxton had won due to a disqualification, only to later correct the verdict to a technical knockout in favor of the still undefeated boxer.

Saxton didn't get away unscathed either, as he put across about the same level of effort as Felton. Naturally, questions regarding integrity surfaced especially, in the light of recent events. In his previous Garden fight, on January 25 against Livio Minelli, Saxton's performance was also questionable despite a knockout victory.[16] Both events added to what appeared to be a growing list of peculiarities inside the City Ring.[17]

Pulling the Lid Off the IBC—Part One

The alleged monopoly in the promotion of professional boxing took a turn on March 17, when an antitrust suit was filed in Federal Court charging the International Boxing Clubs of New York and Illinois, two of its officers and the Madison Square Garden Corporation with conspiring to restrain professional championship boxing business in the United States. It was all about control and extended to the media, contests, contracts, and contenders.

In addition to the corporations, two defendants were named, James D. Norris and Arthur M. Wirtz, both directors of the IBC. (The defendants and the Garden owned controlling interests in the organization.) Joe Louis (Barrow), whose trustees also owned a percentage of the company, was not named as a defendant.[18] However, the government stated that the boxer had entered an agreement with the defendants to retire as undefeated champion in 1949 and that he received $150,000 upon retirement and exclusive rights to the services of four primary contenders: Ezzard Charles, Gus Lesnevich, Lee Savold and Joe Walcott. The suit was extensive and covered numerous topics from purchasing contracts to the exclusive control of venues.[19]

An American boxer, Giuseppe Antonio Berardinelli (1922–2001), a.k.a. Joey Maxim, was a world light heavyweight champion. Stealing his moniker from the first fully automatic water-cooled machine gun, or the Maxim gun, the fighter was lightning fast with his combinations.

THAT OLD MAXIM

Ray Robinson retained his middleweight title on March 13 by defeating Carl "Bobo" Olson in a fifteen-round decision held in San Francisco, and again on April 16, when he knocked out Rocky Graziano in the third round of their battle in Chicago. Questioned about his future after the Graziano fight, the Harlemite confirmed his willingness to defend his middleweight title. But when asked about moving up he was more hesitant. Robinson had no interest in fighting Joey Maxim, who sat atop the light heavyweights, despite the interest by the IBC in promoting such a contest; the organization had presented the Robinson versus Graziano bout, which was a financial success. Finding it difficult to take no for an answer, James Norris continued to press Robinson's manager, George Gainford. When the two finally came to terms, not a surprise to either party, the only concern became the title. Robinson thought he had the option to choose either designation should he win the fight. He did not. NYSAC confirmed that he would have to relinquish his middleweight title if he defeated Joey Maxim for the latter's light heavyweight crown. This ruling was also supported by the National Boxing Association.[20]

As a crowd of more than 47,000 filed into Yankee Stadium on June 25, the oppressive heat was apparent on the faces of all.[21] Referee Ruby Goldstein, who had received the call for the event, was overcome by the temperature and had to be superseded by Ray Miller after the tenth round. It got so hot ringside that Robinson suffered from heat exhaustion and could not answer the bell for the fourteenth round. Although the conclusion appeared valid, skeptics surfaced. Maxim's manager Jack Kearns believed Robinson's behavior was an alibi for a fighter on the verge of defeat. At the time of the stoppage, however, the middleweight champion was ahead on virtually every score sheet. As for the old record book maxim, as in Joey, it was KO14.[22]

The second half of the year saw a bulk of the better fights shift to locations outside of New York.

Forgotten Rounds

Fairfield heavyweight Bernie Reynolds, who had been floored early in a March 7 fight, regained his composure and dropped his adversary, Jim Parker, three times en route to a fourth-round knockout.

On Friday, May 30, heavyweight Roland LaStarza took a ten-round unanimous decision over Philadelphia fighter Dan Bucceroni—the same fighter who outpointed had him the previous December. La Starza just dominated his rival, sending him to the canvas five times en route to victory. The event was the first fight ever held inside Madison Square Garden on Memorial Day weekend.

Carl "Bobo" Olson took a ten-round unanimous decision over New Canaan, Connecticut's Jimmy Beau on June 6—it was Olson's Garden debut. Olson had battled Ray Robinson twice, and though they were losses, he had shown a solid talent, so the result of his bout with Beau wasn't surprising. The attendance of just over 2,400 spectators certainly was.

Johnny Bratton, at 54–19–3 following an eighth-round knockout of Joe Miceli on October 31, decided to turn his attention to the middleweight division. On Friday, December 5, Bratton tackled Yonkers fighter Ralph Tiger Jones in front of just over 3,600 Garden fans. Bratton was such a favorite that Jones, with a record of 23–5–2, was given no chance to win. Nevertheless, from the opening bell to the gong to end the tenth round, Jones hammered Bratton like a cheap steak. And the man who had no chance obtained a unanimous decision.

In conclusion, Brooklyn's unbeaten Johnny Saxton knocked out Cuban Raúl Pérez at the 2:17 mark of the opening round of their bout on December 12. For Saxton it was his thirty-fourth consecutive victory. Let's just say the bout didn't go over well with NYSAC Chairman Christenberry, who asked to see the IBC boxing director following the bout to discuss matchmaking.

Fighter of the Year

Marciano, the "Brockton Blockbuster," who was clearly the sport's fighter of the year, also picked up the world heavyweight title along the way.

Inside the City Ring: Johnny Saxton posted a 3–0 record, but so did Chico Vejar. On December 18, 1952, a thirty-one-year-old Ray Robinson officially announced his retirement. The colorful and talented pugilist left the ring with a record of 131–3–2, having only lost to Joey Maxim, Randy Turpin and Jake LaMotta. Although he didn't fight inside Madison Square Garden in 1952, his presence was always felt inside the City Ring. He was that good.

1953

Twenty long months had passed since Willie Pep was last in a New York boxing ring— his lifetime suspension for his disgraceful brawl with Sandy Saddler was the reason. But his sentence had been commuted, and he was ready to resume one of the most brilliant careers in ring history. At thirty years of age, or a year younger than the retired Ray Robinson, Pep wasn't ready for the nursing home. On June 5, he knocked out Coney Island's Pat Marcune at the 0:14 mark of the final round. Pep's superior skills shined from the onset, as he displayed his superb footwork and precision jabs.

Madison Square Garden unveiled their latest acquisition on July 22, a new lightweight aluminum boxing ring to replace its old steel and wooden structure that was installed in 1935. The ring, which was designed by Lionel K. Levy, had a price tag of $35,000, which was in stark contrast to the $8,000 they paid for the old version.[23] The new piece of multifunctional equipment was scheduled to debut on September 24 inside the Polo Grounds, at the Roland LaStarza v. Rocky Marciano bout for the world heavyweight championship.[24]

ROCKY MARCIANO V. ROLAND LASTARZA II

In their second meeting, Rocky Marciano, who tipped at 185 pounds, beat Roland LaStarza, who weighed in at 184¾ pounds, by way of an eleventh-round technical knockout (TKO). Nearly 45,000 spectators found their way inside the Polo Grounds to witness the event, which was scheduled for fifteen rounds. It was Marciano's second defense of the heavyweight crown, and to little surprise, he was a betting favorite (4–1). The champion looked overanxious in the early rounds and even a bit wild at times with his punches. Referee Ruby Goldstein gave Marciano four warnings in six rounds, and even took the sixth round away from him for a low blow. On the other hand, LaStarza, a.k.a. the "Bronx Express," looked calmer and more composed.

Once Marciano settled down, which wasn't until the seventh round, his combinations became more effective; accordingly, the points started falling in his favor as the punches started to land. La Starza took a beating from this point forward and had cuts around both eyes and one on the bridge of his nose. In the eleventh round, two rights and a left sent LaStarza's shoulders back to the top rope before a crushing right hand catapulted him between the two lower ropes and onto the ring apron. LaStarza, although erect at Goldstein's count of five, was still groggy. Wasting no time, Marciano rushed in for the kill. It was only a matter of time before the referee waved it off.

HAWAIIAN EYE

It was finally set: Carl "Bobo" Olson, of Honolulu, Hawaii, would meet Randy Turpin, of London, England, at Madison Square Garden on October 21 for the world middleweight championship. It was a long time coming, but many were convinced it would be worth the wait. Amongst the media, both fighters were the heirs apparent to the throne vacated by Sugar Ray Robinson. The only question was: Who would have the better day?

An American boxer, Carmine Orlando Tilelli (1930–2008), a.k.a. Joey Giardello, was the world middleweight champion from 1963 to 1965. He holds victories over Chico Vejar, Dick Tiger, "Sugar" Ray Robinson, and Rubin "Hurricane" Carter.

Dominating the first four rounds, Turpin almost scored a knockdown in the first round. But Olson eventually took command. Hoping to draw Turpin in and make it a fight at close quarters, the Brit was slow to take the bait—clinches became as common as tissues at a funeral. As the fight progressed, Olson locked on his target, he scored knockdowns in the 10th and 11th rounds on the way to a unanimous decision.

Forgotten Rounds

Vince Martinez took a unanimous ten-round city decision over Carmine Fiore on January 30. It was the youngster's thirteenth consecutive victory and took his record to 27–1–0. This account is even more impressive when you sandwich in a six-month stint as a member of the New Jersey National Guard.

East Sider Billy Graham outpointed Philadelphia welterweight Joey Giardello over twelve rounds in a unanimous decision on March 6. It was the third meeting between the pair, and Graham's first bona fide victory over his rival. Graham's experience shined, as he outperformed his twenty-two-year-old enemy.

On March 13, a large crowd turned out to witness twenty-one-year-old Chico Vejar take a ten-round united verdict over rookie sensation Vince Martinez of Paterson, New Jersey. In fact, it was the largest Garden throng, over 11,000, to witness a boxing bout since the Marciano v. Louis event on October 26, 1951. Vejar, who was a considerable underdog, took command of the fight and held it for a majority of the conflict—only in the seventh round did the Connecticut fighter exhibit any sign of vulnerability.

Paddy Young took a unanimous twelve-round decision over his nemesis Ernie "The Rock" Durando on March 27. It was envisaged a semifinal of the American middleweight championship elimination series. Finally, on July 8, Garden attendance was so poor that management wouldn't release the actual figure. Only a decade earlier, nobody would have believed such a decline possible.

Death of a Salesman

Mike Strauss Jacobs, arguably the most significant figure in the sport of boxing for the past two decades, died on January 24 of a heart attack while at Mount Sinai Hospital. He was 72 years of age. Having retired three and a half years earlier, the man who once ruled Madison Square Garden had spent his time enjoying the sunshine and traveling back and forth between his home in New Jersey and his retreat in Florida.

Jacobs, who had the challenging task of following in Tex Rickard's footsteps, did so with a swagger and approach all his own. His biggest gate, that of the June 1946 fight between Billy Conn and Joe Louis, brought him just under $2 million. And while Rickard might have rolled over in his grave once or twice, Jacobs hardly gave it a thought to charge $100 for ringside seats.

His meal ticket was Joe Louis, whom he stood behind for every one of his twenty-three title defenses. In the end, whether it was Louis who made Jacobs or vice versa, it didn't matter. It was the finest boxing available and everyone knew it. During the war years, both men were uncompromising in their patriotism: one of Jacobs's shows brought in the sale of $36 million in War Bonds.

FIGHTER OF THE YEAR

Archie Moore, the world light heavyweight champion, went 9–0 on the year. But he didn't battle once in New York City in 1953. For the City Ring, it wasn't a stellar year. While the Marciano versus LaStarza II bout was clearly the best promotion outside the venue, the finest inside was Olson versus Turpin, and for that, Carl "Bobo" Olson deserves recognition as the fighter who shined the most light on the City Ring in 1953.[25]

1954

PULLING THE LID OFF THE IBC—PART TWO

On Thursday, February 4, Federal Judge Gregory F. Noonan dismissed the Government's civil antitrust suit that was filed against the major promoters of professional boxing. As you recall, named in the 1952 suit were the International Boxing Clubs of New York and Illinois together with their principal stockholders, the Madison Square Garden Corporation, James D. Norris of New York, and Arthur M. Wirtz of Chicago. Since the Supreme Court had ruled that baseball was a form of entertainment and therefore was not subject to the antitrust laws, the issue was: where does professional boxing fall in comparison? Judge Noonan confirmed that boxing was in the same realm as baseball and dismissed the action. The government's position on the case was that boxing was "big business." Yet the judge saw it as a byproduct of a sport and not the sport itself. Additionally, the government also failed to separate boxing from the sport of baseball. This put the federal court in a position to define a Supreme Court ruling, something they would not do. The prosecution failed in many aspects; some issues were never even addressed, such as monopolizing arenas or boxers.

Born Archibald Lee Wright, American boxer and long-reigning world light heavyweight champion (December 1952–May 1962) Archie Moore (1916–1998) had one of the longest professional careers in the history of the sport, competing from 1935 to 1963, with an official record of 186–23–10 with 131 KOs.

MISSTEP FOR PEP

Willie Pep had held the position atop the 126-pound division twice, and at the age of thirty-one, wouldn't have minded another crack at it. On February 26, he would enter the Garden confines against Brooklyn boxer Lulu Perez only to have that dream shattered. The former two-time featherweight champion of the world was knocked out at the 1:53 mark of the second round of a scheduled ten-round battle.

The first three minutes of the fight were supposed to be routine—the characteristic jab play, measuring of punches, watching the footwork, looking for angles, you name it—but Pep took a solid left from Perez in the first exchange that backed him off a bit. While he had hoped for an early knockout of the youngster, he was far less confident after the opening round.

When the bell sounded for the second term, Pep fired off some nice lefts that hit their mark, but Perez didn't budge. The twenty-year-old had come out cannons loaded, and began to fire. A combination sent Pep to the canvas for a nine count. Yet Pep appeared to shake it off. The damaging blow came from a right uppercut that struck Pep's chin with perfection, before a straight right dropped him for a second time. When Pep hit the canvas for the third time, it was automatically over—the three-knockdown rule was in effect. In one hundred and ninety fights, this was only Pep's sixth loss. According to some, you could smell the fight from the Second Avenue Deli.[26]

Joey Giardello

Carmine Orlando Tillelli was born in Brooklyn, in the Bedford-Stuyvesant district, on July 16, 1930. While he was still in the crib, the family moved over to Flatbush. Young Carmine paid his street dues by answering challenges, probably more than he should have. At the age of fifteen, which coincided with the end of World War II, Carmine bought a birth certificate from an elder cousin named Joe Giardello, and joined the U.S. Army, becoming a paratrooper in the 82nd Airborne Division. This lasted until his parents caught him and he was discharged.

Carmine, a bit lost as to which direction to turn, decided to head to Philadelphia. It was there—he had scrapped a bit in the city while in the Army—that he looked to the ring to make a few bucks. He made his professional boxing debut in Trenton, New Jersey, and once again he used the name of Giardello. He took a few one-off bouts to pick up some cash before settling in and maintaining his base in Philly.

Giardello lost his first Garden appearance to Gus Rubicini on May 25, 1951. Nevertheless, he bounced back and won his second appearance against Tommy Bazzano, drew Sammy Giuliani, then broke out with his victory over Billy Graham on December 19, 1952. In 1953, he posted a record of 6–2, taking losses from only Billy Graham and Johnny Saxton. This year, Giardello would add the same number of wins to his record and take only one loss, to Pierre Langlois.

Color Television

The first (official) color television boxing broadcast from Madison Square Garden came on Friday, March 26, 1954. The event, conducted by NBC, featured middleweight Gustav Scholz against Al Andrews. To accommodate the technology, some alterations needed to be done to the ring and to the fighters. Ring elements that appeared in white were changed to the color of gray. And one fighter needed to wear blue trunks with gold stripes, and the other gold trunks with blue stripes. By the way, Scholz defeated Andrews by a united verdict.

Pulling the Lid Off the IBC—Part Three

On Tuesday, May 25, the Supreme Court agreed to hear the government's appeal of the lower court's dismissal of its antitrust suit. The emphasis of this appeal was in the specific differences between the sport of boxing and baseball, most notably the sale and control of motion picture, broadcasting and television rights. It was this, the government believed, that put boxing into interstate commerce and thus subject to antitrust laws.[27]

A disquieted James D. Norris had hoped to match Marciano for a February defense in Miami, but Al Weill, who was now managing the heavyweight champion, didn't take the bait.[28] The early view appeared to have Marciano defending twice this year, which was precisely what he did.

MARCIANO V. CHARLES I

With summer just around the corner, it was high time for the big boys. Scheduled for fifteen rounds inside Yankee Stadium on June 17, the heavyweight championship of the world was on the line. The titleholder, Rocky Marciano, was facing a former champion, Ezzard Charles. The champion had held the title since September 23, 1952, and had won every professional fight he had ever participated in, all forty-five of them. Charles, the former champion—having won the championship on June 22, 1949, by defeating Jersey Joe Walcott following the retirement of Joe Louis—was certainly no stranger to ring success. The Cincinnati boxer lost the title back to Walcott in 1951, before losing to the fighter again in an attempt to retake the title the following year. It was Walcott who lost the title to Marciano. Charles was attempting to do what no other heavyweight ex-champion had done: win back the crown.

In the first four rounds, the champion was lethargic and bore no resemblance to the Marciano in highlight reels. Charles, with those brilliant flailing arms of his, tied his opposition into knots, giving him no breathing room—he also opened a deep wound over the champion's left eye. While Charles turned on the defense in the fifth round, he had little choice as Marciano had established the pace. To the champion's credit, he wisely took the battle to close quarters, ever mindful of his challenger's reach advantage. Charles fought a good fight but tired in the final rounds—this opened him up to the champion's relentless combinations that eventually took their toll. When the final distance had been met, the champion had retained his title with a concordant verdict.

GIVE US MOORE

As hard as it was to believe, it was true: Archie Moore's first Madison Square Garden appearance didn't occur until August 11, 1954. Moore, who had been fighting professionally since 1935, entered the City Ring to meet Philadelphia boxer Harold Johnson. It was Moore's fourth fight of the year and the second time this annum that he was defending his light heavyweight title; having successfully protected it against Joey Maxim in Miami, or Moore's hometown, back on January 27.

Although Moore was favored in this clash, you wouldn't have known until the fourteenth round, when the fighter appeared to discover a renewed right hand. As if sent from the gods, Moore discharged a right to the chin of Johnson that staggered the fighter. Having been down in the tenth round, Moore knew he needed a solution and quick. A stunned Johnson then took combination fire before Moore dropped him with a solid left hook. Up at the count of four, Johnson underwent a mandatory eight count that referee Ruby Goldstein administered by mistake. Oops. The fight continued briefly before Goldstein, having seen Johnson endure enough of Moore's punishment, ended the fight. It was a "KO14" for Moore and another successful title defense.

CARMEN MEETS CARMINE

Canastota, New York's Carmen Basilio was tough as nails. No, make it spikes—the railroad type. The vicious ex-Marine had only one direction, forward, and he used it to his advantage. He had gone 4–1 so far in 1954, before entering the Garden on September 10. In the feature battle, Basilio took a unanimous ten-round decision from Brooklyn's Carmine Fiore. Not one to waste time, Basilio dropped Fiore twice in the first round with his trademark left hook. But Fiore, who had plenty of crowd support, fought on. It was Basilio's second victory over Fiore, whom he knocked out back in April of 1953.

MARCIANO V. CHARLES II

The fight, originally scheduled for Yankee Stadium on September 15, was moved to the following night, before being postponed again. Finally, on Friday, September 17, it was time. Marciano, who looked far better than in their first meeting, knocked out Ezzard Charles in the eighth round—the championship fight, as usual, was scheduled for fifteen rounds. The champion had dropped the "Cincinnati Cobra" earlier in the round to a count of four, before finishing him off with a left hook and a right cross to the chin; Charles had also been sent to the canvas in the second round. An estimated crowd of 25,000 witnessed the battle; the poor attendance was attributed to the multiple postponements.

"THE ROCK"

Rocco Francis Marchegiano was born on September 1, 1923, in Brockton, Massachusetts. Rocco was the oldest of six children born to Piecino and Pasqualina Marchegiano; his father was from the town of Ripa Teatina, in the region of Abruzzo, Italy, while his mother was from San Bartolomeo in Galdo, in the region of Campania, Italy. Rocco's father was a hard-working Italian immigrant and a shoemaker, who raised his family in typical American fashion.

Excelling at baseball and football, Rocky fell in love with sports. It wasn't until he was drafted into the Army in 1943 that the sport of boxing caught Rocky's attention; he was on a two-year stint that found him stationed in Swansea, Wales. Soon, he started to participate in camp boxing tournaments, and proved quite proficient as a heavyweight. After the war ended—he completed his service in March 1946 at Fort Lewis, Washington—Marciano continued to box.[29] Following his discharge, he wasn't certain as to which direction to take, as he loved baseball—he once had a trial with the Chicago Cubs—but also enjoyed the sweet science.[30]

Regardless of the fact that he had one professional fight (against Lee Epperson on March 17, 1947, in Holyoke, Massachusetts) on his record, Marchegiano began fighting permanently as a professional boxer on July 12, 1948. Fighting out of Providence served him well, except the ring announcer always had trouble pronouncing his name, so Marciano's handler, Al Weill, suggested they create a pseudonym. After rejecting a few suggestions, they ended up with Marciano—the fighter liked it because it sounded Italian. The Brockton boxer may have had some power behind his punches, but it took trainer Charley Goldman to sculpt Marciano into a competitive heavyweight.

Reaching Madison Square Garden on December 30, 1949, Marciano nearly killed his adversary prior to a sixth-round knockout. Thankfully, Carmine Vingo survived. However, the fight that thrust the heavyweight into the spotlight came on March 24, 1950, when he met an undefeated Roland LaStarza, then handed him his first loss.

Sugar Ray vs. Saxton

On October 20, Ray Robinson announced he was returning to the ring. Having not fought competitively since June 25, 1952, he would gradually ease himself into a fighting mindset. Understanding that to be competitive he needed to follow a proper workout regimen, Robinson systematically scheduled his competition. This, he believed, would guarantee success.

A stable of fighters, like that of horses, has to stay viable in order to be profitable. So when a star performer begins to fade, or exhibits signs of vulnerability, he needs to be replaced. One of the workhorses for the IBC was welterweight champion Kid Gavilan, and when his keepers sensed the inevitable, they turned to a replacement. Johnny Saxton was four years younger, and minus a barrel chest, essentially a clone of Gavilan, minus the Cuban's skill set, of course. On October 20, at Convention Hall in Philadelphia, during a fifteen-round dance marathon, the two performed an exchange of vows and Saxton walked away with the welter crown. On the day of the fight, the word on the street was a fix, and the rumor was supported by the flood of Saxton money. In a flash, bookies wiped the fight off the boards, meaning that they weren't accepting any more bets. The fight was slow, dull, and predictable, with a result antithetical to those sitting ringside.

Patterson v. Gannon

Capturing the Olympic middleweight crown in 1952 at Helsinki, Finland, Floyd Patterson was turning heads. The maturing nineteen-year-old Brooklyn light heavyweight was making his Madison Square Garden feature debut on October 22 in a scheduled eight-rounder against Joe Gannon of Washington. If the name Gannon sounded familiar, it was because the boxer was a sparring partner of Rocky Marciano. No stranger to the City Ring, Patterson had fought inside the confinement as a Golden Gloves amateur and in his third pro contest. As a professional, he had won all but one (Joey Maxim) of his seventeen fights. On this day, Patterson, who aspired to become a champion, took a big step toward that goal by defeating Joe Gannon in a thrilling eight-round united verdict. As he trailed in points, Gannon's only hope of victory in the final round was a knockout, but the fighter just could not do it.

Forgotten Rounds

In a lightweight championship that was held on March 5 inside the City Ring, Brooklyn boxer Paddy DeMarco, who had won only five of his last ten battles, took a unanimous fifteen-round decision and the lightweight crown from Jimmy Carter, also of the Bronx. To some the Carter bouquet wasn't right, but the recent slope of speculation in the Garden had been steep.

South American middle Eduardo Lausse stopped Boston boxer Joe Rindone at the 1:28 mark of the second round on June 4. For Lausse it was the fortieth knockout victory of his career, and a dramatic one as he left Rindone beaten against the ropes.

Philadelphia feather Percy Bassett took an upset victory over Lulu Perez by knocking out the Brooklyn fighter in the eleventh round of their scheduled twelve-round duel. Most knew Bassett as the "interim feather champion" while Sandy Saddler served out his Army obligations. Bassett catapulted Perez through the ropes in the eighth round with a powerful left to the stomach that dropped the fighter down to a count of eight.

In the six-round semifinal of the Moore versus Johnson fight on August 11, Keyport, New Jersey's Joe "Rocky" Tomasello put on a stunning display of fistic prowess by dropping his Brooklyn opponent, Phil Rizzo, twice in the first round, once in the second, and had him all but out in the final round. Tomasello, who possessed a solid left hook, wasn't afraid to use it. In a night of refereeing blunders, Rizzo, who was up at two, was given a mandatory eight count. Embarrassed by the event, Rizzo stood up only to be put to the canvas once again. The verdict, as many believed, was as simple as predicting tomorrow's sunrise, or was it? The decision went to Rizzo.

On November 19, on the undercard of the Patterson versus Slade feature, was a pair of gladiators who gave a sound performance. Pittsburgh's Tommy Barto fought furiously to take a questionable eight-round decision over Gaspar Ortega. Both fighters were so fatigued by the final round that they could barely lift their arms. While the crowd screamed for a draw, the decision turned to Barto.

On November 26, Hartford's Teddy "Redtop" Davis, in his 107th professional bout, took a twelve-round unanimous decision over Philadelphia boxer Percy Bassett. It was the quickness of Davis, along with his commanding left jab, that delivered him the fight. The two had now met four times, with two decisions apiece.

Finally, Big Bob Baker from Pittsburgh took a unanimous ten-round decision over Harlem's Coley Wallace on Friday, December 17. This was in front of a meager Garden crowd estimated at only 2,000. It was the third meeting between the heavyweight duo, and Baker's third victory.

Fighter of the Year

The boxing year belonged to heavyweight champion Rocky Marciano. Defending his crown twice against former champion Ezzard Charles, he remained undefeated.

Inside the City Ring, Gaspar Ortega went 1–1–1, and Niño Valdéz went 2–0. Nonetheless, the fighter who shined the ring most in 1954 was Joey Giardello, who went 4–1.[31]

1955

James D. Norris, president of the International Boxing Club, had spent more than one January sleepless night contemplating his promotions for the year. You can't blame him for his concern, as the previous year had seen the Garden's average attendance for its thirty boxing shows dip below the 4,000-spectator mark, as not a single Garden show attracted more than 10,000 people. When compared to the same 1953 mark, the average attendance had decreased by over 1,000 fans. The significant decline was blamed first on the lack of competitive matches, followed by a saturation of televised boxing, and needless to say, the cloud of suspicion hanging over the City Ring. For those who had followed the fight game, it was hard to believe that over three times as many fans, on average, saw a Garden boxing match in 1945. And that was just a decade ago.

Pulling the Lid Off the IBC—Part Four

On January 31, the United Sates Supreme Court, under Chief Justice Earl Warren, ruled that the legitimate theatre and professional boxing were subject to antitrust laws. The government could move forward with antitrust suits against the defendants in the case. The suits, as you recall, were dismissed in the lower courts due to a reaffirmation of a 1922 judgment that baseball was not covered underneath the antitrust statutes.[32]

In testament to the decline of the sport but not the venue: On Thursday, March 3, a crowd of 22,000 packed Madison Square Garden to see Billy Graham. Yet only a day later, a crowd of fewer than 5,000 turned out to watch Billy Graham. The former was the evangelical preacher and author, whose full name was William Franklin Graham, while the latter was an established welterweight boxer, whose full name was William Walter Graham, Jr. While Graham the preacher lived up to expectations, Graham the boxer lost a controversial ten-round split decision to Stamford, Connecticut's Chico Vejar. The contentious verdict was only because Graham turned on the engines in the final rounds, not to mention igniting a partisan home crowd. In the one hundred and twenty-five fights of his career, Graham had only lost fourteen times. While the evangelical preacher would see another crusade inside Madison Square Garden, the fighter would not.

By summer, the Madison Square Garden Corporation was undergoing some changes: six directors had resigned; James D. Norris succeeded John Reed Kilpatrick as president, while the latter took over as board chairman commensurate with heading a new corporation that would operate the New York Rangers hockey team.[33]

It took a while, not to mention some grueling deliberations, but Archie Moore finally obtained his goal of being matched with Rocky Marciano. The fight would take place at Yankee Stadium on Tuesday, September 20.[34]

The Upstate Onion Farmer

With Carmen Basilio, analogies were endless: He was as durable as steel, he was so rough that he made sandpaper seem like a dust cloth, and he had so much grit that he made test pilots feel insecure. Born on April 2, 1927, in Canastota, New York, Carmen was one of ten children of tenant farmers and Italian immigrants, Joseph Basilio and Mary Picciano. Raising such a large family on Barlow Street in Canastota was no easy task, but the Basilios, like

An American boxer who was the world champion in both the welterweight and middleweight divisions, Carmen Basilio—born Carmine Basilio—(1927–2012) was perhaps most famous for defeating the great Sugar Ray Robinson to take the middleweight title.

so many of their neighbors, persevered—everyone pitched in. From age five, he worked the rich black soil of the onion fields of central New York. The adverse conditions of a laborer were hard, damn hard—the incessant bending developed muscles he never knew had, while challenging his fortitude—and it didn't take long for Basilio to consider his alternatives. And as if he weren't tough enough, the Marines would finish the job.

In 1948, following not only his Marine boxing but some local bootleg battles, Basilio turned pro and fought all across central New York. Standing five-foot-six-and-a-half inches tall and fighting in an orthodox stance, Basilio was primed to meet any welterweight opponent, or so he thought. He went 4–0 in 1948, and had compiled a record of 15–2–2 by the end of 1949. Basilio's breakout year came in 1953, as he took decisions over Ike Williams and Vic Cardell before knocking out Carmine Fiore. On June 6, 1953, he defeated Billy Graham to win the New York State welterweight title, before retaining it by drawing Graham the following month. In 1954, he posted a record of 7–0–1, while trying to fight his way back into the welterweight mix. And in 1955, he did precisely that by defeating Peter Mueller in Syracuse, before knocking out Tony DeMarco in the twelfth round of their June 10 meeting to capture the world welterweight title.

THE UNFORGETTABLE SIXTH

It lived up to every expectation if not more—or Moore, as in Archie. Rocky Marciano, down in the second round, rose to knock out the thirty-eight-year-old former light heavyweight champion at the 1:19 mark of the ninth round. The September 21 battle, which was scheduled for fifteen rounds inside Yankee Stadium, didn't go the distance, but not one of the 60,000 spectators complained. For as unbelievable as it was to see Marciano on the canvas, it was inconceivable to see Archie Moore sent to the canvas five times before being counted out. All this action was from two fighters who not only looked great, but performed at a level of excellence demanded of a champion.

It would be the sixth round, however, that would be etched into boxing history as one of the greatest sessions in heavyweight competition. Compact lefts began the round, as they both traded punches. Moore then tossed a left hook to the face, followed by a straight left in the same direction, before delivering a right to Marciano's chin and a right to the body. Marciano didn't waver. Instead, he alertly drove a right into the face of Moore that dropped him to a count of four.

Upon arising, Moore took several rights, some machine-gun combinations and then a hard right. Both fighters then unloaded the arsenal, without even aiming, until Moore dropped to the canvas for a count of eight. Once again on his feet, Moore heroically met Marciano's artillery and would not give ground. As Marciano's volley of punches was answered by Moore's counters, every fan in the arena stood in anticipation of a knockout by either fighter. When the bell finally sounded, both fighters were hardly capable of walking to their respective corners owing to sheer exhaustion. It was truly an incredible exposition by two gladiators incapable of capitulation. To many it was the finest boxing they had ever witnessed.

FORGOTTEN ROUNDS

Harold Johnson can box, and he proved it on February 11, when he knocked out Buffalo's Paul Andrews at the 1:46 mark of the sixth round. Johnson used an array of sharp punches that included an effective jab. Andrews—who, by the way, was trained by Joe Louis—appeared to have forgotten most of the "Bomber's" advice.

Sandy Saddler, having not defended his title since September 26, 1951, scored a unanimous fifteen-round decision over Hartford's Teddy "Red" Davis on February 25. It wasn't particularly entertaining, as Saddler sailed through the final rounds, but noteworthy for the elapsed time.

Argentine middleweight Eduardo Lausse took a ten-round unanimous decision over Yonkers fighter Ralph "Tiger" Jones on May 13. The fight was a slugfest from the very start and surprisingly stayed

An American boxer, Joseph "Sandy" Saddler (1926–2001) was twice featherweight world champion, having also held the super featherweight title. He was best known for capturing three victories during his four-bout series with Willie Pep.

that way. During an era when fatigued fighters tired early and clinched to obtain a breather, this affair had none of that. While Lausse nursed a cut for most of the distance, it didn't stop him from pounding away on his rival with robust combinations.

Lurking on the undercard in a four-rounder was a Bronx fighter by the name of Carlos Ortiz—it was the fighter's first appearance in the City Ring. Fighting at 133 pounds, Ortiz kayoed Jersey boxer Danny Roberts at the 2:55 mark of the third round.

On September 2, Brooklyn's Carmelo "Chubby" Costa took a ten-round split decision over feather Bobby Bell of Youngstown, Ohio. The fight marked the opening of the Garden's tenth season of routine Friday night bouts.

German Isaac Logart took a ten-round united verdict over Philadelphia scrapper Gil Turner on October 21. Both fighters were relentless with their assaults in the first boxing show in the Garden in six weeks.

On November 18, New Orleans boxer Willie Pastrano, in his Garden debut, took a united ten-round judgment over Pennsylvania boxer Joey Rowan. The heavyweight contest took place in front of a Garden crowd of fewer than 3,000 spectators.

South American middleweight Eduardo Lausse took a unanimous ten-round decision over West Jordan, Utah, boxer Gene Fullmer on November 25. Fullmer, in his Garden debut and second straight loss, was simply outpunched by Lausse.

Fighter of the Year

It was a year that saw many good matches conducted outside the New York City area. Praise, which doesn't come easy, has to be given to the New York State Athletic Commission's new chairman, Julius Helfand, who took a tough stance in regard to the sport.

As for boxing, Carmen Basilio went 5–0, which included winning, then retaining, the world welterweight title. Ezzard Charles, Kid Gavilan, Sandy Saddler, Chico Vejar and Billy Graham fought their last battles in the City Ring, while Gene Fullmer and Carlos Ortiz fought their first. As for the City Ring, there was no standout fighter who really shined in 1955.[35]

10

Exercising Control, 1956–1959

> You do not lead by hitting people over the head. That's assault, not leadership.
> —Dwight D. Eisenhower

Allegations against International Boxing Club of New York and Illinois, its officers and affiliates, finally drew to a close at the end of the decade, leaving the question: Could the sport of boxing, along with its premier venue, recover from the damage caused by the spectacle?

Understanding that a knockdown wasn't a knockout, boxing began the difficult task of regaining its composure and building trust in its participants.[1]

1956

The first solid Garden feature of the year came on February 17, when West Jordan, Utah, middleweight Gene Fullmer captured an action-packed ten-round split decision over Philadelphia's Gil Turner.[2] Not only was it a close fight, as one could assume from the split decision, but it was vicious from start to finish. Just how savage was it? It was so ruthless that it drew comparisons to Basilio versus DeMarco.[3] Since neither fighter was complacent to jab his way to a distance affair, both tossed wallops like Sunday morning pancakes.

Pulling the Lid Off the IBC—Part Five

On April 19, it was time for the government to prove their case against the IBC, its officers and affiliates. A non-jury trial in front of the United States District Court would be the forum.

The charge stated that the defendants had "combined and conspired in restraint of and to monopolize interstate trade and foreign commerce in the promotion, exhibition, broadcasting, telecasting and motion picture production and distribution of championship boxing contests in the United States and that they have monopolized the said trade and commerce."[4]

The government then asserted that the defendants had attained a monopoly "by obtaining exclusive control of titles through direct purchase or acquisition; acquiring and thus eliminating an important competitive promoter of championship matches; obtaining exclusive use of key stadiums and athletic arenas; compelling contenders for the title to agree to fight only for the International Boxing Clubs if they won the championships; and systematically tying important boxers and mangers to themselves by making loans of substantial amounts of money to them at no interest and for unlimited periods."[5]

On April 23, the government introduced numerous documents to support their case. One example stated: "The International Boxing Club and its affiliates promoted or participated in thirty-six of the forty-four championship fights staged in this country between June 1949 and May 1953."[6] The case continued for days with recaps posted in the local newspapers.

Fullmer v. Humez

Gene Fullmer gave another impressive Garden performance on May 25, when he took a unanimous decision over Frenchman Charles Humez. Both boxers fought tirelessly during all ten rounds, with Fullmer exhibiting the greater ring command. A cut right eye hampered Humez from the third round onward, but despite the injury his antagonist could not put him away. Like all the middleweights in the mix, the Utahan wanted a title shot, which meant Ray Robinson. The Harlemite, who had mounted a successful comeback, had won the middleweight championship in December, and retained it on May 18 in a rematch with Carl "Bobo" Olson.

Boardman v. Ryff

It was always exciting when a new star graced the City Ring. On June 1, Larry Boardman, a twenty-year-old lightweight from Marlborough, Connecticut did just that by knocking out Frankie Ryff, a popular New York contender, at the 0:46 mark of the ninth round. Ryff, who caught a sporty right earlier in the fight that seemed to daze him, took an even more powerful version to the chin that sent him flat on his back.

El Indio

Born October 31, 1935, in Mexicali, Baja California, Mexico, Gaspar Ortega found the boxing ring at the young age of fourteen. Beginning his career as a flyweight—the weight limit was 112 pounds—the boxer claimed he won over twenty consecutive fights in Mexico before any official boxing record began to chase him. This situation, by the way, was common for many fighters.

Like many talented Mexican fighters, it wasn't

A Mexican boxer, Gaspar "Indio" Ortega (born October 31, 1935, in Mexicali, Baja California, Mexico) was considered one of the best welterweight boxers from Mexico. Enormously popular with New York City fight fans, he appeared inside Madison Square Garden twenty times from 1954 until 1963.

long before Ortega began looking north for better opportunities. On August 25, 1954, he greeted New York City inside, of all things, the City Ring at Madison Square Garden. There the fighter took a decision over Iggy Maldanado in his first City Ring victory.

By 1956, Ortega was 34-3-1, and gradually stepping up the competition. He took victories during the year over Tex Gonzales, Hardy Smallwood and Isaac Logart before turning his attention to the first fighter he ever faced with over fifty career victories, Tony DeMarco. The former welterweight champion was a confident 4-0 on the year and welcomed the chance to meet Ortega. On November 23, in the City Ring, "El Indio" not only took the decision victory in this battle with "The Hub" fighter, he repeated it in a rematch less than a month later. Nuf Ced!

Forgotten Rounds

There were times when preliminary bouts were better than the feature, and times when they were far worse. On February 10, both occurrences happened on the undercard of the Logart v. Fuentes feature event. The semifinal featured Mexican Gaspar Ortega taking an exciting decision over New Jersey boxer Tony "Tex" Gonzalez—it was far better than the feature. Since this was the pair's third meeting, or rubber match, if you will, both wanted to prove their superiority—each entered the battle with a record of 1-1. Casting science to the wind, both fighters fought relentlessly with wild swings and even questionable blows—Gonzalez was penalized in the second for a low blow. The continuous action ended with Oretga taking the victory.

The fight was in sharp contrast to its predecessor, which saw a scheduled six-rounder between Cleveland's Rudy Gwin and Pittsburgh's Reybon Stubbs terminated and declared "no contest." Both fighters would not engage even after numerous warnings. This prompted the referee to finally step between the fighters during the middle of the fourth round and wave them off to their corners, ending a performance that was far worse than the feature.

On March 23, Queens fighter Ralph "Tiger" Jones took an extremely close ten-round split decision from Charley Humez, the European middleweight champion, in the latter's American debut. In front of a Garden crowd—one of the largest in many weeks—estimated at 5,000 spectators, the fighters put on a solid display despite the absence of dramatic highlights.

On the following Friday, and for the second straight week, a French boxer was in the feature event. Cherif Hamia took a ten-round split decision over Brooklyn's Carmelo Costa on March 30. Unlike Humez, however, Hamia was far more aggressive and exhibited a strong set of skills.

Buffalo middle Joey Giambra scored a tough ten-round decision over Atlantic City boxer Rocky Castellani on August 3. Discharged earlier in the year from the Army, Giambra was out testing his trademark left hook, and on this night it was against a clever opponent in Castellani. Giambra, who appeared to get stronger as the rounds progressed, moved his record to 45-4-1.

On October 19, Giambra grabbed a split decision over Philadelphia fighter Gil Turner in a hard-fought ten-rounder. Turner, who was a notorious infighter, could not get Giambra to take the bait.

Puerto Rican feather Miguel Berrios put on a powerful punching display to take a ten round united judgment over Philippine southpaw Gabriel "Flash" Elorde. As clever a boxer as Elorde was, Berrios seemed to always have a successful counter.

On December 21, in the semifinal on the undercard of Ortega v. DeMarco, Cleveland welter Rudy Gwin took a six-round unanimous decision over Philadelphia battler Jimmy Fisher. Gwin, floored in the first frame to a nine count, then dropped Fisher to an automatic eight count in the second round. From that point onward, Gwin just battered Fisher. Following the announcement, Fisher was still being attended to. Later, he had to be carried to the first aid room on a stretcher, and from there he was removed to St. Clare's Hospital; he had suffered from a slight concussion.

Ring Out the Old

It was not a particularly good year in the history of New York City boxing. The conflict between the New York State Athletic Commission, Jim Norris and the Boxing Guild of New York, created an influx of foreign imports and considerable bad blood. At a glance: Carmen Basilio regained his title from Johnny Saxton (Syracuse), Floyd Patterson took the heavy crown by knocking out Archie Moore (Chicago), Sandy Saddler retained his feather crown from Gabriel "Flash" Elorde (San Francisco), and Joe Brown, despite a broken hand, set up shop in the lightweight division (Houston and New Orleans). Rocky Marciano announced his retirement on April 27, thus Patterson. Ray Robinson defended his middle crown once, albeit in a decisive vindication. And Pascual Pérez still dominated the flyweights; he had three successful defenses.

Fighter of the Year

The City Ring saw many new faces, including Joey Archer and Flash Elorde, but also bid farewell to hub fighter Tony DeMarco. If there was one fighter who shined the City Ring during this term it was Gaspar Ortega. The fighter went 3–1, which included back-to-back wins over a very tough Tony DeMarco.[7]

1957

If Madison Square Garden had to select the perfect fight to begin the year, this was it: Sugar Ray Robinson versus Gene Fullmer. Postponed back in December due to the champion's cold, it was now set for January 22. Fullmer, although far younger and with less experience, believed the delay was nothing more than a Robinson ploy to throw him off his game: tactics such as delays, fake press reports, and contentious press conferences were all a part of the fight game.

An American boxer, Lawrence Gene Fullmer (1931–2015) was a former world middleweight champion. Hailing from a West Jordan, Utah, boxing family, Fullmer holds victories over Paul Pender, Sugar Ray Robinson, and Carmen Basilio.

Sugar Ray Robinson
v. Gene Fullmer I

For fifteen rounds, Gene Fullmer did what he did best: he constantly advanced. And what he received as a result of this action was a fifteen-round unanimous decision and the middleweight championship. Nobody disputed the verdict. Fullmer's punches were abundant and almost instinctive, something you saw in a few boxers at his experience level and certainly something the now former champion didn't anticipate. Robinson's featured characteristic of the evening was holding, which he did more of than Fred Astaire and Ginger Rogers. Perfecting the art of the arms, Robinson tied Fullmer in knots and the capacity crowd wasn't hesitant about expressing their dissatisfaction. Despite the clenching, the Utah scrapper just kept moving forward and throwing combinations.

In the seventh round, Fullmer tossed a hearty left at Robinson's head, then drove him with both hands. The action sent the champion through the ropes and onto the ring apron. The count reached six before Robinson bounced back into the ring. He was not hurt. However, it was not the best night for the City Ring, as the ropes had disengaged in the sixth round and had difficulty staying on the ring posts. By the tenth round, the bottom strand had to be removed, so the fight continued with only two ropes. By the eighth, it was clear that Robinson had to step up the scoring. So he took the ninth, eleventh, twelfth and fifteenth, but it just was not enough. The champion had lost far too many earlier rounds and his crown.

It was a spectacular event, and reminded many of the old days in the Garden when boxing still had its luster. Norris was immediately talking rematch—something Fullmer's camp didn't seem to mind. Even so, reeling in the paradoxical Robinson, as Norris well understood, would present the negotiation challenge.[8]

Pulling the Lid
Off the IBC—Part Six

In a civil action, the IBC was found to have been operating in violation of the Sherman Act—the chief antitrust law—on March 8.[9] The government's antitrust charges trail began on April 19, 1956, and concluded on May 3. The federal judge who gave the decision stated that no financial penalties were involved, but he gave the government essentially thirty days to come up with solution on just how to abort the monopoly. The fifty-nine-page opinion ended as follows: "The court concludes that the promotion of championship contests does constitute a unique and relevant market for Sherman Act consideration."[10]

James D. Norris issued the following statement to the press: "The court's decision was, of course, a disappointment to me. All I can say at this time is I hope we will not be prevented from continuing to present Wednesday and Friday night fights which have proved [to be] such popular television and radio attractions. We already have contracted for the Gene Fullmer—Sugar Ray Robinson fight to be held in Chicago on May 1. After that we hope to continue with our summer plans. This will depend, however, on the terms of the decree which will be entered to carry out the court's decision."[11]

On June 24, in a preliminary decree, Federal Judge Sylvester J. Ryan ordered James

D. Norris, Jr. and Arthur M. Wirtz to sever all their connections with the Madison Square Garden Corporation and to dissolve the International Boxing Club of New York and Illinois. Both Norris and Wirtz must also dispose of their stock in Madison Square Garden within five years. Other detailed restrictions were also applied to the defendants. It was very likely that both Norris and Wirtz would make a motion for a new trial or appeal directly to the Supreme Court of the United States. Hours later, Norris continued his negotiations for a middleweight title fight between Sugar Ray Robinson and Carmen Basilio.

On July 2, a sixty-day stay of execution of the injunctions handed down by Judge Ryan against the defendants in the case was granted. This would allow the defendants time to file a request for a further stay with the United States Supreme Court. The court's orders would not take effect until the final disposition of an appeal, if the defendants opted for that alternative. On July 12, attorneys representing the defendants filed a motion for a new trial in the United States District Court, only to later move to the United States Supreme Court.[12]

Robinson v. Basilio

Back to Robinson versus Basilio. Well, it looked good, then bad, then good again, and by August 20, bad again. The middleweight championship fight—scheduled for September 23 at Yankee Stadium—was called off by Robinson. He felt the IBC had violated their agreement. Robinson would only fight if the Teleprompter Corporation handled the closed-circuit television. NYSAC ordered Robinson to defend his title against Basilio—he had signed contracts back on July 31—or risk losing it.

Newspaper articles were quick to call to mind Robinson's experience and physical size over Basilio. Indeed, Robinson was at least six years older, heavier by eight pounds, and taller by four and a half inches. His reach advantage against Basilio was four and a half inches, which can feel like a mile to a fighter. Both fighters were about equal in chest size, neck, and calves. Robinson had bigger wrists. But Basilio had a bigger waist, thighs, biceps, fists, ankles and much larger forearms. For all that, something was overlooked in the equation: desire.

Robinson took 45 percent of the gate, less taxes, and $225,000 for the television rights. Basilio pocketed 20 percent of the gate and $110,000 for the television rights. It was the largest closed-circuit network in the history of the sport.

In the end, it was Carmen Basilio's relentless pursuit and infinite desire that won out. The Canastota, New York native, who suffered a cut left eye in the fourth round, had Robinson all but out on his feet in the eleventh. The split decision belonged to Basilio and the crowd of more than 38,000 agreed; only referee Al Berl sided for Robinson. Since a 90-day return bout agreement had been signed, only the terms remained to be worked out. According to NYSAC rules, Basilio had to surrender his welterweight belt for a middleweight version.

Gene Fullmer

The oldest of three brothers, Lawrence Gene Fullmer was born July 21, 1931, in West Jordan, Utah. He was named after fighter Gene Tunney, or so he claimed, and the association certainly didn't hurt. Gene's two younger siblings, Jay, born March 9, 1937, and Don, born on February 21, 1939, were also professional fighters.

Fighting primarily out of Utah and California, minus a couple one-offs, Gene Fullmer took a record of 24–0 into the Eastern Parkway Arena in Brooklyn on November 8, 1954. It was his first time fighting in New York City and he defeated Jackie LaBua. He would finish the year 9–0.

In 1955, he compiled a record of 6–3, as he slowly worked his way up in competition. In 1956, the Utah fighter posted a record of 5–0, with victories over Rocky Castellani, Gil Turner, Ralph Jones, Charles Humez and Moses Ward. His triumph over Sugar Ray Robinson inside the City Ring on January 2 was attended by victories over Wilfrid Greaves on January 28 and Ernie Durando on February 18, and certainly made for a solid start. Losing the NBA middleweight title to Robinson on May 1 was a disappointment, but only a temporary setback. He finished the year with three consecutive victories and took a record of 43–4–0 into 1958.[13]

Forgotten Rounds

On February 1, in the semifinal of the Logart v. Bahama feature, Chicago middleweight Bill Tate took a split decision over Italian Fernando Spallotta. The two just went at it tooth and nail for the full eight rounds.

Boston welter Walter Byars, in an enormous upset, took a ten-round united judgment over Garnet "Sugar" Hart on March 8; the latter was a favorite (4–1).

Puerto Rican feather Miguel Berrios took a twelve-round split decision over Brooklyn's Carmelo Costa on March 22. The action-packed event was part of the featherweight tournament designed to find a successor to the crown vacated by Sandy Saddler–the ring veteran surrendered it owing to poor health. Berrios, who dropped Costa in tenth term to a five count, forced most of the action.

On October 18, on the undercard of Calhoun v. Castellani was a semifinal pitting Brooklyn's Tony DeCola against Tony DiBase, of Astoria, Long Island. The fight, which was scheduled for ten rounds, only went seven. That's when a young referee, Arthur Mercante, Sr., in his first Garden appearance, halted the fight on the advice of a NYSAC physician. DeCola was victorious by a technical knockout.

Valley Stream, Long Island, welter Gale Kerwin upset Bronx welter Jimmy Archer in a ten-round split decision. Archer, who was making his Garden debut on December 20, had twelve consecutive victories entering the contest, so naturally he was expected to just slide along to victory. But Kerwin had other ideas as he outpunched and outscored his opponent. Also on the card was Jimmy's younger brother, Joey, who took a six-round unanimous decision over Joe Lissy. Young Joey showed promise by remaining undefeated in twenty fights.

Fighter of the Year

While it's true that Floyd Patterson made two successful heavyweight defenses, the year really belonged to Carmen Basilio. Not only did he defend his welterweight crown in February, he defeated Ray Robinson in September to take the middleweight title. In the City Ring, it was a relatively quiet year, but if anyone added luster to the ring it was Gene Fullmer, who went 2–0.[14]

1958

IT'S ALL IN THE GAME

Virgil Akins knocked out Cuban Isaac Logart at the 2:53 mark of the sixth round on March 21. The fight was part of the welterweight tournament to determine a new division champion. Akins would then meet Vince Martinez in the finale of the competition. The fight would not only be recalled for the performance of Akins, but also for twelve subpoenas that were served that Friday evening inside Madison Square Garden by detectives from the District Attorney's office.

A New York grand jury was looking into reports that professional boxing has been infiltrated and controlled by underworld figures. While it had been rumored that D.A. Frank Hogan was looking into the matter, this was the first confirmation. NYSAC's chairman Julius Helfand, who was at the event, believed that any criminality involved with the sport did not belong in his office but with that of the District Attorney. While some had the opinion that the conspicuous betting in the Garden lobby triggered the action, most knew it had been going on for a considerable period of time. It was no secret that Albert Anastasia, who had been murdered the pervious year, Frankie Carbo, and others were connected to boxing, but just how wasn't clear. The only thing that was certain was that D.A. Hogan, who had investigated the shaving of points in college basketball, was resolved to get to the bottom of things.

On March 27, the District Attorney's office seized the accounting records of B. Wollman & Bros., Inc., from partner Herman "Hymie the Mink" Wallman, who was believed to be linked to Frankie Carbo, and the records of the IBC through General Manager Harry Markson. Wallman had a stable of fighters that included Ike Chestnut, Charlie Cotton, Alex Miteff and Orlando Zulueta.[15] To some, the action was a clear indication that the investigation was serious.

James D, Norris resigned as president of the New York and Illinois International Boxing Clubs on April 18. In the move, he also resigned as director of the IBC in New York and was replaced by Harry Markson. The action taken by Norris was as a result of health concerns, according to the corporation's press release. He also stated, "I postponed tendering my resignation at that time, wanting to renew the television contract for the Friday night telecasts, which has been accomplished."[16] According to statements released by Assistant District Attorney Alfred J. Scotti, IBC matchmaker Billy Brown was one of the first to surface admitting that he met with Carbo, spoke in code and was ordered to match a certain fighter.[17] Under tremendous scrutiny, Billy Brown (real name Dominick Mordini) resigned as matchmaker for the IBC on May 23, and was replaced by Jack Barrett.

From this point forward the action was swift. By July, the District Attorney's office was seeking James D. Norris for questioning before the grand jury. However, the attorney for Norris claimed his client was in poor physical health.

On July 2, New York State boxing judge Bertram T. Grant was indicted on charges of accepting bribes to influence his boxing decisions. Also named in the indictment was Herman "Hymie the Mink" Wallman, though not as a defendant. From September 20, 1954, until April 7, 1958, it was alleged that both men conspired to alter boxing bout decisions. Boxing licenses of both men were immediately suspended by NYSAC.

Eight days later, Jimmy White, a matchmaker and promoter and believed frontman for Frankie Carbo, was indicted. Four days later, Norris was served with a subpoena to appear before the court on September 16; the Norris legal team immediately attempted to quash the subpoena.

Gabriel Genovese, described as a close friend of Frankie Carbo, was indicted on charges of undercover management of fighters on July 22. An unnamed boxing manager alleged that he could not arrange bouts for his fighter without giving Genovese a percentage.[18] The legal undertow was drowning the sport at a swift pace.

Amid considerable controversy, the Garden returned to its boxing shows on Friday, May 23; with the exception of only a few dates, the shows would run until the end of August. However, as the IBC's foundation began to crumble, the Garden needed to look elsewhere for assistance.

Carlos Ortiz

Born on September 9, 1936, in Ponce, Puerto Rico, Carlos Ortiz came from a large family of eight children—three boys and five girls. His parents settled in New York City, before sending for the remainder of the family in Puerto Rico—Carlos was about eight years old. New York City could be challenging, especially if you spoke only broken English, but young Carlos endured.

Between the ropes, Ortiz discovered a whole new world. When the trophies from local tournaments began piling up, he and a friend named Vinny Ferguson set their sights on turning pro. It was Ferguson's father who helped guide the youths, acting as both a manager and trainer. Ortiz made his pro debut inside St. Nicholas Arena on February 14, 1955, against local fighter Harry Bell and quickly made him his first knockout victim. Turning the right heads, Ortiz made his debut inside Madison Square Garden on May 13, 1955, and defeated Danny Roberts via knockout. He would finish the year at 12–0. Ortiz loved the exhilaration he felt as a boxer, and to fight in his own backyard made it even more rewarding.

Posting a record of 7–0 in 1956, the fighter continued to succeed. The following year, he went 6–0 with one no-contest, and was beginning to increase his level of competition. By 1958, the experience of his opponents practically doubled. On October 28, 1958, the fighter headed across the pond for his first battle outside the United States. Fighting at 135½ pounds, Ortiz took a ten-round points victory over Dave Charnley at the Harringay Arena in London.[19] Charnley, champion of the British Isles, was a slugger but not quick enough catch Ortiz. In his final fight of the year, the New Yorker met lightweight Michigan boxer Kenny Lane for ten rounds at the Auditorium in Miami Beach. Lane, a successful southpaw, had a record of 55–6–0 and matched well against his adversary. So well, in fact, that Lane had to take the final two rounds to win a majority decision. For Ortiz, he would finish the year 4–2, sending his record to 28–2.

Forgotten Rounds

Italian lightweight Paolo Rosi defeated East Side boxer Johnny Busso in a ten-round feature inside the City Ring on January 3. It was the first Garden fight of the year and was won by a single point. Both judges' scorecards canceled each other out, and referee Teddy Martin had both fighters even in rounds. Therefore, it was up to the points given by the referee. Martin had given Rossi six points and Busso five.

Yvon Durelle was a Canadian fisherman who could pack a punch. On January 31, he caught and delivered light heavyweight Clarence Hinnant via technical knockout at the 1:46 mark of the seventh round. This was the second meeting between the two and Durelle's victory evened up matters.

Providence fighter Harold Gomes captured a ten-round decision over Harlem's Ike Chestnut on March 7. Gomes started slow, but picked up the pace to win the close engagement. The fight won't be recalled for its action; instead it will be remembered as the first Garden feature under arbiter Arthur Mercante, Sr.

Gaspar Ortega fought a draw against Michigan battler Mickey Crawford on August 13. The verdict was proof that even the supplementary points system couldn't eliminate every draw, as Referee Barney Felix scored both rounds and points even. This, according to most, was the first bona fide draw on a Garden card since the system was adopted.

Tacoma, Washington, boxer Pat McMurtry scored a unanimous ten-round decision over the Canadian heavyweight champion George Chuvalo. Perhaps it was nerves, as it was Chuvalo's first Garden appearance, but the Canadian giant, who outweighed his opponent by nearly twenty pounds, looked lethargic. Slipping once to the canvas, and bleeding profusely from his nose, Chuvalo at times appeared helpless.

Lastly, Syracuse heavyweight boxer Mike DeJohn took a ten-round unanimous decision over Milwaukee boxer Billy Besmanoff on November 28. DeJohn, with a superior reach advantage over his opponent, exhibited strong skills as he took command with his jab and scored often with his uppercuts. Carmen Basilio, who was seeking a second's license and assisting the boxer, accompanied DeJohn. Although Syracuse was well-represented by DeJohn, Moses Walker, also from "The Salt City," was knocked out in the first forty-five seconds of his preliminary by Arlington, Massachusetts, fighter Tom McNeeley.

Fighter of the Year

As the IBC crumbled and Madison Square Garden scrambled, the District Attorney's continued its investigation. Like any controversy, youth was blind. The hungry pugilists were out there; Garden management just had to find them. One such fighter was Emile Griffith, who just dominated the welterweights in the Golden Gloves. Given the opportunity, so Garden management believed, some new faces could revitalize the City Ring.

In 1958, the Garden welcomed Don Jordan, George Chuvalo and Doug Jones, but said good-bye to Joe Miceli. Speaking of Jones, he went 3–0 in the City Ring and continued to impress. But the City Ring shined thanks to Carlos Ortiz, who went 2–1, with a nice back-to-back sequence against Johnny Busso.[20]

1959

Turning a Blind Eye

Oregon fighter Denny Moyer, in his Garden debut on January 2, scored a ten-round split decision over veteran Gaspar Ortega. However, many of those who viewed the battle ringside saw it differently: an informal poll noted by the *New York Times* found a majority saw it for Ortega.[21] Which, for the most part, could have been attributed to many factors, until you note that Ortega had been a favorite until just hours before the battle when the odds swung to Moyer. It was the nineteen-year-old Oregon fighter's nineteenth consecutive victory. Following a NYSAC investigation, the objection was sustained.[22]

SUPREME COURT DECISION

On January 12, in Washington, D.C., the antitrust decree issued in 1957, by Federal District Judge Sylvestor J. Ryan of New York was affirmed by the United States Supreme Court. The case had been complex, as the Supreme Court held in 1955 that the Sherman Act covered professional boxing. The antitrust laws are applied to all professional sports except baseball.[23] To violators of the Sherman Act participating in the sport, this was a knockout punch, and was destined to change the face of boxing.

After the first Supreme Court decision, the case went to trial to see whether the defendants violated the Sherman Act. After all, you can't violate an act unless you are certain that a behavior fell underneath it. Judge Ryan determined that the two boxing clubs and their principals controlled all of the sport's championship bouts. Steps were immediately taken to dissolve the IBC with both Norris and Wirtz disposing of stock-the pair held over a forty percent interest. Francis J. Haezel was elected as president and treasurer of the Madison Square Garden Corporation on January 20. The Graham-Paige Corporation, headed by Irving M. Felt, purchased the forty percent share made available by the dissolution. On February 20, Harry Markson was named general manager of boxing at the first meeting of the Madison Square Garden Corporation's new board of directors.

MEANWHILE, BACK IN THE GARDEN

Bronx boxer Frankie Ryff captured a ten-round unanimous decision over California fighter Cisco Andrade in one of the finest boxing exhibitions seen in the Garden in many an evening. It happened on February 13. Ryff, under the control of former champion Barney Ross, glided across the ring like a hot knife through a stick of butter; Andrade was constantly caught off-balance and searching for his adversary. However, when Ryff did catch a punch it cost him: he encountered his customary eye cuts along with a bloody nose. Overall, it was a fine evening and a great way for everyone involved with the fight game to ease away from all the legal imbroglios.[24]

Gene Fullmer, the former middleweight champion, was back in the City Ring on February 20 taking on Detroit boxer Wilfie Greaves. And it was a much closer battle than many expected. Some were aware that Greaves had won thirteen consecutive fights, and after seeing him box, many knew why. He had an arsenal of solid jabs, complemented by a good right cross. And he was wise to avoid Fullmer's fight-ending punches. In proof that you can't judge a book by its cover: When the fight was over, Greaves didn't have a mark, while Fullmer had a cut above an eye and below his nose and thought he might have fractured his right hand. Despite the damage, or the lack thereof, Fullmer took the split decision.[25]

As the Garden bouts were struggling a bit, Markson recruited Teddy Brenner away from the St. Nicholas Arena to handle the matchmaking.[26] Brenner knew New York City boxing like most commuters knew the train schedule. He had worked wonders over at the Eastern Parkway Arena in Brooklyn under the umbrella of the New York Boxing Club, before heading to St. Nick's.

On a positive note, NYSAC agreed to a junior welterweight championship of twelve rounds between New York's Carlos Ortiz and Michigan's Kenny Lane to be held inside Madison Square Garden on Friday, June 12. The last such title match had been held back on April 29, 1946.[27] And on May 19, it was announced that the City Ring would be the site of the United States debut of British Empire middleweight champion Dick Tiger. The Nigerian national would draw Rory Calhoun on June 5, before losing to him in a Syracuse rematch on July 17.

Ingemar Johansson v. Floyd Patterson I

Floyd Patterson, the youngest man ever to win the heavyweight championship, became the youngest ever to lose it. It happened on June 26, inside Yankee Stadium. Ingemar Johansson dropped Patterson seven times on the way to a third-round knockout. For Patterson, who was a very private and self-conscious individual, the experience was humiliating. Having lost to Joey Maxim back in 1954 over at the Eastern Parkway Arena in front of more than 2,000 people was one thing, but to do it in front of more than 21,000, not to mention a television audience, was extremely hard to stomach.

Recently, a Cuban slant to Garden matches was working, so why not continue? In the ten-round Garden feature, on Friday, August 7, Gaspar Ortega met Cuban Benny Paret. Undefeated Cuban Florentino Fernández was originally scheduled but became ill, so Charley Scott was slated. But Scott couldn't get ready in time. Thus, Paret moved up from his supporting preliminary. When Ortega took the close split decision, both the crowd and Paret's corner were upset—Paret's manager Manuel Alfaro protested the verdict, but to no avail. In a ten-round undercard, an undefeated Emile Griffith (13–0) won a unanimous decision over Cuban Kid Fichique.

Doug Jones

How many fighters can say that eight out of their first ten professional fights were held inside Madison Square Garden? Not many, but Douglas David Jones was one. Born on February 27, 1937, in New York City, Jones, like many city adolescents, was trying to find himself. He discovered part of who, and what, he was in the very structured and disciplined environment of the United States Air Force, where he exhibited a passion for the sport of boxing. Leaving the Air Force in 1958, he took his ring interest with him. The six-foot heavyweight—his frame not completely filled out yet, but he was working on it—attracted interest with his boxing prowess, chiseled physique and movie-star looks.

On August 22, 1958, Jones found himself inside the hallowed walls of Madison Square Garden in his first professional fight. Picking up the victory over Jimmy McNair led to two more Garden opportunities and two more wins before the end of the year, over Vince Ferguson and Andre Tessier.

Doug Jones began 1959 inside Madison Square Garden again, and four of his next seven fights would be inside the City Ring. Undefeated in eleven professional fights, Jones looked like a contender by the end of 1959. It would now be up to his team to guide him into the championship mix.

COURTROOM BATTLES CONTINUE

After entering a not-guilty plea, Frankie Carbo, unofficial commissioner of boxing, was released on $100,000 bail. The underworld figure was caught in Haddon Township, New Jersey. Carbo faced a number of charges including conspiracy and acting as an undercover, or unlicensed, manager and matchmaker. All ten counts included in the indictment were misdemeanors. Carbo would face ten years in jail. But when you had a record of fifteen arrests, four for homicide, and a manslaughter conviction, what's ten years?

FORGOTTEN ROUNDS

On June 12, the junior welterweight championship, scheduled for twelve rounds, lasted only two. New York's Carlos Ortiz landed an enormous right-hand punch that dropped Kenny Lane just as the bell tolled for the end of the second term. The punch, which struck above Lane's eyes, opened up a huge cut. One look by the ringside physician ended the fight. Later, it was learned that both fighters had butted heads and that may have resulted in part of the damage.

On October 23, heavyweight Billy Hunter stopped New York fighter Tony Anthony at the 1:04 mark of the seventh round. Referee Arthur Mercante stopped the fight when Anthony became trapped in a corner and unable to defend himself.

In the semifinal of this feature, boxer Dick DiVeronica, who was managed by Carmen Basilio, took a unanimous ten-round decision over Tommy Tibbs. It was another consecutive victory for DiVeronica. Like Basilio, the fighter hailed from Canastota, New York.

To conclude, South African Willie Toweel, having been floored twice in the eighth round, managed to regain his composure and take a very close ten-round split decision from Philadelphia boxer Len Matthews. The November 20 Garden feature was Toweel's first American victory.

FIGHTER OF THE YEAR

From all accounts, and despite the turmoil that surrounded the venue for months, Madison Square Garden finished the year with promise. Which was good, considering that most of the major battles during the year—Davey Moore versus Hogan "Kid" Bassey (Los Angeles), Sonny Liston versus Cleveland Williams (Miami Beach), Joe Becerra versus Alphonse Halimi (Los Angeles), and Gene Fullmer versus Carmen Basilio (San Francisco)—were again held outside New York City. The only exception was Johansson versus Patterson, which was held at Yankee Stadium.

Some outstanding executives, and even a new majority owner, exhibited nothing but promise. The Graham-Paige Corporation had been gradually increasing its ownership of Madison Square Garden—they owned over eighty percent by year's end. In 1959, Madison Square Garden welcomed Emile Griffith and Dick Tiger, but said so long to Gene Fullmer. It was a year that thrust Swede Ingemar Johansson into the boxing spotlight. But Johansson would never fight in Madison Square Garden, so he would not shine the City Ring. For that, you had to turn to Doug Jones, who went 5–0 in the venue and exhibited tremendous boxing skills.[28]

11

A Cloud of Uncertainty, 1960–1962

> My father always told me that all businessmen were sons of bitches, but I never believed it till now.
> —John F. Kennedy

From the Vietnam War (1965–1975), the Civil Rights Movement (1954–1968), and JFK's assassination (1963), to the British Invasion (1964), counterculture (1964–1974) and Woodstock (1969) the 1960s represented, perhaps, the most consequential decade in U.S. history. It was a period of monumental social and political change, altering virtually every aspect of American life for future generations. And while the sport of boxing could have failed to engage, it did not. The emergence of a young boxer named Cassius Clay would be certain of that.

As the decade opened, the sport of boxing was once again under fire, this time by the Senate Antitrust Investigation, followed by New York State's Joint Legislative Committee on Boxing. If boxing wasn't going to clean out its closet, and "clean up its act," others were determined to do it for them or drive them out of business. Under what appeared to be an investigative microscope, boxing felt uncomfortable and looked west to Las Vegas.

1960

Reviving holiday fights kicked the year off on an unfamiliar note. Not since Henry Armstrong knocked out Enrico Venturi in six rounds back in 1936 had pugilists laced 'em up so gallantly inside the City Ring on New Year's Day. And they did it with style by presenting undefeated hub boxer Tom McNeeley, Jr., in a ten-round feature against Boise, Idaho, fighter George Logan. The stocky flaxen-haired boxer scored a fourth-round technical knockout over Logan, the ring doctor stopping the fight after the fourth session due to a pair of cuts over Logan's left eye.

The End of an Era—*Friday Night Fights*

Disappointed in recent years with both matchmaking for the event and its ratings, NBC felt it had little choice but to discontinue *Friday Night Fights*. The National Broadcasting Corporation also decided to withdraw from their partnership with Gillette due to the recent disclosures of underworld influence in the sport. (The contract between Gillette and NBC would expire in June; there was a ninety-day option on the contract.) Since 1944, Gillette had sponsored the fights. Harry Markson, who wasn't particularly thrilled when he found out, reiterated that the Garden's agreement was with the sponsor, and not with the network. To counter the economic impact on the sport, Markson would explore his options.

Later, on March 16, it was declared that the *Friday Night Fights* at the Garden would move to Saturday. The decision was a result of the Gillette Safety Razor Company and the American Broadcasting Company (ABC) signing a new sports programming agreement. So the fights' moving from NBC to ABC meant switching from Channel 4 to Channel 7, if you lived in New York.[1] The Garden had to juggle some events to accommodate the schedule, but they managed.[2]

Friday Night Fights came to an end on May 20.[3] The final card seen on television and heard on radio featured heavyweight Eddie Machen capturing a unanimous ten-round decision over Alex Miteff.

It was only a matter of time before Emile Griffith starred in a Friday night main event at the Garden, as well as his first television appearance. The charismatic Island fighter had shown that much promise. On Friday, February 11, Griffith met Gaspar "Indian" Ortega in a ten-round welterweight contest televised nationally by the National Broadcasting Company. The twenty-two-year-old Griffith enhanced his appeal by taking the split decision over Ortega. However, it wasn't a very decisive verdict, but one laced with confusion—it was announced incorrectly, then corrected.

Go West, Young Man

Before spring, Harry Markson, managing director of the Garden Boxing Club, confirmed that Don Jordan, welterweight champion, would defend his title, not in New York, but in Las Vegas, Nevada, on May 27. Part of the reason for the migration was the city's booming population: from 1950 until 1960, the population of Las Vegas increased by over 160%.[4] Another motivation was new construction: The Silver State Boxing Club believed the bout would be perfect for the modern Convention Center. Markson, aware of his television commitments, felt a location shift was appropriate at this stage of their Friday night programming—the contract was running out, so why not test a new venue? If Vegas marketing professionals could transform "gambling" into "gaming," just imagine what they could do for boxing.[5]

Senate Antitrust Investigation

On June 12, United States Senator Estes Kefauver confirmed that his committee of antitrust investigators was ready for their first round of their inquiry into the business dealings surrounding the sport of boxing. The board was interested in what, if any, connection the underworld might have to the sweet science. Boxer Jake LaMotta was called as the first witness.

LaMotta admitted that he had thrown his Madison Square Garden battle with Billy Fox. The event took place on November 14, 1947. He stated he was only "play-acting." The reason was simple. He wanted a title shot and this was the only way he could get one. LaMotta won the middleweight championship in 1949 from Marcel Cerdan. The fighter also claimed the title shot cost him $20,000, which was paid to Cerdan's manager.

In LaMotta's signed deposition, he claimed that he received an offer of $100,000 to throw the Fox fight. However, he confirmed that he did not take the money, but agreed to drop the fight just for the title shot. LaMotta stated he was offered, but declined, $100,000 to throw his Garden fight against Ohio fighter Tony Janiro. The former champion also admitted "carrying" a few opponents so as not to look too good. Because the statute of limitations had run out, LaMotta could not be prosecuted by the New York District Attorney for his testimony during a previous investigation.[6]

Former IBC secretary Truman K. Gibson, Jr., testified before the Senate subcommittee on December 5 in Washington, D.C., that the organization purchased Frankie Carbo's "goodwill" by making payments that amounted to about $40,000 to the underworld figure's wife (Viola Masters). The IBC, according to Gibson, was also paying large sums to Jack Kearns to counter Carbo's influence—the former manager of Jack Dempsey abhorred Carbo. The reason for the payments was to maintain the supply chain of pugilists to fulfill the Garden's need. Gibson also supplied the names of individuals believed to be associated with Carbo.

Carbo, at this time, was serving a two-year sentence for matchmaking without a New York State license, which for a man with his heinous past was like a child standing in the corner for not eating his spinach.

Those under "some degree of control" by Carbo, according to Gibson's testimony: Bernard Glickman (manager of Virgil Akins); John DeJohn and Joe Netro (managers of Carmen Basilio); Emil Shade and Angel Lopez (managers of Kid Gavilan); Joseph LaMotta (manager of Jake LaMotta); Anthony Ferrante (manager of Bud Smith); and Felix Bocchicchio (manager of Jersey Joe Walcott)

Mentioned as those "close to Carbo," according to Gibson's testimony: Frank "Blinky" Palermo (manager for Ike Williams and Johnny Saxton); Herman "Hymie the Mink" Wallman (manager of Johnny Bratton); Willie Ketchum (manager of Davey Moore); Ernie Braca (former manager of Sugar Ray Robinson), and many more.

On December 6, Herman "Hymie the Mink" Wallman testified before the Senatorial hearing and confirmed that Carbo assisted him in getting Garden bouts. Wallman's stable of fighters included Joe Baksi, Johnny Bratton, Caesar Brion, Alex Miteff and Randy Sandy. Wallman also linked Carbo to James D. Norris. Gibson testified on the same day that the IBC advanced money to many fighters and paid Frank "Blinky" Palermo, who was believed to be running Carbo's boxing empire, in absentia of Carbo.[7]

INSIDE THE RING

Benny Paret, the world welterweight champion, successfully defended his title by taking a unanimous fifteen-round decision over Buenos Aires boxer Federico Thompson on December 10. It was the boxer's first title defense and the same fighter he drew back in March. A crowd estimated at over 6,000 enjoyed the bout, both fighters having developed a strong following thanks to their City exposure.[8] Following his victory, Paret was likely to match with the winner of the Luis Rodriguez-Emile Griffith bout scheduled for December 17 inside the City Ring.

Undefeated (33–0, or 35–0 depending upon the source, with two no-contests) and making his New York debut, Luis Rodriguez, the prime contender for Paret's crown, was as confident as he was talented. But records meant little to Emile Griffith, as the New York welter took the ten-round split decision over the Cuban.

Forgotten Rounds

Welterweight Gaspar Ortega took a ten-round split decision over Honolulu's Stan Harrington on January 8 inside the City Ring. It was one of the most elaborate promotions in ages, as the Garden staff had flown in Harrington, his trainer and even the island's most prominent promoter Sad Sam Ichinose. A welcoming party even took place in the lobby of the United Nations building. Harrington had posted a record of 34–5–1 entering the battle. Also on the card were Emile Griffith, who took a ten-round unanimous verdict over Mexican Bobby Pena, and Doug Jones, who took a ten-round concordant judgment over Clarence Floyd.

Harlem's Johnny Jenkins took a six-round split decision over Tunney Hunsaker, a police chief from Fayetteville, West Virginia, on February 5. It was Hunsaker's first and only appearance in Madison Square Garden. Despite an unimpressive career, the boxer would greet immortality on October 29, by facing Cassius Clay in Louisville, Kentucky. For Clay, the gold medal Olympian, it was his first professional bout.

Philadelphia lightweight Len Matthews, who was a solid puncher, took a ten-round split decision over Algerian-born Lahouari Godih on February 19. Matthews, with a powerful overhand right, floored Godih in the seventh round. The Algerian, however, was a prolific puncher and battled his way back into the fight.

Garden boxing fans were more than happy to welcome Benny Paret back to the City Ring on August 16. Even though it wasn't a welterweight title defense, the scheduled ten-rounder was against a popular adversary in Denny Moyer. The latter rallied in the final rounds to take the split decision.

On November 20, middleweight Gene "Ace" Armstrong, twenty-eight years old and father of three, took a ten-round unanimous decision over Henry Hank, twenty-five years old and father of six, in the Saturday Garden feature. The event put a whole new spin on the old Gans line of "bringing home the bacon."

Finally, Syracuse heavyweight Mike DeJohn dropped Detroit boxer Billy Hunter at the 2:51 mark of the ninth round to win their scheduled ten-round confrontation on November 26. Possessing a memorable crimson mask for much of the encounter, DeJohn took six stitches in his left eyelid after the fight.

Fighter of the Year

Once again, many good fights were conducted outside of the New York City area. Heavyweight Floyd Patterson's fifth-round knockout of Ingemar Johansson, on June 20 at the Polo Grounds, was no doubt the most memorable city battle. Patterson was rocked early in the second round, but came on in the fifth to drop Johansson at the 1:51 mark. With the victory, Patterson became the first former world heavyweight champion to regain the title. Eight previous champions had tried and failed.[9]

Benny Paret battled five times and posted a record of 3–1–1 between the City Ring ropes. But Emile Griffith fought seven times and won every battle. The New York boxer fought back-to-back-to-back, followed later by four consecutive duels and shined the City Ring with his boxing proficiency.[10]

1961

It took considerable time, but technology finally found a home inside Madison Square Garden—closed circuit television (CCTV) technology, that is.[11] Its inauguration was during the third championship fight between Floyd Patterson and Ingemar Johansson held in Miami Beach on Monday, March 13. A four-sided screen that corresponded to the four sides of the Garden ring was initially sought, but management later opted for a single screen measuring thirty by forty feet that was installed on the Ninth Avenue end of the venue. Just the thought of watching the televised battle inside Madison Square Garden had many excited.

In another first, a boxer who had fought inside the City Ring for the first time back in 1930, or a period of exactly thirty-one years earlier, reentered the same venue to once again fight inside its ring on January 24. Former heavyweight boxing champion Primo Carnera, turned barnstorming wrestler, teamed with Bruno Sammartino in a tag team event that drew nearly 15,000 Garden spectators.

And in perhaps another first: middleweights Joey Archer and Don Fullmer, who were matched inside the City Ring on February 4, trained in adjoining rings inside the Eighth Avenue Gymnasium. Those who had been around the sport for years were hard-pressed to recall a similar situation. Archer took the featured ten-rounder by a majority decision. Don Fullmer, the twenty-one-year-old brother of Gene, the recognized middleweight champion, fell short of expectations.

ARCHIE'S LAST TITLE DEFENSE

Nobody ever asked Archie Moore how old he was because those who knew him, or knew of him, knew better; consequently, to do so would prompt a countenance as forbidding as an executioner's. Because he failed to defend his NBA light-heavyweight championship the previous year, Moore was stripped of the title, which was later won by Harold Johnson. But NYSAC still recognized the "Old Mongoose," as did the state of Massachusetts and the folks of Europe, as champion.[12]

Moore was scheduled to rematch against Italian Giulio Rinaldi inside the City Ring on June 10.[13] And the Garden's promotional caravan was pulling out all the stops for his light heavyweight defense. They went so far as to pitch a ring in the parking lot of Leone's Ristorante so that the Italian had all the comforts of home. To complete the stereotypical portrait, they even had Rinaldi, the Italian light-heavyweight champion, briefly occupy the owner's apartment—no word on what the fighter thought of the chicken cacciatore.

All the marketing worked: a crowd of more than 9,500 turned out to witness Archie Moore victorious in a united fifteen-round decision. Unfortunately, the promotion was more exciting than the fight. There were no knockdowns, no fight-ending wallops, or even a dash of Italian trash talk. It was a paradigm for the classic fisticuffs yawner. Moore exhibited little punching power or efficiency and Rinaldi simply couldn't hit. In the end, the Italian blamed his loss on the climate and a blister. Hey, at least it wasn't Leone's marinara sauce.

Archie Moore would be stripped of his light-heavyweight title by NYSAC, on February 9, 1962, for his failure to defend it.

A New Garden—4 Pennsylvania Plaza

They had talked about it for years, but it finally looked like a new Madison Square Garden would be built atop Penn Station. The "House That Tex Rickard Built," on Eighth Avenue between 49th and 50th, was moving down the street between West 31st and West 33rd Street. The complex sitting above the sub-level railroad would include a hotel and a thirty-four-story office complex in addition to two arenas, one that sat 25,000 and a smaller 4,000-seat theater.[14]

In the meantime, Cuban Benny Paret took a fifteen-round split decision over Emile Griffith on Saturday, August 30, to regain the world welterweight championship. A Garden crowd of more than 6,000 turned out to watch the dueling welters who didn't particularly care for one another. A post-fight Paret certainly didn't look victorious: both his eyes were swollen, his face was cut and his mouth bloodied. In contrast, Griffith was unmarked. Not surprisingly, Griffith's manager Gil Clancy believed his fighter was a victim of collusion.

Forgotten Rounds

It was dull, but it was a Fullmer, inside a ring, on a Saturday night. West Jordan's Don Fullmer took a unanimous ten-rounds decision over Buffalo boxer Rocky Fumerelle on July 15. The Utah fighter worked his solid combinations, held Fumerelle at bay with his left jab, and even dropped the Buffalo pugilist in the third term.

Buenas Aires boxer Jorge Fernandez took a ten-round unanimous verdict over Cuban Isaac Logart on August 19. The victory avenged a ninth-round knockout suffered by Fernandez three years earlier, which had been the only knockout of his career; the South American claimed he had been fouled. It was a good battle, despite having no knockdowns. For Saturday night boxing fans, it was rather nostalgic as the two pugilists were the same fighters used to introduce ring announcer Don Dunphy to television audiences during the *Fight of the Week*.

Undefeated heavyweight Doug Jones continued to impress as he knocked out Philadelphia pugilist Von Clay at the 2:21 point of the tenth and final round. The victory, on August 26, marked the third time Jones had beaten Clay, and the first time both had appeared in a feature event.

Lastly, on November 18, Carlos Ortiz survived a two-count knockdown in the ninth round to score a unanimous decision over Bronx boxer Paolo Rosi in a ten-round lightweight feature. Both boxers fought hard, but Rosi appeared to have fought himself out in the ninth. Ortiz then came out strong and won the final round.

Fighter of the Year

So where were the great fights, you ask? Floyd Patterson successfully defended his heavy crown twice (Miami, then Toronto); lightweight champ Joe Brown beat Dave Charnley (London); Brazilian fighter Eder Jofre knocked out bantam Piero Rollo (South America); and Emile Griffith knocked out Benny Paret (Miami Beach). It was clear that the Golden Age of Flying (air travel) made international promotion less intimidating.

NBA light heavyweight champion Harold Johnson had an outstanding year, posting a 4–0 record, but never fought in New York. Carmen Basilio fought for the last time in the

City Ring, while Don Fullmer made his debut. It's hard to choose a fighter who shined the City Ring the most in 1961, but you have to thank the "Old Mongoose" for defending his title between the ropes one last time.

1962

Mexican welter Gaspar Ortega was a prolific fighter, and a matchmaker's dream because he just wanted to do his job. Soft-spoken in his native tongue, the handsome pugilist dressed to the nines on a regular basis. Ortega was scheduled to meet Ralph Dupas in a ten-rounder inside the City Ring on January 6, but Charley Scott had been substituted.[15] The Philadelphia fighter planned to use his speed and precision combinations to defeat his adversary and his strategy proved effective, as Scott took the unanimous decision; Ortega seemed to tire after the ninth term. Action-packed, despite no knockdowns, the event was a strong beginning to a new year.[16]

Cassius Clay's City Ring Debut

Cleveland Williams was scheduled to meet Eddie Machen on Saturday, February 10, in a ten-round feature event at Madison Square Garden. But when it was clear that it wasn't going to happen, Teddy Brenner scrambled for alternatives. Sonny Banks had won ten of his last dozen fights, nine of them by knockout, so he became an immediate option. As for his opponent, well, there was that kid from Louisville, the 1960 Olympian who had scored seven knockouts in his first ten fights. As loquacious as a used-car salesman, he was a smooth talker with an attitude to match. But could his performance live up to his narcissism? It was a gamble and Brenner took it.

Mississippi-born Sonny Banks, only a year older than his cocky opponent Cassius Marcellus Clay, wasn't impressed by his opponent's size—Clay stood six feet, two and one half inches—his skills, or his prophecy. Nevertheless, that would soon change.

Precisely as predicted by the demonstrative Louisville boxer, Clay disposed of Banks in the fourth round of their scheduled ten-round Garden affair. Prognostication was soon to become the fighter's hallmark. During a horrible beating, Banks was saved by the bell in the third and could not recover. Referee Ruby Goldstein stopped the fight at the 0:26 mark of the term.

Clay, having been dropped in the opening round, floored Banks in the second round. Despite his strong performance, Clay became a target for opprobrium—ribbed by the crowd for his attitude, and for his antiseptic white shoes. His vanity bordered on insulting, and his behavior drew comparisons to even Jack Johnson. Never lost for words or actions, the flamboyant victor charted a course toward the heavyweight championship.

Robinson's Final Garden Bow

Recovering from Clay's City Ring inauguration, Garden sports fans watched the Knicks' home winning streak end at five, got excited about the thought of Rod Gilbert joining the New York Rangers, and found it hard to ignore the 86th Westminster Kennel Show. Few, if any, gave much thought to Saturday night's Garden meeting between Portland, Oregon's used-car dealer Denny Moyer and the legendary Sugar Ray Robinson. Moyer, who had lost a tenrounder to Robinson on October 21, respected the skills of his antagonist, but wasn't intimidated by him.[17] As for Robinson, his Garden appearance was just another fight, and Moyer was just another pug garnishing his reputation by boxing the best fighter pound-for-pound.

In New York, you turned your television dial to Channel 7 (ABC) for the televised fights that began at 10 P.M. Even if the fight didn't come in perfectly—often it was simply a matter of adjusting the "rabbit ears" (antenna)—everyone knew they had the correct channel once they heard the distinctive voice of Don Dunphy. The fight began with the customary introductions; on hand were boxing celebrities Barney Ross and Willie Pep.

The fight remained close the first four rounds, with Moyer progressively pressing Robinson. The emeritus middleweight champion was stuck in a clockwise motion that Moyer just couldn't cut off. To cries of "Come on, Denny," Moyer persevered and took some solid punches from Robinson; his nose bled from Round One forward, but it failed to extinguish any of his actions. Robinson, whose mother was ringside, provided the usual choreographed performance with first-class head feints and octopus clinches. His opponent was careful not to make mistakes, as Robinson was instinctive with his counters that could instantly end a fight. By the eighth term, the former champion knew he was behind and landed a nice left hook to Moyer's face. Was it enough? He wasn't certain. Both fighters came on strong in the tenth, with Robinson enduring more damage than he transmitted.

Over 7,500 Garden fans were in attendance as Denny Moyer took the ten-round unanimous decision. A strong left hand, modified a bit to compensate for his reach, was Moyer's winning punch. Robinson, a 2–1 favorite entering the fight, handled the loss with dignity and grace. Congratulating his opponent following the announcement, he turned and headed back to his corner, and not a soul in the building believed it was for the final time. Reviews of the fight noted a fatigued and aging Robinson who was only a shadow of his former self. Yet a shadow of Robinson was still better than most.[18]

Tragedy Besets the Ring— Benny Paret v. Emile Griffith III

On February 27, Benny Paret, world welterweight champion, penned his name to a contract to fight Emile Griffith inside the City Ring. Griffith's camp was furious over the officiating in their fighter's last loss to Paret, so they presented NYSAC with a list of suitable ring officials. Actions such as this can indeed be genuine, or psychological, and Gil Clancy, Griffith's trainer, was a master at both. A rounds system was used by the referee and two judges to score the fight, along with a supplemental point system used to break draws— the winner of each round gets one to four points, the loser none. Few believed the fight would be anything short of an all-out conflict, but nobody would have ever predicted the ending.

On Saturday, March 24, Emile Griffith avenged his loss to Benny Paret to regain the world welterweight championship. The Cuban was knocked unconscious at the 2:09 mark of the twelfth round of their scheduled fifteen-round battle. Failing to respond, Paret was taken by ambulance to Roosevelt Hospital in serious condition and underwent brain surgery on the morning of March 25. Paret was given the last rites of the Catholic Church before he even left Madison Square Garden. The situation appeared grave.

The winning assault by Griffith consisted of multiple flurries—by some counts as many as twenty-five punches were thrown—that began with two sharp right uppercuts to Paret's chin. A City Ring corner post supported Paret while he endured the beating. When referee Ruby Goldstein finally pulled Griffith away, Paret slid slowly down the ropes and onto the canvas. He lay on his back unresponsive while frantic attempts were made to revive him. In the sixth round, Paret had dropped his antagonist to an eight count. Yet the bell saved Griffith, who eventually was able to rebound in the scoring. It was no secret that Griffith abhorred his opponent—he was called a derogatory name during the weigh-in that made him very upset.[19] Be that as it may, no boxer climbs into a ring hoping to permanently injure his opposition.

Paret showed a slight improvement on March 27, when he opened his eyes, but slipped back into a deep coma. Three days later, his mother arrived from Cuba to attend a vigil at her son's bedside. On Monday, April 2, Benny "Kid" Paret died at 1:55 A.M. The District Attorney immediately mounted an accelerated investigation. Referee Ruby Goldstein, who was criticized for not stopping the fight, was absolved by NYSAC.

The New York State Joint Legislative Committee on Boxing (NYSJLCOB)

Frank "Blinky" Palermo was linked to heavyweight champion Sonny Liston through one of the fighter's former sparring partners. It was an association the heavyweight boxer (who had captured the crown with a first-round knockout of Floyd Patterson) could have done without. This information was disclosed to the public by the New York State Joint Legislative Committee on Boxing (NYSJLCOB); the board was established on April 6, following the tragic death of Benny Paret. Palermo, who was currently free on bail, was appealing a fifteen-year prison sentence for conspiracy and extortion. He, along with Frankie Carbo, had been convicted on May 30, 1961, for pressuring Don Jordan, the former welterweight champion, to see boxing from a different point of view. Carbo was currently a resident of the island of Alcatraz, where he was serving a twenty-five-year sentence. NYSAC, as most were aware, had refused Liston a boxing license due to his past criminal record, which included prison terms for robbery and assault, not to mention ties to the underworld: the Senate subcommittee, only two years earlier, had tied Liston to both Carbo and Palermo. NYSJLCOB was considering whether or not to outlaw boxing in the state. Curious about the heavyweight's relationship to certain individuals, the board sought to question him. As for Liston, he just simply refused to testify; he had no New York license, so the state had no jurisdiction.

Forgotten Rounds

Two very good fighters who flew below the radar screen were hard-hitting Cuban Luis Rodriguez and Panamanian Luis Frederico Thompson. Rodriguez, at twenty-four years of age, put on a tireless display to take a ten-round unanimous decision over Thompson on Saturday, January 27. Rodriguez was not only quick, but countered extremely well; if he incurred too much damage at close range, he knew enough to pull back and alter his artillery.

On Saturday, March 3, Brooklyn's Roland Kellem took a six-round decision over neighbor Vernon Lynch. Kellem exerted a body campaign early, while enduring Lynch's facial assault. The crowd, primarily Brooklynites, loved the action and thrilled when Kellem turned his attention to headhunting in the fourth round. The fight was on the Rosi-Alvarez undercard.

On Saturday, June 9, welter Ted Wright defeated Denny Moyer in a ten-round split decision. It had only been two weeks, on May 26, since Wright defeated Moyer's older brother Phil in a unanimous Garden decision. Denny, with a record of 31–7–0, would defeat Wright by a united decision in a rematch on July 7. The Moyer boys could be tough, damn tough.

Luis Rodriguez won his seventh fight in a row with a technical knockout of Gene "Ace" Armstrong—the fight was stopped at the 2:09 mark of the eighth round. The June 30 bout was the feature event on Saturday's television broadcast. Rodriguez, who continued to impress by running his record to over forty wins and only two losses (Emile Griffith and Curtis Cokes), was a force in the welterweight division.

On Saturday, August 4, Private First Class Wilbert "Sketter" McClure scored a uniform ten-round decision over Argentine Farid Salim. For McClure, also a 1960 Olympic light middleweight, it was his tenth professional victory and his first main event at the Garden.

Doug Jones scored an eighth-round technical knockout over Bob Foster, who was substituting for Zora Foley, on Saturday, October 20. The heavyweight bout, which was scheduled for ten rounds, was stopped at the 0:23 mark of the eighth term. Jones, who outweighed his opponent by eight pounds, dropped Foster for a nine count in the very first round.

In a six-rounder on the undercard, New Yorker Frank Narvaez easily defeated Los Angeles fighter Neto Villareal. Many ringside were impressed with the skills exhibited by the New York lightweight in his sixth appearance in the City Ring.

In conclusion, middleweight Rubin "Hurricane" Carter needed only 69 seconds to knock out—no, flatten—Florentino Fernández on October 27. The Cuban boxer never even realized what hit him, as Carter unloaded a precision left directly to his chin.

Fighter of the Year

The bantams had a new fixture, Brazilian Éder Jofre, who unified the title. There was a Tiger in the middleweight division, Dick Tiger, that is, who went 3–0 with victories over Henry Hank and Gene Fullmer, the latter in a title bout. And then there was Cassius Clay. There was nothing to say about the fighter that he hadn't already said himself.[20]

The Graham-Paige Corporation, a name that dated back to 1909, changed its name to the Madison Square Garden Corporation in March, to better reflect its interests. They also proposed a new home over Penn Station—like all previous Garden proposals, it was met with cynicism.[21]

Emile Griffith, Doug Jones and Luis Rodriguez posted 2–0 records inside the City Ring. But Rubin "Hurricane" Carter was 3–1. While it's tempting to say Carter shined the City Ring more than anyone in 1962, you have to acknowledge Robinson. The middleweight master, albeit still years from retirement, chose the City Ring as his final stop in New York City.

12

"I Must Be the Greatest," 1963–1967

> Never doubt that a small group of thoughtful, committed individuals can change the world.
> —Margaret Mead

While a bit of uncertainty surrounded the sport during the first few years of the decade, it would begin to redefine itself in the years that followed.

1963

President Kennedy's assassination in Dallas, Texas, on November 22 shocked the nation, Wall Street watched as the Dow Jones Industrial Average dropped 21 points in 30 minutes on the news, and Broadway suffered one of its worst seasons in recent memory. Some believed that these actions were a prelude to a turbulent decade, and they were correct.

Following the tragic death of Benny "Kid" Paret, boxing needed a distraction, and he came at the perfect time. The new apostle was a twenty-one-year-old heavyweight named Cassius Clay, who, like every zealous pug his age, was pompously counting the days to his coronation. Granted, he was an Olympian, which allowed him a degree of braggadocio, but he still had to deliver. While the "Louisville Lip" had the sincerity of a streetwalker, to say nothing of a mouth like a cab driver, he also brought the sharpest skills to the fight game since Ray Robinson. Dancing to a unique cadence, Clay was a marvel in the ring. His punches were fluid, powerful and accurate. Despite the cocky attitude, he understood that he still had to prove himself—a process that would take time—and everybody, as it would prove, was waiting.

POETRY IN MOTION

Cassius Marcellus Clay swaggered into the Bitter End, a Greenwich Village coffeehouse, not to fight, but to read poetry on March 7. (Hey, this was the Sixties.) The thirty-six-line metrical composition or prediction was penned by his favorite bard: himself. The poem was clear: Clay would defeat native New Yorker Doug Jones inside Madison Square Garden the following Wednesday (March 13), in the sixth round. The publicity stunt or marketing extravaganza worked, as 18,000 seats were sold for the event. It was the very first sellout before the day of the fight in the Garden's thirty-eight-year history; the last "day of the fight sellout" happened six years earlier (Fullmer versus Robinson). Standing-room-only tickets quickly disappeared at $4 a clip, and scalpers were grabbing $200 a pair for ringside.

Clay, who brought a record of 17–0 into the ring on March 13, wanted a crack at Sonny Liston as soon as possible. But the highly ranked Doug Jones, with a record of 21–3–1, also wanted a shot at the champion.[1] Clay, who showed up at the weigh-in with his mouth taped shut, tipped the scales at 202½ pounds, while Jones registered at 188.

Although Clay's distance prediction didn't hold, he managed to defeat his antagonist by a unanimous ten-round verdict. The crowd was none too happy, as cries of "fix" rang out following the clash. Jones took command immediately and even staggered Clay in the very first round with a right that sent the fighter against the ropes—the action provoked Clay to clinch for dear life. By the seventh round it was clear that the Louisville fighter was behind. He needed to rally to grab the fight, and he did—no knockdowns occurred and neither fighter was cut. As for what's next for the undefeated Clay, he believed, a bit of bear (Sonny Liston) hunting was in order.[2]

Joey Archer

Joey Archer was born in the Bronx on February 11, 1938. Growing to the height of five feet ten inches tall, the middleweight had an impressive reach of seventy-three inches. He began fighting as a teenager and turned pro on November 8, 1956, beating tomato can Danny Jones at Sunnyside Gardens in Queens for his first victory. A few weeks later, Archer then repeated the event inside Madison Square Garden during his City Ring debut.

Joey's brother Jimmy, three years older, was also a professional boxer—he won the 1955 *New York Daily News* Golden Gloves 147-pound Open Championship. Having also turned pro that same year, Jimmy was still fighting out of New York in 1959. And while both brothers held victories inside the City Ring by that point, Jimmy's career was struggling—he would quit the sport the following year.

In October 1960, Joey Archer had a boxing record of 30–0, albeit over substandard competition. Yet he was uncertain of his future. In his lone fight of 1961, he grabbed a ten-round Garden victory over middleweight contender Don Fullmer. Following an extended layoff, Joey was back in Madison Square Garden on June 23, 1962. It cost him, however, as he lost a split decision to Puerto Rican fighter Jose Gonzalez. Archer was rusty and it showed. Finishing the previous year with a career record of 32–1, he needed to rededicate himself to the sport.

On Saturday, May 18, a revitalized Joey Archer, 2–0 on the year, took a solid ten-round decision over Argentina antagonist Victor Zalazar in New York. Archer was battling at 161 pounds, and his punches were swift and accurate. He would finish the year 5–0.

As a result of the safety findings by the New York State Joint Legislative Committee and NYSAC, four ring ropes would be used for every bout, and the four-rounders were cut to two-minute terms using only ten-ounce gloves. The actions were applauded by participants and seen as a step toward saving the sport, rather than discontinuing it.

El Feo

By 1960, an undefeated Luis Manuel Rodriguez—thanks to many, especially his manager Angelo Dundee—had refined his skills to a level where he was a serious contender for the welter crown.³ Posting nine consecutive wins, he faced one more hurdle: Emile Griffith, a fighter so exceptional that he kept Rodriguez out of the foreground of the welter picture. On December 17, in the duo's first meeting, the Virgin Islands' fighter took a split decision by a slim margin over Rodriguez.

Rodriguez would post a record of 7–1 in 1961, followed by 7–0 in 1962. On March 21, 1963, Rodriguez took a record of 51–2–0 into Dodger Stadium in Los Angeles, and grabbed a fifteen-round united verdict over Emile Griffith to capture both the WBC and WBA welterweight titles. It was the pair's second meeting and another extremely close battle. The victory was dampened, however, by Davey Moore's tragic loss of life and the fact that it was not nationally televised.[4]

A rubber match was now as certain as sunrise. Griffith, who was seeking the 147-pound title for the third time, got his wish on June 8 inside Madison Square Garden: it was another narrow fifteen-round split decision over Rodriguez. Over 8,000 fans watched, but most, including many of those sitting ringside, did not agree with the verdict. At no time did either fighter have a distinct advantage, as it was that close.

What Dreams May Come

Ever since Billy Bello was a kid—he was born on December 6, 1942, in Bay Shore, New York—he dreamt about battling between the ropes in Madison Square Garden. Not against just any opponent, but a City Ring fixture like Gaspar Ortega. The twenty-year-old would finally get his chance on July 7, and indeed it would be against the imposing Mexicali Indian. A gentleman outside a ring, but a fierce competitor in one, Ortega wasn't intimidated by any fighter, nor would he bow to an antagonist's dreams—the Bay Shore youth could dismiss any thought of winning. Even if Bello understood the challenge he faced, he didn't accept it. The youngster was convinced he was a hitter and could overpower Ortega. He supported the belief by starting his career with five knockouts.

After dropping out of high school, Bello had taken odd jobs to make ends meet. It wasn't until April 10, 1961, when he knocked out Miguel Martinez inside St. Nicholas Arena, that he felt he had finally found a worthy occupation. His record, he believed, spoke for itself and for the Garden program that aided his development.[5] A victory over Gaspar Ortega on national television, in a Garden feature, would thrust him into the spotlight—it would be a dream come true.

Ortega took it to Bello early on, staying out of range and accumulating damage: Bello's nose bled in the first and his eye was cut in the third. As the rounds counted off, the veteran became fatigued in the later sessions, and catnapped to clinches. Contrary to what Bello believed, he didn't have the power to put away his ring adversary. The split decision was close, but it went to Ortega by a round.

For Bello, now 17–6–1, it was a bitter loss that was magnified unfairly by the press. He was treated as if he had won the lottery but forgot to surrender the ticket. Many of Bello's mistakes were due to inexperience; Ortega had over one hundred professional fights and by this point in his career wasn't prone to error. Having dazed Ortega with a left to the chin in the ninth, and even opening a cut on the Indian, Bello just couldn't finish him. He didn't have it. A single punch from immortality, or so he thought, it would be a scenario that he would never forget.

Fourteen days later, Billy Bello was found lifeless in the fifth-floor hallway of a Bronx tenement. Near his body were envelopes that contained powdered narcotics, and an examination revealed needle marks on his left forearm. Only days removed from Madison Square Garden, many wondered, how something like this could happen? Bello, who had been living with his mother at 2115 Washington Avenue, appeared like just another drunk in the hallway. At least that was what the tenants of the building believed—a few passed him hours before his body was discovered.[6] Bello had lost a decision to narcotics.

The 1960s lowered the barrier to illegal drug use. From middle-class Americans smoking marijuana to kids in ghettos pushing heroin, the counterculture was vindicated through its lifestyle and even supported by educators, such as Timothy Leary, a Harvard professor, who urged the world to try LSD. Even professional athletics, considered by some to be the last bastion of male privilege, could not escape its outreach.

Staying Home on a Friday Night

If boxing fans couldn't catch the action live at the Garden, then why not stay home on a Friday night? Depending upon your television set, eight stations were typically available to those living in New York City: 2–WCBS-TV; 4–WNBC-TV; 5–WNEW-TV; 7–WABC-TV; 9–WOR-TV; 11–WPIX-TV; 13–WNDT-TV; and 31–WNYC-TV. Most network broadcasts, and nearly all local programming, continued to be in black-and-white.[7] It was after the mid–1960s that color sets started selling in large numbers.[8]

On a typical Friday evening, home programming really began with the news, which followed dinner for most families. On the night of Friday, October 18, 1963, many families began their evening with *Route 66*, which started at 8:30 P.M. on Channel 2. The program followed two young men (Martin Milner as Todd Stiles and Glenn Corbett as Lincoln Chase) traversing the United States in a Chevrolet Corvette convertible, and the events and consequences surrounding their journeys. Once that program ended, it was only a half-hour until boxing, so many just stayed on Channel 2 to catch *The Twilight Zone*, an American science fiction, fantasy, psychological, and supernatural horror anthology television series created by Rod Serling, which ran for five seasons on CBS from 1959 to 1964.

After the thirty-minute show, it was time to turn the dial to boxing on Channel 7. On this night it was Luis Rodriguez versus Wilbert "Skeeter" McClure. The former dropped the latter to a count of three on his way to a unanimous ten-round decision. It was the first Friday night boxing event in the Garden in three years and proved entertaining to the 4,500 fans in attendance.[9]

On December 23, it was reported that the American Broadcasting Company and the Gillette Safety Razor Corporation had decided to discontinue their boxing television broadcasts.[10] Sponsoring a prizefight was cost prohibitive.

Breaking Ground

On Monday, October 28, demolition crews began resurfacing Pennsylvania Station—the eclectic American style of what was, would soon be no longer. As officials watched, six eagles, weighing 5,700 pounds each, were removed from their roosts above the entrance to the station. The flock had been there since 1910. The new Madison Square Garden was expected to take three years. Fortunately, rail travel continued as scheduled, at least for most

Forgotten Rounds

In one of those rare matches that kept Garden spectators entranced, Paterson, New Jersey, pugilist Rubin "Hurricane" Carter took a razor-close ten-round majority decision over Philadelphia boxer George Benton on May 25. The latter entered the battle a streak of nine consecutive victories. But Carter was an unremitting adversary.

On July 13, middleweight Joey Archer took a ten-round unanimous decision over Argentina fighter Farid Salim. The bout was a bit dull at first—one of those "I think I'll grab a quick cigarette before this fight gets too far along" battles. In the second round, following orders by referee Arthur Mercante to engage, which was an embarrassment, both fighters got serious. Archer suffered a cut above the left eye. The ring magicians in his corner—Whitey Bimstein and Freddie Brown, who saw more cuts than a butcher shop—somehow managed to close the gash long enough to get Archer the decision. It wasn't until a post-fight damage assessment revealed that the injury required fourteen stitches to close that people understood just how fierce the battle had raged.

In an outstanding eight-round semifinal, on the Stable versus Hayward card of August 3, Buffalo lightweight Tony La Barbara slugged his way to a unanimous decision over Bronx boxer Angelo Soto. Both fighters brawled during the first four rounds, trading punches at close quarters. But as Soto began to fade, La Barbara took command with his left jab and swift combinations. In the final round, they fought fast and furious with neither fighter hearing the gong; they had to be separated by their seconds.

Lastly, Joey Archer, who was on the verge of destruction from the third round until the fifth, and again in the seventh, slugged his way back to take a hard-fought ten-round split decision over middleweight Rubin "Hurricane" Carter. Although there was no major gore or knockdowns, a crowd of more than 8,500 seemed to enjoy every exchange. The fight, held on October 25, was not televised.

Fighter of the Year

In retrospect, Sonny Liston's second destruction of Floyd Patterson—the rematch lasted four seconds longer than their first meeting—brought him much of the sport's attention. He was the first ever to win the heavyweight title with a first-round knockout, and it was equally impressive when he retained it in the same fashion.

Madison Square Garden bid farewell to Gaspar Ortega, but still had its fair share of winners in 1963: Ernie Terrell went 2-0, Luis Rodriguez was 1-1 and Rubin Carter compiled a record of 2-2. Nonetheless, nobody put a gloss on the City Ring in 1963 better than Joey Archer, who went 5-0.[12]

1964

On February 25, 1964, in Miami Beach, Cassius Clay turned boxing inside out. He defeated Sonny Liston, the world heavyweight champion, despite being a 7 to 1 underdog.

Slicing Liston's eye in the third, then surviving a tactical assault on his own vision—a burning substance found its way into his eyes—Clay poured out his anger in the sixth term. Liston, whose frustration had hit the boiling point, quit on his stool. The historic event was promoted by Dundee-MacDonald Enterprises, Incorporated.

"Chegüi"

Born on May 3, 1936, in Ponce, Puerto Rico, José "Chegüi" Torres joined the United States Army in 1953, just as the Korean conflict was drawing to a close. As the government of Puerto Rico had been volatile, many youths, including Torres, were seeking a bit of stability in their lives. It was while in the Army that he learned to box, and box well. He captured the light-middleweight silver medal at the 1956 Melbourne Olympics, losing to the indomitable László Papp of Hungary in the final.

Hoping to capitalize on his Olympic success, Torres made what he considered to be an obvious decision. He headed to New York. Hooking up with renowned trainer Cus D'Amato, professor of "peek-a-boo" style boxing, Torres trained at the Empire Sporting Club. D'Amato, who had his hands full with Floyd Patterson, turned the youngster toward the Golden Gloves. In 1958, Torres won the national AAU title at 165 pounds and the Intercity Golden Gloves title at 160 pounds. If Torres did one thing well, it was listening. And the gospel according to Cus was to observe and learn from those who had gone before you. Standing five foot ten inches, Torres found the style a bit awkward at first, but gradually conformed to it.

A Puerto Rican boxer and Renaissance man, José "Chegüi" Torres (1936–2009) won a silver medal in the junior middleweight division at the 1956 Olympics in Melbourne. In 1965, he defeated Willie Pastrano to win the WBC, WBA and lineal light heavyweight championships.

Torres took his professional debut with a first-round knockout of tomato can Gene Hamilton at the Eastern Parkway Arena in Brooklyn, New York, on May 24, 1958. After three more quick victories at the same venue, D'Amato put Torres on the Patterson v. Harris card out in Los Angeles on August 18, 1958. Knocking out Benny Doyle in the first round was a confidence builder and made for a nice night for the veteran trainer, who also watched Patterson knock out Harris in the twelfth round. Entering 1963, Torres was 26–0–1. His very first loss came at the hands of Cuban Florentino Fernández, who would be the only professional boxer ever to knock him out. By the end of 1964, Torres had added eight more victories and one loss to his record, placing him in line for a title shot.

Ringo in the Ring

Not a lot of professional fighters begin their career in Madison Square Garden, but Oscar "Ringo" Bonavena did on January 3, 1964. Defeating tomato can Lou Hicks, the boxer was on his way to winning his first eight fights—five of them taking place in the City Ring, the other three at Sunnyside Garden. Born on September 25, 1942, in Parque Patricios, Buenos Aires, Argentina, Bonavena began his early career in New York State under the management of Marvin Goldberg. A rugged, wild-swinging puncher, he was nicknamed "Ringo" because of his Beatles haircut.

Fighter of the Year

Boxing had a new centerpiece in Cassius Clay, but the skilled young heavyweight didn't find his way into Madison Square Garden during the year.

Of the year's notable Garden performances: José Torres went 3–0, Joey Archer went 2–0, as did Ernie Terrell and Chuck Wepner. But the boxer who added the greatest luster to the ring was Oscar Bonavena, who went 5–0, which included his first professional fight and four consecutive ring appearances.

1965

Sold Out

Word hit the press on Friday, January 29, that the battle between heavyweights George Chuvalo and Floyd Patterson was a sellout. It was a terrific way to begin the year, not only for Madison Square Garden, but for the sport of boxing. The match was scheduled for twelve rounds on February 1, and a crowd of more than 18,000 was expected. The Garden, as many recalled, hadn't seen capacity at a boxing event since Cassius Clay took a decision over Doug Jones, back on March 13, 1963.

Fighting intensely through the bell in both the second and fourth rounds, both fighters remained focused on the task at hand. For Patterson it was a points-and-rounds duel, while Chuvalo favored a short but sweet victory. As Patterson delivered solid combinations, Chuvalo just shook them off. The Canadian's best option was going to the body early, but Patterson knew enough to wrap him up. Chuvalo took Patterson to the ropes in the seventh and just pounded him with headshots, but the fighter endured. The former heavyweight champion was in control for the bulk of the event, because he had to be. He wasn't going to overpower the "granite-chinned" Canadian who had never even been knocked down. In the end, it was Patterson by a unanimous decision. Later, it was learned that the former two-time champion had suffered a bone separation in his left hand.

More Ring Action

Zora Folley, at age thirty-two, had been fighting for a dozen years. This was hard to believe unless, of course, you had seen his seven growing children during that period. The Texas-born fighter was a proud family man, and nobody had to remind that there were mouths to feed at home. On February 26, Folley would enter the City Ring for a ten-round battle against undefeated Argentine heavyweight Oscar Bonavena. However, Folley, who had a record of 68–7–4, wasn't tormented by all the press accolades that had been thrown at Bonavena. How could he be? He had already defeated George Chuvalo, Henry Cooper, Doug Jones and Eddie Machen, all top-rated heavyweights.

A crowd of more than 8,000 turned out to watch the engagement, which many believed would be an aggressive affair, and it was just that. At the opening gong, Folley stepped away from his corner and sent a right hand that struck Bonavena's chin so hard, it catapulted the South American across the ring—had the ropes not been there to catch him, he would have landed on top of those ringside. It was a warning shot to the fighter that he better keep his distance. Unfortunately for fight fans, Bonavena's performance was pathetic, many believing he had only captured one round. When the united verdict was announced, the South American had lost his first fight.

On March 30 in the City Ring, José Torres defeated Willie Pastrano by a ninth-round technical knockout to capture the light heavyweight championship. Torres, who was lightning fast, took it to Pastrano in the first round and never ceased. By the third round, Pastrano was falling apart, as he was cut, swollen and gasping for air.[13]

ALONG CAME A TIGER

Born in Amaigbo, Nigeria, on August 14, 1929, Richard Ihetu, a.k.a. Dick Tiger, was the son of a chicken farmer. Taught how to box by British Army officers, he soon excelled and was persuaded to turn pro in 1952; the country of Nigeria gained its independence from Great Britain in 1960. Fighting out of Lagos, which would eventually become the country's capital, Tiger won a few, and lost a few. The city was far from being a spirited boxing center, and the youngster soon understood that he needed to hone his skills in a proper environment. In 1955, he moved to England, struggled a bit at first, but finally fell into a rhythm by late 1957. Tiger, an orthodox boxer, reached the height of five feet eight inches tall and had a reach of seventy-one inches.

His first American battle was inside Madison Square Garden, on June 5, 1959, when he drew Rory Calhoun in a hard-fought ten-round duel. As Calhoun was an exciting boxer, not to mention a fixture on *Friday Night Fights*, the exposure proved worthwhile for both fighters.[14] Tiger went 3-1 in 1960, which included splitting Commonwealth (British Empire) middleweight title fights against Wilf Greaves up in Edmonton, Canada. Undefeated (4-0) the following year, which included two Garden victories, the fighter believed he was finally in the title mix.

On October 23, 1962, it was then off to San Francisco to meet Gene Fullmer for the vacant WBA world middleweight crown. As the National Boxing Association became the World Boxing Association, this was Fullmer's first title defense under the new umbrella—the Utah fighter having successfully defended the NBA middleweight title seven times. Tiger dominated the fifteen rounds to capture the unanimous verdict. The brawl was also the beginning of an outstanding trilogy between two of the greatest middleweights ever.

Dick Tiger had never looked more unstoppable than he did in 1963.[15] However, he posted a record of 1-1-1 and lost his middleweight crown to Joey Giardello. Fighting three times again in 1964 (2-1), he lost only to Joey Archer. Tiger's only goal for 1965 was to his take back his title from Giardello.

For the first time in eight years, Joey Giardello received a New York State boxing license, clearing the boxer to do battle against Dick Tiger in the City Ring. Giardello, whose last New York duel was in 1956, never renewed his license due to his suspected associations. And, sure enough, Dick Tiger regained the middleweight championship on Thursday, October 21, by taking a fifteen-round unanimous decision over his rival inside the City Ring.

Flash Mob

A ten-round split decision, awarded to Filipino Gabriel "Flash" Elorde over New Yorker Frankie Narvaez, touched off an uproar inside Madison Square Garden on Wednesday, August 4. Narvaez, an 11–5 favorite, witnessed his fans greet the verdict with such a degree of dissatisfaction that a riot broke out. Witnesses stood or scrambled in disbelief as chairs from the mezzanine began raining down like a summer storm. Soon anything breakable became a target, from chairs and windows to even electrical fixtures.

When fire equipment began landing only feet from ringside, Garden police took action. They engaged a fire hose and turned it on the rioters. Shattered glass became a floor covering, and even the organ found a trajectory over a nearby wall. Once outside, the rioters continued their demolition by launching bricks, stones and bottles. Phil Rosenberg, a former boxer and now NYSAC Deputy Commissioner, was struck by an airborne fire ax. As for the rioters, five men were caught and arrested.

Ironically, the ring battle was rather tame compared to the post-fight free-for-all—there were no knockdowns, but Narvaez bled profusely for much of the battle. Judging ringside was indeed close—the press favored Narvaez—but hardly worthy of a major disturbance. The thirty-year-old Elorde, an established ring veteran who was highly respected, had last appeared in the City Ring back in 1956.

In Living Color

On Friday, December 10, feature boxers Emile Griffith and Manuel Gonzalez ushered into Madison Square Garden the age of color television. Teaming with RKO General Broadcasting, which owned WOR-TV in New York City along with five other stations, the Garden hoped to expand its audience by providing a whole new look to the sport of boxing. However, the real question was: How will Don Dunphy adjust his fight commentary in the age of color television? No longer as simple as gladiators adorned in black or white, an entirely new vocabulary consisting of sapphire trunks with chartreuse stripes awaited the legendary announcer.

World welterweight champion Emile Griffith, a favorite (14–5), scored a colorful fifteen-round unanimous decision over Houston boxer Manny Gonzalez inside the City Ring. Griffith, wearing red trunks, dominated Gonzalez, who was adorned in baby blue bottoms, for the entire battle. Griffith's left hook took its toll on the body of Gonzalez, while his straight right worked the head. Gonzalez, who was quick on his feet, saved himself from a knockout more than once. The fight was in stark contrast to the pair's earlier meeting back on January 26, when the Houston fighter took a non-title duel over Griffith.

A retirement ceremony in honor of Sugar Ray Robinson preceded the evening's boxing program. Fans of all ages cheered affectionately for the best pound-for-pound gladiator in the history of the sport. Four of the five men from whom Robinson took the middleweight championship—Carmen Basilio, Gene Fullmer, Carl "Bobo" Olson and Randy Turpin—were on hand to greet the fighter. The other, Jake LaMotta, was markedly absent; NYSAC was keeping him at a safe distance.

Fighter of the Year

Boxing, and its year, belonged to the fists and tongue of Muhammad Ali. Not only did he successfully defend his title twice, he did so in an incomparable manner. Not since Sugar

Ray Robinson, had such a multi-talented fighter graced the sport, and not since the days of John L. had a boxer, and poet, brought with him such an imaginative colloquial language. From the Big Ugly Bear to the Rabbit, one could only imagine just how far down the food chain Ali might feed.

The World Boxing Association stripped Ali of his title because of a return-bout clause in his 1964 fight contract with Liston. The organization had its own champion in Ernie Terrell.

Madison Square Garden bid farewell to Rubin "Hurricane" Carter, Joey Giardello, and naturally, Sugar Ray Robinson in ceremonial terms. And while there were a few good fights, nobody shined the City Ring more than Dick Tiger, who went 3-0 in back-to-back-to-back victories.

1966

Welterweight boxing champion Emile Griffith became the third boxer of his weight class to succeed in adding the middleweight crown to his resume. It happened on April 25, when he defeated Dick Tiger in a closely united verdict inside the City Ring. Only Sugar Ray Robinson and Carmen Basilio had ever done it, while others, like Henry Armstrong, Kid Gavilan, Benny Paret and Mickey Walker, had failed. In the ninth round, Griffith, who took few risks during the duel, also dropped Tiger for the first time in his career. Despite the fact that the crowd of nearly 15,000 cheered the judgment, many of those at ringside disagreed. It was not an exciting battle, nor was it a well-founded verdict. Nevertheless, Griffith would soon inform NYSAC that he planned on wearing two hats at the same time—under commission rules no champion may hold two titles simultaneously.[16]

An American boxer and activist, Muhammad Ali—born Cassius Marcellus Clay, Jr.—(1942–2016) was widely regarded as one of the most significant and celebrated sports figures of the 20th century. From early in his career, Ali was recognized as an inspiring, controversial, and polarizing figure both inside and outside the ring.

Knocked down twice in the second round by Argentine Oscar Bonavena, a very resolute Joe Frazier managed to fight himself into a ten-round split-decision victory. The twenty-three-year-old Philadelphia fighter, perhaps best known for his gold medal at the 1964 Summer Olympics, was a bit lethargic during the first three rounds. Bonavena, who sensed this, lured Frazier within range to deliver two perfect rights during round two. But, Frazier persevered—yeah, he may have got away with a few low blows—and began taking points. Frustrated by the halfway mark, Bonavena began casting a few low punches himself. By the eighth round, the fight became a brawl with no love lost. In the end, it was Frazier by a nose with little argument. The aggressive display was held inside the City Ring on Wednesday, September 21.

Carlos Ortiz retained his world lightweight title on Monday, November 28, when he was given credit for knocking out Gabriel "Flash" Elorde at the 2:01 mark of the fourteenth

12. "I Must Be the Greatest," 1963–1967

round. It was far from an exciting Garden engagement, but Elorde had never been knocked down or knocked out in ninety-six fights.

Harry Markson, the Garden's boxing director, along with matchmaker Teddy Brenner, spent most of the post–Thanksgiving holiday exchanging calls with Muhammad Ali in an attempt to land a February Garden fight. Having reserved February 6, 1967, as the day the champ would defend his title against Ernie Terrell inside the City Ring, Garden management needed to confirm the date. But Ali, through his new manager Herbert Muhammad—the son of Black Muslims leader Elijah Muhammad—wanted a greater guarantee and a larger percentage of the ancillary rights (theatre, television, radio and film). A counter to the Garden's plans came when New York lawyer Bob Arum, a principal in Main Bout Incorporated, stated that the fight would be conducted in the Houston Astrodome on February 6, 1967.[17]

Fighter of the Year

It was not a spectacular year for the Garden, or boxing. Perhaps the best fight of the year was Fighting Harada's victory over Eder Jofre, on June 1, in Tokyo. Harada, the only man to ever beat Jofre, had done it twice.[18]

Of the finest duels in the Garden, Frazier's victory over Bonavena, sticks out. Also, it was great to see Elorde back in the City Ring, even if he was only a shadow of himself. Joe Frazier posted a 2–0 record in the City Ring, as did Emile Griffith and Buster Mathis. But Brooklyn light heavyweight Johnny Persol went 3–0 in the Garden, and an imposing 4–0 during the year. Paying his dues, the fighter was exemplary of every boxer just waiting for a big break.[19]

1967

An American boxer who competed from 1965 to 1981, Joseph William Frazier (1944–2011), nicknamed "Smokin' Joe," reigned as the undisputed heavyweight champion from 1970 to 1973, and as an amateur won a gold medal at the 1964 Summer Olympics.

As the final days of the third iteration of Madison Square Garden slowly drew to a close, it was a good time to review the champions of each weight class on January 1: Heavyweight—Muhammad Ali; light heavyweight—Dick Tiger; middleweight—Emile Griffith; junior middleweight—Kim Ki Soo; welterweight—Curtis Cokes; junior welterweight—Sandro Lopopolo; lightweight—Carlos Ortiz; junior lightweight—Flash Elorde; featherweight—Vicente Saldivar; bantamweight—Fighting Harada; and flyweight—Walter McGowan and Horacio Accavallo.

A Sixteen-Year Drought

Muhammad Ali agreed to meet Zora Folley on March 22 inside the City Ring for the first heavyweight championship bout held inside the Garden in sixteen years. The last one had been on January 12, 1951, when Ezzard Charles beat Lee Oma. With all eyes on a new venue atop Penn Station, Garden management was once again thrilled to have a foot inside the door of the heavyweight division, even if it was likely the last time within the old walls. The question was: Could they stay there long enough to bring a heavyweight championship to the new venue? For Ali, the immediate concern was time, as he had had two appeals rejected by the Louisville draft board; his induction date was scheduled for April 11.[20]

With a record of 28–0, it was the champion's ninth title defense. With an impressive record of 74–7–4, with forty knockouts, Folley hoped that this bout would determine his destiny. Speaking of the future, an impressive ten-round heavyweight undercard battle between Johnny Persol and Ali's sparring partner Jimmy Ellis was also being watched closely.

Folley wasn't in the ring to dance—energy conservation, at least to him, was paramount. However, he did carry the fight to Ali in the early rounds. The Chandler, Arizona, fighter kept his trademark right cocked, but since he was fighting up, he had to compensate for reach. The first few rounds were sparring sessions, but Ali locked in on the range with his left jab by the end of the third term. The champion caught his antagonist in the fourth round and sent him down for an eight count. Bleeding from the blow, Folley managed to finish the round.

The lackluster sessions that followed seemed to pass quickly until the seventh. It was an Ali short right hand to the chin of Folley that ended the fight at the 1:48 mark of the term. Skepticism surrounding the impact of the fight-ending blow was rampant among those sitting ringside. Many believed it just wasn't powerful enough to deliver a fighter as strong as Folley.

For the record, Jimmy Ellis knocked out Johnny Persol at the 2:44 mark of the very first round. For Ellis, it was his third consecutive first-round knockout. Persol had hit the canvas for an eight count early in the round and later stated that the blow altered his vision.

Over 13,000 fans paid a record gate to witness the event.

Nino Benvenuti v. Emile Griffith I

On April 17, Italian Nino Benvenuti, who had been sent to the canvas in the fourth round, decisively fought his way back to capture the world middleweight championship. It was a convincing fifteen-round Garden decision over Emile Griffith. For the striking European fighter with movie-star looks, it was only his third battle outside his native country and the first in the United States.

Taking command in the early goings, Benvenuti dropped Griffith in the second round. But the champion, who hated to be intimidated, fought back strong during the next few sessions and even catapulted the Italian across the ring with a solid right in the fourth. But Benvenuti wisely clinched and avoided punches long enough to clear his head—Griffith had his opportunity to deliver the Italian, but could not. Appearing fatigued during the final rounds, Griffith did little other than watch his championship slip away. This would be the first battle in an outstanding trilogy—the pair were to meet again on July 13.[21]

Hell No, He Won't Go

On April 28, Muhammad Ali refused induction into the armed forces of the United States. Wasting little time, both NYSAC and the WBA stripped him of his world heavyweight championship; consequently, European organizations quickly followed suit.

O Canada

Unbeaten Joe Frazier met Canadian George Chuvalo for a twelve-round bout on July 19—neither fighter favored a prolonged ascension to the heavyweight throne, and both still regarded Ali as champion. The Garden event was independent of a tournament that was sanctioned by the World Boxing Association. That tournament already had a cast of fighters including Oscar Bonavena, Jimmy Ellis, Leotis Martin, Karl Mildenberger, Floyd Patterson, Thad Spencer, and Ernie Terrell. The winner of the Garden bout was assumed to fill the final tournament slot, but that wouldn't be the case—the slot was filled by Jerry Quarry.[22] Frazier, considered the favorite, was undefeated in sixteen bouts, fourteen by way of knockout. In contrast, Chuvalo had lost (13), but had never been knocked down in 62 bouts.

A Garden crowd of about 14,000 watched as Joe Frazier fractured the Canadian's cheekbone with two of his trademark left hooks.[23] Struck in the right eye socket during the early seconds of the fourth round, Chuvalo could no longer see.[24] Referee Johnny Colan had little choice but to stop the fight. The pinnacle of the short contest came in the third round, when both fighters slugged it out at close quarters, Frazier administering the greater punishment.[25] The Philly fighter hoped to next meet the German southpaw Karl Mildenberger, the number-one contender, to the delight of Frazier's 271 shareholders.

First Time Garden Used as Training Facility

It was hard to believe that the City Ring was actually left up after the Frazier v. Chuvalo fight so that Ismael Laguna could use it to train for his upcoming Shea Stadium battle against Carlos Ortiz. But it was there in its full glory so that those who had purchased fight tickets could also enjoy some practice drills. Ortiz, who performed brilliantly, took the fight by a unanimous decision in fifteen action-packed rounds.

Muhammad Ali (Cassius Clay)

What can you say about a man who has already said everything, to everyone, about himself?

Racial unrest was reaching a boiling point in 1967. On the streets, it was the voice of Martin Luther King, Jr., a Baptist minister, civil rights leader and recipient of the 1964 Nobel Peace Prize, whose words rang out strong and true. In the ring, it was the comments and actions of Muhammad Ali, born Cassius Marcellus Clay on January 17, 1942. All races watched in horror as the events that played out before their very eyes were more deplorable than anyone could have ever imagined. Civil rights activism terrorized every citizen in some way, shape or form and stirred the crucible of the very foundation that built America.

In the ring, the temperature was red hot. Muhammad Ali said and did things that were considered rude, indecent, repulsive and unpatriotic. Honestly speaking, others felt the same, but were too scared to articulate their feelings in the same manner. Also, Ali had the protection of the ring and a title, while others had only their parents standing between them and law enforcement. Even if a part of society loved Ali for his tremendous talent and undeniable voice, a portion also hated him for his narcissistic attitude and his unwillingness to defend his country. In a statement to society's ignorance, Ali would later prove true to his convictions, while others never found theirs.

Chiseled like a god, he was six feet three inches and a handsome young man who weighed in between two hundred and two hundred and twenty pounds. He was named for his father, Cassius Marcellus Clay, Sr., who himself was named in honor of the 19th-century Republican politician and staunch abolitionist, Cassius Marcellus Clay. The family was a descendant of slaves of the antebellum South, and was predominantly of African descent, with smaller amounts of other heritages.

While his father painted billboards and signs, his mother, Odessa O'Grady Clay, was a domestic helper and busy raising her family. Nurtured in Louisville, Kentucky, where he grew up amid racial segregation, Ali's experiences molded him like a fresh piece of kaolin. At the age of twelve and searching for a way to vent his anger and frustration, he put on a pair of boxing mitts. As an amateur fighter, he won six Kentucky Golden Gloves titles, two national Golden Gloves titles, an Amateur Athletic Union national title, and the Light Heavyweight gold medal in the 1960 Summer Olympics in Rome.

In his professional debut, which came on October 29, 1960, in Louisville, he won a six-round decision over Tunney Hunsaker. By the end of 1963, Clay amassed a record of 19-0 with 15 wins by knockout. Despite his talent, early fights were not without challenges. He was knocked down both by Sonny Banks, on February 10, 1962, and later by Henry Cooper, on June 18, 1963. Clay's fight with Doug Jones, another contender, on March 13, 1963, was by far his toughest fight during this stretch. Jones staggered his adversary in the first round at the Garden, and the unanimous decision for the flamboyant youngster was greeted by boos from Jones's hometown fans. The rain of debris thrown into the City Ring was a salute Clay wouldn't soon forget.

Whether it was disparaging his opponents or extolling the virtues of himself, Clay served up non-stop prattle meant to rattle any pre-fight battle. He would never shut up. An opponent was "ugly," while he was "pretty"; or his opponent was a "bum" or the "bad man" compared to himself, and it was all part of a marketing technique he attributed to professional wrestling. Following his 1964 victory against Sonny Liston, he was the greatest and told us so. He went 2-0 in 1965, 5-0 in 1966, and 2-0 in 1967.

As the young man pondered his future, the headlines faded, the ropes tightened, and his universe shrunk, but only in proportion to his courage and conviction.

On June 20, a Houston jury convicted Muhammad Ali of violating the United States Selective Service laws by refusing to be drafted. Ali, a.k.a. Cassius Clay, was sentenced to five years in prison and fined $10,000, the maximum punishment. Ali appealed and was freed on a $5,000 bond. Contrary to what the former champion believed, boxing didn't die with his departure, but the headlines certainly did. One boxing hero who flew beneath the radar in 1967 was Vicente Saldivar, who never battled inside Madison Square Garden. But boy, could he fight. He retired unbeaten as featherweight champion after defeating an outstanding Welsh boxer by the name of Howard Winstone.

Fighter of the Year

While New York hosted some outstanding matches, it was indeed a transition year, the high point being a new Madison Square Garden on the horizon. Muhammad Ali's presence inside the City Ring on March 22, 1967, would be his last fight for three and a half years. Fighting only once in the venue, he made us think twice about ourselves. What if it had been his last fight ever, which it easily could have been, and where would he be today?[26]

13

In the Eye of the Storm, 1968–1969

> If opportunity doesn't knock, build a door.
> —Milton Berle, a heavyweight
> in the comedy division

In retrospect, it may have been the most turbulent two years in our country's history. America appeared to be unraveling at the seams. Activist Martin Luther King, Jr., was fatally shot in Memphis, politician Robert F. Kennedy was assassinated in Los Angeles, and even artist Andy Warhol was shot and critically wounded in New York City. During a decade that criticized the ring over safety concerns, many never felt safer between the ropes.

1968

The old Madison Square Garden officially closed at the conclusion of the Westminster Kennel Club Show on Tuesday, February 13, 1968. As one of the Garden's most prestigious events, it was indeed fitting.

ANOTHER MADISON SQUARE GARDEN

The fourth Madison Square Garden opened on Sunday, February 11, 1968, at 8:30 P.M. A "Salute to the USO" (United Service Organizations), hosted by none other than Bob Hope and Bing Crosby, cleared the road for those who would follow. The capacity crowd of 20,000 spectators found their way to the 33rd Street venue and entered through two main entrances, one on Seventh Avenue and the other on Eighth Avenue. Many, having witnessed large crowds at the old Garden, appeared unaffected by the additional spectators. There were taxis and limousines as far as the eye could see and the excitement was invigorating. The fashionable crowd worked their way to four groups of escalators that serviced the four towers of the primary structure—a total of 44 moving staircases enhanced mobility while providing the required orderliness.

The Garden's new color-coding system made it easy to navigate the facility. All a spectator needed to do was to follow the numbers and colors of his ticket. Ticket shades corresponded to the seat color, so a gray ticket allowed a visitor to claim a gray folding chair on the arena's floor. And since there were no obstructed views, unlike the old Garden, a visitor could be assured of an outstanding vista. This feature was made possible by the largest cable-supported roof in the country. As a spectator looked up, he viewed an orange and beige covered ceiling that was almost hypnotic in its design.

Madison Square Garden Center was composed of six facilities: the Arena, the Felt Forum (5,227 seats), bowling center (48 lanes), movie theater (486 seats), rotunda and the Hall of Fame.

On opening night, Bob Hope, under the moniker of "Chicken Delight," sparred against Rocky Marciano, the retired unbeaten heavyweight champion. Marciano's second was Willie Pep, while Hope opted for the beautiful and talented Barbara Eden. Hope also joked with New York City Mayor John Lindsay. The evening's entertainment included Pearl Bailey, Les Brown (with orchestra), Bing Crosby, Phyllis Diller, Joey Heatherton and Jill Jones (formerly Jill St. John). As for Hope and Crosby, it was their first live appearance together since 1942. Also on hand: General Omar Bradley, Jack Dempsey, General Emmett O'Donnell, and Gene Tunney.

Overall, it was just an outstanding evening.

A Double-Header—Opening Night for Boxing

It was a double-header designed to fill the new twenty-thousand-seat-arena, and it featured Joe Frazier versus Buster Mathis for the world heavyweight championship, along with Emile Griffith defending his middleweight title against Nino Benvenuti. Formal attire was requested and tickets scaled at $100 (ringside), $75, $50, $30, $20 and $10. The two title fights took place on Monday, March 4.[1]

There was no questioning Frazier's credentials, but a fair share of the press questioned the recognition given Mathis. Granted the fighter was 23–0, but his victories were over less competitive boxers. Those who followed boxing recalled Mathis's outpointing Frazier in the finals of the 1964 Olympic trials, which quelled some of the skepticism, but the British Boxing Board did not acknowledge the battle. As for the middleweights, Griffith had lost the title to Benvenuti the previous April 17, before winning it back on September 29, so that stage was set.

Joe Frazier delivered a left hook to the face of Buster Mathis that knocked him out at the 2:33 mark of the eleventh round. The 243½-pound heavyweight was catapulted backwards, before heading through the ropes and onto the ring apron. Although Mathis was on his knees at the count of eight, he was clearly dazed and could not arise. The victory earned Joe Frazier championship honors as recognized in the states of Illinois, Massachusetts and New York. The question was: would the public accept him as the true champion?

Italian Nino Benvenuti took a unanimous fifteen-round decision over Emile Griffith to regain the world middleweight crown. The Italian was brilliant, playing possum in the sixth and seventh rounds to lure Griffith into range. When the timing was right, which happened to be in the ninth round, Benvenuti dropped his antagonist. Griffith tried to fight back and even staggered his opposition in the final round, but he could not deliver him.

The Deputy Sheriff

Bob Foster boxed as an amateur before turning pro in 1961. Standing six feet three inches tall, with a seventy-nine-inch reach, the lanky light heavyweight was polishing his

An American boxer who fought as a light heavyweight and heavyweight, Robert Lloyd "Bob" Foster (1938–2015) was one of the greatest light heavyweight champions in boxing history. He won the world light heavyweight title from Dick Tiger in 1968 via fourth-round knockout, and went on to defend his crown fourteen times in total from 1968 to 1974.

skills at an extraordinary rate. Winning his first nine professional fights—four of which were in New York, three in Canada, and the other two in the D.C. area—Foster caught the eye of city matchmakers and landed inside Madison Square Garden for the very first time on October 20, 1962. His opponent would be the familiar face of Doug Jones; the pair had fought each other as amateur middleweights back in 1957 while both were serving in the United States Air Force. Foster suffered a technical knockout at the 0:23 mark of the eighth term of a scheduled ten rounds. His second Garden visit, in 1964, would also be a loss, this time to Ernie Terrell. However, this year, Foster, with a record of 29–4, felt certain his luck was about to change.

Bob Foster v. Dick Tiger

It took a mammoth left hook to the jaw of Dick Tiger, in the fourth round of their May 24 Garden duel, for Bob Foster to capture the world light heavyweight championship (WBC and WBA). A right uppercut had set the stage when it stunned the veteran Biafran boxer, and it was then that Foster, locked and loaded, capitalized on the situation. He kayoed Tiger for the only time in his career at the 2:05 mark. For Foster, who essentially quit boxing in 1965, the victory was long overdue. A crowd of more than 11,000 turned out for the impressive battle and everyone appeared satisfied. Foster, who was much taller and heavier than his antagonist, maximized his eight-inch reach advantage with his dominant left jab; the punch kept Tiger from any thought of infighting.

On the undercard, Brooklyn's Johnny Persol outpointed Puerto Rican fighter Angelo Oquendo in a ten-round bout. As a result of the battle, Persol hoped for a shot at Foster's newly acquired title. Days later, however, Persol was hospitalized to repair a detached retina in his left eye. The injury would derail his career.

The Felt's Debut

The first professional boxing show at the Felt Forum, or the five-thousand-seat arena beneath the main floor of Madison Square Garden, took place on Wednesday, September 11, 1968. The main event saw Jersey City boxer Frank DePaula, the "Jersey Jolter," drop Irish Jimmy McDermott, of Holyoke, Massachusetts, five times in the fourth round on his way to a knockout victory. Referee Mark Conn, witnessing the devastation, tried to get between the fighters to end the fight after the fourth knockdown but failed. McDermott, having seen the canvas twice in the first round, endured a vicious pummeling; ringside physicians took ninety seconds to revive Irish Jimmy.

The orange and yellow seats were a bit different, as was the wall that provided the backdrop for boxing, but the intimacy was clearly evident by the Forum's size, and enhanced by its soft lightning. It would likely take some time for fans familiar with Garden boxing to adjust to the conditions. But for Markson and Company it was clear that the venue, serviced by the City Ring, could become an incubator for arena talent.[2]

Survival Instincts

Following the battle, and proof that dreams really can come true, Frank DePaula was inked to a ten-round light heavyweight bout on October 25 against the thirty-nine-year-old Dick Tiger. With a record of 58-16-3, Tiger, who had arisen to the rank of captain in the Biafran army, had to request a leave to return to the United States. DePaula, with a record of 18-5-3, was over a decade younger than Tiger.

The story of Dick Tiger, his wife, seven children and relatives, had been one of survival. The secessionist state of Biafra, in the Old Eastern Region of Nigeria, had been at war since May 30, 1967. Most of what the fighter once owned was gone. Fighting for far less than what he had once commanded, he had turned back to the fight game to make ends meet. It fed his family and for that he was extremely grateful. Just knowing what this man had been through was enough to root for him—no offense to DePaula, who was an outstanding young fighter.

It was four knockdowns in four rounds, and a toe-to-toe battle between two gladiators: Dick Tiger, a thirty-nine-year-old Biafran warrior, and Frankie DePaula, a twenty-eight-year-old Jersey City pug. And it was a former light heavyweight and middleweight champion, fighting for food money against a young kid, whose dream was only one step away from reality. And in many ways, it was perfect.

A crowd of more than 13,000 turned out—granted as many as half, or so it appeared, had made the journey from Jersey City to view their boy—to witness a spectacle certainly worth the price of admission. With a streak of five knockouts under his belt, DePaula came out strong and dropped Tiger in the second round with superb combinations. Tiger retaliated in the third and sent his antagonist down, not once, but twice to the canvas. It looked like it was over as DePaula was struggling to maintain some sense of actuality. As a chorus of "Stop it" rang out from ringside, the bell finally saved DePaula. Referee Arthur Mercante took the heat of nearby spectators who were mystified by the lack of a stoppage. Had the referee sensed something? Both warriors struggled to reach their corners. In the fourth round, DePaula found his equilibrium and managed to drop Tiger with a solid right. However, in doing so, the Jersey gladiator injured his hand.

The pace slowed in the fifth, as both warriors looked fatigued. Tiger, however, threw more punches during the final half of the battle. In the end, it was Tiger by a unanimous decision.[3]

Dance on a Volcano

The first riot inside the new Madison Square Garden occurred on Friday, November 15, following a majority ten-round verdict in favor of Ismael Laguna over Roman Bianco.

Everything from a press box refrigerator to assorted wine bottles cascaded from the higher elevations—the latter even landing inside the City Ring. It was not only a sad commentary on the game, but an embarrassment to both the Garden and to Ismael Laguna. Of course, NYSAC looked into the issue and agreed that a tactical anti-glass-throwing patrol was needed. The Garden also agreed to close some of the upper tiers during certain events.

The Laguna versus Bianco bout was the feature of three scheduled ten-round battles. It was preceded by David Melendez fighting to a draw against Dario Hidalgo, and former welterweight champion Luis Rodriguez taking a unanimous decision over Joe Shaw.

Speaking of firsts, the Felt Forum hosted a closed-circuit television boxing doubleheader on December 10, its first pay-for-view broadcast. The first bout featured Sonny Liston tackling Amos Lincoln from the Baltimore Civic Center, while the second bout featured world heavyweight Joe Frazier against Oscar Bonavena, broadcast live from Philadelphia. For the record, Liston knocked out Lincoln in the second round and Frazier took a fifteen-round unanimous decision over Bonavena to retain his title.

Fighter of the Year

The deposed champion, Muhammad Ali, still ruled the heavyweight division despite whatever Joe Frazier, who was recognized in five states, or Jimmy Ellis, who was the WBA champion, believed. Ali was still awaiting the results of his appeal to the United States Supreme Court.[4]

New York hosted many of the better fights of the year, the only exception being the stunning victory by Lionel Rose over Fighting Harada that took place in Tokyo on February 26.

As for the City Ring, which would include appearances in both the Felt Forum and the Garden Arena, Joe Frazier won back-to-back bouts, and Chuck Wepner went 2-0. However, the gladiator who many believed graced the sport and the Garden during the year was Bob Foster. The lanky boxer went 4-0 on the year, and finally obtained the light heavyweight title inside New York's premier venue.

1969

The Mysterious Death of Frankie DePaula

On January 22, 1969, Frankie DePaula found himself facing Bob Foster inside the City Ring for the light heavyweight championship. It wasn't pretty, nor was the contest what DePaula expected. Early in the first round, the youngster floored the champion—although it was more of a slip than a drop. Needless to say, it aroused the crowd and the young gladiator. However, when an embarrassed Foster rose from the canvas, he was none too happy. He dropped DePaula three times. And since the three-knockdown rule was in effect, the fight ended at the 2:17 mark of the first term. To DePaula's credit, he wasn't sprawled out on the canvas, and he stood quickly. Over 16,000 spectators, many from Jersey City, turned out to watch their hero's dream fade in one hundred and thirty-seven seconds.

Later, DePaula was arrested by federal agents along with his manager Gary Garafola, and three other men—John DiMaio, John Gardner and Max Griesler—on charges of stealing

$80,000 worth of copper bars from a Port Newark pier on March 11, 1968. Garafola and DiMaio were nightclub owners, while Gardner and Griesler were independent truckers.[5]

DePaula's last fight was a knockout victory over Art Miller inside the Arena in Philadelphia on November 6, 1969. The boxer's trial with regard to the copper heist began on April 14, 1970, at the Federal Criminal Court in Newark, New Jersey. On May 7, 1970, the jury acquitted him of charges of possession and theft, but failed to reach a verdict on the charge of conspiracy.

In the early hours of May 14, 1970, DePaula was shot near his girlfriend's residence on Jersey City's west side. At the Jersey City Medical Center, he developed paralysis and died on September 14, 1970, at the age of 31. The mystery surrounding his death still lingers. He fought inside the City Ring seven times.

Ali's Case Continues

The United States Supreme Court ruled on Monday, March 24, that Muhammad Ali's appeal (made in his given name of Cassius Clay) of his draft refusal conviction sentence must be returned to a lower court for consideration. Should the case be dismissed, Ali, who hadn't fought in two years, would need time to get back into fighting condition. NYSAC had previously stated that if the conviction was overturned, they would withdraw the recognition of Joe Frazier and reinstate Ali as the heavyweight champion.

Heavyweights at Hand

Joe Frazier inked a deal to battle Jerry Quarry inside the City Ring on June 23. Both fighters had looked impressive of late, so it promised to be a good show. The $100 ringside ticket would set a record for a single heavyweight title bout held indoors.[6] Frazier brought an unbeaten record of 23–0 into the ring, while Quarry's record stood at 31–2–4.

It was Joe Frazier's vicious left hook that opened up an inch-long cut under Jerry Quarry's right eye in the third round of their Garden battle. And as the cut swelled, Quarry gradually lost his vision. By the time the bout reached the seventh round, the fighter's eye had swollen shut and forced the ringside medical staff to stop the fight. It was a wise decision, as the cut later took eight stitches to close. Over 14,000 fans turned out to watch the conflict that turned into a bloodbath by the fourth round. Joe Frazier was quick to remind everyone that no heavyweight champion had ever lost his title in Madison Square Garden, and he wasn't going to be the first.

Of notable undercard engagements: heavyweight George Foreman made his professional debut and knocked out noted Golden Gloves boxer Donald Walheim at the 1:54 mark of the third round, and unbeaten Mike Quarry, Jerry's brother, outpointed Ruben Figueroa in a six-rounder.

On October 31, George Foreman won his eighth straight bout since turning professional. He took an eight-round unanimous Garden decision over Peru pugilist Roberto Davilla, the first fighter he faced whom he didn't knock out. And, it was his third appearance in the City Ring.

From the opening bell, heavyweight Jerry Quarry systematically took apart George Chuvalo during their Friday, December 12, Garden feature. By the time the second round rolled around, Chuvalo's cheeks puffed like an October squirrel. Quarry, cut under the right eye, continued to command the fight while putting Chuvalo's countenance under constant attack. But as Chuvalo began losing his vision, he also lost his patience. Angered over his swollen right eye, the Canadian delivered a solid left hook that floored Quarry in the final seconds of the seventh round. Falling backward, Quarry was stunned by the impact. Managing to get to one knee at the count of three, Quarry looked like he was patiently waiting to rise at nine. But he did not, and was counted out at the 2:59 mark of the seventh. In forty-one professional battles he had never taken the count.

Fighter of the Year

Aside from the Frazier versus Quarry fight on June 23, many of the better fights—José Nápoles's victory over Curtis Cokes on April 18 (Los Angeles), Rubén Olivares's knockout of Lionel Rose on August 22 (Inglewood, California), José Nápoles's victory over Emile Griffith on October 12 (Inglewood, California), and Nino Benvenuti's kayo of Luis Rodriguez on November 22 (Rome, Italy)—took place outside New York City.

Making his mark in the sport during the year was welterweight José Nápoles, an outstanding Cuban fighter then living in Mexico, who destroyed Curtis Cokes twice before dominating Emile Griffith.

As boxing nervously awaited the destiny of Muhammad Ali, Madison Square Garden bid farewell to Nino Benvenuti, Buster Mathis, and José Torres, but welcomed George Foreman and Mike Quarry.[7] As for the City Ring, Emile Griffith went 2–0, as did Mike Quarry and Dick Tiger. However, George Foreman went 13–0 in 1969. He won all three of his Garden fights and shined the City Ring at just the right time.[8]

14

New York City Serenade, 1970–1976

> Yea, I shall return with the tide.
> —Kahlil Gibran, *The Prophet*

The Seventies was the fallout from the previous decade—essentially the end of Richard Nixon, the Beatles, the Great American Ride, and the war in Vietnam. It was middle-class comfort from a lounge chair eating fast food and watching television shows such as *All in the Family*, *Saturday Night Live*, or *Monday Night Football*. And once again, boxing, which will include "The Fight," unveiled a self-portrait.

The new Madison Square Garden, in all its opulence, offered nothing but potential. The name alone carried a legacy of unmatched distinction. Just the same, it was management's admirable intent to add to that endowment. The decade would see the uncertainty in the heavyweight division slowly disappear, the exciting emergence of a new breed of welter and middleweights, and "The Fight." The latter would overshadow every event of the decade.

1970

THE GREAT CONTENDER

The Garden spent the greater part of the beginning of the year promoting the February 16 fight between Joe Frazier and Jimmy Ellis. In all fairness, the winner would not be Ali's successor as the media continued to profess, but simply the number-one contender. And boxing fans were tired of Joe Frazier's being described as the champion of six states, and Jimmy Ellis as the WBA champion or Clay's former sparring partner. Reality was: undefeated Joe Frazier was disposing of heavyweight contenders, while Jimmy Ellis hadn't fought for seventeen months, or 517 days.

The fight that everyone believed would be dominated by Frazier was exactly that. Jimmy Ellis, dropped twice in the fourth round, was kept on his stool. His manager, Angelo Dundee, would not let his fighter answer the bell for round five. And no sooner had the fight ended than Ali's name could be overheard from every correspondent covering the engagement. But to nobody's surprise, Frazier was ready to counter. He made himself perfectly clear: no Ali, no Frazier, was his ultimatum. If a fight couldn't be arranged with the deposed champion, Joe Frazier was going to pursue a musical career.

Ali Returns

Circulating for weeks had been rumors of Ali's return. Finally, Muhammad Ali and Jerry Quarry agreed to meet in a fifteen-round contest scheduled for October 26, at the City Auditorium in Atlanta. Ali had been stripped of his heavyweight crown when he refused military induction back in April of 1967, and his last ring battle was against Zora Folley in March of 1967 at Madison Square Garden. Ali formally applied for his NYSAC license on Thursday, September 24, 1970. The reason behind the application was a September 14 ruling by Federal Judge Walter R. Mansfield that a denial of a license to Ali was "an arbitrary and unreasonable departure from the commission's established practice of granting licenses to applicants convicted of crimes or military offenses."[1] It looked like the tide had turned. And it had.

Ali defeated Jerry Quarry via an impressive third-round knockout. He would next meet Argentine heavyweight Oscar Bonavena for fifteen rounds inside Madison Square Garden on December 7. That card would also see Ken Buchanan, the world lightweight champion, battle welter Donato Paduano, in a ten-round non-title duel.

Ringo

In one of those better-late-than-never Garden moments, a volatile Ali left hook caught the jaw of his Argentine antagonist and sent him to the canvas in the fifteenth and final round. When Bonavena got up and attempted to shake off the damage, he was thrown right back into the line of fire. Another left hook sent him to the floor again. Ali waited and watched as his adversary arose once more. He then locked onto his target and fired a solid right to end the battle. Invoking the three-knockdown rule, referee Mark Conn stopped the fight at the 2:03 mark of the final term. With Bonavena removed from the heavyweight mix, the stage was set for the inevitable.

By Wednesday, December 9, two potential sites for the Ali v. Frazier had risen to the top of the list. The Houston Astrodome, with its seating potential of nearly 70,000 and substantial tax savings (no ancillary income tax), was currently the top choice, according to Bob Arum, one of Ali's attorneys and executive vice president of Top Rank, Inc., a closed-circuit television firm. Madison Square Garden was the second—hurt by a lack of matching capacity and a five-percent New York State tax on ancillary income. The potential of a two-million-dollar gate, for the targeted February (15 or 22) date, excited everyone involved, especially the fighters. Markson and Company would need every angle possible—from appealing to fighter loyalty to even the Garden's mystique—to persuade both camps to fight inside the City Ring.

The formal announcement of the fight took place at noon on Wednesday, December 30, 1970, inside Toots Shor's restaurant. Both fighters would receive a flat fee of $2.5 million each to do battle inside Madison Square Garden on Monday, March 8, 1971. Putting up the guarantees was Jack Kent Cooke, the multimillionaire Los Angeles sports team owner, who also designated the Garden as the site of choice.[2] The promoters of the colossal event would be both the Garden and Chartwell Artists (Los Angeles, London and New York), a theatrical agency.

A Garden sellout of 19,000 would yield a gate estimated at $1.25 million, with tickets scaled at $150, $100, $75, $50, $40 and $20. The promoters would not disclose any closed-circuit locations until the venue sold out. The only major item that could affect the promotion would be an adverse ruling by the United States Supreme Court on Ali's appealed draft-refusal conviction.

Forgotten Rounds

Jerry Quarry stirred up the heavyweight mix by knocking out Mac Foster in the sixth round on Thursday, June 18. After a right cross to the head sent Foster through the ropes, the referee stopped it without a count. Nearly 16,000 Garden fans turned out for the Quarry versus Foster battle, many to watch the pre-fight seventy-fifth birthday celebration for Jack Dempsey. Over two dozen former champions were on hand to assist the "Manassa Mauler" in blowing out the candles.

A bright star, however, was on the horizon as George Foreman was signed to his first main event in the Garden on August 4. Turning professional thirteen months earlier, the twenty-year-old heavyweight would confront his most formidable challenger yet when he climbed between the Garden ropes and faced George Chuvalo. It was the "Battle of the Georges," as over 12,000 boxing fans turned out to watch Mr. Foreman stop Mr. Chuvalo in the third round. Referee Arthur Mercante ended the battle at the 1:41 mark of the third term when it was clear Chuvalo, although standing, was not defending himself.

Finally, José Nápoles, a Cuban-born fighter residing in Mexico City, was an indestructible boxer with a passion for knockouts. Ever since taking the world welterweight championship from Curtis Cokes in April of 1969, the excitement surrounding the fighter has been unparalleled—he had not lost a fight since August of 1966. Although it was a non-title bout, over 8,000 fans turned out to watch Nápoles score a Garden victory by way of technical knockout over Pete Toro; the fight was stopped at the 2:32 mark of the ninth round.

Fighter of the Year

Of the memorable bouts held outside of New York: Carlos Monzón knocked out Nino Benvenuti in the twelfth round on November 7 (Rome, Italy). Monzón, who hurt Benvenuti early, had to survive some tough left hooks in the seventh round to eventually capture the middleweight title. And on October 16, Chucho Castillio knocked out Rubén Olivares in the fourteenth round of their battle (Inglewood, California). It was the first loss for Olivares in sixty-one fights.

Naturally, it was great to see Ali back inside the Garden. Of those who graced the City Ring with their presence, none did finer in 1970 than George Foreman, who went 6–0 (includes the Felt Forum).

1971

The City Ring, a "Petrie dish" for our culture since its creation, once again hosted a defining moment in history as Muhammad Ali, a radical symbol of defiance, met Joe Frazier, a superficial model for the establishment. Or at least that's how some sociologists viewed the conflict. Naturally, the symbolism attracted more stars than grains of sand on Coney Island Beach. Anybody who was somebody was there, and even those who thought they were found it hard to resist a ticket at any price.

On January 11, the Supreme Court agreed to decide whether Muhammad Ali, a.k.a. Cassius Clay, was entitled to be deferred from military service as a conscientious objector. The case would likely be heard in April, thus the one open item that could affect the promotion was no longer an issue. Had the Supreme Court declined to hear his appeal, Ali could have faced prison. Ali had insisted throughout his legal proceedings that his Black Muslim faith forbade him to take up arms in the Vietnam War or any other conflict that he might face as a United States serviceman. Ali began his training for the big fight on January 14, inside the 5th Street Gym in Miami Beach, Florida.[3]

THE FIGHT

The only sport that could transcend every major news event was boxing. Outside the United States, nobody participating in the four core sports of baseball, basketball, football and hockey was an international superstar. It took a boxer to cross international borders. As the heavyweight championship was still the most coveted title on the face of the earth, it garnered headlines whenever it became available. And such was the case with "The Fight."

Everything in the solar system seemed to align perfectly for Ali versus Frazier. Boxing had the most controversial athlete of his time, Muhammad Ali; the perfect opponent, Joe Frazier; and the premier venue, Madison Square Garden. It would be the most polarizing sporting event ever held, because it could be.

It was a match between a pair of Americans, two undefeated black athletes who happened to possess extraordinary boxing skills. And it was a superlative pairing of two men who both laid claim to the heavyweight title. If you saw them as more than this, or attached symbolism to each, they didn't mind.

The flamboyant Muhammad Ali, a.k.a. Cassius Clay, was recognized as the public's champion regardless of who denied it. Deposed in 1967, following his tumultuous draft-refusal conviction, the former Olympian refused to be denied. The decision would be reversed three months after "The Fight (of the Century)."

The recognized and politically correct champion was Joe Frazier. Also an Olympian, he had his fair share of detractors, but he also had the championship belt. Emblematic, or so the sociologists believed, of those—many of whom happened to be white—who resented Ali's defiance of the establishment, Frazier had found solace in his role.

The Rub

Dissected from many angles, "The Rub," or the bottom line, came down to each fighter's position regarding many things, not the least being patriotism, religious beliefs, and race. The materials provided to the media presented it in this manner[4]:

> Who are these men? "Muhammad Ali is a narcissist and a charmer. He is unpredictable, electrifying and argumentative."[5] "Joe Frazier is everybody's fighter, white or black."[6]
> When questioned about patriotism, religious beliefs, and race, or the often-cited criticisms of both participants, they responded accordingly.

Regarding his military service Ali stated, "Sweep out the cell, man, here I come. I ain't got no squawk with them Viet Cong."[7] And, regarding his origin, Ali confirmed, "My white blood came from slave masters, from raping. The white blood harms us. It hurts us. When we was darker we was stronger. We are purer."[8]

Regarding Ali's position on military service, Frazier declared: "You tell your friend, Clay, he ought to be ashamed of himself. This country gave him everything he's got and he don't want to fight for it. He don't help the black people. He hurts them. He ain't no leader of the black people. He's just full of 'con.' When the time comes you'll see who's going to beat who's ass. I'm blacker than he is. There ain't one black spot on his whole body."[9]

Regarding Ali's feelings on race, Frazier stated, "He [Ali] believes that the white man and the black man should be different. But, hell, I don't want to live off hate. My kids are going to have plenty of problems, like I had. They don't need any more."[10]

It's Time

Ali, his red velvet robe fluttering about the ring before "The Fight" as if to warn us that we were ultimately responsible for the result, was there by demand. He was a millionaire rebel as defiant as the bag ladies that lined Eighth Avenue. In contempt of his adversary and regardless of anything he stood for, Ali's razor-edge sneer tried to penetrate Frazier's glare, but it could not. The most colorful figure ever to enter a ring lost the fight before it even began.

As the bell rang, the show began. Ali's defiant attitude, enhanced by his flawless physique, seemed to intensify with each passing second. Toying with Frazier, like a captured animal in a shoebox, he pushed, poked, prodded and mocked every movement by his opponent. Wearing him down at every instance, from leaning on his shoulders to pushing him during clinches, Ali believed he could abrade his adversary like a tire on a road course. Then, precisely as he predicted, he would knock out his rival in the sixth round. At least, that was exactly what he believed. Anyhow, it was a miscalculation—a rarity, as he would later be more than happy to confirm. Frazier's indignation for his antagonist was much stronger than anticipated. And it grew round by round—when the Philadelphia fighter dropped his gloves at one point and laughed, everyone knew he had Ali just where he wanted him, as he endured more jabs than President Richard Nixon.

Ali's mentor, Angelo Dundee, admonished his fighter for his behavior, or the "clowning," as the fighter would later call it. Bulling his way through Ali's jabs—the few that didn't strike him, that is—Frazier answered with blows that were accumulating damage. The former champion's countenance and body were being plied like pizza dough. When his unpredictable left hook landed, most spectators marveled that any human, yet alone Ali, could withstand the blow. Strategically, the Philadelphia fighter moved upstairs and hurt his antagonist in the eleventh and twelfth rounds. It was obvious by the final term that Ali needed a miracle to win the fight.

In the fifteenth round, about twenty seconds after the opening bell, Frazier caught Ali with a mammoth left hook that sent him onto his back. Arising slowly to the count of four, trying desperately to think of a way to camouflage the action as anything other than his own vulnerability, Ali resorted to survival tactics. Foremost to him was finishing the fight. When the bell finally tolled, the former champion's head hung low, his swollen jaw was to his chest, and his pride hung on an inevitable decision—shame was private, humiliation was public. On this day, David had traded in his slingshot for a left hook. Upon hearing the verdict, Ali bolted from his corner to his dressing room, then departed for the hospital. His jaw was not fractured, but his pride certainly was.

All the official scorecards read Frazier: Judge Artie Aidala had it 9–6 (rounds), Referee Arthur Mercante had it 8–6 with one even, and Judge Bill Recht had it 11–4. A few days later, the winner entered a Philadelphia hospital, where he was treated for exhaustion, high blood pressure and kidney problems. Ali denied the scorecards and believed Frazier's need of hospital care, which of course he needed as well, was proof of an incorrect verdict. Nobody bought it. Ali's post-fight rant of "I really won" was a delusion. And nobody bought that either, because most had spent all their money on the fight.

The numbers spoke volumes: each fighter received $2.5 million (millionaire Jack Kent Cooke had guaranteed the bulk of the fee), with the Garden taking the difference. The live gate at the venue was $1.3 million (a record for an indoor bout) and the total gross was $20 million.

If truly great events are measured by the frequency of which symbolism was attached, then "The Fight" was truly that.

The Fallout

The fallout from "The Fight" was quick, but far from painless. The Empire struck back first, just to remind employees where they were working—New York State felt it only appropriate to file a jeopardy assessment of $348,000 against both Ali and Frazier's $2.5 M guarantee. In addition to income tax, the state had a five percent tax on both the live gate and the ancillary income. Pocket penetration, or a death warrant as some boxing promoters saw it, would become an enormous factor in negotiating future boxing matches.[11]

Forgotten Rounds

Ken Buchanan retained his world lightweight championship by picking up a united fifteen-round decision over Ismael Laguna on September 13. In the rematch, the "Fighting Carpenter" from Edinburgh, despite the enormous swelling under his left eye, dominated the later rounds and even had the twenty-eight-year-old Panamanian wobbling in the fourteenth.

But the most impressive Panamanian on the card was a twenty-year-old-fighter by the name of Roberto Durán, who dropped Brooklyn's Benny Huertas sixty-six seconds into the semifinal bout. Unbeaten in twenty-five bouts, with twenty-two knockouts, Durán impressed Teddy Brenner so much that the matchmaker inked him into the title mix.

An unbeaten George Foreman returned to the City Ring to meet Luis Pires, the former South American heavyweight champion, on October 29. Pires had lost the championship to Oscar Bonavena. It took Foreman only four rounds to batter Pires into submission. A crowd of almost 7,000, which was fewer than anticipated, turned out for the Garden event. Worth noting, and no offense to George Foreman, Roller Derby the following week attracted a crowd of more than 16,000.[12]

Fighter of the Year

Two notable fights weren't held in New York: Rubén Olivares regained his bantam title with a win over Chucho Castillo on April 3 (Inglewood, California), and Carlos

Monzón defeated veteran Emile Griffith to retain his middle crown on September 26 (Monte Carlo).

Despite the adversity, it was a historical year for boxing and Madison Square Garden. The City Ring hosted "The Fight," or "The Fight of the Century," between Joe Frazier and Muhammad Ali. Without question, nobody shined the City Ring more in 1971 than Joe Frazier.[13]

1972

Known as "The Meat Wagon," the trainer handled fourteen of Joe Louis's opponents, but it seemed like a lot more. The Harlem-raised instructor would walk them to their corner, pump them up, send them out, and cart them away in far more pieces than when they arrived. Louis became so familiar with his face, he thought he was a member of the Garden staff. He was Ray Arcel, perhaps the most gifted trainer the ring had ever seen. The tutor behind names like Jack "Kid" Berg, Jim Braddock, Ezzard Charles, Barney Ross, Freddie Steele, and Tony Zale. And there he was, standing next to another pupil, Roberto Durán. Arcel was preparing him for a shot at Ken Buchanan's world lightweight crown in Madison Square Garden on June 26.

Various disputes with Jim Norris and the International Boxing Club during the 1950s sent Arcel into a premature retirement. Add to this a mysterious lead-pipe assault on the trainer that was never solved, and you had yourself a solid rationale to take a break from the fight game. But Ramil "Ray" Arcel was back. It would be his first evening in a boxer's corner in eighteen years, and if that didn't send a statement regarding the Panamanian's talent, nothing would. It was Carlos Eleta, the wealthy industrialist and an old friend of the trainer, who convinced Arcel that he had found a talent. And boy, had he.

Border Control

Ken Buchanan, the Scottish master, was a smooth stylist who could make an awkward knockout artist like Roberto Durán look foolish. Even if the unbeaten Panamanian had knocked out twenty-four opponents, nine in the first round, the "Fighting Carpenter" wasn't impressed.

In one of the most chaotic endings in boxing history, Roberto Durán delivered an abdominal blow to Ken Buchanan after the bell had sounded to end the thirteenth round. Analogous to previous rounds, the fighters had not heard the gong and punches continued to fly. All of a sudden, Buchanan was on his back holding his groin. The referee had warned Durán earlier in the round to keep his punches up. Buchanan, who was losing the fight, was fatigued by the thirteenth but managed a flurry in the final ten seconds. Referee Johnny Lobianco grabbed Durán from behind only a few seconds after the bell, but Durán had already managed to inflict the damage. The match went into the books as a Durán victory via TKO. The fight footage was indecisive, and most of those sitting ringside did not see or hear the blow. In the dressing room following the fight, Team Buchanan exhibited proof or a dented fighter's protective cup. As they say in Boston, Nuf Ced!

In a very short period of time, Roberto Durán had been able to attract a very loud and loyal following. Much of the popularity was courtesy of the Garden, which capitalized on the fighter's graduation from the streets of Panama City; naturally, the marimba band accompanied by a herd of flamenco dancers certainly didn't hurt. Suffice it to say that Markson knew a mina de oro (gold mine) when he saw it.

ALI RETURNS

On July 6, Muhammad Ali signed a contract to fight Floyd Patterson. The twelve-round Madison Square Garden duel was initially slated for August, but later rescheduled to September 20. The news conference, held in the Felt Forum, had all the excitement of a routine oil change.

For the first five rounds Ali played with Patterson, patiently inflicting minor damage as the moments passed by. Ali didn't care. The graceful boxer, in complete control, would begin his assault when he was good and ready. That time came in the sixth round, when a noticeably aroused fighter landed a solid right hand that slit Patterson's left eyelid. The only questions that remained were: when would he deliver his boyhood idol, and how much damage would the old fighter incur on the way out the door?

By the end of the seventh, Patterson's vision was impaired. Following a damage assessment, referee Arthur Mercante stopped the fight. The play ended, at least to some, exactly as it should: it was Floyd Patterson's last fight in Madison Square Garden and his final professional contest. The torch had been passed.

A TRILOGY BEGINS—
ESTEBAN DE JESÚS V. ROBERTO DURÁN I

Puerto Rican fighter Esteban "Vita" de Jesús scored a unanimous ten-round Garden decision over Roberto Durán in a non-title fight on November 17. The fighter flattened Durán with a left hook in the very first round. Arising at the count of two, Durán became far more cautious in his approach. Taking command and firing at will with long-range artillery—his rights were solid and his left hooks accurate—de Jesús had set the tone of the battle. When it was over, de Jesús not only became the first boxer to knock Durán down, but the first to hand him a loss. It was de Jesús's thirtieth victory in thirty-one fights.

ALI AND FRAZIER: SEPARATE WAYS

In retrospect, the momentum generated by "The Fight" the previous year was dampened in 1972. Ali versus Frazier II never happened. However, Ali went 6–0 for the year, while Frazier, the heavyweight champion, picked up two victories. Three fights outside the city were worth noting: Bob Foster knocked out Chris Finnegan to retain his light heavy crown on September 26 (London); Carlos Monzón defeated Bennie Briscoe in defense of his middle title on November 11 (Buenos Aires); and Muhammad Ali dropped Bob Foster numerous times on the way to an eighth-round knockout on November 21 (Stateline, Nevada).[14]

Foreign dominance was becoming a reality in nearly every division. For example, Panama claimed four titleholders: Roberto Durán, Alfonso "Peppermint" Frazer, Ernesto Marcel and Enrique Pinder. Only two world champions, Joe Frazier and Bob Foster, lived in the United States.

Fighter of the Year

As for those who shined the City Ring, Ken Buchanan went 2-1, including the unfortunate loss to Roberto Durán, as well as his final appearance inside the Arena. However, he would return the following year to fight inside the Felt Forum. Buchanan, at 44-2, already had a brilliant career and he wasn't done yet.

1973

A mere twenty-two days into the month of January, the boxing gods spoke, not from New York City, but Kingston, Jamaica. Distracted by all his mega-offers for an Ali rematch, Joe Frazier failed to recall all the elements that had brought him the championship when he entered the ring against George Foreman. Floored three times by Foreman in the first, Frazier would repeat the process in the second. All Hail King George!

Harry Markson, President of Madison Square Garden, Inc., retired on March 31. The Garden's fifth impresario, like his predecessors, was instrumental in the legacy of the esteemed venue—it all began with Tex Rickard, then Jimmy Johnston, Mike Jacobs, Jim Norris and finally Markson. Teddy Brenner, the Garden's matchmaker since 1959, succeeded Markson. It wasn't comfortable picking up the pieces after Norris, but Markson succeeded in doing it. He removed the layers of the Garden tarnish, one round at a time, in order to recapture the hardest moral principle: integrity.

Brenner's first major announcement came on April 3, when he offered George Foreman a guarantee of $1 million, or an option of forty percent of all revenues, to defend his title against Jerry Quarry on June 20 inside the City Ring. Later, the fighter would choose to safeguard his crown in Canada.

In other news, NYSAC suspended Roberto Durán's boxing license, then reminded him that he must uphold his title against Ken Buchanan in Madison Square Garden within 90 days or lose recognition. Young Vito Antuofermo, the Brooklyn middleweight, picked up a ten-round split decision victory over New Jersey fighter Art Kettles inside the Felt Forum on April 31. The Brooklyn middle looked promising as he took his record to 16-0-1.

Jimmy Ellis, who replaced an ailing Jerry Quarry, fought Earnie Shavers on June 18 inside Madison Square Garden. Ellis, at age thirty-three, was the oldest of the leading contenders, which meant he would be evaluated fight-by-fight for future consideration. Last engaging in the Garden back in 1970, Ellis understood this, but hoped for another title shot anyway. Yet his dream was vanquished with a sledgehammer blow by Earnie Shavers at the 2:39 mark of the first round. The hard-hitting and assertive Shavers quickly placed his name alongside that of Ken Norton, who had recently defeated Muhammad Ali, as another very impressive contender. On the undercard, middleweight Vito Antuofermo captured a second-round technical knockout over Tony "Kid" Durango.

Back to the Future

The summer of 1973 saw boxing once again televised nationally, as it graced the programming of the American Broadcasting Company on a weekly basis. From July 7 through September 1, the Felt Forum was the venue of choice on Saturday afternoons for the first nationally televised weekly boxing in nine years. In a spin of a different sort, Brenner also decided to award American world titles. But would the public buy into his new designations?

On July 7, Sammy Goss of Trenton, New Jersey, took a twelve-round unanimous decision over New York's Jose Fernandez to capture the American Junior Lightweight Championship. Before each fight, Brenner scheduled speakers as well as clinics, for both children and adults; the fights took place at 4:00 P.M. On this occasion that speaker was Muhammad Ali.

Ali versus Frazier II was finally scheduled for twelve rounds inside Madison Square Garden on February 4, 1974, later to be moved up to January 28. The only possible glitch was a ruling by the State Tax Commission. The deal was banking on the fighters' being taxed only on the income derived in New York from ancillary revenue. Although changes in the heavyweight division had taken place since the first pair's battle, it was hoped that the rivalry was strong enough to paint a positive revenue picture.

At age 24, George Foreman was the new heavyweight champion. Meanwhile, Joe Frazier, still wondering what hit him, headed across the pond to pick up a victory over Joe Bugner. Ali also defeated Bugner before having his jaw broken by Ken Norton in a losing effort. Ali then defeated Norton in a rematch before shuffling off to Jakarta to defeat Rudi Lubbers.

In a pair of fights that flew beneath the radar, Arnold Taylor staged an incredible comeback—after being floored four times—to knock out Romeo Anaya to win the bantam title during a fight held on November 3 (Johannesburg); and Bob Foster, the light heavyweight champion, outpointed Pierre Fourie in a December 1 rematch (Johannesburg).[15]

Fighter of the Year

It wasn't a great year for New York City boxing. The departure of Harry Markson from the Garden left an enormous void to fill, even with the talented Teddy Brenner. The reemergence of television as a viable revenue source was a step in the right direction, as were the clinics held in conjunction with events. Both Quarry brothers combined went 3-0-2 for the year in the venue. But nobody added a better shine than Vito Antuofermo. He went 5-1 inside the City Ring, and went 8-1 for the year; every bout but one was held in New York City.

1974

The early bird might get the worm, but the second mouse gets the cheese. Ali versus Frazier II had all the potential, or so the promoters believed, of a "Super Fight," sort of boxing equivalent to the Super Bowl, or even a Hollywood blockbuster. It was like dropping Paul Newman and Robert Redford into an unlimited budget film: how could it not be an epic?

The Fight II

Billed as "The Fight II," it was twelve rounds of heavyweight boxing promoted by Madison Square Garden Boxing, Inc., in association with Forum Boxing, Inc., and Top

Rank, Inc. It would take place back in the "Big Apple," inside the City Ring, on January 28. Once again, it was two gladiators each unwilling to stand in the shadow of the other.

The Sell

The picture looked different. Muhammad Ali, the top contender, sought to avenge his 1971 loss to Frazier to secure a shot at world heavyweight champion George Foreman. Joe Frazier, also a top contender who was dethroned by Foreman, just wanted an opportunity to get his title back.

"I'm the people's champion," Ali proclaimed. "Ask them. They'll tell you I beat Joe Frazier. I sent him to the hospital. His face was all messed up and I came out pretty, didn't I?"[16]

"Got to start all over," Frazier believed, "Got a lot of work to do to get me my title back. I just hope George gives me a chance. I would give it to him."[17]

"I'm going to be the first black fighter you can look at and say, 'There's a wise, wealthy man with property, businesses and two million dollars in the bank," Ali continued. "I found out why boxing's mainly black; why entertainers go broke. While they're making it they forget they're not going to keep going. And they're so great and so good they don't see themselves falling. They don't realize that champions come and go."[18]

"He lies to the people," Frazier claimed. "He gets people all fired up like he's some kind of god or something and all the while he's lying to them."[19]

While many of the leftover undertones remained, the softer sell for "The Fight II" was "hypocritical vs. sincere."

First there was "Smokin'" Joe Frazier, age thirty, a mere three and a half pounds heavier than when he stunned Ali back on March 8, 1971. He was a wiser, more refined boxer who had been taught a lesson by Father Time, a.k.a. George Foreman. Next there was Ali, age thirty-two, no first name needed, a legend in his own mind, a mere three pounds heavier as well.

Frazier was sanguine, quiet, and unyielding, while his opponent was confident, fluid, and antagonizing. Neither fighter was willing to stick his neck out, like they both did last time, with a goofy prediction. An impressive 1,500 spectators went to the weigh-in on Sunday, January 27, at the Felt Forum. Neither fighter saw the other in order to avoid the "scuffle in the studio," or a rerun of the programmed television wrestling match that occurred on national television, which cost each fighter $5,000 in fines levied from NYSAC.

Ali was a favorite (7–5), the Garden was sold out (a record gate for a non-title fight), and although the fighter guarantees were only $850,000, many who followed the sport felt that the revenue generated from other aspects of the venture, such as the ancillary revenue, might allow each fighter to retire comfortably in his own country.

The Outcome

It was front-page news: "Ali Beats Frazier On Decision Here," the *New York Times* boldly stated on Tuesday, January 29, 1974. It was rounds 16 through 27, a mere extension of their first fight back in 1971. But Ali took the twelve-round unanimous decision and naturally his cut of the $1,053,688 gate. The series was now even. That should be enough, right? A mere three sentences into most accounts, including Dave Anderson's *Times* account, the term "rubber match" surfaced.

Solid Ali jabs and combinations prevented Frazier from making a Garden stand. Ali dominated most of the rounds, with his best punch administered to the jaw of the Philadelphia pugilist in the second round; it was a straight right delivered by his bursitis-ridden hand. Ali clowned to a lesser degree, held more, danced a bit less, and retreated better. In the end, Frazier needed a knockout, which he couldn't deliver, to take the fight. Most closed-circuit viewers didn't feel cheated by a relatively close distance decision; Ali was clearly victorious. Of paramount importance to the victor: Just when, and how, to call out George Foreman. Of secondary importance: Ali v. Frazier III, and what it would mean to bring a heavyweight title into play.

The Aftermath

To counter the promotional emergence of promoter Don King, Brenner turned to the second- and third-ranked heavyweight contenders, Joe Frazier and Jerry Quarry for a twelve-round clash in the Garden on June 17. The promotion was part of a closed-circuit double-header that featured Bob Foster, the light heavyweight champion, doing battle against Argentine boxer Jorge Ahumada live from Albuquerque, New Mexico.

The duel between Frazier and Quarry was a rematch of their June 1969 clash that saw Frazier victorious after seven rounds. It was later announced that Joe Louis, the former heavyweight champion, would referee the Garden bout.

Frazier proved far too much to handle for Quarry. The California fighter was badly cut and beaten during their Garden war. Although most the fans were calling out for a stoppage much sooner, referee Louis didn't halt the conflict until the 1:37 mark of the fifth round. Over 14,000 fans watched as Quarry's crimson mask—his wounds later requiring fifteen stitches to close—essentially put an end to his championship hopes. Afterwards, many stayed to watch Foster fight Ahumada to a draw.[20]

A talented yet controversial American boxing promoter, Donald King (born August 20, 1931) was recognized for his involvement in numerous historic boxing match-ups. Often associated with "The Rumble in the Jungle" and the "Thrilla in Manila," King promoted some of the finest fighters in the history of the sport.

CRISIS? WHAT CRISIS?

On Thursday, June 20, Madison Square Garden's new president, Alan N. Cohen, announced his willingness to drop the sport of boxing as one of the venue's main attractions. This action was being taken as a cost-cutting measure. Cohen, who replaced Irving M. Felt, cited New York Governor Malcolm Wilson's veto of a bill that would have given boxers tax breaks as part of the justification. The "boxing bill" would have eliminated the primary hurdle the Garden faced in negotiating many major bouts.[21] The tax was such a deterrent that it nearly cost Madison Square Garden the promotion of "The Fight." Cohen's fear was that, without the tax breaks, the Garden's boxing could not negotiate from a position of strength or maintain profitability.[22]

Only weeks after the announcement, 1,800 fans rioted in the Felt Forum as a result of a draw awarded to Puerto Rican fighter Eduardo Santiago over Vilomar Fernandez. It rained bottles, along with everything that could be broken. At a time when many boxing fans were up in arms over the possibility of losing the Garden sport, this type of immature and violent behavior proved that perhaps it should be considered. By the second week in December, NYSAC warned that another riot at the Felt Forum would result in the end of boxing.[23]

Ali Back on Top

It happened on October 30, in Kinshasa, Zaire, Africa. With an eighth-round knockout of George Foreman, Muhammad Ali became the second man in history to regain the world heavyweight championship. The person behind the battle was Don King, a black promoter. In a sport dominated by black boxers, not only was he racially correct, he was also vice-president of Video Techniques, Inc., a closed-circuit television firm. Having handled the "Caracas Caper," also known as George Foreman vs. Ken Norton, he was confident in his abilities, yet aware of the possible pitfalls.[24] The charismatic promoter was loquacious, connected, and politically savvy.[25]

Emile Griffith entered the Garden on November 22, to fight the twenty-two-year-old Vito Antuofermo, who was only six when Griffith began his professional career. A resident of Brooklyn, Antuofermo was a bona fide fighter with a record of 26–1–1, including nine consecutive victories. Griffith, thirty-five years old, had won the world welterweight title three times and the middleweight title twice.[26] But Vito Antuofermo didn't impress easily. The Brooklyn boxer took the ten-round unanimous decision over Griffith, and never lost a beat. Although there were no knockdowns, it was a hard-fought contest. Antuofermo forced the action and took the battle inside as often as he could, much to the chagrin of his opponent.

Fighter of the Year

The boxing year belonged to Muhammad Ali, who captured the heavyweight title for the second time with his victory in Zaire. Outside of New York, there were fights that couldn't be overlooked: Roberto Durán's knockout victory over Esteban de Jesús on March 16 (Panama City); Bobby Chacon's ninth-round knockout of Danny Lopez on May 24 (Los Angeles); and Rodrigo Valdéz's victory over Benny Briscoe—the only knockout loss of his career—on May 25 (Monte Carlo).

Ali v. Frazier II highlighted the year for the Garden, but the Governor's veto of the "boxing bill," not to mention all the violence inside the Felt Forum, were difficult to ignore. The frequency of good fights had also fallen off, leaving many to wonder just what the future had in store for the venue. Inside the City Ring, without question, both Ali and Frazier, in their final New York City meeting, shined the ring's patina.

1975

In a crushing blow to boxing fans, Monday night fights at the Felt Forum were suspended. Since August 1974, three riotous outbreaks had occurred and tainted the reputation of the facility. Just how this would impact future shows in the facility remained to be seen; however, what was certain was the Garden corporation's president, Alan N. Cohen was committed to decorum and profitability.

Madison Square Garden, Inc., with a bulk of its shares owned by Gulf and Western Industries, and operating in the red (revenue didn't meet operating expenses), was noted as being for sale by consultant Donald J. Trump on April 14.[27] Two unnamed Arab oil interests were believed to be involved. The corporation owned the site of the previous Garden; Two Penn Plaza, which included an office tower (80 percent stake); Roosevelt Raceway; and holdings in Chicago that included two hotels, two race tracks and land. Less than ten days later, the Garden offered Ali a cool $3 million to defend his title against Joe Frazier in a rubber match inside the City Ring. The entire package amounted to $4.5 million with the Garden handling everything, including television.[28]

Three championship fights in a single night—two live and one broadcast—would highlight a sensational evening at Madison Square Garden on Monday, June 30. The program opened at 8:15 and saw Víctor Galíndez defend his World Boxing Association light heavyweight title by picking up a tough fifteen-round decision over Argentine fighter Jorge Ahumada. Next, legendary boxer Carlos Monzón, owner of the WBA middleweight title, knocked out popular Tampa fighter Tony Licata in the tenth round of their duel. This would be Monzón's sole appearance inside Madison Square Garden; he had not lost one fight since October 9, 1964. And on the screens, live from Kuala Lumpur, Malaysia, world heavyweight champion Muhammad Ali outpointed Joe Bugner in fifteen rounds to retain his crown.

THE THRILLA IN MANILA

It wasn't held inside Madison Square Garden—a phrase that was getting hard to swallow—but instead Ali versus Frazier III found its way to Manila in the Philippines on October 1. The "Thrilla in Manila" would witness the champion taking control of the duel with his left jab, while keeping Frazier at bay with his right. Frazier, behind on the cards, ignited in the sixth and maintained his vicious body assault on his opponent until the tenth round. Battered by Frazier's trademark left hook, Ali somehow managed to endure the punishment. Stepping up his game, Ali hurt Frazier in the twelfth round and thrashed him to such an extent that his manager Eddie Futch would not allow his fighter to answer the bell for the fifteenth. It would enter the record books as an Ali fourteenth-round knockout (the bell not having rung). Frazier could no longer see out of his right eye, forcing Futch to stop the contest.

It was an Ali victory. Some saw this fight the best of the trilogy, as both fighters seemed to leave nothing on the table; few boxers could have endured such punishment. The pair would go on to fight another day, but would never again fight each other.[29]

"The Thrilla in Manila" painted a nice international vista for the sport, as did other fights outside of the city, including Roberto Durán's knockout victory over Ray Lampkin on March 2 (Panama City), José Nápoles's controversial victory over Armando Muniz on March 30 (Acapulco), and John Stracey's spectacular sixth-round knockout victory over Nápoles on December 6 (Mexico City).

FIGHTER OF THE YEAR

The year definitely belonged to Muhammad Ali, who defeated Chuck Wepner, Ron Lyle, Joe Bugner and finally Joe Frazier.

In a rare appearance, middleweight Carlos Monzón entered between the ropes of the City Ring for the first, and what would prove to be the last time. His speed, punching power and instinct were still evident, even at this stage of his career. When he finally hung up the gloves, he had compiled a record of 87–3–9, with 59 knockouts. Each of his three losses, which were early in his career, were avenged.

1976

For fifty years, the New York Golden Gloves boxing show had attracted superior talent, while bringing out some of the finest sportsmanship boxing had to offer. On Friday, March 19, over 20,000 people turned out for a commemorative evening, including Governor Hugh L. Carey and former heavyweight champion Floyd Patterson. Catching the eyes of many was a nineteen-year-old Long Island construction worker named Gerald Cooney, who picked up a decision over a New York Recreation Department employee—not to mention Golden Gloves veteran—by the name of Earl Tripp.[30]

Speaking of talented amateurs, the five gold-medal winners on the United States Olympic boxing team—Leo Randolph, a flyweight from Tacoma, Washington; Howard Davis, a lightweight from Glen Cove, Long Island; Sugar Ray Leonard, a light welterweight from Palmer Park, Maryland; and the Spinks brothers from St. Louis, Michael, a middleweight, and Leon, a light heavyweight—had been living a dream, and just when you thought it couldn't get any better, it did. Teddy Brenner, director of boxing for Madison Square Garden, met with Rollie Schwartz, the manager of the team, and offered all the medalists bouts on the Ali v. Norton undercard scheduled for September 28 in Yankee Stadium. Be it patriotism or just plain good business sense, it would prove a wise choice even if no one took him up on the offer. It didn't take a rocket scientist to realize the potential of this team and its members.

Muhammad Ali v. Ken Norton

Ali was a favorite (8–5) against Ken Norton in their fifteen-round Yankee Stadium extravaganza scheduled for September 28. Staged by Madison Square Garden and Top Rank, Inc. (handling the ancillary rights), the event had potential written all over it. And in capturing a fifteen-round unanimous decision over Norton, Ali did not disappoint. As for Norton, the man who broke the champion's jaw back in 1973, the disappointment of the razor-thin defeat was almost more than the fighter could handle. Remember, the benefit of the doubt always favors the champion. Only two heavyweight champions were dethroned by a decision: Max Schmeling (who lost to Jack Sharkey) and Jack Dempsey (who lost to Gene Tunney).[31]

"Mr. Gray"

Nobody pulled more strings at Madison Square Garden than master puppeteer Paul John "Frankie" Carbo, the "underworld czar of boxing," who died on November 10 in a Miami Hospital. He was 72 years of age. Carbo's criminal resume read like a felony dictionary, and included over a dozen arrests, including five for murder. From armed robbery and bootlegging to gambling and vagrancy, if it had an angle, Frankie found it. His underworld acquaintances—friends were nonexistent in organized crime—included Albert Anastasia, Frank Costello and Bugsy Siegel.

By 1959, Carbo and his partner Frank "Blinky" Palermo—the two had worked together as part of "The Combination," a successful fight-fixing organization—owned a majority interest in the contract of heavyweight boxer Sonny Liston. The fighter had a criminal record as long as a city block and had a reach to match; even the police feared him. In 1958, Joseph "Pep" Barone, who was a front man for "The Combination," became Liston's boxing manager. The following year, the fighter's career ignited and he was on a course for the heavyweight championship, which he captured in 1962.

In the late 1950s, Carbo's legal troubles began. First, he was convicted of managing boxers without a license and was sentenced to two years in the New York City jail on Rikers Island. Following his release in 1960, Carbo was subpoenaed to appear before a Senate investigation committee, headed by Senator Estes Kefauver, to testify on his involvement in professional boxing. Carbo took the Fifth Amendment 25 times, answering questions with the response, "I cannot be compelled to be a witness against myself."

Carbo's boxing marionettes included fighters, managers, matchmakers and promoters. In 1961, he was convicted of conspiracy and extortion.[32] Carbo was sentenced to twenty-five years in Alcatraz Federal Penitentiary in California, and subsequently transferred to the McNeil Island Federal Penitentiary in Washington State. Granted early parole due to ill health, Carbo, forever known as a New York City Mafia soldier in the Lucchese crime family, a boxing promoter, and a gunman with Murder, Inc., was released from prison and returned to Miami, where he died on November 22, 1976. To this very day, boxing historians still marvel at his reach.

Big Apple Exodus

By 1976, the boxing scene appeared to be shifting out of New York City. There were, however, a few bouts worth noting overseas. A seventeen-year-old phenom, and future star, by the name of Wilfred Benítez became the youngest boxing champion in history by capturing the junior welter title from Antonio Cervantes in a fifteen-round duel on March 6 (San Juan). On May 22, Víctor Galíndez pulled off a magnificent victory over Richie Kates (Johannesburg). And Carlos Palomino gradually wore down John Stracey to take the welter title on June 22 (London).

A Puerto Rican boxer, Wilfred Benítez (born September 12, 1958) earned his first of three career world titles in separate weight divisions at the age of seventeen and is best remembered as a skilled and aggressive fighter with exceptional defensive abilities.

In the City Ring, no single boxer shined its patina in 1976, but an organization had been doing it for years: the New York Golden Gloves. It was Arch Ward, sports editor of the *Chicago Tribune*, who came up with the idea of a citywide Chicago amateur boxing tournament back in 1923, and it gained sponsorship from the *Tribune* in 1927. Soon, an exciting annual tournament was being held between Chicago and New York. In later years the idea was taken up by other cities, and a national tournament was held. Along with the New York Golden Gloves, the Chicago tournament was viewed as one of the two elite Golden Gloves Championships in the United States.[33]

15

Fade Away, 1977–1978

> I don't want to be a millionaire, I just want to live like one.
> —Bernard "Toots" Shor, saloonkeeper

"Toots" Shor's—at 51 West 51st Street, 33 West 52nd Street, and 5 East 54th Street—was a sports landmark. Its name derived from the wisdom of its proprietor: Naming a joint after yourself wasn't egotistical, only a guarantee that you knew how to spell it. For thirty-five years, Toots Shor, New York's tender tavern owner, ministered to the needs of actors, athletes, authors, entrepreneurs, politicians, stock pushers and beat writers. If a pug wordsmith or baseball beat needed a slant, he knew he could always find it at the joint. Shor died on Sunday, January 23, at New York University Hospital. He was 73 years old.

As the "Ali Era" drew to a close, Garden management priorities were changing. A new breed of smaller charismatic fighters emerged, exhibiting nothing but potential. Finally, that excitement every boxing fan used to feel in his gut was returning.

1977

Originally scheduled for the Garden on January 31, the impressive card of three ten-rounders was moved to February 2. It featured Harold Weston, Jr., the popular New York City welterweight, facing Wilfred Benítez of Puerto Rico, the World Boxing Association's undefeated junior welterweight champion; ring veteran Emile Griffith taking on New Jersey middleweight Christy Elliott; and Pedro Soto battling Pedro Agosto, for what was being billed as the "heavyweight championship of Puerto Rico." The welter division was shaping up as a very competitive weight class thanks to Pepino Cuevas, the WBA titleholder, and Carlos Palomino, who wore the World Boxing Council crown. Weston, confident of his own skills, hoped to bury Benítez first, before taking care of the others. However, that was about as easy as climbing Mount Everest in a spacesuit. Always looking for angles in deals, the Garden later offered $100,000 to the winner of the Palomino versus Stracey welter title fight, if they matched with the victor of Weston versus Benítez.

The biggest surprise of the night came when the unbeaten, and clearly overconfident, Wilfred Benítez decided to clown around with his opponent Harold Weston during the final rounds of their confrontation. The behavior was humiliating to Weston, a local pug who had more than his fair share of support in the audience. The antics, which included the Ali shuffle, punch windmills, and much more, cost Benítez a victory and got him a draw.[1] Christy Elliott lost a majority decision to his idol Emile Griffith, and Pedro Soto took a unanimous decision over sub Brian O'Melia. The Garden boxing show drew 10,000 fans.

On an exciting note, lightweight Howard Davis, Jr., an Olympic gold medal winner, was tentatively scheduled for a Garden undercard in March. He was the first member of the 1976 U.S. Olympic boxing team—arguably the most gifted set of American boxers ever assembled for a major international event—to really test the professional waters. As always, the question for his handlers was the pace to which you move your fighter up in competition. Confidence, as everyone understood, was paramount to a boxer's success. Granted, some former Olympians had still been working their way through the boxing labyrinth, including Ronnie Harris and Ray Seales, but this new group of athletes appeared more self-assured.

Speaking of new talent, a young left-hander fighting out of Brockton, Massachusetts—home of you-know-who—was picking up some decent ink, and his name was Marvin Hagler. The southpaw middleweight finished the previous year with a record of 30-2-1.

Muhammad Ali, who had announced his ring retirement on November 30, showed up in the United States District Court of Chicago to claim his contractual obligation to Madison Square Garden to fight Duane Bobick was null and void. The Garden had filed a $4 million suit on March 16 against Ali, claiming breach of contract. Ali's attorney Henry R. Mason claimed the agreement was not valid because Herbert Muhammad, the fighter's business manager, had not signed it. Accordingly, the defendant (Muhammad Ali) had established his defense of abandonment, and judgment was entered for the defendant and against the plaintiff (Madison Square Garden Boxing, Inc.).[2]

It was a merciless overhand right—a few body blows had set the stage—into the unbeaten and unsuspecting countenance of Duane Bobick that dropped the redhead. Up at the count of nine, he staggered forward before referee Petey Della stopped the fight. Ken Norton was just unrelenting with his arsenal—a crushing overhand right, accurate left hook and crippling right uppercut. The May 11 Garden battle ended with a Norton victory at the 0:58 mark of the opening round. After the fight, Norton immediately tried to call out Ali. Why not, considering the economic potential?

Summer Games

The Garden's Summer Festival of Boxing was held on June 22 and attracted an international crowd of more than 7,000 boxing fans. Alexis Argüello, from Managua, Nicaragua, dominated Juan "Cocoa" Sanchez, of the Dominican Republic. Sanchez was a prolific puncher, but lacked the power of Argüello. After the Dominican was dropped twice in the fourth term, the ring physician had seen enough damage, and Argüello was credited for a knockout.

Sean O'Grady, an eighteen-year-old from Okla-

A Nicaraguan boxer who competed from 1968 to 1995, Alexis Argüello (1952–2009) was a three-weight world champion. He held the WBA featherweight title from 1974 to 1976; the WBC super featherweight title from 1978 to 1980; and the WBC lightweight title from 1981 to 1982.

homa City, took a decision over New York's David Vasquez. O'Grady was a knockout artist who had impressed many with his 43 knockouts in 47 previous victories. Frankie Benítez, Wilfred's brother, grabbed a ten-round unanimous judgment over Cemal Kemaci, and Harold Weston, Jr., took a verdict over Andy Price of Los Angeles.

The excitement continued as over 11,000 hungry Garden fight fans turned out on August 3 for another look at Wilfred Benítez, a.k.a. "El Radar." The exciting junior welterweight systematically defeated (Jose Ramon) Ray Chavez Guerrero over fourteen rounds, before unleashing a nonstop assault that dropped the Venezuelan at the 1:41 mark of the fifteenth round. Having struggled to make the 140-pound weight limit, Benítez was now vowing to move up seven pounds to the welterweight division. His trainer believed the lack of strength was why it took his fighter so long to dispose of his antagonist.

Alex Argüello, the former world featherweight champion, was also included in the evening's card. The Nicaraguan fighter disposed of Jose Fernandez at the 2:06 mark of the opening round. Argüello understood the dilemma faced by Benítez, as he abandoned his 126-pound title to move up; he was now fighting at 131 pounds.

On August 19, Gulf and Western Industries, who had owned 81 percent of Madison Square Garden stock, took over the remainder of the company through a merger vote that took place at a stockholder's meeting. So the Garden, its adjacent office building, Roosevelt Raceway, Arlington and Washington Parks, the O'Hare Hilton (Chicago) and assorted real estate, not to mention the New York Knickerbockers and the New York Rangers, had a new owner.

Ali's Last Call

Earnie Shavers's knockout percentage ranked him first all-time among the heavyweights at .963; Muhammad Ali ranked tenth. The champion's record was 54–2, and although he had been knocked down, he had never been knocked out. Granted, Ali had fought better boxers, but none that hit as hard as the heavyweight who would earn the moniker "Puncher of the Century." In a bout scheduled for September 29 inside the City Ring, Muhammad Ali was taking on Earnie Shavers. Neither fighter would ever battle inside Madison Square Garden again.

Earnie Shavers, 54–5–1, had never gone more than ten rounds.[3] But that's because none of his opponents ever lasted that long. It was a scary thought. Coincidentally, this would be the first heavyweight title bout held in the Garden since Ali versus Frazier I, back on March 8, 1971. Need you be reminded that Ali lost that battle? Yet Shavers had lost his last Garden battle to Jerry Quarry.

As he entered the ring accompanied by the theme music from *Star Wars*, perhaps it was Ali's inner strength, or the "Force," that gave him the ability to withstand Shavers's powerful punches for fifteen rounds. But something did. The champion retained his title by acquiring a unanimous decision—all the scorecards had him ahead in the fight. His corner, which harbored some of the fight game's finest, was well aware that Shavers needed a knockout in the final round to take the title.[4] (In six of his last nine fights, Ali had gone the distance.) Over 14,000 fans saw the fight from inside the Garden, Ali's last ever in the City Ring. And they applauded the verdict in favor of "The G.O.A.T." (The Greatest of All-Time).

Taking a final look: Ali outweighed his last opponent by 13.75 pounds. Johnny LoBianco was Ali's last Garden referee, and he scored the fight 9–5, and one even; Ali's last ringside judges were Eva Shain (the first woman in history to judge a heavyweight championship fight) and Tony Castellano, who both scored the bout 9–6. Ali's last Garden bout was sanctioned by the World Boxing Council Heavyweight Title and the World Boxing Association Heavyweight Title (it was Ali's 10th defense of both). Ali's final Garden fight was broadcast in primetime on NBC and the commentators were Dick Enberg, Larry Merchant and Ken Norton, the #1 ranked heavyweight contender. Ali wore white Mitre trunks trimmed in black in his last Garden duel. The ticket scaling for the event was $100, $75, $50, $40, $30, and $20. There were three ten-round fights on the undercard: Alfredo Evangelista (KO8) vs. Pedro Soto; Alex Argüello (KO2) vs. Jerome Artis; and Mike Rossman (W10) vs. Gary Summerhays, along with a four-round battle, Bernardo Mercado (KO1) vs. Roger Russell. Also worth noting: An image of Vito Antuofermo vs. Mike Nixon appeared on the fight poster, though the pair did not fight each other until October 27.[5]

The painful reminder: New York State law required boxing promoters to pay the state five percent of the gross receipts, including money for broadcast, television and motion picture rights.[6]

Forgotten Rounds

In an amazing display of courage on November 18, Wilfred Benítez, down three times and nearly out at one point, managed to capture a split decision over Bruce Curry. The powerful punching of Curry, hailing from Los Angeles with a record of 13–0 before the fight, nearly pulled off the upset of the year. Over 6,000 Garden fans watched the event unfold, with likely another 6,000 wishing they had attended after reading the reviews. The fight was just so exciting that management booked a rematch for February 3, 1978; also on that card would be Benny Briscoe v. Vito Antuofermo.[7]

A quick corporate note: Garden challenges continued prompting Gulf & Western Industries to bring in David A. "Sonny" Werblin, from the Meadowlands Sports Complex in New Jersey, to take over as president and chief executive officer of the Madison Square Garden Corporation.[8]

Carlos Palomino's remarkable knockout victory over Armando Muniz on January 22 (Los Angeles), Jimmy Young's win over George Foreman on March 17 (San Juan), Carlos Zarate's fourth-round knockout of Alfonso Zamora on April 23 (Inglewood), and Matthew Franklin's twelfth-round kayo of Marvin Johnson on July 26 (Philadelphia), were just a few outstanding contests that took place out of town.

Fighter of the Year

The year in boxing belonged to Carlos Zarate, the unbeaten WBC bantam champion who knocked out Alfonso Zamora, the undefeated WBA bantam king. Zarate then retained his title by stopping Fernando Cabanela, Danilo Batista and Juan F. Rodriguez. Unfortunately for fight fans, Zarate would never fight inside Madison Square Garden.

The City Ring bid farewell to Muhammad Ali, Emile Griffith and Earnie Shavers. But it welcomed Alexis Argüello, and Gerry Cooney—both of whom went 3–0 on the year inside Madison Square Garden.[9]

Emile Griffith fought professionally twenty-eight times in Madison Square Garden, winning 24 and losing only 4; remember, he also fought in the venue as an amateur. His first professional Garden confrontation was back on August 7, 1959, and his last on February 2, 1977. Or, better stated, he was a willing participant and at the beck and call of Garden management for 6,390 days. The City Ring will miss Emile Griffith.

1978

"Time is the longest distance between two places, and it had been ten years since the opening of the new Garden," to modify an old Tennessee Willliams quote. Ten years that had been filled with change. A decade ago it was all about Ali, yet ten years later nobody was even certain of his fight status. Ten years ago, everybody was excited about the possibilities of the Felt Forum, yet a decade later its fight future was in jeopardy. A decade ago it was nostalgia over profitability, yet ten years later it seemed as if it was vice versa.

Dethroned! On February 15 in Las Vegas, Leon Spinks, a 10–1 underdog, defeated Muhammad Ali via a fifteen-round split decision. To add insult to injury, it was Spinks's eighth professional bout. The fight was close going into the final round and could have turned decisively in favor of either fighter with a forceful action. However, such was not the case. It was the champion's time to transfer ownership.

An Infusion of Youthful Talent

Let the sound of youthful exuberance resonate between the ropes. It appeared some new guns had ridden into town. The 1976 Olympic boxing team, with all of its personalities and success, was part of the excitement, but so too was the media. Television journalism, led by people like Jim McKay, who was then hosting ABC's Olympic broadcasts, was exciting viewers. Many of the amateur boxers had charmed their way through our living room screens and into our hearts. Arguably the most handsome and captivating of the entire lot was Sugar Ray Leonard. Others, including brothers Leon and Michael Spinks, were also establishing their own identities as they made their way through the division ranks.

In addition to television, the cinema also contributed to the appeal. *Rocky*, a 1976 American drama film directed by John G. Avildsen and both written by and starring Sylvester Stallone, had romanticized the sweet science. It was a portrayal of the American Dream, or a "rags to riches" story of a fighter. Rocky Balboa was an uneducated but kindhearted working class Italian-American boxer employed as a debt collector for a loan shark in the slums of Philadelphia. Nonetheless, dreams can come true in boxing, and he was given a championship shot.

The appeal of the American Olympians was one thing, but when you combined it with factors such as the growing interest in the lighter weight classes, the allure of an entirely new batch of international stars and a new cinematic hero, it was a winning recipe.[10]

A Night at the Garden—May 15, 1978

In a different spin, Garden management opted for an alternative marketing approach on May 15. If a real-life version of Rocky Balboa was out there, and it was a big *if*, then perhaps he could be identified and given an opportunity to showcase his skills on the sport's greatest stage. Six storylines, or matches if you will, were billed as "co-main events" and attracted over 7,000 spectators.

Back on December 19, 1958, a tough southpaw heavyweight from the Bronx named Bobby Halpern, a.k.a. the "Hebrew Hammer" (also "Crazy Bobby" in the streets), received his Garden debut against Tom McNeeley, an undefeated scrappy fighter out of Massachusetts. The Bronx boxer lost the fight, then seemed to lose his balance; he served seventeen and a half years for armed robbery, assault and kidnapping. While he was riding out his sentence in the pen, his mind never left the Garden. Everything about it, Halpern would recall, was exciting. Back on the streets in 1976, he returned to the gym—if the magic was still there, then why not give it another try?—and began fighting his way back out of White Plains in Westchester County. Halpern's story made it to the Garden and they bought it. They put him on a six-bout card, all scheduled eight-rounders. Halpern met Newark fighter Guy Casale on May 15, but a short right to the chin ended his dream at the 1:13 mark of the third round. Crushed like a wad of paper, the fighter fell through the ropes, still wondering what hit him.

Like Halpern, Bill Sharkey's life had taken a wrong turn: he served three years for manslaughter. The Garden booked him in a match with an undefeated Colombian heavyweight by the name of Bernardo Mercado. However, when the Colombian couldn't make the gig, Greg Sorrentino, out of Syracuse, substituted for him. The Italian, who entered the fight with a record of 9–1–2, took it to Sharkey and picked up the unanimous eight-round victory.

Johnny Turner was a promising 143-pounder from Sheepshead Bay in Brooklyn, who began his pro career in 1975. A good-looking kid, he had also done some acting on the side. In only his eighth fight, he made his Garden debut on September 30, 1975, against tomato can Pete Pagan and took the unanimous decision. In his next Garden appearance, on August 3, 1977, he took a points victory over Julio Garcia. Now, in his third appearance at the Garden, Turner faced Frankie Benítez, who had a record of 24–4–1. Turner stepped up his game and took it to Benítez in the final round. Sending a savage overhand right to the face of the Puerto Rican, he dropped the fighter to the canvas. Although Benítez took a standing eight-count, he was dazed and the referee stopped the duel at the 1:28 mark of the eighth round.[11]

G.G. Maldonado, a heavyweight from New Jersey, was scheduled to battle Gerry Cooney, the undefeated Long Island fighter, but the latter couldn't make it due to a swollen left hand. Nick Wells, a southpaw out of Fort Worth, took the place of another fighter who intended to sub for Cooney—this scenario seldom worked out well. In a fierce attempt to sell Wells, the Garden noted that as an amateur the Fort Worth fighter had stopped Larry Holmes, not once but twice, and even kayoed Scott LeDoux. Maldonado took the unanimous decision.

Popular light heavyweight Kevin Smith, from Jersey City, was booked on the ticket because he could draw spectators, and he did. The Garden staff also wanted to take a closer look at him; Smith had defeated only one fighter with a winning record and was booked to next meet Mike Quarry. Clyde Mudgett, with a record of 8–3, made the pilgrimage from Indianapolis to meet Smith. In the end, it hardly seemed worthwhile for Mudgett, as Smith, who sustained some damage, managed a unanimous verdict.

Marv Stinson, an undefeated heavyweight from Joe Frazier's stable and perhaps best known for losing to John Tate in the 1976 Olympic trials, met the popular Pedro Soto. Touted as "the heavyweight champion of Puerto Rico," Soto was a Garden regular who had turned into a punching bag in recent years—he had lost four of his previous six fights. Stinson, who didn't impress many, but more than Soto, took the united judgment.

All in all, the evening was very reminiscent of the "good ol' days" at the Garden—a worn-out expression folks hate but nonetheless often used. It had been awhile since patrons felt that way, and they liked it.

A week later, Bobby Halpern was shot and critically injured while inside a Bronx store. The event had a suspicious nature to it, leading police to view it as a "hit." Two unidentified men, one wielding a shotgun, while the other used a handgun, just opened fire for no apparent reason. Halpern was taken to the North Bronx Hospital, where he was reported in critical condition.

By mid-July, rumor had it that David A. "Sonny" Werblin, president of Madison Square Garden, was expected to welcome promoter Don King to the venue. King would co-promote events for one year, allowing the Garden right of first refusal on matches. As Teddy Brenner would remain president of the Garden's boxing department, one could only wonder how the dynamics would play out, since there was known tension between the two. The nonexclusive agreement was formalized on July 27.[12]

Ali v. Spinks II

Ali v. Spinks II was held inside the Superdome in New Orleans on September 15. As anticipated, a mammoth crowd of 63,350—the largest indoor attendance ever for a boxing match—turned out to witness history as Muhammad Ali became the only boxer to win the heavyweight title three times. The rematch wasn't even close, as Ali, who was twenty pounds heavier than his opponent, essentially used his left jab, not to mention his experience, to dominate the battle. ABC televised the fight live in the United States, and it was seen in some eighty nations worldwide.

Leon Spinks held the world heavyweight championship for exactly 214 days between the bouts with Ali. As for the new champion, retirement, which had ever been an option, seemed closer than ever before. Let's go out on top, shall we?

Forgotten Rounds

The crowd on February 4 was reminiscent of the past, as over 16,000 turned out to watch Wilfred Benítez capture a majority decision over Bruce Curry. While Benítez was far more cautious than in his previous encounter with the Californian, he was also smarter. He won rounds because he was quicker on his feet and delivered precision combinations.

The co-feature saw Brooklyn's Vito Antuofermo capture a ten-round unanimous decision over Philadelphia pugilist Bennie Briscoe. The partisan crowd seemed to ignite the fighter with their two-syllable bellows of "Vito! Vito! Vito!" It was testimony to the excitement that could be generated both by local fighters and the smaller weight classes.

Roberto Durán, not only the most exciting boxer of the day but the best pound-for-pound, attracted over 17,000 fans to Madison Square Garden to watch him take a unanimous decision over junior welterweight Adolfo Viruet from the South Bronx. Billed as two street fighters throwing down the gauntlet, the match was indeed that. The fight took place on April 27.

Alfredo Escalera vaulted himself back into title contention with a victory over Larry Stanton on July 26 inside the City Ring. The Puerto Rican boxer, who had lost his world junior lightweight crown earlier in the year to Alexis Argüello, stopped Stanton at the 2:13 mark of the third round.

Lastly, on December 8, Roberto Durán came into his Garden bout with Los Angeles fighter Monroe Brooks twelve pounds over the lightweight division limit—a sector of the fight game the Panamanian had ruled for seven years but had gradually left without competitors. Surprisingly, Durán didn't look the least bit sluggish as he pounded Brooks until the fighter finally caught a left hook to the belly that sent him to the canvas for the count; the time of the knockout was 1:59 of the eighth round.

Fighter of the Year

The boxing year belonged to Larry Holmes, a former Ali sparring partner, who outpointed Earnie Shavers before taking on Ken Norton in one of the best Las Vegas heavyweight title fights ever held. With the momentum constantly shifting between fighters, Holmes eventually landed the split decision. Later in the year, the WBC heavyweight champion retained his title with a seventh-round knockout of Alfredo Evangelista.

The City Ring was polished by a number of fighters during the year. Gerry Cooney went 2-0, as did Roberto Durán, but Vito Antuofermo and Wilfred Benítez both went 3-0.[13] Overlooked, however, was Harold Weston, Jr., who beat an undefeated Antuofermo on July 9, 1973, and drew Benítez on February 2, 1977. His impressive career would draw to a close the following year (1979), after he had compiled a record of 26-9-5. In a professional career of 40 fights, 21 of Weston's battles took place inside Madison Square Garden.[14]

16

Your Kingdom Come, 1979–1985

> Don't mistake activity with achievement.
> —John Wooden

It took four kings, as author George Kimball so eloquently noted, to transform the state of boxing: lightweight Roberto Durán, middleweight Marvin Hagler, super welterweight Tommy Hearns, and welterweight Sugar Ray Leonard. Exceptional in so many ways, each combined speed and power with pugilistic prowess. Four rivals, all extraordinarily talented, all with respect for each other. And this was their time. For the record: Roberto Durán battled seven times in Madison Square Garden; Marvin Hagler and Sugar Ray Leonard there fought only once each, while Tommy Hearns never graced the City Ring.[1]

1979

As the most primitive form of conflict, boxing's binary nature can reflect moral virtue, as simple as good versus bad. But boxing can also communicate more complex issues. It can express ideology: Max Schmeling (fascism) versus Joe Louis (democracy). It can reflect ethnic origin: Jack Johnson (black) vs. James J. Jeffries (white). It can reflect a crusade: Muhammad Ali (left-wing anti-establishment) vs. Joe Frazier (conservative right, pro-war). As a sport, or as a practice, it has become a microcosm of human nature.

A scheduled fight between South African heavyweight Kallie Knoetze and Queens boxer Bill Sharkey, in Miami on January 13, was drawing a considerable amount of criticism. The bout was co-promoted by the Garden and CBS, but objections to it originated from the fact that Knoetze, a white former South African policeman, was involved in the shooting of a fifteen-year-old black South African youth in November 1977. Protests, led by the Rev. Jesse Jackson and three other leaders, were planned for the event, which was to take place inside the Miami Convention Hall.

The roots of the issue lay in a policy or structure of segregation. Apartheid was a system of institutionalized racial isolation and discrimination that existed in South Africa between 1948 and 1991. Racial segregation had been applied for centuries, but when the new policy started in 1948, it was strict and more systematic.[2]

On January 9, Kallie Knoetze became the first South African athlete barred from competition in the United States, as a result of the State Department's revocation of his visa on grounds of "moral turpitude." Moral turpitude, a legal concept in the United States and some other countries, refers to "an act or behavior that gravely violates the sentiment or the accepted standard of the community."

THE BEAT GOES ON

The money continued to flow to the smaller fighters as Mexican Carlos Palomino pocketed almost a half million dollars in a losing defense of his WBA welter crown against Wilfred Benítez of Puerto Rico, and Colombian Antonio Cervantes collected a junior welter record guarantee of $150,000 in retaining his WBA title against Dominican Miguel Mantilla. Meanwhile, fighters like Sugar Ray Leonard, age 22, stood on the sidelines salivating at every offer that hit the headlines. Having made his pro debut a year earlier, Leonard sat at 19–0, with eleven knockouts. Following a meticulously prepared path, developed by his trainer Angelo Dundee, Leonard was still maturing. He was attempting, according to Dundee, to master the art of imperturbable tranquility, or the capacity to accept or tolerate delay, trouble, or suffering without getting angry or upset.

The target for many of the smaller fighters was Roberto Durán, who sought to be a champion in three divisions before he decided to retire: lightweight (135-pound limit), junior welterweight (140), and welterweight (147). His competitors saw him as their meal ticket. But even Durán understood that every time you think the lighter division can't get any better, along comes another fighter like Wilfredo Gómez, a self-professed super bantamweight (122 pounds) hailing from Las Monjas, Puerto Rico. The twenty-year-old undefeated fighter held recent victories over Carlos Zarate, Leonardo Cruz, Juan Antonio López, and Dong Kyun Yum. In his Garden debut on March 9, which was also his first fight in the United States, Gómez stopped Colombian Nestor Carlos Jimenez, who had not lost since 1975. The impressive victory allowed Gómez to retain the WBC and lineal super bantamweight titles.

Not long after Sonny Werblin brought in Don King to co-promote in the Garden, Teddy Brenner was ousted as president of Madison Square Garden's boxing department. Credentials in hand, Brenner then turned to promoting. Meanwhile, his close friend Gil Clancy handled shows at the Felt Forum, while King catered to the Arena.

THE GARDEN'S CENTENNIAL

Since 1879, there had been no other venue that matched Madison Square Garden's capacity for entertainment. And while it amused, it also made history. It became more than a place where things happened. It grew into a community. It encapsulated, in miniature, the characteristic quality or features of who and what we were. That was Madison Square Garden.

An American boxer, motivational speaker, and an occasional actor, Ray Charles Leonard (born May 17, 1956), best known as "Sugar Ray" Leonard, was one of the most popular athletes of the twentieth century.

You could watch chariots race there, or even bicycles; ride a horse or pet a dog; preach to someone or be preached to; watch the most gorgeous woman or view the prettiest flower; stand in the same room as a United States president; witness the greatest athletes in the world on a court, on ice or in a ring; listen to the best voices sing a song, or the finest guitarist play one; marvel at a dancer or even an exotic animal. It turned fantasy into reality and it was magic.

Madison Square Garden had become a succession of amphitheaters beginning with a freight depot for the New York and Harlem Railroad. Ironically, today it was a structure built above the platforms of an active railroad station, a venue catering to the needs of the entertainment industry rising above those used for transportation—a dais for the virtuoso over that of the commoner. From its boxing platform, the City Ring, pugilists, like trains, entered the station. Having made numerous stops along their journey, most hoped they reached their final destination. However, most also understood the unlikelihood. But the fact they just reached the station, at least to most, will have been worth the price of the ticket. Let a new century of boxing begin.

Larry Holmes, an active heavyweight champion, battled Mike Weaver on June 22 inside the City Ring.[3] Over 14,000 boxing fans turned out for the Garden event, thanks to a very impressive fight card. Holmes took Weaver late into the eleventh round before catching him with a fierce uppercut that floored the ex-Marine. The bewildered Californian rose to beat the count and the bell, but little else. The referee stopped the fight at the 0:44 point of the twelfth round—Weaver was unable to defend himself.

Also on the docket, Roberto Durán, the former lightweight champion, was scheduled for ten rounds with Carlos Palomino, the former welter titleholder. It was hard to believe that almost seven years had passed since Durán had lifted the title from Ken Buchanan, but they had. In that period, the Panamanian had defended his title eleven times. "Hands of Stone," a moniker Durán had earned thanks to his enormous punching power, had won 65 of his last 66 bouts, 53 of them by knockout.

Having floored Palomino in the sixth round, Durán, with his flicking head and shoulder feints, glided to a unanimous ten-round decision. Hard rights by the Panamanian kept his antagonist off-balance, and his relentless pursuit was just overpowering. The critics, who had buried Durán, had to quickly reevaluate the Panamanian. As the decade closed, Durán was the top welterweight contender for the WBC crown worn by Wilfred Benítez.

Sugar Ray Leonard

Thankfully, boxing has never had to search for its next disciple. The flamboyant and clairvoyant style of Muhammad Ali, the perfect proponent for his time, gave way to Ray Charles Leonard. Born on May 17, 1956, in Wilmington, North Carolina, one of seven children, the youth was granted a gift. Ray's father, Cicero, who worked at a produce market, soon moved the family to Washington, D.C. His mother, Getha, was a nursing assistant, who admitted she hoped her son would be a singer. Later the family would move to Palmer Park, a Beltway community, at about the time the youngster's interest in boxing had escalated.

Blessed with good genetics, his five-foot nine-and-a-half-inch frame, at 147 pounds, was sleek but not cut to the extent of some of his future opponents (Hagler or Hearns). Handsome beyond comparison, with a million-dollar smile, Leonard was a heartthrob—

an Adonis in boxing trunks. Clean-cut, smooth-featured and dulcet-voiced, he wasn't overpowering like Ali—he didn't have to shout to make his point. He was a "soft sell," and a successful one at that. Leonard was humble (more like Tunney, rather than Dempsey), ingenuous and unimpeachable. Another blessing was that the word respect was never far from Leonard's vocabulary. He would not only be good for the job, he would be perfect.

Leonard was reflective of a new era that sought "conformity" over "discord," "patriotism" over "perfidiousness." After he won the gold medal at the Olympics, a part of Leonard believed he was through—he had accomplished what he set out to achieve. The next logical step was to college, but when the financial offers began rolling in like waves along the Maryland shoreline, such as a pug with a mug on a Wheaties box, well, perhaps it was time to rethink the journey.

Leonard's first professional battle was a six-rounder against Luis Vega, on February 5, 1977, which he won by a unanimous verdict. Held in Baltimore's Civic Center, it drew over 10,000—a boxing record for that arena. With a ring record of 26-0, Ray Leonard would finish 1979 with welterweight titles in his hand.[4]

MARVELOUS MARVIN

Meanwhile, the uncrowned king of the middleweights added an adjective to his name and was now Marvelous Marvin Hagler. The southpaw from Brockton, Massachusetts, was having an outstanding year at four wins and no losses. Hagler hadn't been defeated since March 9, 1976, when Willie Monroe took a united decision and handed him only his second career loss.

With his shaved head and Fu Manchu—adorned countenance, Hagler looked tough, and when he talked about the destruction of his opponents, you felt like asking him where he planned to hide all the body parts. He was intimidating and believable. The middleweight was also hungry for a title shot, which he would get against Vito Antuofermo on November 30 in Las Vegas.

DEATH IN THE RING

On November 23 in the Felt Forum, prospect Wilford Scypion, at 12-0, was matched against Puerto Rican middleweight Willie "Macho" Classen (16-6-2). Classen was a difficult fighter who had gone the distance with future middleweight champion Vito Antuofermo back on August 25, 1978. Granted, Antuofermo took the decision over "Macho." But going the distance with the tough Italian was no simple task. Classen, a Bronx resident, was a street fighter. While he was more than thankful for a Garden check, the loss seemed to take a toll on him: since his defeat

An American boxer who competed from 1973 to 1987, Marvelous Marvin Hagler (born Marvin Nathaniel Hagler, May 23, 1954) reigned as the undisputed middleweight champion from 1980 to 1987.

by Antuofermo, he had lost three of his last four bouts. To feed his large family, the fighter also worked as a security guard at a Manhattan supermarket.

In his 24th professional bout, Classen didn't look sharp against Scypion. By the third round, on this night after Thanksgiving, he looked lethargic. Nonetheless, he battled back, and picked up some rounds. When the bell sounded for the final term, he hardly had his gloves in place when Scypion threw a smashing left hook to the face, followed by a right to the chin.[5] Classen fell onto his back unconscious and went through the lower ring rope. Immediately, the doctors knew he was in trouble. After more than fifteen minutes, Classen was placed on a stretcher as his lungs continued vomiting blood. The physicians who treated him feared brain damage. Despite surgery to relieve a blood clot in his brain, Willie Classen died five days later. The twenty-nine-year-old fighter, who made $1,500 from the fight, left behind a wife and four children. There were occasions like this—cyclical in nature, or so it seemed—when the City Ring could make any boxing fan rethink his priorities. The tragedy left Garden fans heartbroken.

The Forum had attracted over 2,500 fans, many there to witness Chuck Wepner, the recently retired heavyweight, who was being honored.[6] As fate might have it, in Scypion's corner during the fight was five-time world champion Emile Griffith. If anyone could empathize with a fighter under these conditions it was Griffith.[7] On Thursday, December 13, NYSAC, reacting to a legislative investigation into the death of boxer Willie Classen, ordered all professional fights in the state halted until new safety procedures could be implemented.[8]

Forgotten Rounds

Undefeated lightweight Howard Davis, Jr., battled against Italy's lightweight champion Giancarlo Usai on Friday, April 20, in the Forum. Davis, who had nine pro fights under his belt and was still under a lucrative television contract with CBS, knocked out Usai at the 0:28 mark of the third round of their scheduled ten-round affair.

Also on the card was fellow Olympian Leo Randolph, who lost an eight-round split decision against Puerto Rican David Capo. It was the first time that the Olympians had been in the same ring since the summer of 1976. (Just as a reminder, only Davis, Leonard and Michael Spinks, of the Olympic medalists, remained unbeaten as professionals.)

Also in the Felt Forum, heavyweight Gerry Cooney extended his unbeaten mark to 18–0 with a second-round knockout of Miami Beach boxer Tom Prater on June 29. The bout was halted at the 2:13 mark of the second round. Cooney, who often depended upon a dominating left jab, exhibited a nice array of punches during the victory.

An American boxer who competed from 1977 to 1990, Gerry Cooney (born August 24, 1956) was often recalled for his expeditious knockout of former world heavyweight champion Ken Norton in the first round of their 1981 Madison Square Garden duel.

Fighter of the Year

The centennial year of Madison Square Garden was tragically altered by the death of Willie Classen. There were simply not enough comforting words for his family. The sport witnessed a bulk of the better fights occurring outside New York City: Matthew Saad Muhammad knocked out Marvin Johnson in the eighth round to take the WBC light-heavyweight title on April 22 (Indianapolis); Danny Lopez knocked out Mike Ayala to retain his WBC feather crown on June 17 (San Antonio); Ray Leonard captured the WBC welter crown by defeating Wilfred Benítez on November 30 (Las Vegas); and Vito Antuofermo fought Marvin Hagler to a fifteen-round draw on November 30 (Las Vegas).

The year in boxing belonged to Ali's heir apparent, Sugar Ray Leonard, who went 9–0, and picked up the NABF welter crown by defeating Pete Ranzany. He also knocked out Andy Price in a single round and stopped Wilfred Benítez with six seconds remaining in the final round.

The City Ring bid farewell to Alexis Argüello and Carlos Palomino and welcomed Billy Costello.[9] The latter was 2–0 in the Garden, as was Saoul Mamby. But nobody shined the City Ring better than Gerry Cooney, who posted a 4–0 record at Madison Square Garden; he fought and won three consecutive bouts inside the Felt Forum.

1980

Oh, how "The Bull" did rage. City boxing fans flocked to the cinema to watch Martin Scorsese's *Raging Bull*. The movie starred Robert DeNiro as middleweight legend Jake LaMotta. Not surprisingly, Scorsese's masterpiece ignited interest in the sweet science.

For the first time since November 23, 1979, boxing returned to Madison Square Garden. The aftermath from the Willie Classen tragedy was evident with the presence of Willie Classen, Sr., and some assorted politicians. While the sport of boxing should have been on its best behavior on January 25, it was not. In a featherweight battle between Brooklyn's Bobby "Wildman" Alexander and the undefeated Carmelo Negron, emotions were running high. Alexander, who was taking a solid beating, had been dropped twice and struck by questionable blows. While referee Joe Santarpi admonished Negron's behavior, it wasn't enough to satisfy Alexander's corner. In the tenth and final round, Alexander's hinges became loose, so Santarpi stopped the fight at the 1:20 mark. Alexander's manager Bob O'Neill then reached his boiling point and kneed Santarpi in the groin. Thankfully, Santarpi, a former Golden Gloves boxer, could defend himself.[10]

On October 2, Greg Page, a promising heavyweight from Louisville, Kentucky, knocked out Dave "Big Foot" Johnson at the 1:51 mark of the sixth round inside Madison Square Garden.[11] It was the featured bout of a live card that preceded the closed-circuit broadcast of the Ali v. Holmes heavyweight championship fight from Las Vegas. Over 20,000 packed the main arena while the adjoining Felt Forum brought in an additional 4,000 spectators.

The Student Bests the Master

A crowd, uncertain of just how to react, watched Larry Holmes systematically destroy his idol—it would enter the fighter's resume as a KO 11. After a layoff of seven hundred and forty-nine days, Ali, at age 38, had nothing to offer. Nothing. Quietly, in almost an eerie lull, Larry Holmes recorded his eighth consecutive knockout as WBC champion, surpassing the record (7) set by Joe Louis. But the night wasn't about Holmes and his success; instead, it was about Ali and his lack thereof.

As for Larry Holmes, he was no longer Ali's former sparring partner; he was the heavyweight champion of the world. Ali's successor had finally removed the monkey from his back, and with it the love for his idol only seemed to intensify. The champion understood it was a historic moment in boxing history, and handled himself with class; boxing on this night couldn't have been in better hands than that of Larry Holmes.

Heading into the '80s

Underscored by the two battles between Roberto Durán and Sugar Ray Leonard, the sport of boxing presented a powerful image at the beginning of a new decade. As the heavyweight torch passed from one generation to the next, it wasn't the performance of that division that stuck out, but rather that of the lighter classes. For example: scoring four straight knockouts before winning the WBA welterweight crown, Thomas Hearns painted the prevailing image of a rising superstar.

It was, however, a horrible year for New York City boxing, as every noteworthy battle was held outside the metropolis. In a pugilistic drought, the Garden saw no sign of water until early the next year. The venue planned a boxing card featuring four world championships on Monday, February 23, 1981, inside the City Ring. The event, promoted by Muhammad Ali Professional Sports and Tiffany Productions, even included a heavyweight battle between Ken Norton and Gerry Cooney, and a duel between Thomas Hearns and Wilfred Benítez.

1981

After losing his title to Ray Leonard, Roberto Durán announced his retirement on November 22, 1980. But as boxing retirements are always subject to one final offer, John Condon, president of Madison Square Garden Boxing, felt offering Durán three-quarters of a million bucks might be enough dinero to lure "Manos de Piedra" (hands of stone) back into the ring to fight Aaron Pryor, the WBA junior lightweight champion. Naturally, the ten-round non-title bout would take place inside the City Ring.[12]

Speaking of promotion, by February 1, it was learned that Muhammad Ali Professional Sports (MAPS), Inc.—the co-promoters of a boxing event scheduled for the Garden on February 23—were under investigation. (The fighter issued a statement that he wanted his name withdrawn from MAPS and any other organization that he had allowed to use it.) As the sport of boxing had long attracted its fair share, if not more, of schemers and con men under the promotional umbrella, everyone was hoping that such was not the case here, and that the Garden show would go on as planned. But by February 5, two of the scheduled bouts were looking for another venue and the entire promotion (four world championship fights) was slowly disintegrating. As anticipated, it was canceled.[13]

A Heavyweight Return

In a tailspin after the MAPS fantasy boxing spectacular, the Garden went after both the Ken Norton versus Gerry Cooney bout, and the Thomas Hearns versus Wilfred Benítez contest, with hopes of landing both on the same card. Team Hearns, however, was leaning toward a battle against Maurice Hope, but Cooney agreed to fight Norton in the City Ring on May 11. By the end of February, it looked like the Garden had an impressive card wrapped up, or the first major fight since the summer of 1979, when Larry Holmes beat Mike Weaver.

Advance ticket sales for the Norton v. Cooney heavyweight bout at the Garden were falling short of expectations by late April, despite a plethora of publicity. Critics were quick to point out that Las Vegas (Caesars Palace), or the current fight capital of the world, had passed on the fight, saying the match lacked drawing power. Outside of New York, few were conscious of the pugilistic prowess of Gerry Cooney. Yet the burden for selling tickets seemed to fall on "Gentleman" Gerry; moreover, some believed Norton couldn't sell a Garden ticket to his mother. The venue was also criticized for scaling far short of the $1.4 million it needed to break even.

An American boxer who competed from 1967 to 1981, and held the WBC heavyweight title in 1978, Kenneth Howard Norton, Sr. (1943–2013) was best known for his trilogy with Muhammad Ali.

Fighter tidbits from both camps, leaked out at the average frequency—okay, perhaps a bit faster—and as always were beat bait, or media food. Word was that Norton was on a weak set of legs and susceptible. But word also was that Norton's legs may still be good enough to handle Cooney—he was still Ken Norton from the waist up. Whispers stated Cooney hadn't beat anyone of note—granted, he beat Ron Lyle and Jimmy Young, yet he had lost to Malik Dozier (fewer than ten pro bouts), and Charley Polite, Austin Johnson and Terry Lee Kidd (three fighters with losing records). Nevertheless, whispers also flew that Norton's victory over "Tex" Cobb and draw against Scott LeDoux weren't overly impressive. Gossip was Cooney dropped his right after a left hook (a reflex action) and it left him open after a left jab. All the same, gossip had it that Norton wasn't quick enough to react to it. If all this hearsay didn't ignite your interest, well, you weren't alone.

Not a single person called it—although Cooney's camp, to their credit, stated emphatically that everyone would soon know who Gerry Cooney was—or predicted it, so to speak. It was the shortest heavyweight main event ever at Madison Square Garden, as Gerry Cooney knocked out Ken Norton at the 0:54 mark of the opening round. Norton was knocked unconscious. An overhand right set up two hooks to Norton's body. That pushed the fighter back onto the ropes, where Cooney's left hook appeared to be responsible for the knockout. The Manhattan-born boxer was expected to next tackle Mike Weaver for the W.B.A. heavyweight title. As for Norton, perhaps retirement may once again be in order.

The Garden took a financial bath, as about 9,500 spectators attended the event. At $200 ringside, many felt Yankees tickets were a better buy.

Battles on the Bayou

On June 25, 1981, Madison Square Garden turned its attention to an interesting live boxing card prior to the closed-circuit television broadcast from the Houston Astrodome (Leonard v. Kalule). Over 10,000 fans turned out to view a card that included Edwin Rosario, an undefeated Puerto Rican featherweight, battling Refugio Rojas, and Marlon Starling, an undefeated Hartford middleweight, taking on Juan Hidalgo. Both, as it would turn out, scored impressive knockout victories.

In a bout scheduled for ten rounds, Rosario, a compact 129 pounds, went right to work and disposed of Rojas, of Los Angeles, at the 0:47 mark of round two. The accomplishment sustained perfection, as Rosario moved to a record of 17–0, with 17 knockouts. Marlon Starling took a bit longer, but put away Hidalgo, of the Dominican Republic, at the 0:42 mark of the fifth round. Starling, impressive at 148 pounds, took his record to 18–0, with 12 knockouts. Also, in an eight-round featherweight contest New York, fighter Héctor Camacho took a decision over Bronx boxer Marcial Santiago.

On June 30, Gil Clancy spent his final day at the Garden as matchmaker. The talented boxing guru would join CBS as a full-time television commentator. Clancy, who had spent two and a half years at the Garden trying to land decent fights under extraordinarily difficult conditions, focused much of his attention on the Felt Forum. Worth noting, in one of those "I told you so" moments: Clancy was not in favor of the Garden taking the Norton v. Cooney fight, but was overruled.

The Year in Perspective

The fight of the year wasn't in Madison Square Garden or even in New York City. It was out in Las Vegas at Caesars Palace Hotel. And

An American boxer who competed from 1979 to 1990, Marlon "Magic Man" Starling (born August 29, 1959) held the WBA, WBC, and lineal welterweight world championships. He was undefeated in his first twenty-five professional battles.

it was Sugar Ray Leonard, the WBC welter king defeating Thomas Hearns, the WBA welter king in a unification bout for the world title.

A nineteen-year-old-Spanish Harlem high school student, Héctor "Macho" Camacho was turning a lot of heads lately and turned even more in the Felt Forum on Friday, December 11. Camacho took a unanimous decision over Blaine Dickson to pick up the North American Boxing Federation's super featherweight championship in only his twelfth professional bout.[14] A near capacity crowd turned out to watch the charismatic Camacho, who entertained during some rounds more than he fought. New Garden matchmaker Harold Weston, Jr., was one of many spectators impressed by the "Macho Man."

None of the outstanding bouts of the year made it to New York City. Sean O'Grady picked up the WBA lightweight title over Hilmer Kenty on April 12 (Atlantic City); Alexis Argüello picked up his third title, the WBC lightweight crown, by a decision over Jim Watt on June 20 (London); Salvador Sánchez, in a miraculous performance, put Wilfredo Gómez through the ropes to add another knockout to his impressive record on August 21 (Las Vegas); and Larry Holmes, who was dropped in the seventh round, managed to dust himself off and knock out Renaldo Snipes in the eleventh round to retain his title on November 6 (Pittsburgh). Clearly, Sugar Ray Leonard had an outstanding year, but hats off to Salvador Sánchez as well.[15]

Fighter of the Year

It was not a noteworthy year for New York City boxing or Madison Square Garden. The Garden lost their shirt on the Cooney versus Norton fight; however, it seemed a small price to pay for finally returning a major bout to the City Ring. On a positive note, the combination live card and closed-circuit television presentations were working well, and some new talent was showing promise. Inside the City Ring, Edwin Rosario went 2–0, while Marlon Starling compiled a 3–0 record. But, without question, Madison Square Garden shined thanks to a newcomer named Héctor "Macho" Camacho. The southpaw was 7–0 inside Madison Square Garden and fought in five consecutive fights.[16]

1982

Madison Square Garden's first boxing event of the year was scheduled for January 22 inside the Felt Forum. It included four ten-rounders with Alfredo Escalera tackling Angel Cruz atop the card. Also planned was the professional debut of Brooklyn boxer Carl Williams; the Garden had inked the top-ranked amateur heavyweight to a sound promotional deal. Williams won both the 1980 New York Golden Gloves sub-novice heavyweight championship and the 1981 heavyweight open championship. The event would be the first to feature the thumbless gloves made mandatory for some (non-championship) bouts by the New York State Athletic Commission.

Cruz, a junior welterweight, took the ten-round verdict over Escalera, while Williams defeated Greg Stephaney in a four-round united decision. With regard to the gauntlets: Escalera didn't care for the gloves, but also didn't blame them for his loss, while Williams also disliked the mitts. The issue had legs, and that concerned promoters.

In a first for Madison Square Garden, or at least for the Felt Forum, a six-bout boxing card, scheduled for January 29, was canceled because of boxing gloves: a half-dozen fighters refused to wear the thumbless gloves mandated by New York State.[17] Everlast, which manufactured the gloves in just three sizes, was the only NYSAC–approved supplier. Although the gloves were safer, the fighters didn't like them because of circulation issues: they resulted in a numbed thumb and forefinger. The canceled Garden card had featured lightweight Héctor Camacho against Raphael Lopez.[18]

Bubbling under the boxing muddle were the discreet financial woes of the Garden, or the Center, a distinct part of the Madison Square Garden Corporation, who the previous summer filed a suit to prevent Penn Central, who owned the land and air rights of the location, from evicting them. The issue was the profitability of the Garden and whether or not it was liable for back rent. At risk was the possible movement of the associated professional sport teams. To counter the uncertainty of the Garden, the corporation had been seeking financial assistance from the city. On April 22, the Garden received an additional $1 million in tax abatement.[19]

Stars on the Rise

In stark contrast to the boxing careers of most of his fellow Olympians, and to the surprise of many, Howard Davis, Jr., seemed to have fallen off the pugilistic radar screen. Making his professional debut back on January 15, 1977, against Jose Resto, he had only fought 16 times since. However, he would emerge to take a unanimous ten-round decision over Angel Cruz inside the Felt Forum on April 16. As the fight wore on, he looked better and better. Taking command before the midway point, Davis, who knew he was a little bit rusty, saw his speed gradually increase, as well as his accuracy. With the victory, and a transition in management and staff, Davis hoped to be able to turn a major corner in his career.

Always looking for a new prince, boxing relished finding Héctor "Macho" Camacho, who contrasted well against the other stars of the junior lightweight division. His talent, looks, personality and flamboyance guaranteed nothing but excitement, and with the right people behind him, the sky was the limit. Just as a reminder, it was the Garden that had him under a promotional agreement. On July 11, inside the Felt Forum, Camacho stopped previously unbeaten Louie "Golden" Loy at the 1:24 mark of the seventh round. A prolific puncher with outstanding speed, Camacho could turn on a dime and unleash a barrage of punches in an instant. If there was a flaw in his armor, it was his lack of punching power. Garden matchmaker Harold Weston, Jr., also needed to get the fighter more established in the rankings, which he would try to do by hopefully matching Camacho against Sammy Serrano, the WBA junior lightweight champion.

The hopes and dreams of Hartford, Connecticut, a mere 120 miles from New York City and a city blessed with an impressive boxing heritage, were placed upon the shoulders of Marlon Starling. A Hartford trial lawyer, F. Mac Buckley, headed a group of thirty investors who had underwritten the youngster's career in exchange for a percentage of earnings. And the gamble looked to be paying off. On July 17, Starling was matched against Las Vegas pugilist Kevin Morgan for the USBA (United States Boxing Association) welterweight title inside Madison Square Garden. Dropping Morgan twice early in the opening round, Starling delivered a pair of nasty left hooks and a right to finish the job. Referee

Vinny Rainone had seen enough and stopped the fight at the 2:06 mark. Busloads of cheering Connecticut fight fans couldn't believe their eyes when the fight was over in less than three minutes. Undefeated in twenty-four battles, Starling was thinking title shot, while, Morgan, 21–9, contemplated just where to divert next.

Salvador Sánchez v. Azumah Nelson

In one of those bouts (and the Garden had more than their fair share over the decades) that every boxing fan wished he had witnessed, featherweight Salvador Sánchez scored an impressive fifteen-round technical knockout over Azumah Nelson. Referee Tony Perez stopped the title fight at the 1:49 mark of the final round. Just over 5,500 spectators turned out on July 21 to witness Sánchez, the WBA 126-pound titleholder, defend his crown for the ninth time. Azumah Nelson, a mere 13 fights into his career, was relatively unknown, yet not intimidated by the champion. Most even had him leading before the duel concluded. Despite being floored in the seventh session, Nelson struggled on and came out for the final round, determined to displace Sánchez, until he ran into a sensational left hook. Bouncing off the canvas at the count of two, more of a reflex than a recovery, Nelson was standing defenseless at the end.

To Nelson's credit, he rocked the granite-chinned Sánchez early in the battle—he was that powerful a puncher. But Nelson, whose confidence was growing round-by-round, left himself open to the counters of Sánchez and it would cost him. The experience was an education for Nelson, and one he wouldn't soon forget. The twenty-four-year-old Ghanian challenger wouldn't see defeat again until May 1990.

In the early morning hours of August 12, Salvador Sánchez was driving his Porsche 928 between Queretaro and his training camp at San Juan Inturbide, some 160 miles north of Mexico City. At about 3:30 A.M. his sports car, traveling at a high rate of speed, collided with a tractor-trailer and Sánchez was killed. The incident was out of character for the champion, who was noted for his training regimen, including road work at 5:30 A.M. Sánchez, who believed he had little left to prove in boxing, hoped to retire by the end of 1983, then pursue a medical career. His fight against Azumah Nelson, which was his Garden debut and unfortunately his last fight ever, was part of a four-fight deal he had with promoter Don King.

An Athlete Dying Young

On November 13, Ray Mancini scored a technical knockout in the fourteenth round over South Korean boxer Duk Koo Kim, during a brutal match that was held at Caesars Palace in Las Vegas. Although Kim regained his balance following the knockdown that prompted the end of the fight, he was removed from the ring by stretcher and taken to the hospital. Following an operation, he never regained consciousness and died on November 18 at the age of 23. The tragic death just devastated Ray Mancini, not to mention many others associated with the battle.

Boxing needed to make some changes, and to their credit, they did. One of the most significant alterations was the WBC's reduction of title fights from fifteen rounds to twelve. Worth noting was that the WBC was not the tragic fight's sanctioning organization, but still made the change. The WBA and the IBF followed the WBC's lead in 1987. When the

WBO was established in 1988, it immediately began operating with 12-round world championship bouts. Another recommendation, this one by the Nevada State Athletic Commission, was to increase the number of ring ropes from three to four to prevent fighters from falling through the ropes and out of the ring.

Fighter of the Year

It was a challenging year for boxing and for Madison Square Garden.[20] Although the City Ring saw the Sánchez vs. Nelson bout, many good fights occurred elsewhere: Ray Mancini's first round knockout of Arturo Frias on May 8 (Las Vegas), Pete Ranzany's ten round decision over Sean O'Grady on October 30 (Las Vegas), Aaron Pryor's fourteenth-round knockout victory over Alexis Argüello on November 12 (Miami), Wilfredo Gómez, eyes swollen shut, managed to kayo Lupe Pinter in the fourteenth on December 3 (New Orleans), and Bobby Chacon's courageous victory over Rafael Bazooka Limón to win the WBC junior lightweight title on December 11 (Sacramento). While lightweight Héctor Camacho went 3-0 inside Madison Square Garden, Mike McCallum, the super welter, went 4-0.[21] The City Ring was lucky enough to have Salvador Sánchez, if only briefly, grace its canvas.

1983

Stand Back

Davey Moore, the undefeated (12-0) WBA junior middleweight champion, was a favorite (5-2) to beat Panamanian fighter Roberto Durán on June 16. But since it was the latter's thirty-second birthday, you could bet, and many did, that others had a different opinion. The odds were insulting to the gifted super lightweight and proved only to ignite the Panamanian. Durán had trained hard for the fight. Even an eighty-three-year-old Ray Arcel couldn't believe his eyes when he saw the newly invented boxer.

A capacity Garden crowd—the 20,061 fans who attended made up the biggest gate since 1974—filled the Arena to see what, if anything, was left in the tank of Roberto Durán. From the onset of the first round, Durán slipped, poked (particularly in the eye) and prodded like the Durán of old. He went close quarters and got Moore to drop his gloves a bit, so he could work his jab against the Bronx boxer's right eye, which had begun to swell. Moore's nose began to bleed in the second. Sensing that some damage had slowed his adversary, Durán took a breather in the third and fourth rounds. The Panamanian dropped Moore with a hard right in the seventh term. As Moore rose at the count of eight, the gong sounded. Saved by the bell. Durán's trainer, Nestor Quiñones, told his fighter to finish it before the eighth ended. It took Durán two minutes and two seconds to persuade Moore's corner to surrender. Having won his first world title at Madison Square Garden eleven years earlier, Durán became the seventh fighter in boxing history to win world titles in three weight divisions.[22]

On the undercard, "Irish" Billy Collins, Jr., was matched against Puerto Rican journeyman Luis Resto. Collins entered the fight as a betting favorite but took a heavy beating and lost by a unanimous decision. At the end of the fight, Collins's father and trainer, Billy

Sr., noticed a variance in the size of Resto's gloves—they felt thinner. The gloves were impounded and a subsequent investigation by NYSAC concluded that Resto's trainer, Carlos Panama Lewis, had removed an ounce of padding from each glove.[23] The gloves became weapons. Collins suffered a torn iris and permanently blurred vision, which left him unable to box. The fight result was changed to a no-contest, but that didn't undo the damage.

Lewis's New York boxing license was permanently revoked. Resto was suspended indefinitely and never fought again. On March 6, 1984, Collins committed suicide by crashing his car into a culvert near his home in Antioch, Tennessee, a suburb of Nashville; many believe that the loss of his livelihood had an enormous impact on him psychologically. In 1986, Lewis and Resto were tried and convicted of assault, conspiracy, and criminal possession of a deadly weapon (Resto's fists); prosecutors felt that Lewis's actions made the fight an illegal assault on Collins. Both served 2½ years in prison. Years later, it was further learned than Resto's hand wraps had been soaked in plaster of Paris before the fight.[24]

OTHER RING ACTION

Ray Mancini defended his WBA lightweight title inside the Garden on September 15 by knocking out Peruvian Orlando Romero in the ninth round. Neither fighter looked particularly good. In Mancini's defense, he had a seven-month layoff due to a broken collarbone. This was Mancini's second Garden appearance and his final fight in the City Ring.

On Thursday, October 7, tragedy once again struck as twenty-four-year-old lightweight Gino Perez died at St. Vincent's Hospital in Manhattan, where he had been comatose since he was knocked out in a Felt Forum battle the previous Friday.

MARVIN HAGLER

Marvin Hagler was born on May 23, 1954, in Newark, New Jersey. At the age of sixteen, having moved from Newark to Brockton, Massachusetts, he wandered into a new gym owned by the Petronelli brothers. The two siblings, both of whom boxed, were no strangers to pugilism, as they grew up only a couple blocks from Rocky Marciano.

Hagler turned pro in 1973. Fighting out of the Boston area, in places like the Brockton High School Gymnasium, Boston Arena, Hynes Auditorium and by 1974, the Boston Garden, he gradually refined his skills. The end of 1983 found the fighter with a career record of 58–2–2, having only lost to Willie Monroe (1976) and Bobby Watts (1976). Hagler held the WBA, WBC, *The Ring*, and lineal middleweight titles.

OTHER CHAMPS

Sugar Ray Leonard had retired back on November 9, 1982. That proclamation came after successful surgery to repair the detached retina in his left eye. A mere 397 days later, or 1 year, 1 month, and 2 days, he announced he was returning to the ring. Leonard had not fought since February 15, 1982, when he beat Bruce Finch by a TKO at the Centennial Coliseum, in Reno, Nevada.[25] The fighter's decision was met with a torrent of criticism from fans and the media, who felt Leonard was taking an unnecessary risk.

Speaking of statements, Larry Holmes declared he was the heavyweight champion of the IBF, or International Boxing Federation. Since he had an undefeated record of 45–0, with 32 knockouts, nobody was going to argue with him. The move to a new organization, struggling to be acknowledged, was an attempt by Holmes to gain more control over his career. In the past, the WBC and Don King represented one set of champions and divisions, and the WBA and Bob Arum represented another. Holmes believed it was time for a change.

Fighter of the Year

Outside the city: Bobby Chacon took a vicious battle over Cornelius Boza-Edwards on May 15 (Las Vegas); Robin Blake, in a punching duel, finally kayoed Tony Baltazar in the ninth round on July 24 (Las Vegas); and Gerrie Coetzee knocked out previously unbeaten Michael Dokes in the tenth round for the WBA heavy crown on September 23 (Richfield, Ohio). Michael "Jinx" Spinks, Leon's brother, who would never fight inside Madison Square Garden, had an outstanding year, the pinnacle being the unification of the world light heavyweight crown.

Taking one step forward, followed by two steps back, at least boxing was consistent. It was good to see Roberto Durán back in New York City and fighting in Madison Square Garden, but it was an insult that the event was marred by an undercard controversy. Roberto Durán would never return to the City Ring. In addition to Durán, the Garden bid farewell to Ray Mancini and welcomed James "Buddy" McGirt.[26] In a relatively quiet boxing year for Madison Square Garden, the City Ring salutes Roberto Durán.

1984

"A champion is someone who gets up when he can't," Jack Dempsey once stated. From 1919 until 1926, there wasn't a more popular athlete on the planet than the Manassa Mauler. William Harrison "Jack" Dempsey succumbed to a heart ailment on May 31 at the age of 87.

Achieving all the goals he had for Madison Square Garden, David A. "Sonny" Werblin gave up his post as chief executive officer to assume a new role with Gulf and Western Industries, the Garden's parent company. Jack Krumpe, the Garden president, filled Werblin's former role. Just how this would affect the Garden's programming was yet to be seen. Later, on September 7, it would be learned that the Penn Central Corporation agreed to sell the land under Madison Square Garden, and the long-term lease between the two organizations to Gulf and Western Industries, who owned the Garden.

Talking about the venue, on Friday, March 23, Brooklyn's Mark Breland became the first five-time champion of the New York Golden Gloves Tournament. It took only 42 seconds for Breland, a two-time world amateur welterweight champion, to defeat Victor Laguer in the 147-pound open class. Perhaps even more impressive was that Breland had him taking a standing eight count less than thirty seconds into the fight. A twenty-year-old lanky boxer, Breland possessed an impressive record of 99–1, 70 wins via knockout. Turning his attention next to the Summer Olympic Games taking place in Los Angeles, he wanted to add a gold medal to his impressive list of achievements that included fifteen Golden Glove knockouts.

The 1984 United States Olympic boxing team, or the next generation of ring stars, consisted of: 106 pounds: Paul Gonzales, Los Angeles, CA; 112: Steve McCrory, Detroit, MI;

An American boxer who won five New York Golden Gloves titles and a gold medal at the 1984 Olympics, Mark Anthony Breland (born May 11, 1963) was pictured here (left) with Marvis Frazier (born September 12, 1960), an American boxer who fought in the heavyweight division.

119: Robert Shannon, Edmonds, WA; 125: Meldrick Taylor, Philadelphia, PA; 132: Pernell Whitaker, Norfolk, VA; 139: Jerry Page, Columbus, OH; 147: Mark Breland, Brooklyn, NY; 156: Frank Tate, Detroit, MI; 165: Virgil Hill, Williston, ND; 178: Evander Holyfield, Atlanta, GA; 201: Henry Tillman, Los Angeles, CA; and +201: Tyrell Biggs, Philadelphia, PA. To no one's surprise, Mark Breland, age 21, had outpointed Louis Howard to grab the 147-pound spot. Michael Tyson, age 18, of Catskill, New York, drew considerable attention but lost his bid to Henry Tillman.

Hagler v. Hamsho II

It was hard to accept that three years had passed since Marvin Hagler sliced Mustafa Hamsho like a Thanksgiving turkey inside the Horizon Arena at Rosemont, Illinois, but it had; the fighter required 55 stitches to close his wounds. Their duel was part of a "Double Dynamite" promotion from Top Rank, Inc., that also featured Mike Weaver against James "Quick" Tillis. Determined that the same type of brawling style would not occur in their second meeting on October 19, Hagler hoped for a quicker ending. Hamsho was ranked #1 by the WBA and WBC.

True to his word, Hagler quickly disposed of his adversary, inside Madison Square Garden. Referee Arthur Mercante stopped the fight at the 2:31 mark of the third round when Hamsho's manager Al Certo entered the ring. Having hit the canvas twice in the third round, Hamsho was defenseless at this point; the knockdown was the first in his nine-year professional career. Hagler moved his record to 60–2–2 with the successful title defense, and also picked up his fiftieth knockout.[27] Hamsho revised his record to 38–3–2.[28]

NIGHT OF GOLD

As part of a two-hour ABC prime-time television broadcast, five American Olympic boxing team stars—Tyrrell Biggs, Mark Breland, Evander Holyfield, Meldrick Taylor, and Pernell Whitaker—made their professional debuts inside Madison Square Garden on November 15. Perhaps even more attractive was the admission: it was free. That's correct: promoter Dan Duva, who had exclusive promotional rights to the five fighters, stated that a bulk of the tickets would be given out as part of a contest conducted by his corporation, Main Events, and the *Daily News*.[29]

The evening had all the excitement of the advanced billing, as all the Olympic boxing stars won their professional debuts. An impressive crowd of 19,000 boxing fans filled Madison Square Garden to watch the event that was also broadcast on prime-time television. Many were there to see homegrown favorite Mark Breland, who had only one brief scare during his first pro victory: Dwight Williams, trying to make a statement, sent Breland into the ropes during the opening ten seconds. Both Holyfield and Biggs went the distance to collect unanimous victories. However, it took the smallest two fighters, Pernell Whitaker and Meldrick Taylor, to deliver the only knockouts of the evening. According to many, Holyfield's distance battle against Lionel Byarm was the most exciting. A tough Philadelphia fighter, Byarm had sparred with numerous light heavyweight champions and it showed; the fighter endured Holyfield's vicious body assault and even rocked the Olympian at one point. As for the prime-time television ratings, ABC wasn't too happy as the boxing show was knocked out by *The* [Bill] *Cosby Show,* and took a TKO against *Magnum P.I.*

FIGHTER OF THE YEAR

With a glimpse into the future, Madison Square Garden welcomed the Olympians by hosting "The Night of Gold." New York City also greeted Marvelous Marvin Hagler, who did not disappoint the crowd with his ring performance. Overlooked, which can happen in a venue like the Garden, was welter James "Buddy" McGirt, who fought in four consecutive ring battles in the Felt Forum and won all four. Notwithstanding McGirt's impressive performance, having Marvin Hagler in the City Ring added a marvelous luster.

1985

The youth movement had emerged and the question was who was going to sign, keep and promote it, before taking it to the next level. Pernell Whitaker was a five-foot six-inch southpaw, with a sixty-nine-inch reach, and a passion for the ring. Born in Norfolk, Virginia, on January 2, 1964, he was the son of a sanitation truck driver. He began boxing before the age of ten, and from that point onward he seldom recalled a time when he didn't have the mitts on. His early career, like those of many boxers, wasn't well documented, but he claimed participation in hundreds of fights. As an amateur, his nemesis was two-time Olympic Gold medalist Ángel Herrera Vera; the Cuban defeated him in the final of the 1982 World Amateur Championships. Be that as it may, everything changed for Whitaker following the 1984 Olympics. He was co-managed by Lou Duva and Shelly Finkel, who were convinced that he was one of the best lightweights in the world. Later, they were proven correct. Taking his Garden debut, he added six more victories to his record and finished 7–0, by the end of 1985.

Julio César Chávez

Born on July 12, 1962, in Ciudad Obregón, Sonora, Mexico, Julio César Chávez learned early in life that he was going to have to fight to survive. His father, Rodolfo Chavez, worked for the railroad, and the family took advantage of whatever options came their way. Julio grew up in an abandoned railroad car with his five sisters and four brothers, which was a challenge, but also a roof over his head. Coming from a poor family, he saw boxing as an opportunity, a way out of poverty. By the age of sixteen, he was boxing as an amateur.

Chávez debuted as a professional on February 5, 1980, in his home of Culiacán, Mexico. A very large and densely populated city, it was located in the northwestern portion of the country. Undefeated in his first thirty-three fights, all of which took place in Culiacán, Guamuchil or Tijuana, Chávez was finally persuaded to travel north of the border, to Sacramento, in December 1982. While it was clear by the end of that year that Chávez possessed the skills of a competitive boxer, he needed exposure and stiffer competition.

A Mexican boxer who competed from 1980 to 2005, Julio César Chávez González (born July 12, 1962), also known as Julio César Chávez, Sr., was considered by acclamation as the greatest Mexican boxer of all time, and one of the most eminent boxers ever.

The fighter added seven more victories to his resume in 1983, six by way of knockout. He was splitting his time between Mexico and California, and the exposure, not to mention experience, was paying off. On September 13, 1984, Chávez captured the WBC super featherweight championship of the world by defeating Mario "Azabache" Martinez in Los Angeles, California.

Still undefeated, the 130-pound Chávez would fight five times in 1985, while defending his title four times against some challenging opponents, including Ruben Castillo, Roger Mayweather, Dwight Pratchett and Jeff Bumpus. He was still relatively unknown to boxing fans, but 1985 would prove to be his breakout year.

The Felt Forum

Controversial Brooklyn boxer Eddie Mustafa Muhammad, a light heavyweight, scored a ten-round unanimous decision over Tyrone Booze at the Felt Forum on Friday, February 8. Muhammad was never far from an issue, or so it seemed; the last time he had surfaced, it had resulted in a canceled fight with Michael Spinks, and a riot involving a Brooklyn motorcycle club. Prior to this fight he was whisked away by sheriffs to New York Supreme Court to answer a contempt of court citation. Granted, the Felt Forum, or the Garden's AAA minor league affiliate, always had an element of uncertainty about it, but occasionally it bordered on disbelief; it could be a forum of opportunity, or a ring of controversy. There were nights when a boxing fan swore he would never go back, and evenings when every round was a delight.

Welter Mark Breland needed no introduction and was scheduled to meet Donald Gwinn for eight rounds. For the Olympic gold medalist, who was 6–0 professionally, this fight was his third eight-rounder. Gwinn hailed from Charleston, West Virginia, and brought a modest record of 8–7 into the Felt Forum on Friday, October 18. Breland knocked out Donald Gwinn at 1:32 of the second round and hit his adversary so hard that Gwinn's corner thought he had fractured his rib cage.

On December 6, Mike Tyson, a promising youngster from Catskill, New York, with a record of 13–0, was scheduled to do battle with Sammy Scaff, who brought a record of 13–6 into the Felt Forum. For Tyson, this was his first professional fight inside Madison Square Garden. A mere seventeen seconds into the battle, a left hook from the Catskill youngster sent Scaff backward with a broken nose. Bleeding heavily from his muzzle, Scaff, having lost his two previous bouts by knockout, was looking to add to his streak. Tyson followed it up with a solid overhand right that found his antagonist's jaw and caused him to retreat. Scaff looked not only uncomfortable, but perplexed. A sharp left hook finally sent the 250-pound fighter back into the ropes and down on his chest at 1:04. Scaff struggled and got to his feet at the count of eight, but the referee waved off the battle at the 1:19 mark of the opening round. This fight was on the undercard of the Iran Barkley vs. Mike Tinley Felt Forum Feature. Barkley won his twelve rounds via split decision.

On Friday, December 13, Leon Spinks, the former world heavyweight champion, who was resuming his career after a 21-month layoff, entered the Felt Forum to take on Kevin "Kip" Kane in a scheduled twelve-rounder. Spinks sent seven uppercuts to the head of Kane before referee Joe Cortez halted the battle at the 1:37 mark of the eighth round. The victory advanced Spinks to a record of 17–4–2, while Kane dropped to 15–2–1.

While the talent may have been inside the Felt Forum, the people weren't, as the average crowd was under 800 paid admissions.

FIGHTER OF THE YEAR

If the year was emblematic of anything, it was a reminder of just how much New York City stood in the shadow of the Las Vegas fight scene. "The Gambling Capital of the World" saw Hagler versus Hearns, Michael Spinks upset Larry Holmes to become the first light heavyweight champion to capture the heavyweight crown, and Donald Curry knock out Milton McCrory to unify the welterweight title. Meanwhile, over in London, Barry McGuigan took the WBA featherweight title from Eusebio Pedroza, ending his seven-year reign. As for boxing, Marvin Hagler, at the height of his popularity, boosted interest in the sport; his wars at the middleweight level were becoming legendary.

Madison Square Garden welcomed Iran Barkley and Mike Tyson. James "Buddy" McGirt had a good year, posting a 4–0 record inside the Garden. But if anybody shined the City Ring in 1985, it was Iran Barkley, who was victorious in seven consecutive Felt Forum battles.[30]

17

Iron Mike, 1986–1990

> Life's battles don't always go to the stronger or faster man. But sooner or later the man who wins, is the man who thinks he can.
> —Bruce Lee

It had ever been the most sought-after title on the planet: the heavyweight championship of the world. While most of those who held the designation had a passion for glory, some had a propensity for self-destruction. A thug, groomed in the poorest neighborhood in Brooklyn, Mike Tyson grew up to become one of the most savage boxers of all time—and the youngest heavyweight champion ever. His undeniable confidence, superior skills and intimidating attitude came at a time when boxing cried out for a "wake-up call." The heavyweight division needed a resurfacing and Tyson was just the pugilist to do it. However, his brilliance and success in the ring were often compromised by reckless behavior. As his ambivalence towards authority grew, so too did his inability to be contained.

1986

Still far from a household name, Mike Tyson appeared destined for immortality—after all, he was a protégé of the legendary Cus D'Amato. You could sense his potential as even the newspapers were picking up on his early fights and listing them in the daily events. The youngster's first battle of the year was against Dave Jaco, a ten-rounder on January 11 at the Empire State Plaza Convention Center in Albany. For Team Tyson, it was a short thirty-four-mile drive north from their home in Catskill, New York.

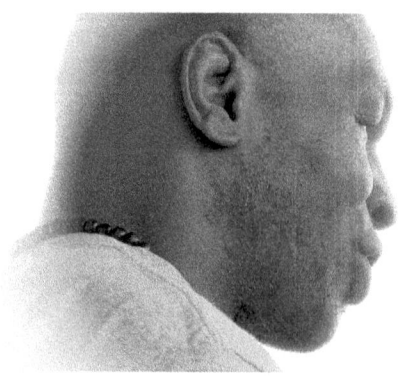

An American boxer who competed from 1985 to 2005, Michael Gerard Tyson (born June 30, 1966) reigned as the undisputed world heavyweight champion and holds the record as the youngest boxer to win a heavyweight title at 20 years, 4 months and 22 days old.

Jaco, from Ann Arbor, Michigan, was 19–5, and had fifteen knockouts in twenty-four professional fights, while Tyson had fifteen knockouts in fifteen professional bouts, eleven in the first round. On this evening, Jaco would hit the canvas three times before the fight was halted at the 2:16 mark of the opening round.

Out in Las Vegas, on April 19, Michael Spinks retained his IBF heavyweight title by taking a fifteen-round split decision over Larry Holmes in their rematch. Oddsmakers favored Holmes (8–5), believing that the pair's last fight was simply an anomaly. They were wrong. Taking his record to 29–0, the undefeated Michael Spinks was in the catbird seat; he could sit back and let the opponents come to him. Meanwhile, Holmes, at 48–2, looked vulnerable—no, he looked ridiculous—for the very first time. Interesting things were happening in the fight game, even if most weren't inside the City Ring.

Welcome to the Arena, Mr. Tyson

If anyone had any doubt about the intentions of Michael Gerard Tyson, they were clarified by his triumph over Mitch "Blood" Green inside the City Ring on May 20. With his twenty-first victory, a ten-round unanimous decision, the youngster believed he was on a path toward the world heavyweight championship. And, following his victory over Green, it looked like it was achievable.

Tyson's assault appeared to overwhelm his opponent from every conceivable angle. Often the twenty-nine-year-old Green, who stood six feet five inches and was ten pounds heavier, had little option but to hold his adamant antagonist in hope of preventing his machine-gun body assaults or damaging overhand artillery. Twice in the early rounds, Green was struck so hard that it dislodged his mouthpiece and sent it flying across the ring, then onto the ring apron; Tyson also knocked it out in the tenth. Criticized for his late-round fatigue during his last fight against James Tillis, Tyson believed this fight had to make a statement. And he did precisely that against the WBC's seventh-ranked contender.

Floyd Patterson, another D'Amato protégé, had become the youngest heavyweight champion at twenty-one years, eleven months. Mike Tyson hoped to break that mark; he would turn twenty on June 30. The youngster, who was managed by Jim Jacobs and Bill Cayton, wanted his next match to be with Trevor Berbick, the WBC champion. There was further hope that he would be added to HBO's heavyweight unification series co-promoted by Don King and Butch Lewis.[1]

Camacho at the Garden

City boxing fans were elated as only twenty-four days later they were treated to another Garden slugfest. On Friday, June 13, over 10,000 fans turned out at the Garden to watch Héctor "Macho" Camacho take a hairline twelve-round split decision against Edwin "Chapo" Rosario to retain his WBC lightweight championship. It was Camacho's first defense of the crown he had won from José Luis Ramírez the previous August.[2] Rosario fought well, as Camacho was dazed and cut in the fifth term and rattled in the eleventh, but it was not enough. With his "stick and move" tactics, Camacho scored points, while avoiding his opponent as much as possible. Wisely, "Macho" would hold when he felt threatened.[3]

The bout also had a rather impressive undercard: Julio César Chávez (47–0, 43 knockouts) stopped Refugio Rojas in seven rounds, Mike Tyson knocked out Reggie Gross in the first round, and Matthew Hilton (23–0, 18 knockouts) took a ten-round unanimous victory over Cheto Ramos. Welcome to New York City, Mr. Tyson.

20 Years, 4 Months and 22 Days

He did it! Mike Tyson became the youngest heavyweight champion in boxing history on Saturday, November 22, 1985. The Las Vegas Hilton hosted the World Boxing Council (WBC) heavyweight championship between Tyson and Trevor Berbick that ended at the 2:35 mark of the second round. Knocked down early in the round with a Tyson left hook, Berbick dropped to his back end. Tyson's mentor Cus D'Amato, who had passed away on November 4, 1985, wasn't there physically, but he was certainly there spiritually. The Tyson heavyweight era had begun.

Later in the year, the heavyweight march continued. After many twists and turns, there was finally a heavyweight confrontation on December 12, inside Madison Square Garden. James "Bonecrusher" Smith, a late replacement for Tony Tubbs, captured the WBA heavyweight crown by knocking out Tim Witherspoon at the 2:12 mark of the opening round. The two fighters had met back in June 1985, only then it was all Witherspoon in a twelve-round decision for the NABF heavy crown.[4] Witherspoon, a twenty-nine-year-old Philadelphia fighter, was put to one knee by an overhand right by Smith. Up at the count of three, he took the mandatory eight count. Sensing the kill, Smith dropped him again with a sharp right to the head. Spitting blood as he rose, Witherspoon was on borrowed time. A powerful Smith right ended the fight with a third knockdown.

Fighter of the Year

Tyson, who finished the year 13–0, reinvigorated a game that needed a kick in the ass. People from all walks of life just wanted to watch boxing again. Interest in the New York City fight game also seemed to improve, as the Felt Forum actually doubled its average attendance.

Some good battles also took place outside the state. Thomas Hearns knocked out the previously unbeaten James Shuler in seventy-three seconds on March 10 (Las Vegas); Marvelous Marvin Hagler, stunned early in a battle against John Mugabi, rallied back to kayo "The Beast" in the eleventh term on March 10 (Las Vegas); Evander Holyfield fought a vicious distance war with Dwight Qawi to take a split decision and become the new WBA cruiserweight champion on July 12 (Atlanta); and Lloyd Honeyghan, in an enormous upset, stopped Donald Curry in the sixth round on September 27 (Atlantic City).

Two notable fighters, Mustafa Hamsho and James "Buddy" McGirt, posted 3–0 records inside the City Ring, but the fighter who shined it the most with his two appearances was Mike Tyson. Unfortunately for New York fight fans, he would never return to fight inside the City Ring.[5]

1987

As new champions, like Mike Tyson, emerged, old ones stepped out of the past. George Foreman committed himself to a comeback. The thirty-eight-year-old, who was tipping at 300 pounds the previous summer, was shaping up nicely and weighing in around the 250-pound mark. Preacher George, having fought only against sin since 1977, hoped to shine his mitts in the ring and grab a title by age forty.

Dusting off the mirror as well was Floyd Patterson, but not in the same manner as Foreman. The former heavyweight champion had been working with his adopted son Tracy Harris Patterson. The skilled super bantam was undefeated in his first fifteen bouts and fighting primarily out of Atlantic City. His record was somewhat deceptive, however, as eleven of the fighters had losing records.

THE FIGHTING FORUM

Madison Square Garden shifted much of its boxing into the Felt Forum. The goal was to ignite interest in Thursday nights inside the venue.

On January 8, Canadian Michael "The Silk" Olajide knocked out Richard Burton at the 1:38 mark of the fourth round. The fighter had been criticized for not having overwhelming power, but he remained unconquered at 21–0 with 15 knockouts. It was middleweight Olajide's third appearance inside the Forum.[6]

Another Canadian, Donny "The Golden Boy" Lalonde picked up a twelve-round unanimous decision over Brooklyn's Mustafa Hamsho on May 7. The victory took the light heavyweight to 29–2 with 24 knockouts. Hamsho, who became noticeably frustrated as the duel wore on, drew a number of warnings from referee Arthur Mercante, Jr., during the fight. The loss took the Brooklyn boxer to 42–4–2 with 26 knockouts.

Boxer Chris Reid, with a record of 17–1–1, had a night he wouldn't soon forget on June 18, when Venezuelan Fulgencio Obelmejias, who stood at 49–4, dropped him to the canvas six times during their bout.[7] The battle was halted at the 1:01 mark of the tenth round and Obelmejias awarded the victory.

On August 6, James "Buddy" McGirt, ranked the number two junior welterweight by both the WBC and IBF, knocked out Roger Brown at the 1:05 mark of the fifth round of their scheduled ten round bout. Dominating from the opening bell, McGirt was spot on with all his punches. The event drew more than 1,400 fight fans.

In one of the better Forum cards of the year, Michael Dokes, who hadn't fought since March 1985, knocked out K.P. Porter at the 0:25 mark of the fifth round in a scheduled ten-round confrontation. Dokes was on a five-year probation as a result of a cocaine possession conviction. Coming out slow, he picked up the pace in the fourth term. Landing some solid combinations, the 245-pound former WBA heavyweight champion sent Porter to the canvas in the fourth round. After Porter took some early damage in the fifth, the referee waved off the fight.

Also on the undercard: Michael Olajide, who dropped his opponent three times, stopped Frank Owens two minutes into the sixth round, and James "Buddy" McGirt impressed everyone with his knockout of John Sinegal at the 1:54 mark of the first round.

ACTION IN THE AGE OF IRON MIKE

Clearly atop the heavyweight division and in the shadow of greatness, Mike Tyson inscribed his saga into the history books as other outstanding fighters wrote their final chapters. The brilliant middleweight Marvin Hagler ended his career, while Sugar Ray Leonard, always one offer short of a comeback, pondered his future. All the same, if you had to pick an exit, Hagler's approach was near perfect. Forever etched in our memory will be his three-fight swan song: Thomas Hearns, John "The Beast" Mugabi, and Sugar Ray

Leonard. Hagler, whose image alone should rest in the dictionary next to the word intimidating, will forever remain timeless.

Las Vegas presented four outstanding battles in 1987: Leonard's split decision over Hagler (April 6); Mike McCallum's fifth-round knockout of Donald Curry (July 16); Thomas Hearns's fourth-round knockout of Juan Rolden (October 29); and the perfect performance by Julio César Chávez in his eleventh-round knockout of Edwin Rosario to capture the WBA junior middleweight title (November 21). Two who impressed: Evander Holyfield went 4–0, with victories over Henry Tillman, Ricky Parkey, Ossie Ocasio and Dwight Muhammad Qwai; and Julio César Chávez, the 130-pound terror, went 3–0, with victories over Francisco Tomas Da Cruz, Danilo Cabrera and Edwin Rosario.

Fighter of the Year

As for New York City boxing, it excelled inside its premier smaller venue. James "Buddy" McGirt, who went 5–0 inside the Felt Forum, continued to polish the City Ring in 1987, while reminding New Yorkers just how great the fight game can be.

1988

On January 11, the United States Supreme Court refused to consider reinstating the triple-murder convictions of Rubin "Hurricane" Carter and John Artis. Both men were convicted by juries in 1967 and 1976, but the verdicts were reversed each time by appeals courts on the ground that the constitutional rights of the defendants had been violated at each trial. Both men had been charged with the fatal shooting of two men and a woman in the Lafayette Bar and Grill in Paterson, New Jersey.

A former middleweight contender, Carter was convicted in two trials and spent nineteen years in prison before his release in 1985. His case drew public attention thanks to numerous celebrities, most notably Bob Dylan, who composed the biographical ballad "Hurricane." Concerts to raise funds for his defense were even held at venues such as Madison Square Garden—a facility where Carter had fought eleven times.

Carter's Garden debut took place on June 23, 1962, against Ernest Burford. He lost the duel by united verdict but vindicated his performance by knocking out Burford in a rematch. Carter also fought in five consecutive Garden bouts, beginning on October 27, 1962, and won four of them, including victories over Holly Mims and George Benton. Compiling a final record of 28–12–0, he may be the sole Garden contestant to ever use the arena as a defense fundraiser.

A Heavyweight Contrast

Having not fought since April 19, 1986, Larry Holmes, having lost back-to-back battles against Michael Spinks, decided to re-enter the ring, and to oppose not just any opponent, but to tackle the undefeated heavyweight champion, Mike Tyson—a man seventeen years younger. So as the last vestige of the Ali era (other than George Foreman), Holmes would close the book. Some believed "Iron Mike," a betting favorite (8–1), might show the "Easton Assassin" a bit of respect, you know, as Holmes did to Ali. It was possible, as Tyson was a student of the fight game; it just wasn't probable. Perhaps if Holmes had been, say, Henry Armstrong, it might have been different. Nobody was betting on Holmes to win, and few, if any, thought he would go the distance of the scheduled twelve rounds.

On January 22, inside the Convention Center in Atlantic City, Mike Tyson knocked Larry Holmes down three times in the fourth round before referee Joe Cortez stopped the fight prior to the end of the term. Tyson had taken command and never relented.

Next, it was "Iron Mike" Tyson versus Michael "Jinx" Spinks, in a confrontation billed as "Once And For All." Two undefeated fighters, each believing he had a legitimate claim to the heavyweight championship of the world, were meeting for the very first time on June 27.

To get a sense of casino economics: Trump Plaza paid $11 million to host (site fee), HBO paid $3 million for delayed TV rights, $2 million was paid for foreign TV rights, and Pepsi paid $1.25 million to sponsor the fight. A sellout crowd of 21,785 attended the event at Convention Hall, or the Convention Center, adjoining Trump Plaza, in Atlantic City and produced a gate of $12.3 million. Ringside seats were priced at $1,500 a pop, although Donald J. Trump wanted the top of the scale at $2,000. In recent years, ringside ticket prices had escalated in direct proportion to casino involvement. Be it Las Vegas or Atlantic City, the escalation was due to one thing ("churn & drop"): statistics. Entice the high rollers with ringside seats and it will pay back in multiples—this was what the Garden was contending with.

If you can't beat them, join them: Madison Square Garden, one of more than 1,000 closed-circuit hosts for the fight, turned out a crowd estimated at 18,000 for their arena event that combined live boxing with the Tyson v. Spinks broadcast. In the live features: The ageless Saoul Mamby, the former WBC junior welter champ, took a ten-round decision over the undefeated Glenwood Brown, and Michael Dokes dropped Andrew Stokes three times en route to a first-round technical knockout.

The atmosphere was stirring in the Garden as fans turned their attention to the live broadcast. Cheers went through the roof with the prefight introductions that included Donald J. Trump and Muhammad Ali. In summary: Tyson delivered a crushing right hook to the body that sent Spinks to his back, his head actually underneath the bottom rope. While trying to regain his senses, Spinks took the ten count, then fell forward at 1:31 of the first round.

Felt Forum Highlights

In New York City, the Felt Forum remained the only venue to stage regular (roughly twice monthly) boxing shows.

On Sunday, March 6, Iran Barkley battered Michael Olajide, Jr., into submission, knocking him down twice before referee Arthur Mercante, Jr., stepped in to stop the fight at the 1:12 mark of the fifth round. Although Barkley dominated the bulk of the fight, he was not without vulnerability, as his aggressor dropped him briefly in the fourth. With the victory, Barkley moved into the forefront of the middleweight division, and on June 6, he would upset Thomas Hearns. As for Olajide, 25–2 with 17 knockouts, he decided to take some time off.

Four exciting battles took place inside the Forum on October 27: Lightweight Edwin Rosario captured his fifth consecutive knockout victory by defeating Juan Minaya at the 1:44 mark of the fourth round. With the victory, Rosario moved his record to 31–3, with 27 knockouts, and hoped to do battle next with Julio César Chávez or Luis Ramirez. Michael

Dokes, the former WBA heavyweight champion, stopped Curtis Isaac at the 2:21 mark of the fourth round. With the victory, Dokes moved to 36–1–2, with 23 knockouts, and hoped for a shot at Evander Holyfield. Heavyweight Alex Stewart made Lorenzo Canady his eighteenth knockout victim at the 2:14 mark of the fourth round. Finally, super bantam Tracy Harris Patterson knocked out Mario Gonzalez at the 1:42 mark of the second round. Patterson moved his total to 27–1, with 18 knockouts, and climbed up the rankings.

Fighter of the Year

Although it wasn't a bad year for boxing at the Garden, thanks to the Felt Forum, many of the better performances took place outside of New York City: Simon Brown, in a bloody battle, managed to rally back and knock out Tyrone Trice in the fourteenth round on April 23 (Berck-sur-Mer, France); Orlando Canizales dropped Kelvin Seabrooks in the fifteenth to take the IBF bantam title on July 9 (Atlantic City); unknown Tony Lopez rallied from being dropped in the eighth round to defeat Rocky Lockridge for the IBF junior lightweight title on July 23 (Sacramento); and Jorge Páez floored Calvin Grove three times in the final round to grab the IBF feather crown on August 4 (Mexicali, Mexico).

A young southpaw featherweight by the name of Kevin Kelley attracted some attention inside the Forum as he made his pro debut in the venue on September 8. Winning four consecutive fights inside the venue, the Queens fighter had exhibited considerable promise.[8] But hard-hitting Edwin Rosario went 4–0 inside the Forum ring, and had not let his loss last year to Julio César Chávez throw him off his championship pace.

1989

James "Buddy" McGirt's first professional loss was to an undefeated Frankie Warren, back on July 20, 1986. His only other loss was to an undefeated Meldrick Taylor on September 3, 1988, at Harrah's Marina Hotel Casino in Atlantic City. That's an impressive duration of 776 days between losses, or 2 years, 1 month, 14 days, excluding the end date. Add to it the ten victories he took between losses, which included names like Saoul Mamby, Frankie Warren in a rematch, and Howard Davis, Jr., and you have a spectacular resume. In his battle with Taylor, McGirt's manager Al Certo rushed through the ropes waving a towel to halt the pounding his fighter was taking. Referee Randy Newman stopped the bout at 2 minutes of the 12th and final

An American boxer who competed from 1982 to 1997, James Walter "Buddy" McGirt (born January 17, 1964) was a Madison Square Garden favorite.

round. It wasn't like McGirt to surrender, but it was like him to lose, either. At 38-2-1, Brentwood, Long Island's premier fighter was battling hard to stay in the division mix.[9]

On Thursday, January 12, McGirt stopped Manuel DeLeon at the 0:29 mark of the sixth round. The light welterweight was glad to be back inside the Felt Forum, in front of his fans, even if DeLeon provided little threat. It was the confidence boost that he needed. Also on the bill, Merqui Sosa, with a record of 8-0, 6 knockouts, stopped Charles Hollis, and Gino Gelormino knocked out Darren McGrew.

In January, it was announced that a plan to replace the current Madison Square Garden had been abandoned in favor of renovation. In order to complete the $100 million refurbishment, the Arena would be closed during the summer months of June, July and August. Also, the Felt Forum would be closed for two years.

THE DEATH OF SUGAR RAY ROBINSON

The best fighter pound-for-pound ever, Sugar Ray Robinson, died on Wednesday, April 12. He was 67 years of age. The coroner's official cause of death was arteriosclerotic cardiovascular disease, a gradual weakening and hardening of the arteries.

A quick, sleek and accurate boxer, Robinson held both the welterweight and middleweight titles. He was recalled not only as a talented fighter but a skilled and challenging negotiator. To take on the champion, you met his terms or he didn't meet you.[10]

Trying to choose Robinson's best fight was like trying to recall Babe Ruth's greatest home run. Robinson fought the best because he was the best. His adversaries included Fritzie Zivic, Marty Servo, Sammy Angott, Jake LaMotta, Henry Armstrong, Kid Gavilan, Randy Turpin, Rocky Graziano, Bobo Olson, Joey Maxim, Gene Fullmer, Carmen Basilio, and Paul Pender.

It was a professional career well worth recalling: Sugar Ray Robinson fought inside Madison Square Garden twenty-five times and compiled a record of 23-2 inside its ropes. His first professional fight, against Joe Echevarria, took place inside Madison Square Garden on October 4, 1940. His last fight in the venue was a unanimous decision loss to Denny Moyer on February 17, 1962. Robinson's first loss inside the City Ring was against Gene Fullmer on January 2, 1957. The fighter with the greatest number of victories to face Robinson in the Garden was Henry Armstrong (134 at the time). The boxer with the greatest number of losses to meet Robinson at the venue was Fritzie Zivic (27 at the time). He never met an undefeated fighter inside the Garden. Robinson fought in four consecutive Garden battles (1941–42) once in his career. His first repeat opponent in the Garden was Fritzie Zivic, and his last was Denny Moyer.

In 1965, Sugar Ray Robinson planned to work his way through the ranks once more for what would have been his 16th middleweight championship fight. It was another case where pride seemed to take a backseat to the pocketbook. He had won the 160-pound championship five times, more than any other man, and the welterweight title once, and he thought that at the age of forty-five he could do it again. While a part of every boxing fan just wanted to believe him, the other part didn't want the memories tainted. We wanted to remember him in his prime. Fighting over a dozen times in 1965—even the record books don't agree on the exact number of fights—in places like Steubenville, Johnstown and Tijuana, Robinson resorted to battling tomato cans to make a buck.

For his final fight, and you have to give him some credit for the selection, he turned to the very talented Joey Archer. With a record of 44–1–0, Archer was a good, but not great, puncher with solid skills, and as the number-one contender, he stood between Robinson and the middleweight champion Dick Tiger. When Robinson hit the canvas in the fourth round, the dream essentially ended; Archer hadn't bottomed a fighter in five years. Robinson also hit the canvas in both the sixth and seventh rounds. He looked like a veteran ballplayer taking a third strike.

Honestly, few recall Robinson's final fight. Instead, and as it should be, they turn to his finer moments, like his rematch with Randy Turpin. It was midway through the battle and Robinson had a serious cut over his eye. Referee Ruby Goldstein was a single favor from calling the ring physician to stop the fight, but the veteran arbiter heeded Robinson's plea for just one more round. Robinson seized the moment and stopped Turpin.

Death Comes for Esteban de Jesús

As a reflection of society, the fight game's participants were vulnerable to challenges. On Friday, May 12, Esteban de Jesús, the former WBC lightweight champion (1976–1978), succumbed to AIDS at his home in San Juan, Puerto Rico. He was 37 years old. Admitting his drug use, de Jesús had been diagnosed as having acquired immune deficiency syndrome early in 1989.

The boxer's first battle inside Madison Square Garden came on April 10, 1972, when he defeated George Foster in the Felt Forum by a unanimous decision. In his fourth Garden appearance, de Jesús handed the undefeated Roberto Durán his first career loss by taking a ten-round united verdict on November 17, 1972. The victory thrust the young fighter into the spotlight and he captured the vacant NABF lightweight title by defeating Ray Lampkin on February 16, 1973, at Coliseo Roberto Clemente in San Juan, Puerto Rico. In a rematch with Durán, de Jesús took only his second career loss when he suffered an eleventh-round knockout. With a record of 45–2, he fought Antonio Cervantes for the WBA world super lightweight title, but lost in a unanimous decision.

Three of his last five fights occurred in Madison Square Garden, his last being on November 9, 1979, which was a victory over Ruby Ortiz. Esteban de Jesús finished his career with over 50 wins, against a handful of defeats; 32 of his victories were by knockout. His trilogy with Durán remains a classic. In late 1980, his life began to unravel. Involved in a traffic dispute, the boxer fatally shot a man and was sentenced to life in prison. It was while in prison that he tested positive for the AIDS virus. His death came a mere two months after his sentence was commuted.

Inside the Felt Forum and Its Stand-Ins

On Thursday, April 13, Bronx boxer Aaron "Superman" Davis took a unanimous decision over Luis Santana from Los Angeles. Davis, a welterweight, had a sensational left hand that just could not be overcome by Santana. With the win, the undefeated Davis ran his record to 23–0, with 13 knockouts.

Michael Dokes, the former WBA champion, took out Bobby Crabtree with a massive left hook to the body. The fight was stopped at the 1:46 mark of the first round. The heavyweight skirmish took place inside the Forum on Thursday, July 13. Dokes, who always seemed a day late and a dollar short when it came to making matches, took his record to 38-2-2. Also on the bill, heavyweight Alex Stewart remained undefeated with his twenty-third knockout. This time his opponent was Fernando Montes, whom he delivered at the 1:50 mark of the second round.

Brooklyn's Alex "The Destroyer" Stewart tied the record of twenty-four consecutive knockouts at the beginning of a heavyweight career by defeating Terry Armstrong in the third round of their Thursday, August 10, battle inside the Felt Forum; Mac Foster had set the record back in 1970. It was Alex Stewart's fifteenth appearance inside the Felt Forum. Proving that you can find a pot of gold at the end of a knockout rainbow, Stewart was then matched against Evander Holyfield on November 4 in Atlantic City. He would fight courageously against Holyfield, but suffer a loss by way of an eighth-round technical knockout; the fight was stopped at the 2:51 mark.

Madison Square Garden's first card at the Beacon Theater, which was the venue of choice as the Felt Forum underwent a facelift, took place on Thursday, September 14. The feature bout saw Aaron Davis take a united decision over Gene Hatcher, the former junior welterweight champion. Located at Broadway and 74th, the "ancient" Beacon Theater held 2,680 seats. To accommodate the spectators in the orchestra seats, the ring legs were lowered to eighteen inches. While the Garden used the facilities at the Beacon, they were further exploring other venues such as the Manhattan Center and Hofstra University over at Hempstead, Long Island.

Fighter of the Year

Keep them playing, whatever it takes, even ringside tickets. That was the gambling establishment mantra. Casino boxing was where the money was, and that's where you were going to find the big-name fighters. With the Garden renovation underway, boxing looked outside of town: Roberto Durán defeated Iran Barkley in a hard-fought split decision on February 24 (Atlantic City); Lupe Gutierrez managed to survive twelve brutal rounds to take a split decision from Jeff Franklin on March 6 (Reno); Evander Holyfield took ten rounds to finally stop Michael Dokes on March 11 (Las Vegas); and Loreto Garza, in a junior welter confrontation, managed to take a victory over Frankie Warren on August 12 (Sacramento).

Boxer Pernell Whitaker had a solid year and took the IBF lightweight title with a unanimous decision over Greg Haugen. He also picked up wins over Louie Lomeli, José Luis Ramírez and Martin Galvan. Madison Square Garden, via its daughter venue, welcomed Junior Jones, and Tommy Morrison, while both Kevin Kelley and James "Buddy" McGirt went 5-0 under its umbrella.

1990

Proof that reality was merely an illusion came on February 11. Buster Douglas, a 42-1 underdog, put on an incredible display of pugilism by knocking out Mike Tyson in the tenth round of their battle in Tokyo. Surprisingly, Douglas controlled the fight from the beginning, effectively using his jab and tying up Tyson whenever the champion got inside. And, just like that, the invincibility was gone.[11]

THE BOYS ARE BACK IN TOWN

Finally, the big boys were back in Madison Square Garden on Wednesday, April 4, as Donovan "Razor" Ruddock faced Michael Dokes for twelve rounds of heavyweight boxing. The main arena had not seen a live card since December 1986.[12]

Over 12,000 turned out to watch the Garden festivities, and it proved to be an interesting evening's boxing. James "Bonecrusher" Smith took a twelve-round unanimous decision over Mike Weaver, which was a little bit of a disappointment, as many believed Smith should have knocked his adversary out. The surprise of the evening was the lightweights. Juan Nazario upset Edwin Rosario to take the WBA world lightweight crown. The referee would not allow Rosario, who had been cut over his eye, to answer in the ninth round. In the main event, "Razor" Ruddock sent three slicing left hands to Doke's head and knocked out the fighter at the 0:53 mark of the fourth round. Dokes was out cold and took oxygen in an attempt to bring him back to his senses. The fight was fairly even going into the decisive fourth round. Afterwards, as Dokes pondered retirement, Ruddock was trying to figure out just how, or even if, he fit into the heavyweight picture.

At a November press conference, it was announced that Sugar Ray Leonard would be making his first fight appearance ever at Madison Square Garden. His resume had not included the historic venue, and he, not to mention New York City fight fans, deemed it time. He would tackle Terry Norris, the WBC super welterweight champion, on February 9, 1991. The eleven-year age difference between the fighters should offer an interesting contrast: Norris with his speed and accuracy against Leonard's maturity and perseverance. Leonard relinquished his WBC super middleweight crown in December of 1989, while Norris won his by defeating John "The Beast" Mugabi in the first round on March 31.

THE YEAR IN PERSPECTIVE

As the Tyson era was fading into the horizon from a number of perspectives, he still defeated both Henry Tillman and Alex Stewart to close out his year at 2–1. Lightweight Julio César Chávez added five victories to his total and stood 72–0. To say he was a dominant force in the boxing would be a soft sell. For the time being, Evander Holyfield, at 24–0, was picking up the pieces of the Tyson heavyweight foundation and rebuilding it to suit his needs.

Outside of New York State, Julio César Chávez floored Meldrick Taylor in a spectacular knockout comeback on March 17 (Las Vegas); Terry Norris knocked out John "The Beast" Mugabi in the opening round to take the WBC junior middle crown on March 31 (Tampa); and Tony Lopez regained the IBF junior lightweight title by defeating Juan Molina on May 20 (Reno). The relative silence of the City Ring was heartbreaking.

18

Comfortably Numb, 1991–1996

> Be regular and orderly in your life like a bourgeois, so that you may be violent and original in your work.
> —Gustave Flaubert

Igniting the Nineties, or the last decade of innocence, was everything from grunge music and flannel shirts to gangsta rap and backwards baseball caps. Socially conscious issues took the forefront, kicking hair bands, Spandex and goofy video games to the curb. The digital age was just beginning, and as predicted, it would change everything entering a new century.

Not only a game but a form of entertainment, boxing was subject to all the advantages and disadvantages of both. So does a venue roll the dice and take a chance on a boxing event, or turn to a performer who has a hit record? The Garden had one goal, profitability, but it had many options, and exercised them accordingly.

During this period, the Felt Forum was renamed the Paramount Theater, heavyweight boxing returned, and women's boxing premiered. However, the Garden's boxing department was kayoed. That's right. From the summer of 1993 (July 8), until late fall of 1995 (December 15), the City Ring was essentially inactive. It would take the "Golden Boy," or Oscar De La Hoya, to awaken it from its slumber.[1] However, months later a fiasco known as Riddick Bowe vs. Andrew Golota I once again led to questions about the legitimacy of the fight game. The toxicity of the period left every boxing fan numb.

Were there glimmers of hope? Of course, and that flicker would eventually turn into a light at the end of the tunnel.

1991

Father Time was traditionally depicted as an elderly bearded man, sometimes with wings, dressed in a robe and carrying a scythe and an hourglass or other timekeeping device (which represents time's constant one-way movement). Ray Charles Leonard, at age thirty-four, was clean-shaven but wore an earring, a robe, and gloves while leaving the timekeeping duties to someone else. However, most could see the resemblance.

On February 9, inside Madison Square Garden, Sugar Ray Leonard, who hadn't fought in fourteen months, entered the City Ring for the very first time to box; it had taken him thirty-nine professional fights to find his way to the prestigious confinement. His opponent, Terry Norris, was eleven years his junior and making his second defense of the WBC super welterweight championship. Despite his lack of fighting frequency, Leonard was a favorite (12–5). Indeed, it seemed he was always the favorite.

Terry Norris, who fought without an earring, was fast on his feet and possessed a knockout punch that faded with rounds. His idol growing up was Sugar Ray Leonard. Whether or not the over 7,000 Garden fans cheered for him, he didn't care. Had he not been inside the City Ring, replaced by another opponent, he too would be cheering for Leonard.

Norris made a statement in the second round when he dropped Leonard with a left hook, then stung the fighter again in the seventh, only this time with a compact right. Instinctively, Leonard understood where had made his mistakes and corrected them. At this point, there was no doubt he would last the twelve-round distance. However, he had not fought since beating Roberto Durán in a super middleweight bout in December 1989, and it showed. After the second-round knockdown, Leonard tried a few classic moves, like setting a trap for his antagonist, but Norris didn't take the bait. When the unanimous decision for Norris was announced, nobody disputed it. And when Leonard took the ring microphone and announced that it was his last fight, nobody believed it.

Mike Tyson was arrested in July 1991 for the rape of 18-year-old Desiree Washington, Miss Black Rhode Island, in an Indianapolis hotel room. On March 26, 1992, the boxer was sentenced to six years in prison along with four years of probation and assigned to the Indiana Youth Center (now the Plainfield Correctional Facility) in April 1992. The action sent the fight game into a tailspin.

A Glimpse at the Champions

With all the legitimate, not to mention renegade, titles being thrown around the fight game it's a good time to review the "alphabet soup" list of the seventeen divisions:

Heavyweight—Evander Holyfield, Atlanta, GA, undisputed*
Cruiserweight—Bobby Czyz, Totowa, NJ (WBA); Anaclet Wamba, France (WBC); James Warring, Miami (IBF)
Light heavyweight—Thomas Hearns, Detroit (WBA)*; Jeff Harding, Australia (WBC); Charles Williams, Grand Rapids, MI (IBF)
Super middleweight—Victor Cordova, Panama (WBA); Mauro Galvano, Italy (WBC); Darren Van Horn, Lexington, KY (IBF)
Middleweight—WBA title is vacant; Julian Jackson, Virgin Islands (WBC); James Toney, Detroit (IBF)
Junior middleweight—Vinny Pazienza, Cranston, RI (WBA); Terry Norris, San Diego (WBC)*; Gianfranco Rossi, Italy (IBF)
Welterweight—Meldrick Taylor, Philadelphia (WBA); James McGirt, Brentwood, LI (WBC); Maurice Blocker, Germantown, MD (IBF)
Junior welterweight—Edwin Rosario, Puerto Rico (WBA)*; Julio César Chávez, Mexico (WBC)*; Rafael Pineda, Colombia (IBF)
Lightweight—Pernell Whitaker, Norfolk, VA, undisputed*
Junior lightweight—Ganaro Hernandez, Los Angeles (WBA); Azumah Nelson, Ghana (WBC)*; Brian Mitchell, South Africa (IBF)*

Featherweight—Yungkyun Park, South Korea (WBA); Paul Hodkinson, Great Britain (WBC); Manuel Medina, Mexico (IBF)

Junior featherweight—Raúl Pérez, Mexico (WBA); Daniel Zaragoza, Mexico (WBC)*; Welcome Ncita, South Africa (IBF)

Bantamweight—Israel Contreras, Venezeuala (WBA); Joichiro Tatsuyoshi, Japan (WBC); Orlando Canizales, Houston (IBF)*

Junior bantamweight—Khaosai Galaxy, Thailand (WBA)*; Sungkil Moon, South Korea (WBC); Robert Quiroga, San Antonio (IBF)

Flyweight—Yongkang Kim, South Korea (WBA); Muangchai Kittikasem, Thailand (WBC); Dave McCauley, Great Britain (IBF)

Junior flyweight—Myung Woo Yuh, South Korea (WBA)*; Humberto Gonzalez, Mexico (WBC)*; Michael Carbajal, Phoenix (IBF)*

Mini-flyweight—Hiyong Choi, South Korea (WBA): Ricardo López, Mexico (WBC)*; and Fah-Lan Lookmingkwan, Thailand (IBF)

Tyson or not, this was an extraordinary list of boxing talent, and proof that the fight game had built itself a solid foundation for the next decade. Those with asterisks after their names considered elite fighters.[2]

Tyson, the market driver for professional boxing, was stumbling, so the question was: Which boxer would take his place? Julio César Chávez, Pernell Whitaker, Meldrick Taylor, or Evander Holyfield seemed to be obvious choices to some. But it remained to be seen.

Forgotten Rounds

Three battles that flew under the radar: Robert Quiroga, badly cut over his left eye, lost a brutal unanimous decision to Akeem Anifowoshe, who collapsed after the fight on June 15 (San Antonio).

Buddy McGirt turned in an outstanding performance in defeating the invincible Simon Brown to win the WBC welter crown on November 29 (Las Vegas).

There was a magnificent draw, if there was such a thing, between Tony "The Tiger" Lopez and Brian Mitchell on March 15 (Sacramento).

Fighter of the Year

In 1991, the City Ring was lucky enough to host both Terry Norris and Sugar Ray Leonard; moreover, for both fighters, it was the first and only time in their professional careers.

1992

Boxing on regular television, which was once common, was now a rarity. Cable television, with networks such as ESPN, the MSG Network and the USA Network, still catered to fans, but not for most of the championship bouts. For big fights, it was a matter of premium cable, like HBO or Showtime, or their pay-per-view extensions TVKO and SET.[3] But because the technology was still limited, the best exposure options remained network or cable television. Becoming a household name, which was every fighter's dream, was not likely if a pugilist remained on pay-for-view television. Boxing managers understood this, and as carefully as picking opponents, they were selecting the proper technology for each of their fighters.[4]

THE PARAMOUNT THEATER— THE FORMER FELT FORUM

A solid evening of New York City boxing was long overdue. So, on January 10, an entertaining night of boxing, featuring Iran Barkley, Roy Jones, Jr., and Frank Tate, was delivered. Over 3,000 boxing fans filed into the Paramount Theater and couldn't help noticing the new seats and upgraded lighting. It smelled new, looked brighter, and yet still had a degree of intimacy with it. Accomodating 5,190 spectators, the venue hoped to be able to host a schedule of regular boxing shows beginning on February 18.

Bronx boxer Iran "The Blade" Barkley, at thirty-one years of age, entered the Paramount on January 10, and took out Darrin Van Horn at the 1:33 mark of the second round to win the IBF super middleweight title. Van Horn, a victim of the three-knockdown rule, not to mention a Barkley left hook, was simply no match for his opponent. With the victory, Barkley hoped to entice Thomas Hearns, from whom he had won the WBC middle title back in 1988, into a rematch.[5]

The 1988 Seoul Olympics silver medalist, Roy Jones, Jr., turned nearly every head in the complex with a stunning first-round knockout over former world champion Jorge Vaca. With the victory, Jones, who fought at 158 pounds, remained undefeated. In his record of 16-0, all his wins had come by way of knockout.

Frank Tate went eleven rounds before stopping Andrew Maynard at the 1:52 mark. With the win, he picked up the NABF light heavyweight crown and took his record to 29-2, 16 by way of knockout; it was Tate's first and only Garden appearance. Everyone involved in the opening the Paramount Theater could not have been more thrilled with the evening.

On February 18, the fabulous featherweight from Flushing, unbeaten Kevin Kelley, fought valiantly to take a unanimous decision over Troy Dorsey. Taking his record to 27-0, Kelley lit up the Paramount with his performance.

An American boxer who competed from 1989 to 1996, and from 2004 to 2008, Riddick Lamont Bowe (born August 10, 1967) reigned as the undisputed world heavyweight champion in 1992, and as an amateur he won a silver medal in the super heavyweight division at the 1988 Summer Olympics.

Brooklyn boxer "Poison" Junior Jones retained his USBA (United States Boxing Association) bantamweight title by stopping San Antonio's Eddie Rangel fourteen seconds into the seventh round of their twelve-round scheduled skirmish. Paramount's audience seemed to enjoy the incessant punching of Jones, who dropped his opponent three times on the way to the September 17 win.

You got the sense that it was more than an important fight, and it was just that. Riddick Bowe, at the age of twenty-five, pounded away on his thirty-year-old antagonist Evander Holyfield for twelve rounds. In the end, it was Bowe with a unanimous decision, and the game had a new king. With the November 13 victory in Nevada, Bowe won the WBA, WBC, IBF, and lineal heavyweight titles.

As for the heavyweight champion, on December 14, he tossed his green WBC title belt in the trash can during a London news conference before stating he would defend his remaining two titles on February 6, 1993, inside the City Ring.[6] The reaction from the WBC was to crown Lennox Lewis as the new champion; the belt had been unified since 1987. As for Holyfield, he would ponder retirement.

By late December, Bowe confirmed that his initial title defense would be against Michael Dokes inside Madison Square Garden. Billed as "The Homecoming," it was the perfect setting for the city to welcome back their favorite son. Being raised in the Brownsville section of Brooklyn, Bowe started boxing at the age of eleven in the Kid Gloves at the Garden program. Later, he would become a Brownsville household name by picking up four New York Golden Gloves titles in the City Ring. The fight would be the first for the champion, who had signed a six-fight package with premium channel owner HBO.

The Year in Review

The economy of the fight game came into play in 1992, as without Mike Tyson, everyone involved was having difficulty sorting through the financial potential of television, be it premium cable or pay-for-view. Holyfield v. Holmes proved the benefit of doing a market potential analysis prior to signing a fight agreement; suffice it to say, the bout fell short of financial expectations. Among those fighters making strides were Buddy McGirt, James Toney, Azumah Nelson, Julian Jackson, Lennox Lewis and Roy Jones, Jr.

Boxing continued to use the Olympics as a glimpse into its future. The 1992 Summer Olympic Games, officially known as the Games of the XXV Olympiad, were dominated by

A British boxer who competed from 1989 to 2003, Lennox Claudius Lewis (born September 2, 1965) was a three-time world heavyweight champion, twice lineal champion, and remains the last heavyweight to hold the undisputed title.

Cuban boxing, but the United States had some standouts, including Oscar De La Hoya, Chris Byrd and Tim Austin. Casino boxing continued to dominate. Nevertheless, the Garden took some ground back thanks to the Paramount Theater and those who shined it, like Iran Barkley, Junior Jones, Roy Jones, Jr., and Kevin Kelley.

1993

An adrenaline rush! That's what city fight fans felt when learning that James "Buddy" McGirt, of Brentwood, Long Island, would be making the second defense of his WBC welterweight title (147 pounds) against Mexican Genaro Léon inside the Paramount on January 12. Ever since he won the title in a decision over Simon Brown back in on November 29, 1991, McGirt's popularity had soared.

While the champion certainly wanted to win one for his fans, he also wanted to stay sharp, and for good reason: he had a $1 million payday awaiting him against Pernell Whitaker on March 6 inside the Garden arena. To fight Léon, who had a record of 42-2-2, was a risk, but one the champion felt had to be taken. The pairing was originally on the undercard of the Holyfield versus Bowe fight, but had to be postponed owing to McGirt's tonsillitis.

Despite suffering from a troublesome left shoulder, Buddy McGirt was able to defend his title to pick up a united verdict over Genaro Léon. The injury limited McGirt's arsenal and truly tested the fighter's perseverance. In the twelfth round, he was dazed by a Léon right hand that sent him into his own corner. Perceiving capitulation, Léon struck again, but both fighters were so fatigued this late in the fight that neither looked capable of putting the other away. In an earlier bout, Flushing's Kevin Kelley stayed undefeated by knocking out Brooklyn boxer Peter Nieves in the sixth round. Overall, it was a wonderful evening of New York City boxing.

WBC President José Sulaimán flew to London, not to sightsee, but to present a new version of the heavyweight championship belt to boxer Lennox Lewis. As the first British heavyweight champion since Bob Fitzsimmons, Lewis planned to make his initial defense on April 24, in London, likely against Tony Tucker.[7] The event was part of a four-fight multimillion-dollar deal the new champion struck with HBO.[8]

Heavyweight Championship Boxing Returns

Riddick Bowe, with a record of 32–0, including 27 knockouts, didn't pick a simple title defense when he signed to meet his next adversary on February 6. Michael "Dynamite" Dokes, hailing from Akron, Ohio, held a version of the championship in 1982, and had a current record of 53-3-2, with 32 knockouts. He was no tomato can, but neither was he heir to the throne.

Just in case, the twenty-five-year-old was training hard, and seemed to be taking the role of heavyweight champion seriously. This garnered him praise from the media and the person directly responsible for keeping him on that path, his 81-year-old trainer Eddie Futch.[9]

Despite slow initial ticket sales, all parties remained optimistic. After all, this was the first heavyweight title fight at Madison Square Garden since 1986, when James "Bonecrusher"

Smith knocked out Tim Witherspoon for the WBA crown. Bowe's camp received continued criticism for their choice of Dokes, who wasn't on a short list of contenders. All the same, when fight night at the Garden arrived, nobody cared about who was on the card.

Boxing was back in New York, and the Garden atmosphere was intoxicating. You could feel it, hear it, see it, taste it and smell it. Those who frequented the Garden understood this perfectly. A Rangers or Knicks game seldom felt like a heavyweight boxing match—a court doesn't smell like an ice rink, or a boxing ring. You could close your eyes and instantaneously be catapulted back in time to the Ali-Frazier days or even the Louis-Baer era. Since 1916, when Willard fought Moran, heavyweight title fights at the Garden belonged to two men: Joe Louis, who fought in eight, and Joe Frazier, who fought in five.[10] Boxing history was in the Garden, because it flourished there.

The media coverage of the event was extensive and having HBO carry it live just added to the excitement. As an insurance policy, the Garden boxing staff was pulling out all the favors in the hope of a sell-out (18,841); management's sense of urgency was apparent, even if it wasn't immediately clear as to why.[11]

When the bell sounded for the first round, Bowe anticipated Dokes would try to come out and intimidate him, so he prepared for such an assault.[12] Instead, Dokes was delayed a bit in his corner. Bowe started to take control of the fight with his jab in the center of the ring. Both fighters were flat-footed with little movement. Three left hooks to the side of Bowe's face marked Dokes's first assault. The champion continued to measure with the jab, while keeping his overhand right locked and loaded.

With 1:45 left in the opening round, a sharp left by Bowe staggered his adversary. But, Dokes rebounded almost by instinct. The fighter had virtually no head movement and made himself a stationary target. Ten seconds later, Bowe's powerful left struck the face of his antagonist and he fell back into the ropes-his right hand catching the second strand. Bowe then went at him.

With 1:26 remaining in the round, Dokes took a standing eight count-the expedient response by Referee Joe Santarpia was controversial, as the Ohioan never hit the canvas. Pinned into a corner, Dokes did his best to counter Bowe's attacks but could not withstand the champion's combinations. Standing dazed in his corner, the helpless fighter had few alternatives. The Referee pushed Bowe back and waved off the fight. The entire Dokes team jumped into the ring to protest the stoppage. As the crowd in unison chanted "Bullshit!" The official time of the knockout was 2:19 of the first round and the official attendance was 16,332.[13]

McGirt vs. Whitaker

The evening of March 6 would be a big payday for both James "Buddy" McGirt, 59–2–1, who would defend his WBC welter crown for $1 million, and Pernell Whitaker, 31–1, who would not defend his IBF junior welter crown (140 pounds), but still take home $1.25 million. And the winner hoped to cash in further by meeting Julio César Chávez.

For weeks, Buddy McGirt insisted that his left shoulder was fine, but it was not, and it cost him his title. Even a fighter as good as McGirt isn't going to defeat a sensational boxer like Whitaker without a complete arsenal. In front of more than 10,000 Garden arena fans, Whitaker, who had stepped up in weight, walked away with a unanimous decision and the WBC welter crown.

Of interest on the undercard: Brooklyn's Junior Jones took his record to 28–0 with a fourth-round knockout of Mexican Juan Pablo Salazar, in a scheduled ten-round bantam skirmish. After the fight, many learned that Whitaker would indeed do battle against Chavez, Lennox Lewis had signed to meet Tony Tucker, and Bowe looked certain to meet Holyfield. Later, on March 15, McGirt underwent shoulder surgery to reattach a tendon. This was his final fight in Madison Square Garden.[14]

Garden's Boxing Department Kayoed

If they took a standing eight count, nobody was aware of it. Announced on May 7, Madison Square Garden would bid farewell to its boxing department during the summer. Bobby Goodman and his five-person division had been kayoed. The reason was simple: It had become an unprofitable portion of the company's business.[15] Yet the Garden management, who understood the value of the name, still hoped to stage fights using licensed outside promoters.[16]

It had been the Paramount, or the smaller auditorium, that had hosted most of the contemporary Garden fight cards, the main arena having been relatively inactive with regard to the sport. Even if the typical attendance at the Paramount wasn't overwhelming, the venue provided a nurturing environment for new talent. The problem was that nurturing can take years, and the process was not turning a profit quickly enough to satisfy the need of the corporate balance sheet.[17]

And then there was the question of competition. Casino boxing didn't just happen overnight. Everyone who followed the fight game saw it coming and was waiting for venues like the Garden to mount a viable challenge to the gaming industry. However, that confrontation never came, because it was far easier to turn to another form of entertainment. Had there been no viable options, perhaps things would have turned out differently. The money flow, be it in Las Vegas or Atlantic City, had made casino boxing the venue of choice, and it looked like it was going to stay that way. Casinos offered perks like guaranteed ticket sales, free accommodations, and even a staff at the team's disposal. These were concessions other venues simply could not make.

A contrite gathering of 1,706 turned out at the Paramount Theater on Thursday, July 8, to bid farewell, at least for now, to boxing at Madison Square Garden. Closing the curtain: Boxer Kevin Kelley disposed of Mexican Adolpho Castillio in the second round, Aaron "Superman" Davis knocked out Harold Bennett in the second round, and New York's own Lonnie Bradley kayoed Marcel Huffaker in the opening round.[18] Kelley was having a sound year: he defeated Peter Nieves in January and Jesus Poll in May. If someone had to turn off the lights, Kelley was an excellent choice.

Fighter of the Year

No longer was there a Garden boxing department, only the name of a venue with all the glorious connotations surrounding it. It was simply difficult to believe. Boxing was consumed by casinos, and their guarantees; premium television, with its pay-for-view; and alphabet-soup sanctioning bodies, with their champions by the pound.

In another sign of the changing times, the lower weight classes were emerging once again as a home to the stars, such as Michael Carbajal, Oscar "Golden Boy" De La Hoya and Kevin Kelley. All three of the aforementioned boxers made it an interesting year for the sport, but if anyone shined the Paramount it was Kevin Kelley, who went 3–0 inside its ring and shut off the lights.

1994

Over in the heavyweight division, Dan Duva, who promoted Evander Holyfield, was filling in the champion's schedule. Following a bout with Michael Moorer, Holyfield would most likely fight someone in August, followed by a November title contest (likely Lewis). Frank Maloney, who managed Lennox Lewis, matched his fighter against Phil Jackson on May 6, followed by Oliver McCall. Rock Newman, Bowe's manager who alienated his rivals during his fighter's title reign, believed there was an anti-Bowe plot underway and wasn't sure just where his fighter was going to end up—somebody find Rock a "grassy knoll." Then there were boxers like Larry Holmes. Still battling about just waiting for a title shot, Holmes would take a unanimous ten-round decision over punching bag Garing Lane on March 8 at Foxwoods Resort Casino in Ledyard, Connecticut. New London County was to Connecticut what Atlantic County (Atlantic City) was to New Jersey, a geographic area welcoming the gaming industry with open arms.

As for the fight game, it was another back-to-the-future year: Big George Foreman, who was enjoying million-dollar endorsement deals, had himself another heavyweight championship. I kid you not, or was the kid you're not?[19]

A fight that slipped between the cracks: WBA middleweight champ Jorge Castro shocked John David Jackson with an incredible left hook that floored his challenger in the ninth round. Castro finished the job by dropping the fighter two more times before the battle was stopped. The fight took place on December 10, at the Estadio de Beisbol in Monterrey, Mexico. For Madison Square Garden, the ring silence was deafening.

1995

Mike Tyson, whose original release date from prison was May 9, had it modified to March 25. The reduced term lit a fire of urgency under the bottoms of nearly every heavyweight hoping to land a big payday: even a sacrificial lamb could walk away with a year's salary following a bout with "Iron(s) Mike." But the best-laid plans of promoters and pugilists often can go awry, so only time would tell. Let the scramble begin.

Roy Jones, Jr.

Roy Jones, Sr., had four daughters, plus a son named after him. The girls had a role model in his wife, Carol, so he turned a considerable amount of his attention to his oldest child, Roy. Born on January 16, 1969, in Pensacola, Florida, Roy Levesta Jones, Jr., was blessed with good genetics. Jones the Elder had been a talented athlete. When the son turned age nine, he told his father that he wanted to be a boxer.

By the time Junior was a teenager, he was showing outstanding abilities in the ring and the fight game was becoming more than an avocation. As an amateur, he was almost faultless and compiled an impressive record of more than one hundred victories against few defeats.

Making the 1988 United States Olympic Boxing Team, an unofficial platform for a future in the sport of professional boxing, was a dream come true for many youngsters, including Roy Jones, Jr.[20] As a member of that team he would fight at 156 pounds and be joined by fellow teammates Michael Carbajal (106 pounds), Arthur Johnson (112), Kennedy McKinney (119), Kelcie Banks (125), Romallis Ellis (132), Todd Foster (139), Kenneth Gould (147), Anthony Hembrick (165), Andrew Maynard (178), Ray Mercer (201) and Riddick Bowe (201 plus).[21]

Jones simply dominated his opponents, never losing a single round en route to the finals. It was never a question of if he was going to get there, only when. Controversy erupted in the title bout when he was defeated in a 3–2 decision by South Korean fighter Park Si-Hun. Jones pummeled Park for three rounds and outpunched him by two to one, but the judges saw it differently. Few could believe the verdict. Allegedly, Park himself apologized to Jones afterward, and the referee told Jones that he was dumbstruck by the judges' decision. Later, all three judges who voted against Jones were eventually suspended.[22] Although the incident led organizers to establish a new scoring system for Olympic boxing, Jones, silver medal in hand, had taken a very unfair fall.

With a tremendous amount of experience under his belt, Roy Jones, Jr., turned professional on May 6, 1989, knocking out Ricky Randall in two rounds in Pensacola at the Bayfront Auditorium. Some quick Jones facts: his first Garden bout was in the Paramount on January 10, 1992, where he defeated Jorge Vaca (48-9-1) in an opening-round knockout. Jones defeated Percy Harris (1992) to capture the vacant WBC Continental Americas super middleweight title. He beat Bernard Hopkins (1993) for the vacant IBF World Middleweight Title. Jones took a technical knockout victory over Thomas Tate (1994) in defense of the IBF world middleweight title, then grabbed a unanimous decision over James Toney (1994) to add the IBF world super middleweight title to his resume.

Jones would make three successful IBF super middleweight title defenses in 1995, all by way of technical knockout: Antoine Byrd was vanquished in the opening round on March 18; Vinny Pazienza lasted until the sixth term on June 24; and Tony Thornton was licked in the third session on September 30. An undefeated Roy Jones, Jr., looked like a nonpareil champion.

Mike Is Out

Mike Tyson was released from prison on March 25, after serving three years and six weeks of a six-year sentence for a rape conviction. He departed the Indiana Youth Center Prison in Plainfield, Indiana, at 6:15 A.M. By Tyson's side, with his light-socket hair, Cheshire Cat smile and bellowing voice, was promoter Don King. And the master of evocative elocution and banditry wasn't apt to leave it anytime soon.

As the fight game, with all of its bizarre twists and turns, played out before fans, the City Ring was lying in storage, dusty from its lack of use; it hadn't been assembled for a big fight in more than two years. It was dragged out for a few Paramount battles, but that too came to an end. However, a few champions, like Roy Jones, Jr., and Oscar De La Hoya, hoped to convince Garden management to reassemble its most treasured possession. Both fighters understood tradition, and the value of adding their name to the list of pugilists who had graced Madison Square Garden. Granted, there were obstacles to overcome—things like expenses, including insurance and taxes—but compromise could be had, even if greed nearly always conquered nostalgia.[23]

When the International Boxing Federation mandated that its heaviest champion meet Axel Schulz in October, George Foreman declined. So the heavyweight picture looked as follows: The IBF title was vacant, Bruce Seldon held the WBA title, Oliver McCall held the WBC, and Riddick Bowe held the WBO. As always, everyone hoped for a title unification—the road to amalgamation, for all participants, was paved with gold. And the person most believed capable of the task was Mike Tyson.[24]

Naturally, every time Tyson even sneezed, it landed some form of media coverage. And the criticism, which was unrelenting, be it pro or con, was really not about Tyson, but our society as a whole. Hey, if you're going to blame something or someone, why not turn to the sweet science? Right? When society looks closely at its reflection, using the mirror of pugilism, it sees only what it wants to see.[25]

THE RETURN OF MIKE TYSON

In late May, it was announced that Mike Tyson would meet Peter "Hurricane" McNeeley at the MGM Grand in Las Vegas on August 19. The fight lasted all of 1 minute 29 seconds, before McNeeley's manager jumped into the ring, thus disqualifying his fighter.

Just the facts: The National Anthem lasted about a minute longer than the fight; Mike Tyson received about $300,000 per second for the encounter; over a million Americans watched the fight at an average of forty bucks a crack; and all 16,736 seats to the event were sold, grossing a cool $15 million.

Before you could remove the hook, line and sinker from your mouth, the farce was over, but the "He's Back," Part II post-fight news conference was just beginning. Tyson's next opponent was Buster Mathis, Jr., on November 4. However, that fight was postponed due to a Tyson broken thumb; it was later rescheduled for December 16.

RETURN TO THE MECCA

Madison Square Garden, in an enormous step to bring boxing back to the City Ring, announced that on January 12, 1996, Roy Jones, Jr., would do battle against Merqui Sosa, the NABF light heavyweight champion. The event to take place four weeks after the Garden fight between Oscar De La Hoya and Jesse James Leija, scheduled for December 15. Both boxing matches had fans citywide excited for the first time in years.[26]

In many ways, it was perfect, as Oscar De La Hoya loved the idea of fighting inside Madison Square Garden. He was the undefeated World Boxing Organization's lightweight champion, and the only member of the 1992 Olympic boxing team to bring back gold. De La Hoya was handsome, colorful, articulate and incredibly talented. And, as an ambassador for the sport, he successfully crossed ethnic lines. It was the first major boxing event at the Garden in two and a half years.

On December 15, in front of a crowd of more than 16,000, including every city celebrity from Walter Cronkite to Eddie Murphy, Oscar De La Hoya (19–0) scored a second-round

TKO over Jesse James Leija (29–1–2). Also on the card: Arturo Gatti took a unanimous decision, along with the IBF junior lightweight crown, from Tracy Harris Patterson; Shannon Briggs grabbed an opening-round TKO over Calvin Jones; and Mitchell Rose upset Eric Esch, a.k.a. Butterbean, by way of a second-round TKO. With the victory, De La Hoya decided to leave the lightweights (135-pound limit) to focus on Julio César Chávez at the 140-pound mark. Of all the bouts, perhaps the Gatti battle surprised most, as few realized what a warrior he had become. Overall, it was a magnificent night for New York City boxing.

Katherine Anne Porter, an American journalist, novelist, and a political activist, once quipped, "The past is never where you think you left it." Well, maybe, just maybe, Garden boxing was back to where it was left. The City Ring was finally dusted off and its patina shined once again.

1996

Show Me the Money

What better way to begin the New Year than by showcasing the athlete many believed to be the best pound-for-pound fighter of his time? With a record of 30–0 that included 26 knockouts and an IBF super middleweight championship, Roy Jones, Jr., stepped inside the City Ring on January 12 to confirm his willingness to meet and greet contenders at every level. Across the ring from him on this evening was Merqui Sosa, a light heavyweight who hoped to make it a competitive ten-round contest. There were no signs of intimidation, just Jones being Jones, forever confident in his abilities.

For a minute or so, it looked like Jones was inhaling the intoxicating Garden experience—something every fighter fantasizes about—but he understood that he had a job to do. As the bell rang, an enthusiastic crowd of more than 11,000 was placed immediately at the edge of their seats watching the knockout artist, who was cut like a 171-pound Greek god, slice through his opposition like a hot knife through butter. Sosa, an outstanding fighter who had never been horizontal, caught a wrecking ball right in the second round that dropped him. Up at three, he took a mandatory eight count, but it still looked as if the elevator wasn't stopping on all floors. At this point, Jones had his quarry; consequently, it was only a matter of finishing the kill. An unanswered machine-gun volley provoked referee Ken Zimmer to step in and wave it off at the 2:34 mark.

Everything felt right about the evening, and the Garden's new regime, headed by Dave Checketts, was pleased by what they saw and what they felt. It was an impressive gate considering the horrible weather. On the undercard, Tim Witherspoon, a thirty-eight-year-old gladiator, took a ten-round unanimous decision over Al "Ice" Cole, Michael Grant took a six-rounder over Bradley Rone, and heavyweight Lou Savarese took a second-round TKO over Lyle McDowell.

The Toughest Adversary

Boxer Tommy Morrison, the former WBO heavyweight champion, became the third prominent athlete to allegedly test positive for HIV, the virus that causes AIDS; the other two athletes were Magic Johnson and Greg Louganis. The announcement, which was the outcome of testing by the Nevada Athletic Commission, came on February 12, and shocked the boxing world. In Nevada, testing had become mandatory in 1988; California, New Jersey and New York had no mandatory testing. The twenty-seven-year-old boxer expressed regret regarding his carefree lifestyle, which may have given rise to contracting the illness. Morrison last fought on October 7, against Lennox Lewis, and was badly beaten.

Mike Rolls On

Four fights into his return to boxing, Mike Tyson had yet to hit a speed bump. Having regained the WBC heavyweight title with a third-round TKO of Frank Bruno on March 16, then regaining the WBA heavyweight title with a first-round TKO of Bruce Seldon on September 7, Tyson relinquished the WBC title to fight Evander Holyfield instead of the mandatory challenger, Lennox Lewis.

First Blood

The brilliant African-American author Zora Neale Hurston, who understood a struggle when she saw one, observed, "Through indiscriminate suffering men know fear and fear is the most divine emotion. It is the stones for altars and the beginning of wisdom. Half gods are worshipped in wine and flowers. Real gods require blood."[27]

On Saturday, March 23, the gods spoke inside Madison Square Garden's Theater. Two former bantamweight champions met, as Brooklyn's Bushwick boxer Junior Jones tossed mitts for twelve rounds with Orlando Canizales. It appeared a draw to most, but the verdict was awarded to Jones in a split decision. As an opening act, it framed the milieu, without handing you the picture.

A crowd of about 4,000 dedicated observers arrived a bit earlier than normal due to the talented opener. Granted, some were drawn thanks to HBO's late-night series *Boxing After Dark*, which was covering the event, but many were the boxing regulars just out for a quick dose of "March Mayhem," as it was being billed.

The co-feature was Arturo "Thunder" Gatti vs. Wilson "Black Label" Rodriguez. For the 130-pound Gatti, it was his first defense of the IBF super featherweight

An American boxer who competed from 1989 to 2002, Junior Jones (born December 20, 1970) was a two-weight-class world champion, having held the WBA bantamweight title from 1993 to 1994, and the WBO super bantamweight title from 1996 to 1997. Additionally, he held the IBO featherweight title from 1999 to 2000.

championship. Rodriguez, a 128-pound Dominican who was living in Spain, had a record of 44–8–3 and had won five of his last six contests.

Gatti wasn't afraid of heights. He was afraid of edges. Yet, he fought on the edge of a stoppage throughout this entire crusade. Thankfully, at least for the fighter, referee Wayne Kelly was familiar with Gatti's "wait and see" approach. Rodriguez, who endured some belt-line punches, was mindful of Gatti's left hook and avoided it early. Enduring a good deal of punishment, Gatti was dropped in round two at the 1:14 mark. He rose quickly, swabbed his swollen right eye with his right mitt, and went about his business.

As usual, the edge proved only to motivate the fighter. He came out strong in round three looking for a knockout and delivered some sound volleys, but Rodriguez decisively countered, focusing on Gatti's puffy eye, especially during the final minute of the round. Kelly, or should I say ringside physician Stephen Gelfman, damn near stopped the duel in the third as he, along with everyone else, was wondering what was keeping Gatti up.[28]

Rodriguez was unstoppable in the fourth, as he stalked his rival while delivering his devastating combinations. Quick on the trigger, he was only waiting for his moment. Gatti's only solace was found backed against the ropes or corner post, desperately trying to cover, as inspiring cheers of "Gat-ti! Gat-ti" filled the venue. Miraculously, as if commanded by some divine force, the half-blind gladiator began to fire back. As the round ended, Gatti looked and acted as if he had not an ounce of energy left. In defense of his first belt, his twenty-sixth pro fight was supposed to be routine, or so he believed.

After losing a point for a low blow in the fifth term, "Thunder" floored Rodriguez with a perfect left to the body. Thirty-six seconds remained in the round. Remarkably, Rodriguez arose and nearly had Gatti silenced during the final ten seconds. Everyone was mesmerized by the momentum shifts.

After landing many borderline body blows in round six, Gatti knocked out Rodriguez with a left hook to the head with fifty-five seconds remaining. It would take more than a minute for Rodriguez to get off the canvas and reach his corner.

By the end of the fight, Gatti, with his cut right eye swollen, looked like he had been through pure hell, because he had. The statistics, if you put your faith in numbers, had the fight even. The war, dubbed the "Fight of the Year" by *The Ring* magazine, would have impressed any Garden fan from any boxing era.[29]

Summer Games

The 1996 Summer Olympics took place in Atlanta, Georgia, from July 19 to August 4, 1996. The International Olympic Committee voted in 1986 to separate the Summer and Winter Games, which had been held in the same year since 1924, and place them in alternating even-numbered years, beginning in 1994. The 1996 Summer Games were the first to be staged in a different year from the Winter Games. Atlanta became the fifth American city to host the Olympics, and the third to hold a Summer Olympic Games.[30]

Boxing immediately captured the spotlight, as Muhammad Ali lit the Olympic torch and later received a replacement gold medal for his boxing victory in the 1960 Summer Olympics. The members of the 1996 U.S. Olympic boxing team included Albert Guardado (106 pounds), Eric Morel (112), Zahir Raheem (119), Floyd Mayweather (125), Terrance Cauthen (132), David Diaz (139), Fernando Vargas (147), David Reid (156), Rhoshii Wells

(165), Antonio Tarver (178), Nate Jones (201), and Lawrence Clay-Bey (201 plus). David Reid would prove to be the lone (gold) medal-winner.

TRIPLE FEATURE AT THE GARDEN

On Friday, May 10, it was another outstanding, if not a bit nostalgic, night of boxing at the Garden. Three main events graced the card as Evander Holyfield met more-brains-than-brawn Bobby Czyz, Lennox Lewis met more-brawn-than-brains Ray Mercer, and Tim Witherspoon met more-mass-than-marvel Cuban Jorge Luis González.

Holyfield, clearly in the heavyweight mix, disposed of blurry-eyed Czyz at the end of the fifth round. Referee Ron Lipton declared the Atlanta heavyweight the winner by way of a technical knockout. Czyz had complained of a substance on his opponent's gloves that was blurring his eyes, but no such material was discovered. With the win, Holyfield ran his record to 32–3, with 23 knockouts, while Czyz, a former cruiserweight titleholder, slipped to 44–7.

Lennox Lewis had a much harder time of it as the free-spirited Ray Mercer, with little to lose along his comeback trail, tried hard to derail the Briton. In the end, however, it was a majority decision for Lewis. Although there were no knockdowns, both

An American boxer who competed from 1984 to 2011, Evander Holyfield (born October 19, 1962) reigned as the undisputed champion in both the cruiserweight and heavyweight divisions, being the first and to date only boxer in history to do so, which earned him the nickname of "The Real Deal."

fighters incurred some damage—their mouths dripped blood and left eyes were swollen. Lewis, despite the verdict that took his record to 29–1, did not give an impressive performance.

Tim Witherspoon managed to stop Jorge Luis González in the fifth round with an incessant battering of right hands that left the Cuban Brobdingnagian clinging to the ropes until the fight was stopped at the 2:54 mark. Witherspoon fought well and negated the Cuban's jabs by coming to close quarters. There he invoked his jabs, but measured and fired his trademark right whenever an opportunity presented itself. The victory moved Witherspoon to 45–4, with 30 knockouts, while González fell to 24–2.

An impressive crowd of more than 17,000 turned out for an event that corroborated the city's commitment to the sport, even if it added little clarity to the heavyweight picture. To many, Holyfield should have flattened Czyz, and Lewis should have decisively delivered Mercer. As for Witherspoon, at the pinnacle of his career, his performance mirrored his last seven successful crusades.

Meanwhile, Tyson was ducking and playing Lewis, in hope of matching with Bruce Seldon, while also negotiating with Holyfield.[31] And Riddick Bowe planned to meet Andrew Golota on July 11 at Madison Square Garden.

De La Hoya in Vegas

It took less than a minute for Oscar De La Hoya to open a cut over the eye of Julio César Chávez. Yet, from that eye would flow with the blood of victory. Having little choice, referee Joe Cortez stopped the WBC super lightweight championship in the fourth. Chávez, whose nose was also broken by a De La Hoya left's hand in the fourth term, had blood all over himself. The event, held on June 7 at Caesars Palace in Las Vegas, was the broadcast, or more interesting portion, of a dual Garden event.

You Can't Be Serious

The Fighters

Andrew Golota was twenty-two years old when he left Warsaw, Poland, six years earlier. He never dreamed, although he later hoped, that he would one day fight inside Madison Square Garden. A former Olympic bronze medalist (Seoul 1988), European champion, and Polish heavyweight champion, he was popular in his native country, but a stranger outside of it. When he came to the United States, he moved to Chicago to become a truck driver. But the ring called him back. While he had knocked out 25 of his 28 opponents, it wasn't his casualty list that impressed. It was the size of Golota himself, who stood six feet four inches tall and weighed 243 pounds. Having a bit of a reputation as a dirty fighter, not to mention a stare that could melt steel, only added to the fighter's allure.

New York City was Riddick Bowe's home. For him, the thought of fighting anyone inside Madison Square Garden, including Andrew Golota, was exciting. "Big Daddy" had won his last four fights, against the likes of Larry Donald, Herbie Hide, Jorge Luis González and Evander Holyfield. In fact, he hadn't lost a fight since his first meeting with Holyfield back on November 13, 1992.

The Fight

Although advanced ticket sales were slow, the Garden remained optimistic. And it was easy to understand why. Just take a look at the undercard: Roberto Durán versus Craig Houk, Arturo Gatti versus Feliciano Corea, Merqui Sosa versus Karl Willis, and Montel Griffin versus Matthew Charleston.

A crowd of more than 11,000 boxing fans, not counting all those watching live on HBO World Championship Boxing, turned out on July 11. And they were about to be treated to a rather memorable evening. In the seventh round, Golota, who was clearly winning the bout and en route to a major upset, continued to fire his devastating combinations. But as the fight wore on, the punches began dropping to the belt-line or below; consequently, each fighter was fatigued and frustrated that his opponent would not capitulate.

Golota, having already lost points for low blows in the fourth and sixth rounds, could not afford to continue his behavior. Yet another low blow in the seventh doubled over Bowe; the fighter had hit the canvas earlier as a result of the action, and a point had been deducted. Finally, with Golota's fourth low shot, referee Wayne Kelly had seen enough and waved his arms and ended the fight. No sooner had Golota thrown the punch than he began shaking his head, aware of his miscalculation and inevitable disqualification.

The Riot

At that moment, two individuals, who appeared to originate from Bowe's corner, came racing across the ring to confront Andrew Golota. One person, later identified by police as Jason Harris, struck the fighter on the back of the head with a walkie-talkie. Within seconds, a riot ensued, involving nearly everyone in proximity to the ring. Bowe's manager Rock Newman entered the ring to tend to his fighter, followed by Bernard Brooks, Sr., a Bowe associate. Punches flew from boxing seconds, managers, associates and fans, as the situation spiraled quickly into pure chaos. The young attacked the old, Bowe fans battered Golota followers, and even spectators assaulted security guards, all with complete disregard for authority, consequence or safety.

The private security force at Madison Square Garden was ineffective and unable to control the situation; there was no training for a riot of this magnitude. Security guards were beaten, pushed and assaulted at will. As a Warsaw-born fighter, Golota had attracted fans carrying Polish flags, who immediately became a target for Bowe fans seeking retribution. A couple of those arrested were still holding their colors as they commenced their free journey to Rikers Island.

When police reinforcements—estimated at about 150 officers—arrived, some individuals were handcuffed in an attempt to bring them under control.[32] But, no sooner was one confrontation diffused than another erupted. Tempers were flaring as those being restrained turned their hatred toward those around them, including authority figures; fights continued to erupt even on the exiting escalators. Over an hour passed before police could finally clear the venue. The following day, police filed charges against Jason Harris, a member of Bowe's entourage; Stephen Bowe, Riddick Bowe's brother; and William Wright, believed to be part of the Bowe group. At least eight others were likewise arrested.

The reported number of casualties varied, but over a dozen were rushed to the hospital as a precautionary measure. Amid the ring chaos, Lou Duva, the seventy-four-year-old trainer for Golota, was struck by a walkie-talkie and hit the canvas; most of Bowe's entourage carried the communication devices. There was immediate concern expressed by observers, but no way to reach the trainer, who had a history of health issues. Duva had trouble breathing and was finally removed by stretcher and taken to New York University.

Outside the Garden, police in full riot garb rerouted traffic on 33rd Street and Seventh Avenue. The goal was to immediately block the entrance into the facility, while removing individuals from inside the venue. Most of the fans removed were stunned by what they had just witnessed. Their emotions were easier to understand than the cause—by some accounts racially motivated—of the incident.[33]

In the co-feature, by the way, Héctor "Macho" Camacho stopped Craig Houk in the second round. Thankfully, Lou Duva spent only a day in the hospital before being released.

The Fallout

The adverse incident was not just harmful to the victims of the event, but it left a cataclysmic scar on the sport of boxing. From Home Box Office to the careers of everyone associated with both fighters, not to mention Madison Square Garden, the effects were felt for years.

Just two and a half years earlier, Garden owner Paramount Communications had shut down the venue's boxing operation, for some of the same reasons that resulted in this event.

Under the current ownership of Cablevision Systems and ITT, the fight game was exhibiting signs of a nostalgic renaissance. Everybody, and I mean everybody, associated with the sport was excited until this fiasco.[34]

On Friday, July 12, NYSAC froze Riddick Bowe's $5 million purse due to the actions of those in his entourage. Later, the organization would state that more arrests were likely and that of those apprehended, none were licensed by the state. On August 1, NYSAC sought the revocation of Lou Duva's manager's license, along with a fine for his protest and bumping of referee Wayne Kelly due to the disqualification of his fighter, Andrew Golota. NYSAC also fined and suspended the license of Rock Newman's Spencer Promotions; the organization would not be allowed to promote a New York State fight until next July 31.[35]

As for the Garden, a day after the brawl they announced they were still in the boxing business. And, as proof that maelstrom begets opportunity, a Bowe vs. Golota rematch was scheduled for December 14, at the Atlantic City Convention Center in Atlantic City.

The Rematch

So how do you get beyond one of the most traumatic embarrassments in professional boxing history? Simple. Recreate another imbroglio not nearly as bad, but still tragic. On December 14, Riddick Bowe was awarded a ninth-round victory by disqualification over Andrew Golota in a rematch. Once again, Golota was ahead in the scorecards. And once again, he fell prey to his own dirty habits. He had points deducted for a second-round head-butt, a fourth-round low blow, and a final groin combination. Bowe, who was down in the second and in the fifth, somehow managed to struggle his way through the rounds.

FIRST WOMEN'S PROFESSIONAL BOXING MATCH

Andrea DeShong, with a record of 12–2, with 5 knockouts, met Kathleen Collins, with a record of 2–0–1, in a six-round, 140-pound event inside the Garden Theater on August 20. The Garden's first women's professional boxing match was on the undercard of feature bout Lou Savarese versus Tim Puller, the latter a replacement for Buster Mathis, Jr. Also on the card, Héctor Camacho fought Arturo Nina. The event was televised on USA Network's *Tuesday Night Fights*.

Collins, with her superior defensive skills, upset DeShong, the only woman to defeat the popular Christy Martin. The women's showing was actually more impressive than the men's performance. Lou Savarese knocked out Puller at the 2:51 mark of the second round. In addition, Camacho took a ten-round decision over Nina, Oleg Maskaev took an eight-round judgment over Fernely Feliz, and Junior Jones grabbed a ten-round verdict over Wilson Santos. Attendance for the event topped 2,500.

As this was the first fight in the Garden since the July 11 riot, the Garden went out of its way detailing their new protection policies, which included limiting credentials, increased visibility of security, stronger and improved positioning of security, and an improved ringside seating arrangement.

JONES VS. BRANNON

Turning back to the Garden Theater on October 4, Roy Jones, Jr., the IBF super middleweight champion, did battle against contender Bryant Brannon (16–0, with 10 knockouts). Billed as "The Next Chapter in Boxing History," the fight was broadcast live on HBO; the premium television network conducted a very robust advertising campaign for the event.

At the bell, Brannon sprinted across the ring at Jones and commenced firing a haphazard assault. It was an approach that seldom worked. With 38 seconds remaining in round two, Jones delivered Brannon to the canvas for the final time. With the victory, Jones ran his record to 33–0, with 29 knockouts.

By the end of November, he was looking to conquer any class within in his reach. On November 22 in Tampa, Jones took a unanimous twelve-round decision over Mike McCallum to grab the WBC light heavyweight championship. Jones was absolutely tenacious in his title pursuit.

THE YEAR IN PERSPECTIVE

The gender barrier was finally broken in 1996, as professional female boxers, most well-trained and exhibiting fine boxing skills, finally fought inside Madison Square Garden. Also, inside the Garden ropes, Junior Jones went 3–0, and Héctor Camacho went 2–0, as did Arturo Gatti, Roy Jones, Jr., and Tim Witherspoon.[36] A salute to the Garden staff, who would not surrender to adversity around the sport.

19

Captain Hook, 1997–2002

It is not enough that we do our best; sometimes we must do what is required.
—Winston S. Churchill

On September 11, 2001, 2,977 victims were killed in a terrorist attack at the World Trade Center in New York City, at the Pentagon, and in rural Shanksville, Pennsylvania. American Airlines Flight 11 and United Airlines Flight 175 were hijacked and crashed into the World Trade Center's Twin Towers. Also, American Airlines Flight 77 was hijacked and plunged into the Pentagon, and United Airlines Flight 93 was hijacked and crashed into grassland in Shanksville, due to the passengers fighting to regain control of the airplane. The World Trade Center towers collapsed as a result of the crashes. Life as we knew it forever changed.

Boxing, as we knew it, also changed. After suffering his first career defeat in 1997, Roy Jones, Jr., wouldn't be denied again until 2004. The brilliant light heavyweight, a.k.a. "Captain Hook," shredded opponents like vegetables at a delicatessen. As he finished 2002 at a record of 47–1, only four men lurked in his shadow: Bernard Hopkins, who would finish 41–2–1; Shane Mosley, who would stand at 38–2; Vernon Forrest, who would conclude at 35–0; and Floyd Mayweather, Jr., who would finish 29–0. Of these talented pugilists, including Jones, only Mayweather wouldn't see the inside of the City Ring during this period.

1997

With a record of 66–6–0, Larry Holmes last fought on January 24, when he lost to Brian Nielsen, an undefeated Denmark heavyweight.[1] On July 29, he entered a Madison Square Garden ring for the third and final time—a confinement he had never lost in. His opponent was a virtually unknown target by the name of Wilbur Maurice Harris, a.k.a. Moe Bettha or Sugar Moe, with a record of 9–9–2. Holmes, who was 47 years of age and was 43 pounds heavier than his adversary, took the close split decision over his twenty-two-year-old opponent. The uninspiring event drew almost 4,000 to the theater and was broadcast live on USA Network. Three one-off fights from the end of a magnificent career, Holmes deserved a better ride out of town than he received.[2]

The Lighter Weight Divisions

If there was a division to save boxing from itself, perhaps it was the welterweights, home to three undefeated champions: Felix Trinidad, at 31–0, was the IBF titleholder; Oscar De La Hoya, at 25–0, held the WBC version; and Ike Quartey, with a record of 34–0, held the WBA variety. On August 23, Garden boxing returned to the arena for the first time in more than a year; the last fight had been the Bowe vs. Golota debacle. Felix "Tito" Trinidad knocked out Australian Troy Waters; William Joppy lost a unanimous decision to Harlem's Julio César Green; Wilfredo Vazquez, the WBA featherweight champion, took a united judgment over Roque Cassiani; and Christy Martin, the WBC women's lightweight champion, grabbed a unanimous decision over Isra Girgrah.[3]

Prince Naseem Hamed, of Yemeni descent, 28–0, with 26 knockouts and the WBO featherweight champion, brought his extravagant theatrics—the fighter was known for his dramatic fight entrances—to the United States and into Madison Square Garden on December 19. Staring opposite him inside the ring was Kevin Kelley, the WBU featherweight champion. The champion was already inside the City Ring when the drama unfolded. A crowd of nearly 12,000 boxing fans watched as Hamed took seven minutes to find his corner.

The opening extravaganza, as it would prove, was almost as long as the battle itself. In an absolutely passionate duel, in which both fighters hit the canvas three times, Hamed sent a rocket left to the chin of Kelley that knocked out the boxer at the 2:27 mark of the fourth round. On the undercard, Kennedy McKinney upset Junior Jones with a fourth-round knockout to capture the WBO super bantam crown. Hamed, hoped to move on to do battle against Arturo Gatti. It would be Hamed's only City Ring appearance.

Forgottten Rounds

The man noted for knocking out Mike Tyson seven years earlier, one James "Buster" Douglas, was on the comeback trail and coming to the Madison Square Garden Theater on February 12. In a rather lackluster event, Douglas defeated Dickie Ryan via a ten-round decision; there were no knockdowns.

A healthy crowd of more than 4,000 turned out for the event, which included a strong undercard: Three 1996 Olympians—Vassily Yirov, Daniel Santos and Eric Morel—won preliminary bouts. Also, New York City police officer Ricky Frazier took a ten-rounder and Eric "Butterbean" Esch captured a four-rounder.

The Year in Perspective

Madison Square Garden welcomed some new faces, like Hamed, and UK super lightweight Ricky Hatton.[4] James "Buster" Douglas made his City Ring debut, as did the undefeated Mexican minimum weight Ricardo López and welter Felix "Tito" Trinidad. But the venue also bid farewell to the familiar faces of Edwin Rosario and Larry Holmes. The thought of being a New York City boxing fan and having a chance to see Ricardo López, Edwin Rosario and Larry Holmes in a local ring for the final time was exhilarating.[5]

1998

A fresh face surfaced among the super featherweights, that of the 1996 Atlanta Olympic Games bronze medalist, Floyd Joy Mayweather, Jr. The Michigan-born Olympian, with a professional record of 12–0, was expected to headline his first card at the Grand Casino in Biloxi, Mississippi. The television station ESPN2 planned to feature his bout against Hector Arroyo, who carried a record of 16–4–2.[6] Mayweather, on the path to stardom, would defeat his adversary on January 9, via a fifth-round TKO.[7]

Garden Heavyweight Championship Boxing

Not since Riddick Bowe knocked out Michael Dokes, back on February 6, 1993, had Madison Square Garden hosted a heavyweight championship fight. But that was about to change, or so it seemed, on June 6. Evander Holyfield was scheduled to meet Henry Akinwande inside the City Ring. The impressive undercard of the event included William Joppy, Jr., versus Roberto Durán, Lou Del Valle against Dario Matteoni, Christy Martin meeting Nieves Garcia, Johnny Tapia versus Carlos Hernandez, and Ray Mercer against an opponent that had yet to be determined.

Days before the duel, ticket sales, at prices ranging from $100 to $1,000, were off, or lower than anticipated. Those involved blamed everything from the Belmont Stakes, being held on the same day, to the weather. The fight was also being broadcast live on pay-per-view by Showtime Event Television ($39.95). Some even faulted a jejune Holyfield for the lack of interest.[8]

On June 5, the day before the event—which was billed as "D-Day," as fate might have it—was called off. The events surrounding the cancellation included: two participants tested positive for hepatitis (Akinwande and Mercer); one participant was pregnant (Garcia); and one participant was guilty of unpaid child support (Durán). Ironically, a boxer not even on the card, Lennox Lewis, may have suffered the biggest loss, as HBO withdrew a $20 million contract extension. Hey, it's boxing.

Madison Square Garden lit up on July 18, as light heavyweight Roy Jones, Jr., 36–1, did battle against his former sparring partner, Bronx boxer Lou Del Valle. Although Del Valle was cut over the left eye from an accidental butt in round seven, it didn't appear to slow him much as he put Jones down for the first time in his professional career with a left cross in the following term. Entertaining a crowd of more than 4,500 inside the Theater, the fight went the twelve-round distance and to the cards. And the unanimous decision went to Jones. Del Valle, a southpaw, shook off many of the blows by his opponent, but they were having a cumulative effect and he knew it.

Also on the card, Derrick "Smoke" Gainer upset Queens boxer Kevin Kelley, the former two-time featherweight champion, in a ten-round united verdict—the latter hit the canvas twice. Gainer, who was taller as well as six years younger, simply accumulated rounds and was not intimidated in the least by Kelley. It was hard to believe that this was the first Garden boxing card of the year, but nevertheless it was nice to see the City Ring occupied.

Just mention the name Don Dunphy, and instantly his voice is called to mind. The television and radio sports announcer specialized in boxing broadcasts. Noted for his fast-paced delivery, realism and enthusiasm for the sport, Dunphy had become synonymous with the sweet science thanks to the *Friday Night Fights*. The legendary mouthpiece passed away on July 22, 1998. He was 90 years old.[9]

TNT IN THE THEATER

The expansion of cable television continued to offer viewers options with regard to the sweet science. TNT, an American basic cable and satellite television channel owned by the Turner Broadcasting System, and later a division of Time Warner, threw its hat into the ring by announcing their inaugural boxing show on September 22, inside the Theater at Madison Square Garden. While the original purpose of the channel was to play spillovers from its sister channel TBS by airing classic film and TV shows, the dynamic nature of television soon provided the network with other viable options.[10]

The six-bout card they had configured featured Shane Mosley (28–0), the IBF lightweight champ, versus Eduardo Morales (26–0) of Argentina, and Angel Manfredy (24–2–1) versus John Brown (18–4).

In his Garden debut, Shane Mosley was nothing short of spectacular as he ruthlessly battered Argentinian fighter Eduardo Morales into a droopy corner mass before the referee stepped in to stop the fight in the fifth round. The previously undefeated Morales hit the canvas not once, but twice. Mosley displayed his sensational skills to a Garden crowd of more than 4,000 who enjoyed a splendid evening of boxing. Also, Angel Manfreddy took a close but unanimous decision over John Brown.

Finally, Evander Holyfield would meet Lennox Lewis in a heavyweight unification bout on March 13, 1999, inside Madison Square Garden. The fight was billed as "Kings' Crowning Glory." Holyfield was guaranteed $20 million, while Lewis would grab $9.5 million. From the Garden's perspective, it paid a site fee of $8.3 million, with hope of a sellout and a possible $10 million return. Tickets for the event were rumored to start at $100 and go as high as $1,500.

More and more, television in every form was grabbing a bigger piece of the fight game. Control of the sport was as dynamic as it was delicate for those involved. The sanctioning bodies and their rankings remained a mystery, no better exemplified than by the pitiful five-punch performance of the WBC's Patrick Charpentier, the organization's top-rated welterweight contender, who was destroyed by Oscar De la Hoya. Such mismatches served no purpose.

FIGHTER OF THE YEAR

In his Garden debut, "Sugar" Shane Mosley ruthlessly battered Argentina fighter Eduardo Morales; moreover, it was TNT in the Garden, as a touch of "Sugar" shined the City Ring.[11]

1999

All of boxing shifted its attention to Madison Square Garden on February 20, as Felix "Tito" Trinidad, Jr., age 26, dominated Pernell Whitaker, age 35, for twelve rounds. The latter, having not fought in sixteen months primarily due to drug suspensions, looked every bit as deficient as one might have expected. Whitaker, who was dropped by a solid right in the second round, scoffed at the only knockdown of the contest. Later, he was taken to a hospital with a fractured jaw. Trinidad, who retained his IBF welterweight crown, looked sharp and landed over twice as many punches. The conclusion of the fight was a prelude to the obvious, De La Hoya versus Trinidad.

It didn't take long for the media hype surrounding the Holyfield versus Lewis fight to begin. It started heating up about three weeks prior to their March 13 battle inside the City Ring. Lewis was up in the Poconos with Emanuel Steward preparing for the conflict and trimming off some weight; the fighter hoped to drop about fifteen pounds before the bout to enter the ring tipping at about 245. With a record of 34–1, the Briton believed this was one of the biggest fights of his career. Dedicated to the task at hand, Lewis did his best to eliminate distractions. As for Holyfield, he stepped outside of character—the fighter had never been prone to trash talk—to predict that he would knock out Lewis before the third round.

Evander Holyfield v. Lennox Lewis I

It just doesn't get any better, or so most boxing fans believed, than a heavyweight unification bout inside Madison Square Garden. Like an October seat inside Yankee Stadium, it was a guaranteed memory. The March 13 event, which attracted a capacity crowd of more than 21,000, was also televised live on TVKO, HBO's pay-per-view company. It was a moneymaker from every perspective because it had to be.

On the line were the championship belts: World Boxing Council heavyweight title (5th defense by Lewis), World Boxing Association heavyweight title (4th defense by Holyfield), and the International Boxing Federation heavyweight title (2nd defense by Holyfield). Since the fight sold out two months in advance, most of the media hype targeted pay-for-view sales.

The fighters stacked up like this: Lewis was three years younger, thirty-one pounds heavier, and three inches taller. Lewis also had a reach advantage of seven inches. Overall Lewis was a bigger fighter, and had larger biceps, forearms, thighs and calves; he also had a two-inch thicker waist. Holyfield brought a record of 36–3 into the City Ring, while Lewis stood at 34–1. To some, Lewis didn't have the same level of credibility—an abstract measurement that invited a subjective analysis—as Holyfield. And his desire and stamina had been challenged. At the same time, Holyfield had been denounced for his middle-round catnaps and weak chin.

From the opening bell, Lennox Lewis withdrew the jab from his holster and kept firing. He was as prolific—Lewis landed nearly twice the number of punches—as he was commanding. The Briton backed off a bit in the third round, when Holyfield briefly awoke, but soon the assault continued. Assessing the damage: Lewis suffered a small cut over the bridge of his nose in the fifth round, while Holyfield's left eye began to swell in the seventh. There were no knockdowns.

The verdict was a suspension of the tenable, in favor of a preposterous pronouncement. The twelve-round draw between Evander Holyfield and Lennox Lewis was a statement about the absurdity of an anachronistic system with far too much subjectivity. Upon hearing of the stalemate, the capacity crowd booed and hissed, having witnessed and concluded that Lewis had unified the title. Putting his own life at risk, promoter Don King uttered the "R" word, or *rematch*. It easily could have been his last expression.

All three sanctioning bodies, the IBF, WBA, and WBC, agreed and mandated a rematch. Investigations were conducted (by the State Senate Investigation Committee), opinions from every direction conceivable were printed, and boxing was once again under a microscope. The use of open scoring, or having the judges' scores posted in public view, once again surfaced.[12]

Heavyweight Theater

On June 19, the Theater at Madison Square Garden conducted a heavyweight doubleheader as Michael Grant (29-0) met Lou Saverese (39-2), and Jeremy Williams (31-1) faced Maurice Harris (14-9-2).[13] Grant, who stood six feet seven inches tall and weighed 250 pounds, was one of the most promising new faces of the heavyweight division. At the age of 26, he was also the North American Boxing Federation's (NABF) heavyweight titleholder. But Saverese took George Foreman the distance—granted, no pun intended, it was a losing affair—and kayoed Buster Douglas. So Grant had himself a challenge.

Over 3,500 spectators were drawn to the pugilistic proceeding. Grant, traditionally a slow starter, didn't find his rhythm until the third round, and took command from that point forward. With his imposing uppercuts, he began finding angles on Saverese that just punished the fighter. Going into the tenth and final round, Grant dropped his opponent twice, but just could not put the finishing touches on Savarese. The verdict was a unanimous decision in favor of Grant.

The co-feature saw Maurice Harris, who thought he broke his hand in the third session, take a ten-round unanimous decision over Jeremy Williams. Worth noting on the undercard, welter Vernon Forrest (29-0) knocked out Ed Goins (16-13-2) at the 2:57 mark of the fourth round. Sitting ringside was Lennox Lewis, the WBC heavyweight champion, assessing the skills of Grant as a future opponent.

Boxing and the Bottom Line

This brings up the complex topic of boxing economics. Every participant, be it a fighter, manager, promoter or ancillary vendor, views it differently, and unfortunately with little empathy for each other.

Only a couple of years earlier, HBO had signed Prince Naseem Hamed to a six-fight, $12-million deal, then spent millions marketing the flamboyant English featherweight. It was an enormous gamble, but the premium television network was willing to take the risk.[14]

Naturally, the action set a precedent for future agreements. In October, both Floyd Mayweather, Jr., the WBA junior lightweight champion, and David Reid, the WBA super welterweight champion, rejected contract offers from HBO. For example, Mayweather, who believed he was worth $3 million a fight, turned down a seven-fight, $12.5-million contract and dismissed it as an insult.[15] The financial underpinnings of the fight game were always being challenged, some wisely, some not so much.

Boxing in the Dock

On November 4, in a groundbreaking move, a 32-count indictment was handed up in United States District Court (Newark) that accused top officials of the IBF of receiving a total of $338,000 in payments for manipulating the rankings to allow boxers to qualify for lucrative fights. The culture of corruption needed to cease in order to preserve whatever integrity was left in the sport.[16]

Speaking of integrity, NSAC (Nevada State Athletic Commission) was going out of its way to avoid controversy at the rematch between Evander Holyfield and Lennox Lewis, on November 13 at the Thomas & Mack Arena in Las Vegas, by carefully selecting all three judges and referee without outside input. This action, so NSAC believed, should preclude the controversy—one judge for Holyfield, one judge for Lewis, and one judge calling it draw—that arose during the first fight.[17]

The dynamics of boxing found the sport once again apologizing for itself, as Holyfield versus Lewis I made as much sense as most pulp fiction; Trinidad (W) versus De La Hoya, held in Las Vegas, didn't hit every note; and nobody was buying lemonade at the stand set up by the International Boxing Federation.[18] Then, in proof of the apocalypse, at least to some: Muhammad Ali's daughter Laila was fighting, and parrying well, in a boxing ring.[19]

2000

The poet W.H. Auden once quipped, "What the mass media offers is not popular art, but entertainment which is intended to be consumed like food, forgotten, and replaced by a new dish." Somebody hand me a boxing menu.

THE GOLDEN BOY

On February 26, the spéciale du jour was the "Golden Boy," or Oscar De La Hoya. The fighter (31–1) had only one thing on his mind: the destruction of Derrell Coley (34-1-2). It was a welcome home of sorts for the twenty-seven-year-old De La Hoya, as he had a large New York City following, to say nothing of the fact that he hadn't fought in Madison Square Garden since December 15, 1995; as you may recall, he retained his WBO world lightweight title with a victory over Jesse James Leija. A conclusive victory over Coley, he believed, would ease the pain he still felt from his loss to Felix Trinidad the previous September.

The bout was scheduled for twelve rounds, but nobody thought that it would go the distance. Prolific and accurate, De La Hoya, the former WBC welterweight champion, delivered a booming left hand to the body of Coley at the end of the seventh round, and it was over. A lively crowd of nearly 14,000 was on hand to watch De La Hoya's commanding performance. With the victory, the "Golden Boy" picked up the IBA welterweight title, which had been vacant, and set himself up for a WBC welterweight title shot, or so he believed. Later, De La Hoya was awarded the WBC title as Felix Trinidad moved to super welterweight.

On the undercard, Arturo "Thunder" Gatti, who tipped at 141 pounds at the weigh-in, knocked out Joey Gamache in the second round. However, at fight time, Gatti appeared much larger. Gamache's manager, Johnny Bos, astounded by the size of Gatti, would later claim his fighter suffered a severe concussion during the bout and needed to be hospitalized. Since Gatti tipped unofficially at 160 on the evening of the fight, Bos protested; and the Manhattan District Attorney's office in turn subpoenaed NYSAC's records. "Thunder," who would later admit to the heavier weight, also confessed to the ability to add, or dispense with, pounds at will. Although this is a common talent among boxers, his amount of weight gain within a short period of time was certainly impressive. The event sparked action by the commission: Gatti could claim responsibility for NYSAC's moving fight weigh-ins back to the day of the event, or where they had traditionally been.

Physical Graffiti

Madison Square Garden hosted "13 Feet and 500 Pounds of Fight," or Lennox Lewis (35-1-1) versus Michael Grant (31-0), in a heavyweight standoff that promised to be exciting just based upon physical size. Although Lewis wanted to battle Tyson before Grant, he faced a major obstacle: Tyson had an exclusive contract with Showtime, while Lewis was locked into a contract with Home Box Office, and neither network was bound to let their fighter battle on the screens of a competitor. It would be the final time Lennox Lewis would grace the City Ring.

It was short, and it was sweet for the champion, who knocked Grant down three times in the first round and once in the second round. Lewis unleashed a robust uppercut that landed flush to the face of his adversary in the second term and ended the April 29 bout. "The Lion," a moniker used by Lewis, had roared.

Obviously, one could question Grant and his trainer Don Turner's decision to try to bully Lewis—a miscalculation that saw Grant winded and unsteady four minutes into the fight. To the credit of Lewis, he anticipated the approach and countered with his magnificent uppercuts.

Lewis, who threw and landed twice the number of punches, exhibited superior skills. It was the fighter's seventh defense of the World Boxing Council heavyweight title and his first for the International Boxing Federation heavyweight title; Lewis surrendered his WBA crown in order to fight Grant. A Garden crowd of more than 17,000 appeared to enjoy the skirmish despite its brevity. Part of the reason was an entertaining undercard that saw Paul Ingle retain his IBF feather crown with an eleventh-round TKO of Junior Jones. In addition, Arturo Gatti disposed of Eric Jakubowski by way of technical knockout with forty-four seconds remaining in round two.[20]

Also on the undercard, Ukrainian Wladimir Klitschko, the 1996 Olympic heavyweight gold medalist, made his American debut. The impressive heavyweight improved his record to 33-1 by destroying David Bostice by way of a second-round technical knockout.

As for Lewis, who still wanted Tyson, he would defeat Frans Botha (40-2-1) by way of a second-round TKO in July (London), and grab a unanimous decision over David Tua (37-1) at the Mandalay Bay Resort and Casino (Las Vegas) in November.

A heavyweight update: Evander Holyfield, in another step toward immortality, won the heavyweight championship for the fourth time by taking a unanimous decision over John Ruiz on August 12 in Las Vegas. This was the WBA title that Lewis was stripped of because of his fight with Grant.

Sugar Shane Mosley

Shane Andre Mosley, born on September 7, 1971, stood five feet nine inches tall and began fighting out of Pomona, California, where he fought in over 250 amateur contests.

Jack Mosley, his father, trainer and mentor, raised a family of three, which included an only son whom he wanted to mold into a fighter. Turning pro in 1993, Shane picked up the IBF lightweight championship of the world by defeating Philip Holiday on August 2, 1997, and charted his course. Successfully defending the title eight times, against names like John-John Molina, Eduardo Morales, and Jesse James Leija, to name only a few, he had nothing left to prove in the division.

Presenting a rather modest image, Mosley would rather surround himself with a few very close friends and family than an enormous entourage. If an opportunity to meet the "Golden Boy" surfaced, so Mosley hoped, why not take it? Knockout victories over Wilfredo Rivera and Willy Wise set up the battle. It was time, or so Shane believed, for Oscar de la Hoya to relinquish the welterweight crown. On June 17, 2000, Mosley met De La Hoya in Los Angeles for the WBC, IBA and vacant lineal welterweight titles. The atmosphere was charged, as this was also the first boxing event to take place at the newly built Staples Center.[21]

It wasn't pretty, but it wasn't meant to be. The duel was pure war driven by the instinct to survive. The swift combinations delivered by both fighters could be felt ringside. The twisting and turning Mosley, who never looked balanced, found angles many thought De La Hoya didn't have. Both had swollen faces at the end and De La Hoya was bleeding from the nose for several rounds.

After twelve rounds, Mosley emerged with a close split-decision victory.[22] For the twenty-eight-year-old, who ran his record to 35–0, it was time for some leisure activities before looking at an autumn defense. As for De La Hoya, a bit of uncertainty surrounded the boxer, who was looking beyond the ring and into areas such as acting and music.

Mosley defended his newly won titles on November 11, 2000, in the Theater at Madison Square Garden against Mexican boxer Antonio Diaz (35–2, 24 KOs). A one-sided affair, scheduled for twelve rounds, it lasted only six before referee Arthur Mercante, Sr., waved it off at the 1:36 mark of the term. Diaz had been down twice in the round and three times during the fight. The Mexican was Mosley's 33rd knockout victim.[23]

On the undercard of the event was Héctor Camacho, Jr., who was no less flamboyant than his father. Fighting out of Orlando, Florida, Junior had a record of 29–0, with 17 knockouts and was putting it up against Indianapolis boxer Joe Hutchinson (18–1–2). The junior welterweight battle went the distance and with a unanimous decision in favor of Camacho, Jr.

Meanwhile, Roy Jones, Jr., defended the WBC, WBA, and IBF light heavyweight title belts three times. On January 15, in the first boxing show ever held at New York City's Radio City Music Hall, Jones won a twelve-round unanimous decision over David Telesco (23–2–0). On May 13 he scored an eleventh-round technical knockout of Richard Hall (24–1–0) in a bout held at Conseco Fieldhouse in Indianapolis. And in his final bout of the year, Jones scored an eleventh-round technical knockout of an undefeated Eric Harding (19–0–1) at the New Orleans Arena. This would take Roy Jones, Jr., to a record of 43–1–0.

The Year in Perspective

It was a good year for New York City boxing, as fans had an opportunity to see Oscar De La Hoya, Arturo Gatti, Junior Jones, Lennox Lewis, Shane Mosley and even Wladimir Klitschko at the Garden. Seeing another "Sugar" in the ring was certainly promising.

2001

It was the perfect way to initiate the year, as six members of the 2000 United States Olympic team made their professional debut inside the theater at Madison Square Garden on January 27. And while none of the former Olympians were wearing gold medals from Sydney, Australia, their pride was in their hearts and their dreams inside a pair of boxing mitts. The event, promoted by Lou DiBella of DiBella Entertainment, was exciting, and a large portion of the program was being broadcast by HBO.

Silver medalist Ricardo Williams, Jr., a talented Cincinnati lightweight, was the most heralded of the lot, and he met Anthony Simpkins (5-0-1). Williams, who won a gold medal at the 1998 Goodwill Games at the Garden, was no stranger to the venue. Putting on an impressive display, Williams took a fourth-round TKO over Simpkins; the fight stopped at the 2:10 mark of the term.

Also doing battle: Heavyweight Michael Bennett quickly knocked out Andrew Hutchinson (1-1-1) at the 1:46 mark of the opening round. Welterweight Dante Craig knocked out Darren Fallen (1-0). Junior bantam José Navarro took a fourth-round unanimous decision over Puerto Rican Kenny Berrios. Navarro, a Golden Boy Enterprises fighter—the promotional company run by former champion Oscar De la Hoya—was originally scheduled to meet Mario Rodriguez. Middleweight Jermain Taylor knocked out Chris Walsh (17-4-1) with a powerful right hand in the fourth round. And Bantam Clarance Vinson, who was a bronze medalist at the Olympics, took a fourth-round unanimous decision over Mexican Adrian Valdez (3-2-2). Jerson Ravelo, a member of the Dominican Republic Olympic team, was also on the bill and knocked out Bronx boxer Miguel Guittierrez.

A crowd of more than 4,000 turned out for the Olympians. To watch these youngsters begin their professional careers in such an extraordinary fashion was a delight.

BERNARD HOPKINS

Bernard Humphrey Hopkins, Jr., was born January 15, 1965, to Bernard Hopkins, Sr., and his wife Shirley. Growing up with his family in the Raymond Rosen housing project in Philadelphia was challenging, to say the least. Hopkins, like some of those around him, turned to crime early in his life. Mugging people as a young teen became commonplace, but being stabbed three times was not. At seventeen, Hopkins was sentenced to 18 years in Graterford Prison for nine felonies.

Prison life, with its everyday violence and haunting voices, wasn't easy to handle; Hopkins witnessed the murder of another inmate in an argument over a pack of cigarettes. The best offense was a daunting defense, so he learned to box. After serving almost five years, Hopkins was released from prison in 1988.

A convert to Islam, Hopkins credited the transition to getting his life back in order. The youngster joined the professional boxing ranks as a light heavyweight, but lost his debut on October 11, 1988, to Clinton Mitchell in a bout held at the Resorts Casino Hotel in Atlantic City, New Jersey. Now what?, Hopkins thought.

After a sixteen-month layoff, he decided to resume his career as a middleweight, and took a fourth-round unanimous decision over Greg Paige at Philadelphia's famed Blue Horizon on February 22, 1990. Between February 1990 and December 1992, Hopkins scored

21 wins without a loss; sixteen of those fights were won by way of knockout, 12 coming in the first round. In his bout with Wayne Powell, on December 4, 1992, he picked up the vacant USBA middleweight title—perhaps not the most prestigious title, but certainly a confidence builder.

But reality, or Roy Jones, Jr., had a way of quickly putting a fighter's skills into perspective. Hopkins met Jones on May 22, 1993, for the vacant IBF middleweight title inside the Robert F. Kennedy Memorial Stadium in Washington, D.C. Dominated throughout most of the fight, Hopkins lost the twelve-round unanimous decision as all three judges scored the fight 116–112 for Jones.[24]

In his ensuing eighteen fights, Hopkins would add sixteen victories, one draw and one no-contest to take his record to 38–2–1. At age thirty-six, his forty-third ring battle (includes no contest) would be his first inside Madison Square Garden.

Hopkins, the IBF middleweight champion, would do battle with Keith Holmes, the WBC middleweight belt owner, inside the Garden Theater on April 14. The joint production by Don King and Lou DiBella was a unification duel televised on HBO. Hopkins had his mind set on a victory and his heart set on an eventual rematch with Roy Jones, Jr. The battle was part of a middleweight championship series that would also see William Joppy (32–1–1), the WBC belt holder, do battle against Felix "Tito" Trinidad (39–0), the WBA super welter and the IBF junior middle champion, who was stepping up to the 160-pound division; this battle was to be held at the Garden on May 12. Once both winners tackled each other, likely in September, that victor would then face Jones. As might be expected, Hopkins, who had defended his title 12 times, felt he was in the best position.

It took Hopkins twelve rounds to defeat Keith Holmes, but it was mission accomplished. Taking the unanimous decision in stride, he immediately turned his attention to the winner of the Joppy vs. Trinidad contest. Although there weren't any knockdowns in his battle with Holmes, the crowd of more than 4,200 in the Theater seemed to enjoy the brawl. Hopkins, who could be a bit of a slow starter, took command in the third round and would not be deterred. To the credit of Holmes, who was battling a cut over his left eye through most of the fight, he went the distance and fought hard during the final three rounds.

Trinidad vs. Joppy

Felix "Tito" Trinidad, the undefeated four-time world champion who dominated welters and super welters, felt he found a home at 160 pounds, or the middleweight limit. Even a rematch with De La Hoya or Fernando Vargas wasn't going to drag him back to 154 pounds, or so he claimed. Unifying the middleweight title, something that hadn't been done since the days of Marvin Hagler,

A Puerto Rican boxer who competed from 1990 to 2008, Félix Juan Trinidad García (born January 10, 1973), also known as "Tito" Trinidad, was a three-weight-class world champion, and considered among the best boxers in Puerto Rico's history.

was his goal. Once Trinidad disposed of antagonist William Joppy, it would be on to Hopkins and unification. That was his strategy, and one he shared with his manager and trainer Felix "Papa" Trinidad.

Joppy, the WBA middle titleholder, was Trinidad's first hurdle. Having suffered a broken vertebra in his neck during a 1999 auto accident, the twenty-nine-year-old understood determination and perseverance. He had no intention of being pushed aside by Trinidad. Although he was the underdog against Trinidad, so was Hasim Rahman, who had recently knocked out Lennox Lewis in the fifth round of their April 22 bout at Carnival City in Brakpan, Gauteng, South Africa. Joppy was friends with Rahman and saw firsthand that a long shot needs only one shot to defeat a rival.

The Garden duel scheduled for May 12 didn't begin until 12:03 A.M. the following day, but proved worth the wait. Felix Trinidad, in his first middleweight outing, stepped up and took Joppy's WBA crown with a fifth round technical knockout. Referee Arthur Mercante, Jr., stopped the Garden battle with 35 seconds remaining in the term. Joppy, who started strong, was surprised at how much power Trinidad put behind his punches; he found that out early when he caught a Trinidad left hook that sent him backward to the canvas with 12 seconds left in the first round. Trinidad did a magnificent job of countering and his speedy combinations overwhelmed his opponent. Joppy was dropped to the canvas by two right hands and a left hook in the fourth round.

A festive Garden crowd of more than 18,000 waved Puerto Rican flags, sang and chanted "Tito" for their favorite son. Joppy, joined in the ring by Hasim Rahman, entered the ropes a bit late and had a modest following.

Worth noting on the undercard: Chris Byrd (33–2) grabbed a unanimous decision over Maurice Harris, and Vernon Forrest won the vacant IBF welter title by taking a unanimous decision over Raul Frank.

Echo of a Classic Garden Bout

How do you recreate perhaps the greatest moment in City Ring history? Easy: just replace the main characters with their daughters. On June 8, in Verona, New York, just a jab from Canastota, Laila Ali took a majority decision over Jacqui Frazier-Lyde. The surnames were the same, even if everything else wasn't. A crowd of more than 6,500 couldn't resist making the trip to the Turning Stone Resort Casino, even if it was only to catch a glimpse of "Smokin' Joe" Frazier ringside; Muhhamad Ali did not make the journey. It's tough to recreate a memory, even with the same DNA.

Hopkins vs. Trinidad

The terrorist attacks of 9-11 forced the rescheduling of the Hopkins versus Trinidad Garden battle. Originally slated for September 15, the date was moved to September 29. Hopkins (39–2–1, 28 knockouts) confirmed that the rescheduling of his duel with Trinidad (40–0, 33 knockouts) would not impact his eventual victory. Conversely, Trinidad thought otherwise.

Bernard Hopkins, as he predicted, became the undisputed middleweight champion, defeating Felix Trinidad by way of a technical knockout at the 1:18 mark of the twelfth round. Floored by a powerful Hopkins right, Trinidad struggled to reach his feet at the count of ten. Referee Steve Smoger, sensing the imbalance, wisely grabbed the fighter and waved off the battle. By this point Felix Trinidad, Sr., had also entered the ring.

Over 19,000 Garden fans were treated to a terrific, but long, night of boxing. And they witnessed some history as Hopkins successfully defended his IBF middleweight title for the fourteenth time, matching the record held by the great Carlos Monzón. The fighter now looked ahead to another enormous payday, be it against Oscar De La Hoya, Fernando Vargas, or Roy Jones, Jr.

Forgotten Rounds

To bring you up-to-date on a few fights that flew beneath the radar: On January 20, Floyd Mayweather, Jr., dominated Diego Corrales to successfully defend his WBC Super Featherweight Title (Paradise, Nevada). Corrales was knocked down five times, before his corner threw in the towel in the tenth round.

On April 7, following a fourteen-minute introduction, Naseem Hamed lost a distance battle to Marco Antonio Barrera by unanimous decision (Paradise). Barrera, known as a brawler, surprised most by easily outboxing Hamed.

On July 13, Lowell fighter Micky Ward defeated Emanuel Augustus in a ten-round unanimous decision (Hampton Beach, New Hampshire).

On July 28, Roy Jones, Jr., defended the WBC, WBA, and IBF light heavyweight titles against Julio César González (27–0) by a united verdict (Los Angeles). He had also defeated Derrick Harmon on February 24 (Tampa).

Fighter of the Year

Bernard Hopkins truly had a magnificent year and solidified his position in boxing history. Even so, to acknowledge him alone would be tantamount to forgetting another great fighter, Ricardo López. In his very last professional fight, and in only his second appearance in Madison Square Garden, López, a minimum weight, finished his career undefeated at 51–0–1, having only drawn with Rosendo Alvarez.[25]

2002

'Twas something fascinating about the January 26 welter match between Shane Mosley and Vernon Forrest; the latter was the last person who had defeated the former in the ring, and the loss prevented Mosley from making the 1992 Olympic team. Granted, Mosley, with a record of 38–0, overshadowed Forrest and held the WBC welter belt, but one just had to wonder if he wouldn't mind just a bit of revenge. As for Forrest, with a record of 33–0, his decision to take the lucrative battle against Mosley cost him his IBF welter crown, which he was mandated to defend against Michele Piccirillo. So, "Sweet Revenge," as promoter Cedric Kushner labeled it, or Mosley's fourth defense of his championship, was set for January 26, inside the Madison Square Garden Theater.

Most thought Mosley would walk over Forrest, like a hiker over a log. They were wrong. Forrest's robust right hand dropped Mosley twice in the second round. "Sugar" also suffered a cut on the hairline from an accidental clash of heads early in the same term. "The Viper" negated Mosley's trademark hand speed by clinching and taking him to close quarters. Forrest also feinted and jabbed with precision. At the end of twelve rounds, it was a Forrest victory by a unanimous verdict. When they met again on July 20 in Indianapolis, Forrest would once again win by a twelve-round united decision. Forrest, who hailed from Augusta, Georgia, naturally drew comparisons to another area boxer, Sidney Walker, a.k.a. Beau Jack.[26]

On the January 26 undercard, Arturo Gatti bid a fond farewell to Madison Square Garden by defeating Terron Millett (26-2-1) in a fourth-round TKO; the fight was stopped at the 2:23 mark of the term. It was Gatti's sixth battle inside the historic venue. Millett had hit the canvas three times. For Gatti, it was the last fight before his famed trilogy against Micky Ward.

McCline vs. Briggs

As Van Gogh painted his dreams on canvas, fighters display their athletic prowess on one. Harlem's Jameel McCline (27-2-3) was a fighter who dreamed about fighting on the canvas inside Madison Square Garden. And he finally would get his shot on April 27. He was scheduled to meet Shannon Briggs (36-3-1) inside the City Ring. The latter was a known commodity, a man who had already made his mark by defeating the likes of George Foreman. In contrast, McCline dined on tomato soup until the previous year, when he defeated Alfred Cole, Michael Grant and Lance Whitaker. Both were monsters: Briggs tipped just over 268 and stood six feet four inches, while McCline was two inches taller and four pounds lighter. The theater event would also feature IBF feather champion Manuel Medina (60-11), from Mexico, against Albuquerque's Johnny Tapia (51-2-2).

For ten rounds McCline outpunched Briggs, thanks to a quicker and more efficient left jab, to take a unanimous ten-round decision. The highlight was a sixth-round McCline combination to the head that sent Briggs promptly to his bottom for a five count. For Briggs, who showed little polish during the debate, it was his second defeat since his loss to Lewis back in 1998. For McCline, the dream continued as he next met Wladimir Klitschko.[27]

Also, Johnny Tapia conquered Manuel Medina to add a third different weight class championship (won IBF featherweight title) to his resume. It was a controversial twelve-round judgment, however, as many ringside saw it differently; it was likely more of a draw than a majority verdict.

Fighter of the Year

The year's most celebrated fight saw Micky Ward take a bitter hard-fought ten-round majority decision over Arturo Gatti on May 18 at Mohegan Sun Casino and Resort in Uncasville, Connecticut. The super lightweight non-title bout evoked memories of many of the great fights of yesteryear such as Zale versus Graziano. Yes, it was that good. Later in the year, on November 23 in Atlantic City, the pair dueled once more, only it was Gatti who took a ten-round unanimous decision.

In the biggest upset of the year, Vernon Forrest handed Shane Mosley his very first loss. It happened, as if appropriate, inside Madison Square Garden during a year that saw very little boxing inside the City Ring. The fact that he defeated Mosley again, in a rematch, only proves to reinforce his choice as the fighter who shined the City Ring the most during 2002.

20

The Final Rounds, 2003–2007

> Then there is the other secret. There isn't any symbolism. The sea is the sea. The old man is an old man. The boy is a boy and the fish is a fish. The sharks are all sharks no better and no worse. All the symbolism that people say is shit. What goes beyond is what you see beyond when you know.
> —Ernest Hemingway, *Ernest Hemingway Selected Letters 1917–1961*

No man was the City Ring, yet every man who stepped, perspired or bled on it was part of its rich heritage. Men weren't born in it, but their legends were. For some it was their first claim of notoriety, while for others it was their final landscape. Although it can be seen from a variety of perspectives, the important point is what you see.

2003

Forever dynamic, the heavyweight division would witness the departure of Lennox Lewis, observe only the second light heavyweight champion to win a heavyweight title in Roy Jones, Jr., see IBF heavyweight champion Chris Byrd indecisively defend his title against Fres Oquendo and watch IBF cruiserweight titleholder James Toney knock out four-time former champion Evander Holyfield.[1] What was once a neatly packaged, and somewhat easy to understand, weight division was once again being redefined.

Word was that Lennox Lewis, the World Boxing Council (WBC) champion, was no longer interested in fighting on a regular basis. Simply put: the alphabet soup titles, with all their rules and regulations, didn't guarantee maximum profitability. In fact, Lewis would fight only once in 2003, against the giant Ukrainian Vitali Klitschko on June 21 in Los Angeles.

Klitschko, who replaced Lewis's original opponent Kirk Johnson on two weeks' notice, put on a spectacular performance.[2] During the first two rounds it looked as if it was going to be an enormous upset. All the same, champions are champions for a reason. Lewis went to work. He opened a cut over Klitschko's left eye thanks to a textbook right hand in the third round. The momentum shifted, then shifted again. On the edge of their seats, spectators at the Staples Center were afraid to relax. But at the end of the sixth round, Dr. Paul Wallace, the ringside physician, ruled that Klitschko's cut was too severe for him to continue; the Ukrainian, who was ahead on the cards, required sixty stitches to repair four cuts on his face and one cut in his mouth. Naturally, Klitschko, who looked as if he had just walked through a plate-glass

20. The Final Rounds, 2003–2007

An American boxer who competed from 1988 to 2017, James Nathaniel Toney (born August 24, 1968) was a three-weight world champion, having held the IBF and lineal middleweight titles from 1991 to 1993; the IBF super middleweight title from 1993 to 1994; and the IBF cruiserweight title in 2003.

door, protested and demanded a rematch. As for Lewis, notably fatigued, he was uncertain as to his future.[3]

Distraught over his performance, Klitschko was determined not to lose his standing amongst the heavyweights. To counter any criticism, he understood, required a position statement. Since he hadn't fought inside the City Ring in three years, there was only one logical place to conduct business.

On December 7, inside Madison Square Garden, Klitschko met Canadian Kirk Johnson, whose only previous loss was to John "The Quietman" Ruiz. Despite blizzard conditions, over 10,000 onlookers turned out to watch the World Boxing Council title eliminator. After Johnson hit the canvas twice, referee Arthur Mercante, Jr., wisely waved it off at 2 minutes 54 seconds of the second round of the scheduled twelve rounds. Johnson could no longer endure the Ukrainian's powerful body punches, nor could he manage to get off the ropes. It was, just as Klitschko hoped, a powerful declaration.[4]

OUTSIDE THE CITY

If there was anything Roy Jones, Jr., couldn't do, nobody told him. The fighter became only the second light heavyweight champion to win a heavyweight title. Jones scored a twelve-round decision over Latino John Ruiz to capture the World Boxing Association (WBA) title on March 1 at the Thomas & Mack Center in Las Vegas, Nevada. With the judgment, Jones became the seventh boxer in history to earn world titles in four weight divisions, and the first former world middleweight champion since Bob Fitzsimmons in 1897 to conquer a world heavyweight title. Examining events from the top, Jones wisely dropped back down to the light heavyweight division.

If Jones wan't impressive enough, there was also Bernard Hopkins. The unified WBA, WBC, and IBF middleweight champion defended his title twice, knocking out Morrade Hakkar in the eighth round on March 29 in Philadelphia and winning a twelve-round decision over William Joppy on December 13 in Atlantic City. It was Hopkins's 17th successful defense, as he continued to edit *The Ring Record Book*.

Still enormously popular, Oscar De La Hoya had a disparate year. He defended the WBC and WBA super welterweight (junior middleweight) titles with a seventh-round knockout of Yory Boy Campas in Las Vegas on May 3; the fight was stopped at the 2:54 mark of the term. Campas, who couldn't land a punch to save his life, was sorely defeated.

Then, on September 13, also in Las Vegas, De La Hoya lost a twelve-round decision and both titles to Shane Mosley, who had also beaten him in a 2000 welterweight contest. De La Hoya, who was cut from a head-butt in the 3rd round, actually threw more punches, but they lacked the forcefulness to prove his point.

Flying beneath the radar was a notable feather altercation on November 15. Philippine fighter Manny Pacquiao (37–2–1), down in the first round, upset Marco Antonio Barrera (57–3–0), who was down twice, with an eleventh-round technical knockout at the Alamodome in San Antonio. The fight was stopped at the 2:56 mark of the term.

WBA welterweight titleholder Ricardo Mayorga knocked out WBC prizewinner Vernon Forrest in the third round of their January 25 battle in California. It was an enormous upset as Forrest, who was knocked down twice, was considered a rather scientific fighter with strong skills. The colorful Mayorga, who never met a camera he didn't like, beat Forrest again on July 12 at the Orleans Hotel & Casino in Las Vegas. However, the boxer's championship reign was brief. It came to an end on December 13, when he was outpointed by Cory Spinks in a twelve-round battle held in Atlantic City.[5]

Proof of the growing popularity in female boxing: Laila Ali, 16–0, the daughter of former heavyweight champion Muhammad Ali, knocked out Christy Martin in the fourth round of a bout held on August 23 in Biloxi, Mississippi. The pay-per-view purchases topped 100,000.

THE YEAR IN PERSPECTIVE

Compelling with all its twists and turns, boxing seemed to have picked up some ground in its popularity. Watching both Jones and Hopkins alone was enough to reinvigorate any former boxing fan. Although New York City boxing had seen more prolific years, it was nice for boxing fans to have the opportunity to view the skills of Vitali Klitschko firsthand. It would be the fighter's final time battling inside the City Ring.[6]

2004

Announcing his retirement on February 6, 2004, Lennox Lewis, with a record of 41-2-1 and the reigning heavyweight champion, left the sport of boxing at the top of his game. Father Time was catching up with him, and while his mind was sharper than ever, his physical skills were diminishing; a fighter can sense it, even if his mind refuses to accept it. Lewis grew leaps and bounds near the end of his

An American boxer who competed from 1994 to 2014, Hasim Sharif Rahman (born November 7, 1972) was twice the world heavyweight champion, having held the unified WBC, IBF, IBO, and lineal titles in 2001, and the WBC title again from 2005 to 2006.

career thanks to trainer Emanuel Steward, who began fine-tuning the Brit back in 1995. One wonders what the fighter would have been like had Manny got to him sooner.

After taking the British and European heavyweight titles from Gary Mason (35-0, 32 knockouts) in 1991, Lewis defeated Tony Tucker for his first world championship in May 1993, then turned his attention to winning over British boxing fans by defeating Frank Bruno in October 1993. When Hasim Rahman became heavyweight champion, he insulted Lewis to the point of anger; to "The Lion," he was such a chav. In November 2001, a single-punch knockout of Rhaman fixed that. Smart enough to realize that, title or no title, he still had to beat Mike Tyson, Lewis set out to gain the one missing portion of the respect he sought. That came on June 8, 2002, with an eighth-round knockout of "Iron Mike." "The Lion" had roared.

Sorting Through the Heavyweights

Without Lewis, there was uncertainty in the sport's premier division. The first to make his case was IBF titleholder Chris "Rapid Fire" Byrd (37-2-0), who defended his recognition inside Madison Square Garden on April 17 in a twelve-round draw with Andrew Golota (38-4-0). The exciting evening was billed as "The Next Era of Heavyweights" and also included a WBA title confrontation that saw John Ruiz stun Fres Oquendo in an eleventh-round TKO.[7]

A crowd of more than 15,000 watched in anticipation of just who would rise to the surface. Chris Byrd proved that he was a legitimate contender for the title, as his verdict attracted little criticism. The crafty southpaw, who was outweighed by twenty-seven pounds, managed to elude Golota, or the "Foul Pole" if you will. Nevertheless, Golota, who had become accustomed to an arbiter's admonition, fired a few shots below the Mason-Dixon line, not to mention a belated blow or two. Having drawn Golota, and defeated Fres Oquendo the previous year and Holyfield in 2002, Byrd looked solid. Standing six feet and one inch, with a 74-inch reach, the Michigan southpaw was refining a jab that was difficult to counter.

On November 13, Byrd took a twelve-round split decision over behemoth Jameel McCline (31-3-3) inside the City Ring. Outweighed by 56 pounds, Byrd survived a second-round knockdown to retain his IBF heavyweight title in a very close engagement and his last in Madison Square Garden. He had little choice but to put everything on the line, so the defensive Byrd did his best to stay out of harm's way. In the end, it was another entertaining night of boxing, and the fact that the fighters were good friends added a fresh twist to the evening.

New England—born John Ruiz, standing six feet two inches tall with a 78-inch reach, wasn't ready to let anyone just roll over him. He had fought an entertaining trilogy against Evander Holyfield (2000–2001), defeated Kirk Johnson, lost to Roy Jones, Jr. (2003), and was victorious over Hasim Rahman. Having defeated Fres Oquendo, he moved on to Andrew Golota. On November 13, Ruiz successfully defended his WBA title in a twelve-round united verdict over the Polish fighter inside Madison Square Garden.

Other Ring Action

Nobody seemed to fall harder in 2004 than Roy Jones, Jr. Defeating both John Ruiz (38-4-1) and Antonio Tarver (21-1-0) the previous year, a confident Jones looked to a May

15 rematch with Tarver in Las Vegas. But a single left hook to the head sent the fighter to dreamland. The upset victory earned Tarver the WBA and WBC light heavyweight titles. Nothing more than a twist of fate, or so Jones believed, as the boxer attempted to regain his composure. He charted a comeback against IBF light heavyweight titleholder Glen Johnson, but was knocked out by the Jamaican in the ninth round on September 25 in Memphis. Johnson had won the vacant IBF belt earlier in the year with a twelve-round decision over Clinton Woods. One of the most gifted fighters of his era, Jones had suffered the improbable: back-to-back knockout defeats.

As for the middleweights, it was all about the undisputed champion Bernard Hopkins. The collapse of Jones sent all "pound-for-pound" eyes, or boxing critics, to the Pennsylvania-born boxer for a closer evaluation. And, as expected, Hopkins did not disappoint. He knocked out Oscar De La Hoya with a tremendous left hook to the body in the ninth round on September 18 at the MGM Grand in Las Vegas. The only thing more impressive than the knockout was the purse: it was the second-largest grossing non-heavyweight fight of all time.

Having not fought since May 11, 2002, Félix "Tito" Trinidad, the three-division former titleholder, decided to return to the sport. "Back with a Vengeance" would take place inside Madison Square Garden on October 2. Scoring an eighth-round knockout of former unified welterweight champion Ricardo Mayorga, Trinidad impressed: he sent Mayorga down three times in the term. Referee Steve Smoger stopped the bout at the 2:39 mark. The closest Trinidad had come to the canvas was touching his glove in the third round. The near-capacity Garden crowd delighted in the HBO pay-per-view event: it was the third-highest live gate in Garden history. It was also Trinidad's last City Ring appearance, though he would return to a modern Garden confine in 2008.

Forgotten Rounds

A couple of title exchanges that flew below the radar: Zsolt Erdei defeated Julio César González to become the WBO light heavyweight on January 17.

Winky Wright became the undisputed light middleweight champion after defeating Shane Mosley by unanimous decision on March 13. He beat him again in a November 20 rematch.

Fighter of the Year

As for New York City boxing, the heavyweights were back once again in the Garden. Of those who shined the patina of the City Ring, Chris Byrd takes the honor.[8]

2005

On November 9, 2005, the World Boxing Council (WBC) heavyweight titleholder, Vitali Klitschko (35–2), announced his first retirement. His only two losses were at the hands of Chris Byrd and Lennox Lewis. In a division that was just starting to sort itself out following the Lewis retirement, "Dr. Ironfists" decided to hang up the mitts. The decision was supported by injuries, particularly a damaged right knee, that Klitschko had endured. Later, the WBC would award the heavy crown to Hasim Rahman.

Meanwhile, over at the World Boxing Association (WBA) John Ruiz was attempting to exert his heavyweight legitimacy with two title defenses. The first was a very controversial twelve-round loss to James Toney on April 30 inside Madison Square Garden. Down in the seventh round, Ruiz fought to go the distance but lost the unanimous decision. Later, James Toney tested positive for a banned substance and the decision was changed to a no-decision by NYSAC, and the title reverted to Ruiz. For Toney, his troubles were just beginning: he was suspended for ninety days and fined $10,000 before being served by Ruiz with a $10 million financial damage lawsuit.[9]

Next, on December 17 in Berlin, Russian Nikolai Valuev won a controversial twelve-round decision over Ruiz to take the title. Valuev, who was seven feet tall and weighed 324 pounds, was the tallest and heaviest boxer to win a major title.[10]

A Ukrainian boxer, Vitali Volodymyrovych Klitschko was a three-time world heavyweight champion, and the second-longest-reigning WBC heavyweight champion of all time.

All good things must come to an end, but all great things can endure a lifetime. Or at least that was the hope of a forty-year-old Bernard Hopkins (46–2–1), who faced a pair of back-to-back losses at the hands of an undefeated Jermain Taylor. Having unified the middleweight title back in 2001, Hopkins defended it a record twenty times while compiling over 45 victories. If—and it was a big if—this was the end of Hopkins's title run, he'd step away from a brilliant career.

Félix Trinidad (41–1), in hope of a comeback, hit a brick wall when he was matched against southpaw middleweight Ronald "Winky" Wright on May 14 at the MGM Grand in Las Vegas. A superb defenseman, Wright, who was coming off back-to-back victories over Shane Mosley, was confident and primed for battle. He captured the victory, by way of a united verdict, over his rival and sent him back into his rocking chair.

Forgotten Rounds

Of the fights that seemed to slip between the cracks: Zab Judah knocked out Cory Spinks in nine rounds (St. Louis), to become the new undisputed welterweight champion on February 5.

Érik Morales defeated Manny Pacquiao (39–2–2) by unanimous decision on March 19 (Las Vegas).

Antonio Tarver defeated Glen Johnson (42–9–2) by a united verdict in their rematch on June 18 (Memphis).

Floyd Mayweather, Jr., destroyed Arturo Gatti (39–6–0) in a six-round technical knockout to capture the WBC light welterweight title on June 5 (Atlantic City).

Finally, the undefeated Nikolai Valuev (42–0) defeated John Ruiz to win the WBA heavyweight title on December 17 (Germany).

Fighter of the Year

Of the few, very few, Garden battles that come to mind, the June 11 super welterweight duel that saw Miguel Cotto beat Muhammadqodir Abdullaev by TKO at the 0:57 mark of round 9, of a scheduled twelve-rounder, was a solid display. HBO had billed it as a rematch of the 2000 Summer Olympics bout, where eventual gold medalist Abdullaev would beat Cotto. Having taken the vacant WBO world super lightweight title by defeating Kelson Pinto the previous year, Cotto, a prolific puncher, just looked like a force to contend with. But most of all, he loved his initial battle inside the City Ring at Madison Square Garden.[11]

2006

Just when a fighter thought it was safe to enter the heavyweight mix, along comes another Klitschko. This time it was brother Wladimir "Dr. Steelhammer" Klitschko (46–3, 41 knockouts) who won the International Boxing Federation (IBF) title with a dominant seventh-round knockout of Chris Byrd at the SAP-Arena in Mannheim, Germany, on April 22. Of note: Klitschko was seconded by trainer Emanuel Steward and by older brother Vitali Klitschko. Steward directed his fighter like a navigator through an iceberg-filled channel. The 35-year-old Byrd, who had made four successful defenses of the belt he won from Evander Holyfield in 2002, fought gallantly, but it was not enough.

In a statement that rang loud and true, the venue of choice for Klitschko's first defense was Madison Square Garden. On November 11, he knocked out the previously unbeaten Calvin Brock (29–0) in the seventh round. The Ukrainian, who now lived in New York, landed a left hook, followed by a thunderous right hand that knocked Brock to the canvas face-first. When Brock opened a small cut over the corner of Klitschko's left eye in the fifth, his corner became concerned and pushed Klitschko to try to finish the fight as quickly as possible; accordingly, the fighter gladly obliged. This was Klitschko's second battle inside the City Ring.

Russian ring dominance took front and center in the heavyweight division. Regardless of their current address, there was a new breed of fighter: Nikolai Valuev of Russia held the WBA heavyweight title, while Oleg Maskaev held the WBC international heavyweight title.

De La Hoya Returns

After his loss to Bernard Hopkins back on September 18, 2004, Oscar De La Hoya was a bit uncertain about his future. A twenty-month layoff found him evaluating his aspirations and perhaps putting his life into perspective. Deciding to re-enter the ring against Ricardo Mayorga, the WBC super welterweight champion, at the MGM Grand in Las Vegas on May 6, De La Hoya was entering the "Danger Zone," as it was billed. Dangerous or not, De la Hoya scored a sixth-round knockout of Mayorga (27–5–1) to capture the WBC super welterweight title. It was his tenth world title in six weight classes. "The Golden Boy" still had it.

Zab Judah

On January 7, southpaw welterwight Zab Judah lost a unanimous decision twelve-round decision to Carlos Manuel Baldomir inside Madison Square Garden, the latter being far more aggressive, prolific and accurate than the former. Although many saw it as the upset of the year, nobody was quite sure what was at stake. Even Judah—who had won the WBC, WBA, and IBF titles by knocking out Cory Spinks on February 5, 2005—was in doubt. While Baldomir should have been the unified welterweight champion, he had declined to pay the IBF and WBA sanctioning fee, so the IBF continued to recognize the defeated Judah as champion, and the WBA declared the unified title vacant. Oops!

Next on Judah's agenda was the undefeated "Pretty Boy" Floyd Mayweather, Jr. (35-0), whom he met at the Thomas & Mack Center in Las Vegas on April 8. Despite understanding the strength of his opposition, Judah, a.k.a. "Super," took the fight anyway.

Judah lost the IBF belt to Mayweather via a twelve-round decision. But as sometimes can be the case, at least in boxing, the incident was tainted by a last-minute melee. Near the end of the tenth, a frustrated Judah fouled Mayweather twice. The first was a wake-up call below the Mason-Dixon line, followed by a shot to the back of the noggin. "Pretty Boy" doubled over in pain. Before referee Richard "The Man of" Steele could react, Mayweather's uncle and trainer, Roger Mayweather, stormed into the ring and assailed Judah. The dugouts emptied and it was a free-for-all, even though the battle hadn't been concluded. When order was eventually restored, it was up to the Nevada State Athletic Commission to sort it all out. Fines and suspensions followed as licenses were revoked faster than a Larry Holmes left jab.[12]

While the welterweight division imploded, the lightweights were impressing. The competition at the 130-pound level between Manny Pacquiao, Marco Antonio Barrera, and Érik Morales was as captivating as it was financially successful. When Pacquiao avenged his 2005 decision loss to Morales by knocking out his adversary in the tenth round of a rematch, it generated enormous pay-per-view sales.[13]

As the dust settled on the Mayweather v. Judah fiasco, boxing was still grappling with their math. For example, when Marco Antonio Barrera took his first decision victory over Rocky Juarez on May 20 in Los Angeles, it was originally announced as draw. A mistake in arithmetic was discovered on one judge's scorecard and the verdict was amended. Barrera, who retained his WBC super featherweight title, also took their September rematch.

Fighter of the Year

Finding their way into the City Ring during the year were Wladimir Klitschko, Miguel Cotto, Paul Malignaggi, and even Kevin Kelley for the final time. The "Flushing Flash" (Kelley) had shined the City Ring over fifteen times and was always popular with New York City fight fans. While he lost his final Garden battle to Manuel Medina on November 11, few shined the City Ring like Kevin Kelley.

2007—Last Call

So it came down to this, the final battle atop the most hallowed ground of pugilism. On Saturday, June 9, 2007, inside Madison Square Garden, Miguel Cotto (29-0, 24 knockouts), at 146½ pounds, would make his second defense of the World Boxing Association welterweight title against Zab Judah (34–4, 25 knockouts), who tipped at 145; the bout was scheduled for twelve rounds. Billed as "X-plosive!" the event was live on pay-for-view thanks to the folks at Home Box Office.[14]

For Cotto, a $2.5 million purse plus a share of the pay-for-view profits would greet him upon the conclusion. The five-foot seven-inch Providence-born fighter, who was now living in Caguas, Puerto Rico, had never been defeated. He held victories over five undefeated fighters: Carlos Quintana (23–0), Paul Malignaggi (21–0), Ricardo Torres (28–0), Kelson Pinto (21–0), and Carlos Maussa (17–0).

Zab Judah, his adversary, stood five feet seven-and-one-half inch. He was a Brooklyn-born southpaw, who was now calling Las Vegas his home. Judah held victories over Cory Spinks, Rafael Pineda, Reggie Green and Micky Ward. Honestly, his last three fights had been a disaster. He lost unanimous decisions to Carlos Manuel Baldomir and Floyd Mayweather, Jr., and took a no-contest against Ruben Galvan. The Mayweather fiasco was likely the biggest scar on his reputation. It was time for Judah to prove himself.

The referee for this evening's event was Arthur Mercante, Jr., and the judges ringside were Tom Schreck, John McKaie, and Nelson Vazquez. The ring announcer was Michael Buffer. Behind the HBO microphones were Jim Lampley, Emanuel Steward and Larry Merchant. As the national anthems of Puerto Rico and the United States were sung, views of New York City, along with cuts to the dressing room, played for spectators watching the large television screens that dotted the venue. The City Ring, decked out in blue canvas and adorned with five Corona Extra logos—one for each corner, with the premier logo at the center—and that of Madison Square Garden, featured the traditional four ropes wrapped in red coverings along with two white cornerposts, one red cornerpost and one blue cornerpost. Each cornerpost featured Corona or Puerto Rico tourism markings as well.

Taking a look at the Tale of the Tape: Judah was three years older (29), and ¾ inch taller. Cotto had longer arms and was a pound and half heavier (the limit was 147). The unified regulations in place for the fight: there was no three-knockdown rule, only the referee could stop the fight, and a fighter could not be saved by the bell.

Consistency reigned in the Cotto corner: not only was their fighter undefeated, but this was the third consecutive year Cotto had fought inside the City Ring on the eve of the Puerto Rican Day parade. As referee Mercante directed everybody out of the City Ring except chief seconds and their fighters, the crowd was filled with enthusiasm.[15] Disregarding all the parallels between antagonists drawn by those covering the fight, the real question was: which Zab Judah was going to show up?

In one of the finer ring battles of the year, Miguel Cotto cemented his position as a top welterweight by defeating former undisputed welter czar Zab Judah in an eleventh-round TKO.

Looking at the highlights: During the first round, at about the 1:41 mark, it looked as if Judah had hurt Cotto with a solid left. Team Judah was well aware that their opponent was a slow starter. Although both fighters looked in perfect condition, Judah's hand speed appeared quicker. Then at the 1:15 mark, the Brooklyn southpaw caught a low blow and went to the canvas. While Judah had five minutes to recover, he took far less, and Cotto appeared apologetic for the action.

In Round Two, Cotto worked combinations to the body, then covered as Judah, gloves at chin level, hoped to land then slip away. As the crowd began chanting "Cotto, Cotto,

Cotto," the fighter continued to look to the body while also firing belt-line. Judah, far from prolific, had some angles for his left hand—be it a straight or uppercut—but didn't take them.

In Round Three, Judah was dropped again from a low blow at the 1:49 mark. Following the recovery, which was likely stretching the definition of the action, Cotto, bleeding from his bottom lip, appeared aggravated. Again, Judah had opportunities for the left that he didn't take. Between rounds, referee Mercante went to Cotto's corner to inform him that a point had been taken away and that he better keep the fight clean.

Round Four: Judah had a slight cut on the right eye from an accidental head butt. Cotto was far more aggressive this round and his strength was clearly evident; he also went to southpaw to improve his countering.

The fight took a breather in Round Five. Cotto was noticeably bothered by cut near his right eye in Round Six. At about the 1:10 mark, Cotto stunned his rival with a right hand to the chin. But Judah managed to slip away. As the aggressor, Cotto was using his physical strength to his advantage.

Round Seven saw Judah fire far more combinations and exhibit the hand speed that he should have been displaying earlier in the fight. It was his best term since Round One.

The fight slowed a bit in the Eighth.

In the Ninth, the Puerto Rican continued the onslaught by firing far more punches than Judah. The fighter wasn't hesitant to switch stances to confuse Judah. By the midway point in the round, Judah's right eye was swelling. Following some nice flurries by Cotto, Judah went to a knee at the 1:07 mark of the term. Taking an eight count to gather his thoughts, Judah rose. Cotto, sensing the kill, began headhunting and hoping for a fight-ending blow. Judah hit the gas during the final ten seconds to grab what punches he could to try to save the round.

A rather even Round Ten set the stage for what followed. In the Eleventh, the question was: which fighter had the skills and endurance to end the fight? Both warriors continued to be bothered by cuts. But before Judah could even settle in, he was put to the floor at the 2:44 mark by a Cotto combination. Although up quickly, he was holding onto the ropes with his right hand as Mercante executed a nine count. The dazed fighter wisely tied up immediately. Referee Mercante grabbed Judah by the head at about the 2:10 mark to call the fight, the official time coming at 0:49 of the round.

It was a memorable fight, and an outstanding way to close the book on the City Ring.

"So we beat on, boats against the current, borne back ceaselessly into the past."
—by F. Scott Fitzgerald, *The Great Gatsby*

21

Retirement, September 19, 2007

> Was there, here, something that he had missed? Some richness of the spirit? Sadness crept over him. Yes, he should have become acquainted with the classics. Long ago. Now, alas, it was too late....
> —Agatha Christie, *The Labours of Hercules*

If boxing were a church, which may be a stretch in some cases, then its most talented would be considered the apostles of pugilism, and an item such as a boxing ring from Madison Square Garden would be considered a relic. In fact, a first-class relic, or an item directly associated with the events of its most revered individuals. Such an artifact would be sought and preserved for purposes of veneration—a tangible memorial, if you will. As relics are important to many religions, they are also important to other aspects of life, such as sports. A reliquary, or a Hall of Fame, is a shrine that houses one or more relics pertaining to its subject.[1]

On September 19, 2007, MSG Sports Properties, part of Madison Square Garden, LP, owned by Cablevision Systems Corporation, made a decision to retire a (New York) City Ring symbolizing eighty-two years of historic boxing. It represented "more championship bouts than any other ring in existence and throughout the years has become the place where champions became legends."[2] The corporation's holdings at the time included the New York Knicks (NBA); the New York Rangers (NHL); the New York Liberty (WNBA), the Hartford Wolf Pack (AHL); MSG Entertainment, which included concerts and events at Radio City Music Hall, Madison Square Garden, the WaMu Theater, and the Beacon Theatre; MSG Media, which comprised MSG and FSN New York; and the Madison Square Garden arena complex, located in the heart of the New York metropolitan area. A new era began on October 6, 2007, when a brand-new ring was introduced for the heavyweight championship bout between champion Oleg Maskaev and challenger Samuel Peter.

There are simply not enough words to describe the appreciation felt by worldwide boxing fans for such an altruistic act on the part of MSG Sports Properties. Never has four hundred square feet of materials meant so much; it was where souls came to prosper or to die a slow and perhaps painful death. It was as if Martin Luther himself had it in mind when he stated, "Every man must do two things alone; he must do his own believing and his own dying." The loneliest moments in a fighter's life have always been those seconds when he climbed between its ropes: Dempsey felt it, Louis praised it, Marciano revered it, and Ali extolled it. Those who believed inside the ropes prospered, while those who did not languished.

When it left its fourth-floor storage room at Madison Square Garden, the ring was unassembled for transportation purposes. The relic then made the 270-mile journey north to its retirement home, the International Boxing Hall of Fame in Canastota, New York. Its final days, as only appropriate, would be spent intact. After all, dreams are never found in pieces.

Canastota, New York

Located inside the Town of Lenox in Madison County, New York, the charming hamlet of Canastota had a population of about 4,100 when its favorite son, Carmen Basilio, was born on April 2, 1927. Although the village had been home to a United States Representative from New York, one Milton De Lano, it was an iron-chinned Basilio, an Italian-American professional boxer and the world champion in both the welterweight and middleweight divisions, who really gained the town a level of notoriety. Famous for defeating the great Sugar Ray Robinson on September 23, 1957, to take the middleweight title, Basilio was

A few of the faces of the fighters who made the pilgrimage to Canastota (left to right, from top to bottom): Tony DeMarco, Chuck Wepner, Ray Mercer, Andrew Golota, Marco Antonio Barrera, Don Fullmer, Beau Jack, Leon Spinks and Ray Mancini.

The City Ring, along with a few familiar Canastota faces (bottom, left to right): Dick DiVeronica, Billy Backus, and Tony Graziano.

notorious for his relentless pursuit and incomparable courage. Later, the former champion turned his attention to his nephew Billy Backus, who became a world welterweight champion by defeating the legendary José Nápoles on December 3, 1970.

The idea for a boxing hall of fame, which was nothing new but hardly fully realized, germinated out of a town's love for two of its hometown world champions.[3] In 1982, residents of Canastota, which included standout boxer Dickie Di Veronica and trainer Tony Graziano, to name only a few, decided to honor their favorite sons with a commemorative showcase. That showcase, located across the street from the International Boxing Hall of Fame, was dedicated on August 18, 1984.

The success and enthusiasm for that project encouraged the town's prominent residents to explore the possibility of establishing the sport's first international hall of fame and

Opposite top: A few of the faces of the fighters who made the pilgrimage to Canastota (top to bottom, left to right): Antonio Tarver, William Joppy, Christy Martin, Miguel Cotto and Winky Wright.
  Opposite bottom: A few of the faces around the fight game who made the pilgrimage to Canastota (left to right, top to bottom): Arthur Mercante, Angelo Dundee, Eddie Futch, Larry Merchant, Emanuel Steward, Joe Cortez and Bert Sugar.

museum. That project was completed on June 8, 1989. More than two dozen former champions participated in the ribbon-cutting ceremony that opened the reliquary to pugilism, and for the first time it felt like boxing had truly found a home.

A year later, the first class of boxing legends entered the shrine. Since then, the Hall of Fame has added one wing to the Museum, on August 15, 1992, and a ten-thousand-square-foot event pavilion adjacent to the Hall in 2003. The event pavilion, which also includes a business office, enabled the museum to accept the gift of the Madison Square Garden boxing ring, or City Ring. It was assembled, then put on permanent display for the enjoyment of all boxing fans.

A View from Its Former Owner

The twenty-four by twenty-four feet square "is unique in every aspect and includes four distinctive brass corner posts, plywood flooring and a one-ton iron infrastructure, which hook together without the use of nuts and bolts. The strong frame, which consists

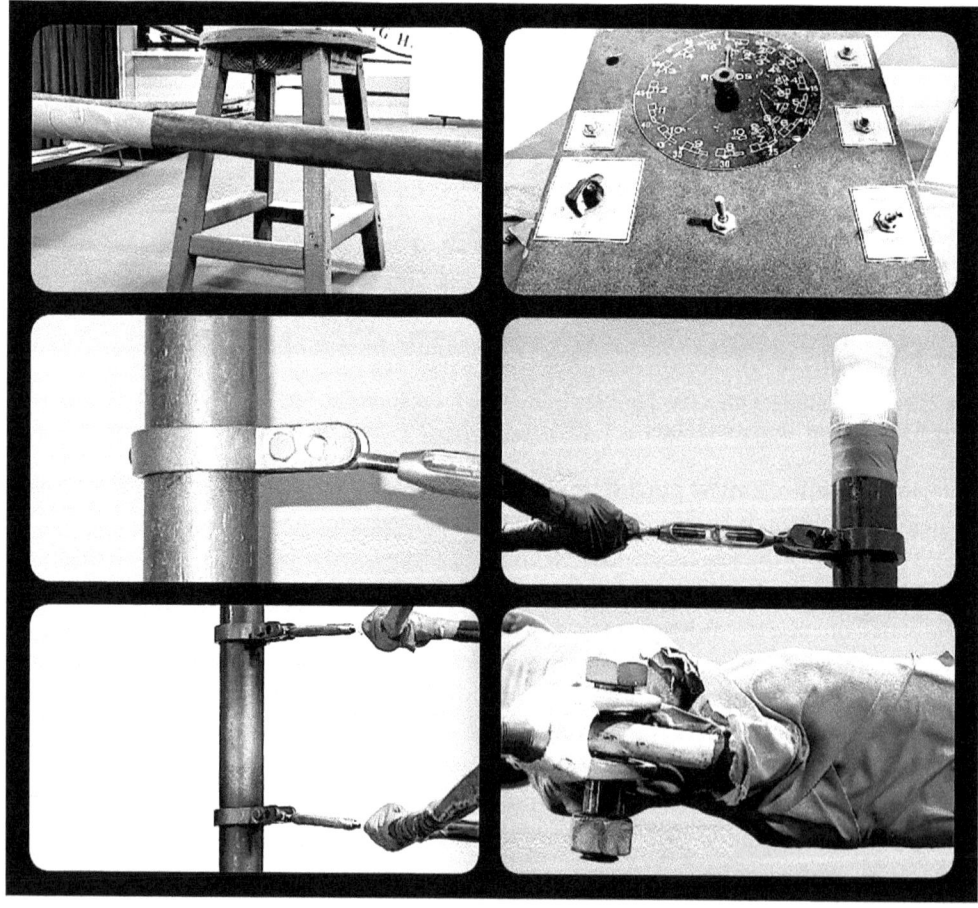

Inside the City Ring (left to right, top to bottom): Corner stool inside the ropes, timekeeper's board, corner post connection, corner post light, rope connections to corner post, and detail of rope connection to tension adjustment.

of over 25 iron beams, ten feet in length, and nine posts, creates a four-foot-high platform that supports the floor. Over the years, the aesthetics of the ring have changed including the corner pads, the floors cushion padding, the bullropes and their respective velvet covers and the canvas." Also, "because the positioning of the ring's four corner posts are so unique, inset to allow a one-foot apron on the outside of the ropes, the renowned boxing supplier Everlast has a special 'MSG canvas' that only fits the Garden's ring."[4]

Some elements of the ring evolved based on need. For example, the addition of red lights atop the four corner posts. In 1940, following the Lew Jenkins versus Lou Ambers fight on May 10, corner post lights were installed on the City Ring. Al Weill, who managed Lou Ambers, claimed his fighter had been hit by two rights after the bell for the second round had sounded. The lights were installed to confirm the end of a round. Later, they were used during matches involving hearing-impaired boxers.

Since it was only fitting to keep one relic behind, Madison Square Garden decided to continue to honor its past through a lone artifact:

> The bell that adorns the ring has a certain mystical appeal in the boxing annals. Many say that the solid-brass bell, which resembles a bell one might find on an old vessel, is original to the ring, while others say it was taken from a sunken ship and was installed in the late 1940s. Because of its status, legend has it that the bell was always locked in a secret room within the Garden and was brought to ringside just minutes prior to each fight. The bell is the one and only artifact of the legendary ring that will actually continue its service and will adorn the new ring, which is set to be unveiled on October 6, 2007.[5]

Perhaps one day it too will find a home in Canastota.

Tale of the Tape

Looking at some City Ring measurements: inside the ropes tapes at eighteen feet six inches by eighteen feet six inches. The height from the floor to the platform is four feet, with five more feet added to reach the top of the ropes.

According to those who know, it takes four hours to assemble the City Ring. A crew, consisting of four men, assembles the infrastructure and installs the canvas, mat, padding and ropes. The one-ton structure includes iron beams and supports. The floor that rests on this foundation consists of eighteen pieces of wood that each measure ten feet by two and a half feet. Atop the floor rest twenty-four pieces of one-inch sub padding. Twenty-four pieces of four feet by eight feet one-inch padding then sit atop the sub padding. The total number of pieces, which includes the four brass corner posts and their hardware, tops one hundred and thirty.

Although primarily used indoors, the City Ring, in whole or in part, functioned where and when needed by its owner.

Not Just a Ring

The City Ring would be just another boxing ring if it weren't for its owners. All four iterations of Madison Square Garden added richly to the history, performance and tradition the name represents. Picking up the legacy left behind by the confinements before it, the City Ring continued to host the greatest names in pugilism. By doing so, most of the lineal champions, in nearly every weight division, can be traced along the Garden path.

Although the City Ring was not created as a national symbol, it became one. Its engagements conveyed meaning about the nation's history, myths and ideals. To individuals these meanings evoked emotional attachment, be it personal or public, to something greater than themselves. The City Ring became an epicenter for expression, particularly for diverse societies. Although most of us never fought between its ropes, we saw ourselves in it. That was its beauty.

New York, New York

> Everybody needs his memories. They keep the wolf of insignificance from the door.
> —Saul Bellow

To those who see it for the first time, the ring appears larger than they imagined. And imagine they do. Every generation has a favorite fighter they recall, be it Marciano, Ali or Tyson. One of the most popular recollections of the City Ring recalls a famous spectator who just happened to be in its shadow. It places one Francis Albert Sinatra, camera in hand, adorning a corner post, ringside. Imagine if you can, just how special an event had to be to attract one of the most popular and influential musical artists of the 20th century as a spectator.

"The Fight," a promotional nickname given to the first meeting between champion Joe Frazier (26–0, 23 KOs) and challenger Muhammad Ali (31–0, 26 KOs), was held on March 8, 1971, at New York's Madison Square Garden. If you were somebody, you were there. From actor and director Woody Allen, to jazz great Miles Davis, the carnival-like atmosphere reeked of wealth and prosperity. Frankly speaking, more snaps were taken of Sinatra than either one of the fighters.

The commentators were play-by-play announcer Don Dunphy and former light heavyweight champion Archie Moore, with color commentating by none other than actor Burt Lancaster—which I suppose made sense, as all you needed to do was to stir in Montgomery Clift, Deborah Kerr and Donna Reed and you had a blockbuster like *From Here to Eternity*. *LIFE* Magazine, which featured Sinatra's cover photography, even hired author Norman Mailer to write a story about the fight, aptly titled—for Ali, for Frazier, and for Mailer—"Ego." And, if that were not enough, Signet even printed a ninety-six-page paperback of Mailer's commentary—the author's *King of the Hill*—priced at a buck.

But like so many City Ring battles, it was more than a social event; it was a collective metaphor. The "bad guy" was Muhammad Ali. Painted as everything unpleasant about the present, he was a brash black sports superstar who refused to fight in a war he did not understand and was disciplined for it. His opponent, or the "good guy," was Joe Frazier. He represented everything that was pleasant about the here and now; quiet and respectful, he was a black sports superstar, who wasn't controversial, and therefore reflective of middle-class white America. It was a war of ideologies, better fought in a ring than in Indochina, so most thought.

As tickets were tough to come by, "Ol' Blue Eyes" found an alternative route: he was snapping for Mailer—not a bad assignment if you could get it. As some recalled, Sinatra had backed Patterson to beat the loud-mouthed Ali years ago, and given an opportunity would have gladly shoved his Nikon down the throat of the "Louisville Lip." To think that the "Chairman of the Board" grabbed the most-coveted prize in the history of photography! The cover on *LIFE* Magazine still blows the minds of many. Which raises the question: where on earth were Neil Leifer, Tony Triolo and James Drake sitting?

A woman attending the induction weekend at the International Boxing Hall of Fame went over to the corner post and kissed it, and stated that's for Frank. When I asked how she knew it was *that* corner post, she turned, smiled and said it's "just one of those things."

An Exclusive Club

To do battle between the ropes of the City Ring was confirmation that an athlete, in this case a boxer, had reached the pinnacle of his sport. It was a pugilist's Yankee Stadium, Montreal Forum, Lambeau Field and Boston Garden, rolled into a canvas and anchored by four corner posts. For decades Madison Square Garden hosted the ring's finest participants, who saw fit to defend their ring prowess at the venue. In doing so, it gave birth to some of the sport's finest rounds and rivalries, trilogies and championships. Each exceptional ring performance shined the patina of the City Ring. It was five hundred and seventy-six square feet consecrated by the greatest gladiators of their generation.

During its time, the (New York) City Ring represented the most accurate reflection of who we are as a society. There was no better portrait and there never will be.

Appendix I

Boxing Lineal Heavyweight Champions

Madison Square Garden should not be confused with the Madison Square Garden Bowl (Long Island City, Queens) or Madison Square Garden Stadium (Miami). Former names for the Garden's smaller venue: Felt Forum (1968–89); Paramount Theater (1991–97); Theater at Madison Square Garden (1997–2007; 2009-present) and WaMu Theater (2007–09).

Key: Lineal Heavyweight Champion*, reign, # of MSG fights—year (times that year), FF—Felt Forum, T—Theater, *italics*—never fought inside MSG, ** indicates first professional fight was also held inside the City Ring.

John L. Sullivan (1885–1892), 3—1885, 1884, 1883
James J. Corbett (1892–1897), 1—August 30, 1900
Bob Fitzsimmons (1897–1899), 1—August 10, 1900
James J. Jeffries (1899–1905), retired, never fought in MSG.
Marvin Hart (1905–1906), 1—May 3, 1906
Tommy Burns (1906–1908), never fought in MSG.
Jack Johnson (1908–1915), never fought in MSG.
Jess Willard (1915–1919), 5—1912 (3), 1913, 1916
Jack Dempsey (1919–1926), 1—December 14, 1920
Gene Tunney (1926–1928), 7—retired, 1921 (2), 1922 (3), 1923 (2)
Max Schmeling (1930–1932), 4—1928, 1929 (2), 1937
Jack Sharkey (1932–1933), 6—1926, 1927, 1928 (3), 1929
Primo Carnera (1933–1934), 7—1930, 1931, 1932, 1933, 1935 (2), 1936
Max Baer (1934–1935), 6—1930, 1931 (2), 1932, 1938, 1941
James J. Braddock (1935–1937), 15—1927 (3), 1928 (3), 1929 (3), 1931 (2), 1933, 1934, 1935, 1938
Joe Louis (1937–1949, retired), 12—1935, 1937, 1938, 1939, 1940 (2), 1941, 1942 (2), 1947, 1951 (2)
Ezzard Charles (1949–1951), 5—1947, 1948, 1951, 1952, 1955
Jersey Joe Walcott (1951–1952), 6—1946 (3), 1947, 1950 (2)
Rocky Marciano (1952–1956, retired), 5—1949 (2), 1950, 1951 (2)

*Lineal champions are established in combat sports when a reigning champion in a given weight class is defeated by a challenger. In professional boxing, lineal champions populate a list of "who beat who" going back to the advent of gloved prizefighting under the Queensbury Rules.

Floyd Patterson (1956–1959), 10—1952, 1954 (2), 1955 (2), 1956, 1965, 1970, 1972 (2)
Ingemar Johansson (1959–1960), never fought in MSG.
Floyd Patterson (1960–1962), see above.
Sonny Liston (1962–1964), never fought in MSG.
Cassius Clay, changed name to Muhammad Ali (1964–1970, boxing license suspended)
Joe Frazier (1970–1973), 10—1966 (2), 1967, 1968 (2), 1969, 1970, 1971, 1974 (2)
George Foreman (1973–1974), 8—1969 (3), 1970 (4), 1971 **
Muhammad Ali (1974–1978), 7—1962, 1963, 1967, 1970, 1971, 1972, 1977
Leon Spinks (1978) 1—December 13, 1985 (FF)
Muhammad Ali (1978–1979), retires 6/79, see above.
Larry Holmes (1980–1985), 3—1973, 1979, 1997 (T)
Michael Spinks (1985–1988), never fought in MSG.
Mike Tyson (1988–1990), 3—1985 (FF), 1986 (2)
James "Buster" Douglas (1990), 1—February 12, 1997 (T)
Evander Holyfield (1990–1992), 4—1984, 1996, 1999, 2004 **
Riddick Bowe (1992–1993), 2—1993, 1996
Evander Holyfield (1993–1994), see above.
Michael Moorer (1994), never fought in MSG.
George Foreman (1994–1997), see above.
Shannon Briggs (1997–1998), 4—1993 (PT), 1995, 2002, 2005 (T)
Lennox Lewis (1998–2001) 3—1996, 1999, 2000
Hasim Rahman (2001), 1—November 13, 2004
Lennox Lewis (2001–2004), retired, see above.
Wladimir Klitschko (2009–2015), 4—2000, 2006, 2008, 2015
Tyson Fury (2015–2016; vacated), 1—April 20, 2013 (T)

Appendix II

Noteworthy Ring Adjustments

In 1931, NYSAC ordered that a two-foot extension be added to all ring floors, meaning that from the ropes to the edge of the ring would measure three and one-half feet.

In 1932, the General Electric Corporation answered the Garden's need for improved lighting and installed a system making it over three times brighter above the ring. The area was prone to difficult illumination, so the company installed thirty-six 1,500-watt fixtures.

In 1935, a new ring, made of steel and wood at a cost of $8,000, was installed at Madison Square Garden.

In 1940, following the Lew Jenkins (W) vs. Lou Ambers fight on May 10, corner post lights were installed on the City Ring. Al Weill, who managed Lou Ambers, claimed his fighter had been hit by two rights after the bell for the second round had sounded. The lights were installed to confirm the completion of a round.

In 1951, as NYSAC continued to experiment with ways of making the ring safer, they turned to the Garden on January 5, and tried out a new floor covering. The padding was made up of three-quarters of an inch of foam rubber and an inch and a quarter of felt. If used, it would replace the current composition horsehair flooring. The organization would later mandate the pad.

In 1953, on Wednesday, July 22, Madison Square Garden unveiled their latest acquisition. A new aluminum boxing ring, designed by Lionel Levy, was purchased to replace its old steel and wooden structure that was installed in 1935. The price tag was $35,000, which was in stark contrast to the $8,000 they paid for the old version.

In 1954, to accommodate color television technology some alterations were made to the ring and to the fighters. Any element of the ring that was white was changed to gray, and one fighter needed to wear blue trunks with gold stripes, and the other gold trunks with blue stripes.

In 1957, during the January 2 fight between Gene Fullmer and Ray Robinson, a rope alteration was made. It was not the best night for the City Ring, as the ropes had disengaged in the sixth round and had difficulty staying on the ring posts. By the tenth round, the bottom strand had to be removed, so the fight continued with only two ropes.

In 1963, as a result of the safety findings by the New York State Joint Legislative Committee and NYSAC, four ring ropes were used for every bout, the four-round opening bouts were cut to two-minute terms, and the fighters used only ten-ounce gloves.

In 1982, the Nevada State Athletic Commission increased the number of ring ropes from three to four to prevent fighters from falling through the ropes and out of the ring. Other commissions were expected to follow their lead.

In 1989, to accommodate the spectators in the orchestra seats at the Beacon Theater, the legs of the boxing ring used were cut down to eighteen inches. While the Garden used the facilities at the Beacon, they were also exploring other venues such as the Manhattan Center and Hofstra University over at Hempstead, Long Island.

Chapter Notes

Introduction

1. As such, casinos gradually impacted Madison Square Garden's ability to present the sport's premier events
2. Bert Randolph Sugar, *Boxing's Greatest Fighters* (Guilford: Lyons Press, 2006).

Chapter 1

1. "The Prize Ring in America," *New York Herald*, May 22, 1871, p. 7. Just a century later, the social event of the season was "The Fight."
2. *Ibid.*
3. There were times when the British Howe brothers played George Washington like Jack Johnson played Jim Jefferies, and that might be giving the Commander in Chief of the Continental Army too much credit.
4. *Ibid.*
5. *Ibid.*
6. *Ibid.* Yankee Sullivan was born on March 16, 1815, at Bandon, near Cork, Ireland. His American victories had included Vincent Hammond, Tom Secor, William Bell and Robert Caunt. The longest of these battles was sixty-three rounds, or one hour and three minutes, against Secor. Sullivan trained for the Hyer fight at Shaw's on Long Island.
7. Broughton instructed and operated a boxing arena in Hanway Street, London, from 1742 until his death. He was the inventor of mufflers, the precursors of modern boxing gloves. As "The Father of the English School of Boxing" and the "Father of the Science of the Art of Self-Defence," Broughton was buried in Westminster Abbey in remembrance of his contribution to English boxing.
8. In 1838, the London-based Pugilistic Society decided to advance "Broughton's Rules" with a list of their own. See "London Prize Ring Rules," Wikipedia: https://en.wikipedia.org/wiki/London_Prize_Ring_Rules (accessed January 23, 2018).
9. John Sholto Douglas, ninth Marquess of Queensberry, from whom the regulations take their name, sponsored the canons. See "Marquess of Queensberry Rules," Wikipedia: https://en.wikipedia.org/wiki/Marquess_of_Queensberry_Rules (accessed May 2, 2018).
10. The popular American Civil War song "When Johnny Comes Marching Home" was attributed to Louis Lambert, aka Patrick Gilmore.
11. "Boxing," *New York Herald*, January 1, 1879. Appearing on the undercard of the benefit as well was Billy Edwards v. Arthur Chambers.
12. Mr. Gilmore's home was at 164 West Eighty-sixth Street in New York. He was buried in Calvary Cemetery, Queens, New York.
13. *Ibid.*
14. Sullivan's ninth-round knockout of Paddy Ryan in Mississippi City on February 7, 1882, entitled him to the World Bare Knuckle World Heavyweight title.
15. In the last round, Kelly was hissed when he inappropriately struck Murphy while he was addressing a problem with his glove.
16. *Ibid.*
17. A grand jury also indicted Richard K. Fox, proprietor of the *Police Gazette*; William E. Harding, one of the *Gazette*'s writers; and Charles Johnson, the master of ceremonies for the fight. Other arrests followed.
18. The inspector observing the fight stepped between the ropes when the first serious blow was thrown. A few sources incorrectly list the fight as a KO1 victory for Sullivan. Four-ounce gloves were used.

Chapter 2

1. "The New Madison Square Garden," *Evening World*, June 17, 1890 (5 O'Clock Special), p. 2.
2. "Truly A House Wonderful," *Sun*, September 27, 1890, p. 5. Stanford White (1853–1906) was an American architect and partner in the architectural firm McKim, Mead & White, the frontrunner among Beaux-Arts firms. He designed a long series of houses for city gentry, along with numerous public, institutional, and religious buildings. White's design principles embodied the "American Renaissance" (1876–1917).
3. An estimated crowd of over 500 people watched Corbett train during the day from the seats and boxes. From lifting weights to even handball—a handball court had been constructed on the east end of the big oval—Corbett's every move was noted. In the evening, a large crowd of between 3,500 and 4,000 spectators paid a dollar each to watch the Californian spar. Corbett arrived late, around 11:00 in the evening, before entering the ring. However, he did not impress.
4. Garden management understood: Americans will fight for what they believe in, or in other words, a passion for confrontation exists; they will fight under a set of rules to prove a point; they will witness a conflict if it is convenient and even pay to do so; and, in doing so, an association will be made between a location and a conflict. But they also understood they were treading a fine line with the legality of the sport.

5. "John L. Describes Tussle With Old John Barleycorn," *New-York Tribune*, p. 18.
6. *Ibid.*
7. Nat Loubet, editor, *The 1979 Ring Boxing Encyclopedia and Record Book* (New York: The Ring Book Shop, 1979), p. 87, estimates "John L. Sullivan's Earnings" at $1,221,470, which would equate to $31,672,232.40 in 2016 dollars (average inflation rate at 2.98% per year).
8. "By Boxing Won $297,000," *Evening Statesman*, August 14, 1905, p. 2.
9. Loubet, p. 87.
10. Joe Gans, born Joseph Gant, died of tuberculosis on August 10, 1910, at the age of 35.
11. On November 28, 1901, Young Corbett, aka William H. Rothwell, so enraged his opponent Terry McGovern that it sent him into an uncontrollable frenzy. It will be noted as the first documented use of psychological warfare (cognitive conflict, aka trash talk) as part of a modern ring battle.
12. The next decade will witness heavyweights James J. Jeffries (1899–1905), Marvin Hart (1905–1906) and Tommy Burns (1906–1908), yield to Jack Johnson (1908–1915); the light heavyweight division was just emerging. Tommy Ryan will hold his middle crown until 1907 before passing it to Stanley Ketchel (1907–1908, 1908–1910) and Billy Papke. The welter division will be a bit more confusing as Matthews passed it to Rube Ferns (1901), before it moved through the hands of Joe Wolcott (1901–1904), the Dixie Kid (1904–1905), Honey Mellody (1906–1907), and Mike Twin Sullivan (1907–1908). and then was claimed by three individuals (Harry Lewis, Jimmy Gardner and Jimmy Clabby). From Frank Erne, the lightweight title passed to a dominating Joe Gans (1902–1908) before both Battling Nelson and Jimmy Britt claimed it. Nelson would hold the crown from 1908 until 1910. The feather crown essentially went from McGovern to Young Corbett II (1901–1904), over to Brooklyn Tommy Sullivan (1904–1905), then into the hands of the preeminent Abe Attell (1906–1912), and finally to a confusing list of bantamweights—Harry Harris, Harry Forbes, Frankie Neil, Joe Bowker, Jimmy Walsh, Frankie Conley, Monte Attell and Johnny Coulon were all in the mix—where claims were as common as a sunrise.
13. "Fights Resumed At The Garden," *Evening World*, May 3, 1906, p. 1.
14. "Fight In Garden Lifts The 'Lid' in Sad Fashion," *Evening World*, May 4, 1906, p. 14.
15. "Thaw Kills Stanford White," *New York Tribune*, June 26, 1906, p. 1.
16. *Ibid.* Thaw remained calm throughout the entire incident, even while handing over his firearm and submitting to arrest. He claimed White ruined his domestic life and was the reason for his wife's unhappiness. Mrs. Thaw, or Evelyn Nesbit, was well known as a prominent model and chorus girl before her marriage to Thaw.
17. "Madison Square Garden," *Alexandria Gazette*, December 9, 1916, p. 6.
18. Looking back at a couple of the notable New York City bouts from this period: On September 15, 1911, Fireman Jim Flynn pounded Carl "White Hope" Morris for ten bloody Garden rounds to the required no decision. Al Palzer, miraculously recovering from being dropped twice and nearly out on his feet, knocked out Bombardier Billy Wells in the third round of their June 28, 1912, Garden confrontation.

Chapter 3

1. "Rickard, Showman-in-chief," *New York Tribune*, May 29, 1921, p. 64.
2. Tex Rickard's Death Certificate.
3. "Tex Rickard, Great Boxing Promoter, Once Gambler," *Bridgeport Evening Farmer*, January 2, 1917, p. 17. Later articles, and there were many, contradict many aspects of Rickard's life.
4. *Ibid.*
5. "Receipts of Big Fight and How Cash was Divided Up," *El Paso Herald*, March 27, 1916, p. 10.
6. The purse was $127,500, divided $100,000 to Willard and $27,500 to Dempsey. Tickets for the event ran $60, $50, 40, $30, $20 and $10.
7. "May Box In East," *Topeka State Journal*, March 12, 1919, p. 3.
8. As insightful as this conflict was to society, it would be overshadowed by another disagreement, that of the Eighteenth Amendment to the United States Constitution. It established the prohibition of alcoholic beverages in the United States by declaring the production, transport and sale of alcohol (though not the consumption or private possession) illegal.
9. Benny Leonard's notable Madison Square Garden battles during this period: fought to the required no-decision against Johnny Dundee (3/8/1916 and 11/15/1916), as well as Freddie Welsh (3/31/1916). Leonard also took a united verdict over Rocky Kansas (7/4/1922).
10. This was the first fight sanctioned by the new National Boxing Association. The NBA would change its name to the World Boxing Association in 1962.
11. There were likely more unrecorded battles.
12. Sources vary considerably with regard to legitimate fights versus exhibitions.
13. Remember, Dempsey had only faced Tommy Gibbons this annum, so the contrast would be striking.
14. As the Temple of Fistiana turned off its lights for the final time, a tear fell from Diana, the St. Gaudens statue that rested atop the Garden, as she would not accompany her friends to the new venue. Once a famous city landmark, she had rested atop the tower of Madison Square Garden from 1893 until 1925. (Her predecessor, also named Diana, was larger but didn't possess her grace or longevity.) Diana's hollow copper figure was graceful enough to rotate with the wind, precisely as her creator had envisioned. So elegant, she was the first statue in history to be lit by electricity.

Chapter 4

1. On the night of November 28, a cycling sprint race, which preceded the annual six-day bike race that would start two days later, became the venue's first event. The advanced opening gave the facility time to work out some of the operational issues. The gala, or formal opening, wouldn't take place until December 15.
2. Berlenbach won the light heavyweight championship of the world by defeating Mike McTigue on May 30, 1925.
3. In the ring's second major battle, on Friday, December 18, Louis "Kid" Kaplan retained his world feath-

erweight crown by defeating Californian Babe Herman in a fifteen-round main event.

4. Also, Fidel La Barba grabbed a six-round victory over Lew Perfetti.

5. Surprisingly, the event, with a gate of over $2 million, did not sell out.

6. "Garden Crowd Apathetic," *New York Times*, September 24, 1926, p. 7.

7. Roderick James "Jess" McMahon Sr. (May 26, 1882–November 22, 1954) was a professional wrestling and boxing promoter (co-promoted Willard v. Johnson, 1915), not to mention the patriarch of the McMahon family. He was founder of the New York Lincoln Giants, a black baseball team, and the Commonwealth Big 5, black professional basketball team.

8. "Flowers Retains Title, Beats Greb," *New York Times*, August 20, 1926, p. 12.

9. Naturally, the Garden's fight frequency increases the odds of an inclusion underneath this subtitle.

10. The boxing world mourned the death of former middleweight champion Harry Greb on October 23. An indefatigable warrior, Greb, or the "Human Windmill," was relentless in his pursuit of an adversary. Size meant nothing to the thirty-two-year-old fighter. His unconventional style bewildered most opponents, many of whom spent more time trying to defend themselves rather than actually engaging with the warrior. Greb held victories over Tommy Gibbons, Gene Tunney, Tommy Loughran, Johnny Wilson and Mickey Walker, placing him among the elite in his sport. Said to have engaged in over 300 ring battles, the fighter was believed to have amassed a small fortune before his death.

11. SEC, or Securities and Exchange Commission, filings by the Madison Square Garden Corporation, 1926.

12. Aiding Rickard in his efforts was matchmaker Jess McMahon, along with the vice-president and treasurer of the organization, William S. Carey.

13. In the preliminaries: Wyoming Warner knocked out George Gerger in twenty seconds of the first round, Johnny Grosso took a decision over Jim Savage, Tom Kirby beat Lou Bogash, Ernie Schaaf took a decision over Murray Gitlitz, and James J. Braddock drew with George La Rocco.

14. Numerous non-championship boxing match records, such as gate receipts and attendance, were set at the Jack Dempsey–Jack Sharkey battle in the Yankee Stadium. A total of 50 radio stations, from coast to coast, were said to have broadcast the fight. Leo P. Flynn was managing Dempsey at this time.

15. As for the preliminaries: Harlem's Phil Kaplan would grab an eight-round decision over Babe McGorgory; light heavyweight James J. Braddock would pick up an eight-round decision over Syracuse heavyweight Paul Swiderski; Jake Warren, a Chicago heavyweight, won an eight-round decision over Jimmy Byrne; and Tony Ferrenti knocked out James Gehrman in the first round of the evening.

16. McMahon used the press to clarify his position. See: "Rickard Makes Bid For Risko Services," *New York Times*, March 26, 1928, p. 16.

17. It was the speed at which Sharkey performed that caught people off-guard.

18. The secondary cause of Rickard's death was acute gangrenous appendicitis, which is a condition in which the appendix becomes gangrenous because obstruction of its lumen blocks the flow of blood to that body part.

19. Office of Vital Statistics, Death Certificate, Florida State Board of Health, State No. 427.

20. According to records, Rickard's first wife was Leona Viola Rickard (1875–1895) and the couple had one child. Rickard married Maxine at Lewisburg, West Virginia, on October 10, 1926, and the couple had a young daughter, Maxine.

21. "$27.50 Top Allowed For Dempsey Bout," *New York Times*, p. 11. Chicago was also vying for the Tunney fight. Rickard's non-fixed seating for Yankee Stadium needed to be approved by the Fire Department and the Bureau of Buildings, Borough of Bronx, in whose jurisdiction the battle would be fought.

Chapter 5

1. Risko was born Mesto Bohunico on August 18, 1902, in Austria. His professional record is incomplete, but it is believed he fought in over 100 contests and won a majority of his bouts. He fought primarily out of Ohio.

2. *The Ring* magazine subsequently recognized the win as its "Fight of the Year."

3. An amazing crowd, considering the limitations of its location: Miami Beach had hotels, but no railroad at the time.

4. Billed as "Jack Dempsey, By Arrangement With Madison Square Garden Corporation, Presents Under the Auspices of Miami Beach American Legion Post 85, Jack Sharkey versus Young Stribling," the fight had every promotional and legal angle covered. The name Dempsey, who had a stake in the fight, speaks for itself, and "under the auspices of the American Legion" was required by Florida law.

5. Just over 50 years of age, Carey had fashioned a reputation for himself as a railroad builder. He was involved in the construction of the new Garden and later that of Boston Garden.

6. This was a common trick used by many boxers out of frustration.

7. NYSAC demanded that Schmeling meet Phil Scott.

8. For the event, the maximum admission charge was $26.50. Leaving New York immediately following the bout, Sharkey headed for his New England home and commented little regarding the fight.

9. It was the first lightweight title bout held indoors since 1921.

10. Williamsburg is a neighborhood in the New York City borough of Brooklyn, bordering Greenpoint to the north; Bedford–Stuyvesant to the south; Bushwick, East Williamsburg, and Ridgewood, Queens to the east; and Fort Greene and the East River to the west.

11. Brownsville is a residential neighborhood located in eastern Brooklyn in New York City.

12. DeGrasse would land in a few motion pictures, followed by the U.S. Army and then the United States Postal Service. Feldman would battle for nearly 200 bouts, establishing himself as a leading contender for the lightweight championship.

13. The City Ring wasn't polished by just noteworthy championship battles. Many fabulous undercards, at a variety of lengths, contributed to its legacy.

14. From a historical perspective, it's not just the fighters and officials who entered the ring who were important, but the many faces of those who existed around it. While it would be impossible to acknowledge everybody who shined in the City Ring in a work this size, perhaps a couple of tactful remembrances may be in order: Eddie Munson died on March 27, 1930. For fifteen years, Munson served as the official timekeeper at the Garden and became known for shouting "Ten seconds–and he can't go out" to the knockdown timekeeper near the close of every round. Leo P. Flynn, who had worn virtually every hat in the fight game, died on Monday, May 19, 1930, as a result of pneumonia. Many remember him through his association with Jack Dempsey. Flynn advised and trained the former heavyweight champion in preparation for his bouts with Jack Sharkey and Gene Tunney (second battle). However, those around Madison Square recall his matchmaking days in the old Garden–a time he cherished working alongside Tex Rickard. Flynn also had a stable of fighters including the hard-hitting heavyweight Bill Brennan.

15. This was for the lightweight and junior welterweight crowns.

16. The three scheduled preliminaries were also interesting: Dave Shade, the veteran middle, took on the West Side's Joey LaGray, Harlem's Johnny Pena met Freddie Miller, and East Side light-heavy Bob Olin matched with German Adolf Heuser.

17. Battling Battalino relinquished his world featherweight title on March 2, 1932.

18. They may have been the two best body punchers ever to meet inside a ring.

19. As of 2017 the property was home to car dealerships, a toy store, a bridal shop and wholesale liquidators.

20. Jacobs was suspended "for actions in the ring detrimental to boxing."

21. Madison Square Garden announcer Joe Hanrahan died in Canada on September 2, 1932. In addition to being a former boxer and referee, the gifted announcer filled the rafters with his silver tongue. Also, on October 12, James "Jimmy" DeForest passed away. The gifted advisor, manager, matchmaker, promoter and trainer worked with many fighters including Jack Dempsey, Luis Firpo and Kid McCoy.

22. "20,000 See Cranera Knock Out Schaaf," *New York Times*, February 10, 1933, p. 18. Schaaf was taken to Polyclinic Hospital exhibiting concussion symptoms. It was later determined that he had suffered an intracranial hemorrhage and partial paralysis.

23. Additionally, on February 27, they added five new regulations: NYSAC must approve ring introductions (limited to three persons); NYSAC must approve announcements of future ring attractions; a boxer cannot participate directly or indirectly in the earnings of another boxer; both managers and boxers are prohibited from being identified with any corporation licensed to promote shows; and finally, no person will have an indirect or direct association with more than one corporation conducting a promotion.

24. Also of note in 1933: East Side's Benjamin Morris Jebalotsky, aka Ben Jeby, knocked out Canadian Frank Battaglia in the twelfth round of their scheduled fifteen-round contest to pick up the world's middleweight crown on January 13. It wasn't a pretty fight, but Jeby's confrontations never were.

25. Carnera's contract with the Garden expired on September 30. In 1933 boxing lost William Muldoon, the "Iron Duke" of athletics, who among many skills trained the great John L. Sullivan and served as New York State Athletic Commissioner. Muldoon died on June 3 at 88 years of age. Also, John C. Baxter, builder of the Madison Square Garden Bowl, was struck and killed on July 26. He was 55 years old.

26. The battle was named *The Ring* magazine's "Fight of the Year" (1934).

27. The Madison Square Garden Corporation and wholly owned subsidiaries, whose fiscal year ended on May 31, announced a net loss for the year.

28. The old Garden lost the familiar face of Pete Stone, known also as Pete the Goat, who died on August 8 at the age of 42. As a teenager, Stone got involved with professional boxing most notably as a one-time matchmaker under Tex Rickard.

Chapter 6

1. Ambers was favored to beat the heavier Dublinsky, even if the Chicago battler had taken a decision over Tony Canzoneri and was far from a tomato can, or human punching bag.

2. In the four-round opener, Brooklyn's Frank Scarpati defeated Herkimer's Frank Moran–just a tidbit for upstate boxing fans. Also, Scarpati's name will surface again.

3. Additionally worth noting: there was one less professional boxing event held indoors, and its outdoor boxing event drew far better than the single outdoor event held last season. All this while NYSAC was still restricting Garden matchmaker Sam McQuade to forty rounds of boxing at the Friday night shows unless permission was otherwise granted.

4. Statement issued by the Madison Square Garden Corporation on January 19, 1935. No amateur boxing statistics were included in the numbers.

5. As for Mrs. Braddock, she hesitantly listened to the radio broadcast from her parents' home at 50 25th Street in Guttenberg, New Jersey. When the radio broadcast the results, she would not wake the couple's three small children, who slept in a nearby bedroom. It was often this aspect of a pugilist's life that received little attention.

6. Joe Louis Barrow, age 21, married Marva Trotter, a 19-year old Chicago secretary, just before his Yankee Stadium battle.

7. It was reported by the *New York Times* that gamblers were offering even money that Louis would knock out Paulino in the fourth round.

8. Feel free to draw your own conclusions regarding the Garden's generosity.

9. Only about 3,000 fans attended.

10. Louis compiled forty-three knockouts in fifty-four bouts, while picking up seven winning decisions against only four losses.

11. Two other summer conflicts worth recognition: Tony Marino staged a remarkable comeback to knock out Baltasar Sangchili in the fourteenth round on June 29, inside Dyckman Oval, to win the bantamweight title. On July 11, inside Civic Stadium in Seattle, Washington,

Freddie Steele took a fifteen-round unanimous decision over Eddie "Babe" Risko to pick up the NBA and NYSAC middleweight title.

12. McLarnin's accepted (IBHOF) final record in 77 bouts was 62-11-3, with one no decision. Twenty of his victories were by knockout.

13. Edgewater is a borough located along the Hudson River in Bergen County, New Jersey.

14. All of boxing lost a very dear friend in Joe Humphreys, the famed ring announcer, who died in his home on July 11. He was 63 years old. For forty-three years, his golden voice was as much a part of a boxing event as the fight itself. With his trademark opening of "Quiet, please!" and traditional close of "the win-nah and new champion," Humphreys stood alone as the voice of not only the City Ring, but of every ring he entered. Also, the man who formed the world's greatest circus, John Ringling, died on Wednesday, December 2, at his home on Park Avenue. He was 70 years old. Ringling had assisted Rickard in building the new Garden, only to see his circus take a back seat to boxing on Friday nights.

15. Later, his resistance of the Nazi party elevated his status once again to that of a hero in postwar Germany.

16. An added feature for his Garden battles would be a modern air-conditioning system that was due to be completed on August 14.

17. Al Weill resigned as matchmaker of the Garden on March 8, 1938, and turned his attention to managing fighters.

18. Fight fans were given the rare opportunity to witness simultaneous Madison Square Garden battles thanks to three rings that were situated in the center of the arena. The noteworthy event–the first occasion that such a multiple-ring format had been established inside an East Coast venue–was the fourteenth annual Golden Gloves competition, conducted by the *Daily News* A.A. on February 23.

19. Whether or not the selection was a quid pro quo for allowing Jacobs to use the Madison Square Garden Bowl for the Ross v. Armstrong fight on May 26, was speculated but not confirmed.

20. Additional ticket levels were: $5.75, $7.75, $11.50, $16.50 and $20. There were forty rows of seats ringside. Additional markets that were vying for the epic event included Chicago, Detroit and Philadelphia. The promoter, never one to burn a bridge, praised each of these cities in the media following his selection.

21. The fight was also broadcast by radio over the NBC Blue and Red networks that included 146 stations. Five short-wave stations also broadcast the fight across the globe.

22. The agreement would terminate on May 31, 1942.

23. Lewis retained his title against Jock McAvoy (1936), Len Harvey (1936), Bob Olin (1937), Emilio Martinez (1938) and Al Gainer (1938).

24. "Exciting Bout Mark Golden Gloves Finals Watched by 18, 231 at the Garden," *New York Times*, March 7, 1939, p. 29. Robinson would be back in the Garden on March 13, as the New York Golden Glove boxing team, of which he was a member, was opposing a group made up of various eastern locations (Atlanta, Buffalo, Newark, Philadelphia, etc.). Picking up two victories that evening, Robinson advanced to the semifinals.

25. Having debuted on July 24, 1924, the Louisiana-born fighter and New York resident had nothing to prove. He had already fought 18 world champions and was the second boxer in history to win world titles in three weight divisions.

26. The man who succeeded Tex Rickard at the Garden as acting general manager and was responsible for the growing popularity of ice hockey, Colonel John S. Hammond, died on December 9 at his Park Avenue home. He was only 59 years old. Inking Conn Smythe to manage his hockey team solidified his reputation as a visionary.

Chapter 7

1. Over the years there had been much speculation as to just when these indicators were added to the City Ring.

2. The dynamic nature of betting lends itself to change.

3. The new champion was the youngest of five brothers, all of whom boxed. Fritzie was born on May 8, 1914, to Croatian parents in Pittsburgh and turned professional eight years prior to this battle. His manager was Pittsburgh's Luke Carney.

4. General John J. Phelan, the elderly chairman of the New York State Athletic Commission, was sitting ringside and left his seat in an attempt to find somebody who would stop the assault.

5. Of all the opponents–Red Burman, Gus Dorazio (D'Orazio), Abe Simon, Tony Musto, Buddy Baer, Billy Conn and Lou Nova–that the champion faced in 1941, only one would eventually find himself among the elite of boxing: Billy Conn.

6. In the sixth round, Baer was sent to the canvas three times. The first fall was due to a right to the face, the second a result of a combination to the jaw, and the controversial third–after the bell had supposedly rung–was another right to the chin. When the bell sounded for the seventh term, Baer's manager Ancil Hoffman placed himself in front of his sitting fighter and refused to vacate the ring; Hoffman believed Baer had been fouled. This was a joint promotion between Ray Alvis and Michael S. Jacobs.

7. "Sharp Rise Is Noted In Boxing Interest, Garden has drawn 185,895 to 13 shows this season," *New York Times*, January 21, 1941, p. 25.

8. Four of the top ten gates during the Garden's indoor season had involved Fritzie Zivic. Zivic, whose two older brothers boxed, actually picked up some tricks from his siblings, who weren't shy about putting the youngster in his place. One such technique was looping his left hand behind an opponent's head to draw him in for a right uppercut. Also in the Zivic arsenal were elbows, eye pokes, gouging, groin assaults, head butts, heeling, and kneeing. His popularity was no doubt attributable to his subterfuge.

9. Immediately reacting to the announcement, the organization named four outstanding contenders to vie for the title through an elimination series. Those four fighters were Anton Christofordis, Gus Lesnevich, Tommy Tucker and Jimmy Webb. The venue of choice for the series was Madison Square Garden. Clearly, Conn wanted in on the mix.

10. Dumont featured 14-inch and 16-inch models, and television prices ranged from $200 to as high as $1000.

11. Nova's powerful rights floored Baer twice in the eighth round. After the second incident, Referee Art Donovan stopped the fight. Unfortunately, the U.S. War Production Board halted the manufacture of television and radio equipment for consumer use on April 1, 1942. The ban was lifted October 1, 1945.

12. Initially scheduled for September 12, the date was moved to November 28 because Zale complained of a painful skin ailment and had to be hospitalized. From a middleweight perspective, it worked out well for Jacobs, as he had a 160-pound clash scheduled the week before between Billy Soose and Ken Overlin.

13. The City Ring saw some historic events. Two greats, Lou Ambers and Max Baer ended their careers inside its confines. Some great fighters emerged, including Beau Jack, who fought three times in the ring and won all three battles. And three talented boxers made their debut: Jake LaMotta, Bob Montgomery and Willie Pep.

14. Sinatra often opened his show with the melody "Stardust," a popular song composed in 1927 by Hoagy Carmichael with lyrics added in 1929 by Mitchell Parish.

15. Forty of those knockouts came in the very first round.

16. Simon would donate part of his purse to the same effort.

17. The ticket range for this event began at $2.50 for unreserved seating and went as high as $25 for reserved. In addition to turning over his purse, Louis also bought a block of tickets for his Army buddies.

18. Connecticut was so busy supplying the war effort that the state ran out of affordable housing. Many temporary homes, and even trailer parks, were established near area employers.

19. Giulio Gallucci (1924–2006), aka Johnny Duke, was a Hartford, Connecticut-born boxer and coach. Duke fought professionally from 1942 to 1946.

20. Wright worked many odd jobs, from harvest picker and chauffeur for Mae West, to Pullman waiter and even salmon fisherman.

21. The World War II years were about sacrifice, on both the front lines and the homefront. As a premier sport, boxing also felt obligated to set an example.

22. Inside the City Ring, Beau Jack fought five times and won every battle, Joe Louis fought in back-to-back victories, the courageous Tami Mauriello fought four times, and an indefatigable Willie Pep went 3–0. A couple of great rivalries were born between the ropes: Robinson versus LaMotta, and Pep versus Wright.

23. This was the first fight in which Robinson's moniker of "Sugar" really began to take hold with both the fans and the media.

24. NYSAC did not mention their position with regard to how other organizations, such as the NBA, viewed "duration champions."

25. His knockout victory over Tippy Larkin inside the City Ring garnered him the New York State Athletic Commission version of the world lightweight title.

26. Both combatants insisted that the most expensive seat be priced at $16.50.

27. In other interesting Garden goings-on: Ned Irish, basketball promoter, former sportswriter and publicity director, was named acting president of Madison Square Garden on January 19 (Brig. Gen. John Reed Kilpatrick, who reported for active duty with the Army the previous March, formerly held the position); Angelo DeStanza, aka boxer Terry Young, having been convicted of robbery, was sentenced on November 16 to a 2½- to five-year term in Sing Sing Prison. As a lightweight contender, Young fought ten times inside the City Ring.

28. These figures were provided to the public on December 22 by promoter Mike Jacobs, the lord high plenipotentiary of pugilism, to borrow a term by writer Joseph C. Nichols.

29. The number provided by the Boxing Writers Association of New York was 4,100, or 60 percent of this country's pugilists.

30. Since the second Zivic meeting, Davis had fought in twenty battles, won fourteen, lost four and drew twice. He knocked out twelve of his opponents.

31. "Ruffin and Greco Fight Savage Draw," *New York Times*, December 16, 1944, p. 22.

32. Harold Green was a tough Jewish welter and middle from Brooklyn who never received a title shot in either division, which was a shame. His career was postponed when he joined the U.S. Army in 1943, but when he returned to the ring, he won over twenty straight fights. Green went 2–1 in his trilogy with Graziano, and the battles are often overlooked. Retiring in 1952, Green owned a marine equipment business. He died on September 4, 2001.

33. Graziano floored Cochrane seven times in the final 5 minutes and 37 seconds of the contest.

34. On a sad note: on November 21, Al "Bummy" Davis was drinking with friends and enjoying his evening at Dudy's Bar, a joint that he had recently sold, at 826 Remsen Avenue over in Canarsie. The Area was a working-class residential and commercial neighborhood in the southeastern portion of the borough of Brooklyn. Around 2:45 A.M., four men, who unbeknownst to Davis had recently robbed six other taverns to the tune of about $1,400, entered the bar and attempted to rob it. Davis attacked the robbers, and even knocked one of them down, but was shot three times. During an attempt to pursue the robbers he was shot a fatal fourth time.

Chapter 8

1. The international picture was unclear but would gradually fill in as opportunities presented themselves.

2. The highest ticket price Jacobs had pushed for was $40 at the Louis v. Schmeling bout on June 19, 1936. Rickard had pushed the $50 level ringside at the Dempsey v. Carpentier championship in 1921.

3. Zale sustained an upper lip injury that wouldn't stop bleeding and the aforementioned battered right hand. Graziano, for his efforts, had a bloody nose and some facial scarring.

4. Zale wouldn't meet Graziano again until July 16, 1947, in a fight held in Chicago.

5. Bell floored Robinson in the second round, and Robinson dropped Bell in the eleventh.

6. Twentieth Century Sporting Club, press release, Friday, January 3, 1947.

7. James J. Johnston, the vibrant boxing manager, matchmaker and promoter, died of a heart attack on May 7. He was 70 years old. A familiar face at both the old and new Madison Square Garden, the cocky little man with

the tilted derby was never one to mince words. Managing the likes of Johnny Dundee, Harry Greb, Petey Latzo, Ted "Kid" Lewis and Jack Sharkey, to name just a few, he later went on to direct boxing at Madison Square Garden. Over 1,500 attended his funeral, and most believed he would have been shocked to learn he made so many friends.

8. Joe Louis stated in an April 24, 1947, news conference that he wished to fight only two more times before hanging up his gloves.

9. The questioning took place on January 25, 1947.

10. Under Commission Rule 64 it is incumbent upon any licensee to report a suggestion or a request that a contest shall not be conducted honestly and fairly.

11. The District Attorney reviewing the case was also looking into the financial records of the Twentieth Century Sporting Club. Later, questions regarding his Army record surfaced.

12. Robinson would only fight a handful of times in New York City until 1952.

13. The Los Angeles welter, with a record of 42-6-3 entering the contest with Robinson, had won his five previous bouts. Doyle, who debuted on May 6, 1941, held victories over Danny Kapilow, Ralph Zannelli and Lew Jenkins. The fighter's only appearance in the City Ring was back on January 12, 1945, when he defeated Frankie Terry.

14. Robinson would later offer to box and turn over his purse to the family of the late Jimmy Doyle. Some sources list the fight as a ninth-round TKO. Robinson, according to sources, dreamed of this happening, although some of the details vary.

15. On October 4, NYSAC refused to renew the license of Nat Rogers, claiming the matchmaker's "actions detrimental to the sport."

16. Later, Jake's wife Vikki would state to the author that she had no idea that he threw the fight. She stated he had suffered an injury while training and almost called off the bout. It wasn't until he later testified before a Congressional subcommittee that she learned the truth. LaMotta also kept two sets of financial records.

17. The fight was originally listed as an exhibition, but was elevated by NYSAC to a championship contest.

18. This was Walcott's fourth Garden appearance.

19. On December 14, 1946, Tommy Sullivan, from South Boston, was matched up against Al Priest in "The Hub." The two pugs had a large and very dedicated local fan base and as a result produced the largest gate ever attracted at an indoor boxing match in Boston up to that time.

20. An American professional boxer, Stefano "Tami" Mauriello (September 18, 1923–December 3, 1999) battled from 1939 until 1949. He lost back-to-back light heavyweight championship fights inside the City Ring to Gus Lesnevich in 1941. Mauriello's terrific trilogy (2-1) against Lee Oma brought him accolades, as did the eleven consecutive knockout victories leading up to his losing battle against Joe Louis. He fought nineteen times inside the City Ring (11-7-1), and his last conflict took place on October 31, 1947, against a fighter he battled four times but never defeated, Gus Lesnevich.

21. While many noted the passing of Henry K. Shaw, a couple of other individuals were overlooked. Walter St. Denis, a popular sports editor and boxing publicity man, died on February 15, after suffering a stroke. He was 69 years old. It was St. Denis who became the press agent for the Twentieth Century Sporting Club after it was formed in 1934. William "Billy" Gibson died on July 21, in his room at the Hotel Paris in New York City. While nobody was sure of his age, what was certain that he was the only boxing manager to have two champions retire undefeated: Gene Tunney and Benny Leonard. Gibson also directed boxing at the old Garden.

22. Sol Strauss and the TCSC were a bit concerned about the availability of pugilists to fill some enormous voids being left by retiring fighters and even those thinking about it.

23. NYSAC's public statement, made by Chairman Edward P.F. Egan, was on February 13, 1948.

24. At one point rumors of a fix flew, but NYSAC chairman Eddie Eagan, who witnessed the fight, felt it was legit.

25. A couple of familiar faces lost during the year: Daniel H. McKetrick, former boxing manager and promoter for the old Madison Square Garden, died on May 22. He was 66 years of age. While McKetrick managed numerous fighters including Joe Jeannette, Willie Lewis and Frank Moran, he was also the Eastern representative for Jack Kearns during Jack Dempsey's heyday.

26. According to the United States government, one dollar in 1949 had the same buying power as $10.23 in 2018.

27. Saddler's camp would protest the decision, claiming the referee Eddie Joseph was favorable to Pep. It was rejected by NYSAC on February 15, 1949.

28. Jacobs left just in time to avoid the New York Boxing Managers Guild disapproval of Madison Square Garden's offer of a settlement concerning television fees.

29. On a sad note: Marcel Cerdan was killed in a plane crash in the Azores on October 28. The former middleweight champion of the world—he took the title from Tony Zale on September 21, 1948—was one of the most popular postwar French athletes. Born in Algeria on July 22, 1916, he spent his childhood in Casablanca, Morocco, which he would forever call his home. His pro career began in 1935 and he compiled an impressive record of 106-4-0 with 61 knockouts.

Chapter 9

1. One reason for the narrow margin of victory was the penalty suffered by Marciano in the eighth round.

2. Col. Edward P.F. Eagan, chairman of the New York State Athletic Commission, introduced his 4-point scoring system in 1948. The idea was to supplement the round-by-round system and avoid a draw if the rounds came out even. Under the Eagan system, a boxer received from 1 to 4 points for each round, depending on his effectiveness, knockdowns and so on. The system continues to be used in New York, except when the rules of the World Boxing Council or of the World Boxing Association supersede the state regulations.

3. Two tragedies befell the sport: Middleweight boxer Lavern Roach died on February 23 from injuries sustained in his ten-round bout against Brooklyn's Georgie Small. Roach was knocked out in the final round of the pair's ten-round bout inside St. Nicholas Arena. In addition, Al "Sonny Boy" West died on December 21 from injuries

sustained in his seven-round bout against Percy Bassett, also at St. Nicholas Arena. West, knocked out in the seventh round, failed to regain consciousness. A well-regarded veteran lightweight, he fought and lost to Ike Williams in the Garden back in February and was working his way through the division mix.

4. The flooring was a composition horsehair mix.

5. The previous record: 3,649 spectators (Eugene Hairston v. J.T. Ross, December 29, 1950). The Garden season ended on Friday, June 8, 1951.

6. An organized crime figure that surreptitiously owned prizefighters and fixed fights, Frank "Blinky" Palermo (1905–1996) was best known for fixing the Jake LaMotta versus Billy Fox fight in 1947. An associate of the Philadelphia crime family, Palermo also ran the City of Brotherly Love's biggest numbers racket. Blinky's partner was Mafioso Frankie Carbo, a soldier in New York's Lucchese Family who had been a gunman with Murder, Inc. Other fighters under the Palermo umbrella: Virgil Akins, Clarence Henry, Sonny Liston, Johnny Saxton, Coley Wallace, and Ike Williams.

7. The event attracted over 18,000 fans.

8. It was his trademark short left hook, which he had used so effectively for years, that caught a beaten and bloodied Lee Savold and sent him down for the count.

9. Graham took their first meeting on February 10, 1950, and Gavilan the November 17 rematch.

10. The momentum of the fight contributed greatly to the discourse. The fight would be regarded by historians as another one of the most controversial decisions in the history of the sport; nearly every account had it even.

11. Historians consider the fight as Robinson's finest performance.

12. For several weeks the Department of Justice had been examining the International Boxing Club and its operations with a concern regarding unfair practices. Christenberry would also assist in the investigation.

13. No conclusion had been given regarding the investigation.

14. A trio of tragic losses captured the interest of boxing fans: William F. Carey died on February 23 at his California ranch. He was 72 years of age. Carey was best known to New Yorkers as the former president of the Madison Square Garden Corporation; he succeeded Tex Rickard in the role on March 20, 1929. Brooklyn welterweight George Flores died on Monday, September 3, from injuries sustained in his fight with Roger Donoghue at Madison Square Garden on August 29. He was 20 years old. Flores was knocked unconscious during the semifinal of the Gavilan v. Graham title fight. William J. Sullivan, a popular New York and New Jersey sports announcer, died on November 16. He was 72 years old. Known to fans of the sweet science as the man who announced the Golden Gloves boxing bouts, Sullivan's prominent voice echoed through the rafters of the old Madison Square Garden so proficiently that he didn't need a microphone.

15. In fairness to Lester, a pupil of Eddie Futch, he was a good feinter.

16. In what appeared to be an unprecedented act, Referee Ruby Goldstein stopped the fight between Johnny Sexton and Livio Minelli in the seventh round of a scheduled ten-round contest on January 25 and ruled the event an "uneven match." NYSAC rules allowed an arbiter to stop a bout should he consider it too one-sided, which was the observation of Goldstein.

17. The IBC, no doubt under tremendous pressure to take action, decided to set aside any future consideration of Johnny Saxton, or at least that's what they said.

18. James Dougan Norris (November 6, 1906–February 25, 1966) was an American sports businessman, with interests in boxing, ice hockey, and horse racing. Norris was the son of James E. Norris. In 1946, James D. Norris was one of a group that purchased the Chicago Blackhawks along with others including Arthur M. Wirtz Sr. As president of the International Boxing Club of New York from 1949 to 1958, Norris dominated boxing in the U.S. in the 1950s, and was involved with organized crime figures. An American entrepreneur, Arthur Michael Wirtz (January 23, 1901–July 21, 1983), was the founder of Wirtz Corporation, a holding company that owned Chicago Stadium, the Bismarck Hotel in Chicago, the Chicago Blackhawks, and the Chicago Bulls.

19. Harry Mendel, an IBC press agent, and Truman K. Gibson Jr., the IBC secretary, approached Norris with an idea back in 1949. The trio chatted and modified some thoughts before taking the idea to Norris's partner, Arthur M. Wirtz of Chicago. The anchor of the idea was heavyweight champion Joe Louis, the sport's most successful drawing card. Resigning as champion, Louis would assign his exclusive contracts to IBC and let IBC promote an elimination tournament to pick his successor. The successor would then be the exclusive property of IBC. That successor would likely be one of the four leading heavyweight contenders (Ezzard Charles, Joe Walcott, Lee Savold and Gus Lesnevich). Announcing his resignation on March 1, Louis, having put the four contenders under contract, traded the contracts for $150,000. Having picked up Mike Jacobs's Garden lease, the IBC then focused on other viable venues.

20. The NYSAC rule read: No individual may hold a world championship title in two or more weight classes at the same time, but the holder of one such championship title may enter a contest for the world championship of another class. In the event that such an individual wins in such other class, his original world championship title is automatically vacated.

21. As for the details: It would be Maxim's title on the line for fifteen rounds at 175 pounds. The estimated starting time of the feature event was 10:00 P.M., with the first preliminary beginning at 8:30 P.M. Of the preliminaries there would be five six-round events and two four-round bouts. The referee would be appointed at ringside. The stadium gates opened at 6:00 P.M. Ticket prices began at $3 for general admission, with levels at $5, $10, $15, $20 and $30. There was no local broadcast of the fight; however, it was carried by Theatre Network Television, Inc., in thirty-nine theaters in twenty-five other cities. Each fighter grabbed 30 percent of the net gate.

22. NYSAC started off the second half of the year by announcing the indefinite suspension of light-heavyweight champion Joey Maxim and his manager Jack Kearns for failure to adhere to a London fight contract. The pair had committed to London promoter Jack Solomon to defend Maxim's championship against Randy Turpin.

23. Before he designed the New York Coliseum and office-tower complex for the Triborough Bridge and Tunnel Authority, Mr. Levy was best known as the architect

associated with Mike Jacobs. Levy's trademark brilliance is evident in the City Ring.

24. See also: "New Garden Ring Ready," *New York Times*, July 22, 1953, p. 33.

25. James P. Dawson, talented boxing editor of the *New York Times*, died on March 6 after suffering a heart attack. He was 57 years old. Fight fans knew him as the man wearing the cap in the corner at ringside: he wore a cap for protection from the lights and possible debris, and sat behind the referee's ring post or where the arbiter waited between rounds. Dawson became boxing editor at the *Times* in 1915 and stayed in that position for the next thirty-eight years.

26. Years later, Pep would reiterate to me how hard Lulu Perez could hit. But he never had a solid answer as to why Perez was a favorite (6–5) on the afternoon of the fight, with even better odds at the start of the contest. Many oddsmakers took the fight "off the boards." After the fight, Dr. Vincent Nardiello, the New York State Athletic Commission physician, claimed Pep could no longer defend himself. Pep denied the claim. He would fight 51 times after losing to Perez, but he would never again box in New York.

27. Brief filed by Solicitor General Simon E. Sobeloff, United States Supreme Court, Washington, D.C., May 24, 1954.

28. In 1952, Weill left Madison Square Garden to become the manager of boxer Rocky Marciano.

29. While awaiting his discharge, Marciano represented the army in its amateur competitions, and even won the 1946 Amateur Armed Forces boxing tournament.

30. Marciano fought in the Golden Gloves All-East Championship Tournament in March 1948 and was beaten by Coley Wallace.

31. A couple of sad notes: Roderick Jess McMahon, a well-known boxing and wrestling promoter, died on November 21 from a heart ailment. He was 72 years old. Perhaps best known as Tex Rickard's last matchmaker, he was also a successful wrestling promoter. Also, former Canadian welterweight champion Johnny Greco was killed in an automobile accident on December 12 in Montreal. He was 31 years of age. During his fourteen-year career, he fought fourteen times in Madison Square Garden, eleven of them in main bouts. Greco's name often surfaced for his record welter gate receipt battle against Beau Jack in 1946.

32. *United States v. International Boxing Club*, 348 U.S. 236 (1955), No. 55.

33. Mr. Norris testified on May 19, during a NYSAC investigation into boxing irregularities, that he knew Frankie Carbo, an ex-convict who had shadowed the fight game and was said to have an interest in some fighters.

34. The champion was to pocket forty percent of the net receipts, compared to Moore's twenty percent, with the latter signing a rematch clause—to occur within 120 days—should he prove victorious.

35. A couple of sad notes: Daniel Francis "Dumb Dan" Morgan, noted boxing manager and sports editor of the *New York Journal*, died in his New York home on July 7. He was 82 years of age. Morgan's marketing expertise was even employed by both Mike Jacobs and Jim Norris to assist in their fight promotion needs at Madison Square Garden. Also, Joseph Robert Loscalzo, aka Midget Wolgast, died on October 19. He was 45 years old. The former flyweight titleholder won his crown inside Madison Square Garden on March 31, 1930, by beating Cuban Black Bill; the crown had been vacated by Fidel LaBarba. The former boxer had been working as a trainer over at the Broad Street gymnasium.

Chapter 10

1. However, politics outside the City Ring remained intense and complex. For example, *New York State Athletic Commission v. the Boxing Guild of New York* was a discreet battle raging for some time. On January 5, the Guild voted unanimously to ignore NYSAC's order of dissolution. The decision would prove detrimental to almost everyone involved.

2. An American welterweight boxer, Gil Turner was born on October 9, 1930. After winning the 1950 AAU Welterweight Championship, the Philadelphia fighter decided to turn pro. Posting a record of 13-0 in 1950, he went 14-0 the following year. A strong defense prolonged his nine-year career, as did television, but Turner lacked a knockout punch. Before hanging up the mitts in 1958, Turner posted victories over Johnny Saxton, Italo Scortichini, Gene Fullmer, and Virgil Akins.

3. Both Basilio v. DeMarco battles ended up with the same result, a "KO12" in favor of Basilio—the second battle only two seconds longer than the first. Both engagements were brutally fought early on, with Basilio banking that the final rounds worked in his favor.

4. Justice Department Complaint, April 19, 1956, 51 pages.

5. *Ibid.*

6. According to the government, exclusive rights to the championship services of welterweight Ray Robinson, Ike Williams and Willie Pep, were difficult for the IBC to obtain.

7. Three former Garden figures passed in 1956: Sam Langford, Boston's "Tar Baby," died in a nursing home on January 12. He was 75 years old. Langford claimed to have fought over 600 times during a career that spanned over twenty years, but the records, which were incomplete, credit him for less. Harry Mendel, the publicity guru for the International Boxing Club, died on July 29 after suffering a heart attack. He was 63 years of age. And Bob Olin, former light-heavyweight boxing champion, restaurant owner and entertainment personality, died of a heart attack on December 16. He was 48 years of age. On November 16, 1934, inside Madison Square Garden, Olin defeated Maxie Rosenbloom to take the light-heavyweight crown. Olin was also a World War II veteran.

8. The former champion never saw a set of terms and conditions that met his initial approval.

9. The case was set in motion by the government way back on March 17, 1952.

10. Federal Court Opinion filed by Judge Sylvester J. Ryan, March 8, 1957.

11. Federal Court Opinion filed by Judge Sylvester J. Ryan, March 8, 1957.

12. The defendants filed a copy of the appeal on October 14, 1957.

13. Just a reminder to City Ring fans: Gene Fullmer's first City Ring appearance was a loss on November 25,

1955; lightweight brother Jay's first appearance was a win over Itzy Wallach on November 15, 1957; and brother Don's first appearance was a loss to Joey Archer on February 4, 1961.

14. On the promotion front: The IBC continued to have a monkey on their back, while keeping one eye on Emil Lence of Brooklyn, who surfaced to promote the Patterson v. Jackson bout.

15. His aliases included: Hymie the Mink, Papa Chaimi, Chaim Welkowitz, Hyman Wallman, Herman Walkowitz, Hymie Wallman, Ayman Wollman, and Chaim Velkovich, to name a few, but he was Chaim (Herman) Wallman (Velkovich). He was born on March 25, 1901, in Shklov, Belarus, and died at Budd Lake, New Jersey, on December 2, 1982. Wallman was a New York fight manager, furrier, and close associate with Frankie Carbo. Wallman stated to the Senate subcommittee on antitrust and monopoly that Norris was the "big boss" and Carbo the "small boss."

16. Press release, International Boxing Club, New York, April 18, 1958.

17. Public statement released by District Attorney's office by Assistant District Attorney Alfred J. Scotti on April 25, 1958. Carbo was believed to be acting as an undercover boxing manager, which was a misdemeanor in New York State.

18. Genovese was a cousin of Vito Genovese, a reputed leader of the Mafia.

19. This was the final fight card staged at the fabled Harringay Arena, which was converted shortly after to a warehouse.

20. Boxing also had Joe "Old Bones" Brown, who won the world lightweight title in 1956 and went 6–0–1 the following year. In 1958 he posted a record of 4–1; his only loss was to Johnny Busso. Brown was a Navy veteran who took part in seven Pacific invasions and won the All-Service Lightweight Championship. Following his discharge from the service in 1945, it took him awhile, but Brown was finally convinced he had some boxing talent. Boy, did he.

21. "Moyer Outpoints Ortega in Ten-Rounder at Garden for Nineteenth in Row," *New York Times*, January 2, 1959, p. 13.

22. Newly appointed NYSAC chairman Maj. Gen. Melvin L. Krulewitch attended the investigation that confirmed the organization's view.

23. Baseball was held by a contrary decision in 1922.

24. In what some viewed as a sign of defiance, Jim Norris and Arthur M. Wirtz surfaced again in the boxing world on February 23. Having migrated to Chicago, the duo formed National Boxing Enterprises (NBE), Inc., under the umbrella of the Chicago Stadium Corporation. Also joining the duo was Truman Gibson, a former IBC president, and Joe Louis, former heavyweight champion. The NBE planned to focus on television along with major promotions.

25. Jay Fullmer, who fought to a draw against Jackie Hayden, was also on the ticket. The pair put on a solid display and the crowd enjoyed their efforts.

26. He would replace Jack Barrett, who had been acting in the role at the Garden.

27. This bout utilized six-ounce gloves; there was no mandatory eight-count after knockdowns; and the fight may or may not be stopped if one of the fighters was downed three times.

28. A couple of familiar faces were lost in 1959: Gerald Slaughter, aka Baby Joe Gans, former fighter and trainer, died of a heart attack on April 20. He was 59 years old. While Gans fought many a good fighter, including Vince Dundee and Barney Ross, it was as a trainer of over 100 Golden Gloves champions that he shined most. And Tony Canzoneri, former featherweight, lightweight and junior welterweight champion, was found dead on December 10 in his room at the Bryant Hotel. Often recalled for being the first fighter to regain the lightweight championship after having lost it, Canzoneri was also a businessman, entertainer and popular Broadway restaurant owner.

Chapter 11

1. Saturday, October 8, was the scheduled debut of ABC's *Saturday Night Fights*; alternate locations were used when the Garden was unavailable. Unlike *Friday Night Fights*, the Saturday events weren't broadcast on radio.

2. Management was hoping to hold about twenty-eight boxing events during the year.

3. The fights had been on radio since 1941. Television coverage began in 1944, when Willie Pep and Chalky Wright battled over the featherweight crown.

4. Source: United Sates Census, 1960.

5. In retrospect, it may have been Markson's most significant business decision.

6. On September 27, 1960, James Dougan Norris renounced boxing and ended the National Boxing Enterprises, his promotional organization. Norris and partner Arthur M. Wirtz owned Chicago Stadium. Many felt the move by Norris was in response to the Congressional hearings on boxing.

7. Promoter Bill Rosensohn (Rosensohn Enterprises, Inc.) also testified with most of his remarks relating to Charlie Black, Cus D'Amato, Irving Kahn (TelePropTer, Inc.), James D. Norris, Anthony "Fat Tony" Salerno, and Vincent Vellela.

8. It was Thompson's third appearance this year in the Garden.

9. Johansson v. Patterson was a Feature Sports Inc. promotion. The eight previous champions who failed: Jim Corbett (2 times), Bob Fitzsimmons, Jim Jeffries, Jack Dempsey, Max Schmeling, Joe Louis, Ezzard Charles (3 times) and Jersey Joe Walcott.

10. John Reed Kilpatrick died on May 7 of cancer; ironically, he was chairman of the New York City Committee of the American Cancer Society. He was 70 years old. The former soldier (both World War I and World War II), builder and college athlete (Yale) headed Madison Square Garden from 1933 until 1955. The retired brigadier general of the Army Reserve was a leader and brilliant businessman.

11. This form of television was the use of video cameras to transmit a signal to a specific place, on a limited set of monitors. It differed from broadcast television in that the signal was not openly transmitted.

12. Jack Murphy of San Diego gave him the moniker.

13. Moore had lost to Rinaldi last year during a non-title bout.

14. NYSAC, still sorting through investigative material,

revoked the boxing licenses (manager and second) of Herman "Hymie the Mink" Wallman and fined him $5,000 for paying gratuities to commission boxing judge Bert Grant. It happened on five occasions between 1954 and 1958, and three of the five occasions were in the City Ring: Ward versus Kilgore (1954), Chestnut versus Claudilli (1957) and Miteff versus Valdes (1958).

15. Actually the original plan was to have Sugar Ray Robinson meet Denny Moyer, but a hand injury forced the former to withdraw; therefore it was Ortega versus Scott, both welterweight contenders.

16. Scott would lose a ten-round decision to Ralph Dupas on February 3, 1962.

17. Moyer was only an infant when Robinson turned pro, so the youngster never really saw him in his prime.

18. Louisville's Jimmy Ellis defeated Philadelphia pugilist Johnny Alford in a six-round anticlimactic semifinal.

19. A television audience estimated at 14 million viewers witnessed the fight. The Cuban had upset Griffith at the weigh-in by taunting him as a *maricón* ["faggot"]. Although it was an open secret that Griffith was "different," the bigoted remark was disgraceful.

20. A few good matches were held outside the city: Giardello versus Hank (Philadelphia), Ortiz versus Brown (Las Vegas), and Liston versus Patterson (Chicago).

21. In July, management also altered their ticket prices to $1.50 for general admission, $3 for reserved, and $5 for ringside. Women accompanied by an adult male continued to pay only the tax charge of thirty cents.

Chapter 12

1. Depending upon the source, Jones was either the number two, or number three, ranked contender.

2. Sitting patiently ringside, as if any venture capitalist ever does, were Clay's investors. The fighter had eleven sponsors—ten Louisville businessmen and one New York executive—who paid him a yearly salary, while underwriting his expenses. They also shared in the profits.

3. In his fourteenth professional fight, he handed Benny "Kid" Paret, who had a record of 20-2-0, his third loss by virtue of a united decision.

4. Moore died on March 25, 1963, aged 29, as a result of injuries sustained in a match against Sugar Ramos.

5. In an attempt to develop talent, MSGC was assisting club fighters.

6. An autopsy confirmed that Bello had been using heroin for a period of time.

7. Although the advent of color television was in the 1950s, color TVs wouldn't become fixtures of the middle class until much later.

8. When it was announced that over half of all network prime-time programming would be broadcast in color in the fall of 1965, that began driving the sale of color television sets.

9. Just for comparison purposes, the following night's wrestling, which featured Bruno Sammartino and Gorilla Monsoon, drew a sellout crowd of 18,969.

10. The General Cigar Company also underwrote some of the cost of the weekly fights.

11. Madison Square Garden Center, Inc., was a majority owner and operator at seventy-five percent.

12. The passing of two individuals shook Garden followers during the year. Gladys Gooding's voice was familiar to everyone who frequented Ebbets Field or Madison Square Garden. Her crisp soprano during the National Anthem filled the rafters and created the first level of excitement to many an event. Gooding died on November 18 of a heart attack. She was 70 years old. John Leo McKernan, aka "Jack Kearns," but also known as "Doc" Kearns, was born in Michigan in 1882. Managing many a fighter, including Kid Scaler, Dick Hyland and Billy Murray, he finally found a champion and a meal ticket with Jack Dempsey. Kearns later managed Mickey Walker, Archie Moore and Joey Maxim. He passed away on July 17.

13. Tickets ranged in price from $5 to $30. Participants wore eight-ounce gloves and any fighter knocked down three times in a single round was disqualified.

14. Calhoun, born Herman Calhoun on September 29, 1935, in McDonough, Georgia, fought out of White Plains, New York. Campaigning from 1954 until 1962, his fearless approach made him extraordinarily popular with those who followed the fight game. A world-ranked middleweight contender from late 1956 until early 1961, he defeated many good fighters including Dick Tiger, Rocky Castellani, Joey Giambra, Ralph (Tiger) Jones and Randy Sandy, to name only a few. He also fought Joey Giardello, Bobo Olson, Florentino Fernández, Eddie Cotton and Jimmy Ellis.

15. Many of his later competitors may debate this claim.

16. On August 1, 1966, the Supreme Court upheld the NYSAC ruling barring Emile Griffith from holding simultaneous titles.

17. Speaking of Ali, on December 5, José Torres offered the heavyweight champion a $250,000 guarantee to box him-there was no response from the Ali camp.

18. Also, ring veteran Eddie Cotton, lost a heartbreaking close decision to José Torres on August 15, in Las Vegas.

19. On a sad note: Randy Turpin, who was best known for capturing the world middleweight boxing title from Sugar Ray Robinson, was found dead from a gunshot wound at his home in Leamington, Warwickshire, England. He was 37 years of age. His two-year-old daughter Carmen was beside her father, also suffering from gunshot wounds. The fighter had run into rough times following his career as a boxer. Turpin declared bankruptcy in 1962.

20. Houston's board agreed to review his status as a conscientious objector because of his Black Muslim beliefs; Ali was claiming the city as his home. On April 28, the fighter went before military induction officials inside Houston's Military Entrance Processing Station building and refused to step forward for induction when his name was called. He was later arrested. This came after the fighter had made three separate appeals to have his draft status changed. His legal team, which intended to exhaust all options on behalf of the champion, believed any final decision was still months away.

21. It was *The Ring* magazine's "Fight of the Year" (1967).

22. Just a note: Spencer defeated Terrell; Ellis defeated Martin; Quarry defeated Patterson; Bonavena defeated Mildenberger; Ellis, Ali's sparring partner, defeated Bonavena and would tackle either Spencer or Quarry for the title in 1968.

23. Some reports state a combination was responsible for the damage.

24. Chuvalo was also cut near his left eye.

25. Chuvalo moved in tight, placing his left foot between Frazier's feet, and at one point nearly sent Frazier through the ropes. As Frazier led with his head, Chuvalo tried to keep him on his left side to make room for a right uppercut. By doing this, however, he took his fair share of punches south of the border, so to speak. Frazier's head movement was superb.

26. In a couple of sad notes: Barney Ross died of throat cancer on January 18, in Chicago. He was 57 years of age. Ross became just the third boxer in history to win world titles in three weight classes: lightweight, junior welterweight and welterweight. And Evelyn Nesbit, the last survivor of the infamous Thaw–White murder case of six decades earlier, died on January 17 in Santa Monica, California. She was 82 years of age. Nesbit achieved worldwide notoriety when her husband, multimillionaire Harry Kendall Thaw, shot and murdered Stanford White on the rooftop theatre of Madison Square Garden on the evening of June 25, 1906, leading to what the press would call "the Trial of the Century."

Chapter 13

1. Among the former ring stars on hand for the festivities were Paul Berlenbach, Billy Conn, Don Fullmer, Tony Galento, Joey Giardello, Joe Louis, Rocky Marciano, Willie Pep, Jack Sharkey and Tony Zale.

2. Also appearing on the evening's fight card: New Jersey boxer Pat Murphy knocked out New Yorker Juan Rueda in the second round of a duel that followed the main event, or the "walk out" bout. Bronx fighter Bobby Melendez scored an eight-round unanimous decision over Philadelphia fighter Mario Saurennann. In a six-rounder, New Jersey boxer Mike Mamarelli drew Jersey City boxer Tony Cruz. New Yorker Roland Trotman scored a four-round unanimous judgment over Paterson's Adolphus McClendon. Finally, Long Island boxer Walter Sealey grabbed a majority decision from New Yorker Rocky Orengo.

3. In early December, DePaula was inked to combat Bob Foster on January 22, 1969, inside Madison Square Garden. The Jersey pug had his wish, and in the light heavyweight champion's first title defense.

4. Both were constantly asked to compare themselves to the former champion.

5. DePaula was released on $25,000 bond.

6. While the first boxing show in the Garden the previous year had seen $100 ringside tickets, it was for two title matches, not one. Some still recalled that the Louis v. Conn fight at Yankee Stadium, and the Patterson v. Johansson bout in the Polo Grounds, were both tagged at $100 ringside, but those were outdoor venues.

7. José ("Chegüi") Torres fought seven times inside the City Ring (5–2).

8. Lou Stillman, owner of Stillman's Gymnasium, which closed up shop in 1959, died on Tuesday, August 19, in a nursing home in Santa Barbara, California. He was 82 years of age. Armand Al Weill died on October 10, at the age of 75. On August 31, former undefeated champion Rocky Marciano died in a plane crash with two companions, Frank Farrell, 23, and Glenn Bells, 37, thirty miles east of Des Moines, Iowa. As he was on his way to visit friends, the single-engine Cessna 172 plane he was traveling in crashed near Newton Airport during its approach.

Chapter 14

1. Federal court order filed by Judge Walter R. Mansfield, September 14, 1970.

2. The Garden would cover $500,000 of the guarantee.

3. Meanwhile, an athlete named Robinson was appointed to NYSAC on February 19. It wasn't the Robinson many expected, but Jackie Robinson, the fifty-two-year-old member of the Baseball Hall of Fame. Although Robinson was recognized as the first black player in Major League Baseball, the first black NYSAC member was Dr. Clilan B. Powell, the publisher of the *Amsterdam News*, who had been named nearly three decades earlier.

4. The symbolism attached to "The Fight" seemed never ending. It was "Radical America v. Patriotic America," "Black Militant v. Black Tom," even "Middle America v. Poverty."

5. Press Brochure, *Madison Square Garden Boxing, Inc.*, March 8, 1971, Muhammad Ali, p. 1.

6. *Ibid.*, Joe Frazier, p. 2.

7. *Ibid.*, Muhammad Ali, pp. 1, 6.

8. *Ibid.*, Muhammad Ali, p. 3.

9. *Ibid.*, Joe Frazier, pp. 6–7.

10. *Ibid.*, Joe Frazier, p. 2.

11. Ancillary income had never been more important to the sport of boxing than it was after "The Fight." Revenue numbers, as anticipated, were just staggering.

12. It is important to note that Madison Square Garden had entertainment options and that each form had drawing power.

13. In a pair of tragic notes: Dick Tiger, twice the world middleweight boxing champion, died at his home in Aba, Nigeria, on December 14. He was 42 years old. It was believed the cause of death was cancer of the liver. And Johnny Addie (Addonizio), the ring announcer for more than 100 world championship bouts in Madison Square Garden and other prominent New York venues, died of a blood infection on December 20. He was 69 years of age. Addie followed in the footsteps of Harry Balogh and Joe Humphreys and his voice was soon familiar to millions, which was quite a feat when you consider that his role was only an avocation.

14. Speaking of Ali: On June 25, *The Ring* magazine founder Nat Fleischer died in New York City at age 84. Years later, Fleischer will be recalled for his steadfast commitment to the sport and even for his anomalies, such as continuing to list "Clay/Ali" as world heavyweight champion even while he was inactive.

15. This was the first racially mixed professional boxing match held in South Africa; Foster had won the previous fight in Albuquerque on August 21, 1973.

16. Press Brochure, *The Fight II*, Madison Square Garden Boxing, Inc., January 28, 1974, Muhammad Ali, p. 1.

17. *Ibid.*, Joe Frazier, p. 2.

18. *Ibid.*, Muhammad Ali, p. 3.

19. *Ibid.*, Joe Frazier, p. 5.

20. The appearance of Joe Louis, who was once again inside a New York City boxing ring, added an element of nostalgia for the event.

21. The bill would have permitted nonresident fighters and entertainers not to pay state tax on out-of-state income derived from their New York performances. There was no doubt that major bouts attracted far more tangential tax money, but there was a fine balance–something both promoters and fighters often forgot.

22. Landing competitive heavyweight fights was a concern. While the sport had its demons and always will, Garden boxing needed to evolve and become more efficient. If that meant being bottom-line conscious, then so be it.

23. In another sign that the Damon Runyon era had drawn to a close, Jack Dempsey's Restaurant, located in the Brill Building at 1619 Broadway between 49th and 50th streets, closed its doors on Sunday, October 6.

24. The fight took place in Venezuela on the basis that all taxes would be waived. However, a day after the fight, the government reneged on the offer and insisted that they collect 18 percent of the fighters' purses, which was $700,000 for Foreman and $200,000 for Norton.

25. Having served a four-year prison term for manslaughter that was completed in 1971, King was known for racketeering in the Cleveland area.

26. Having won 24 fights and lost only 3 inside the City Ring, the fighter adored the atmosphere.

27. Donald John Trump, born June 14, 1946, was elected as the 45th president of the United States. Before entering politics, he was a businessman and television personality.

28. Later, OTB would make a controversial bid for the venue.

29. Over 2,000 fans watched Ali v. Frazier, III, from inside the comfort of the Felt Forum, while over 19,000 spectators jammed the Arena above, not only to watch the closed circuit broadcast but also to get into the spirit by witnessing some live boxing. Light heavyweight Mike Quarry picked up a unanimous ten-round victory over Mike Rossman in the featured live confrontation.

30. Also of interest was Paul Christiana, a United States Military Academy cadet, who took a decision over Clyde Vaughn, of the Peekskill Police Association.

31. It would be Ali's seventeenth title defense and his twentieth appearance in a world heavyweight championship.

32. This was against the National Boxing Association welterweight Champion Don Jordan.

33. Winners from selected states and regions headed to Chicago to meet in the Chicago Golden Gloves, while winners from other sections of the U.S. faced each other in the New York Golden Gloves tournaments.

Chapter 15

1. As for Benítez and his clowning, he was two years from his first loss and five years removed from his fall from grace.

2. See 430 F. Supp. 679 (1977), *MADISON SQUARE GARDEN BOXING, INC., Plaintiff, v. Muhammad ALI, Defendant*, United States District Court, N.D. Illinois, E.D., April 29, 1977.

3. Some sources claim an additional draw.

4. Following each round, the television viewers were made aware of the scoring.

5. Antuofermo defeated Mike Nixon, who had been knocked down three times.

6. Separate actions were taken to Manhattan's Supreme Court, on November 6, naming Caesars Palace Productions, Don King Productions, Madison Square Garden and Main Event Boxing Corporation for moneys owed.

7. The date for this battle was Friday, February 3, 1978. Some sources state the date incorrectly.

8. Michael Burke, senior vice president of sports and entertainment, along with Stuart B. Freeman, senior vice president of real estate and finance, and Joseph F. Joyce, Jr., senior vice president of racing, fell beneath Werblin on the organization chart.

9. A Nicaraguan professional boxer, Alexis Argüello (April 19, 1952–July 1, 2009) competed from 1968 to 1995, and later became a politician. He held *The Ring* magazine and lineal featherweight titles from 1975 to 1977; he held *The Ring* lightweight title from 1981 to 1982, and the lineal lightweight title in 1982. Later, he was often recalled for his two light welterweight world title loses to Aaron Pryor. Cooney fought in the Golden Gloves as an amateur.

10. The latest breed of professional fighter also attracted more clubs and even new venues. Just a few years earlier, the perceived promotional monopoly at the top of the fight game encouraged smaller promoters to nurture amateurs. And those who did were beginning to see signs that the strategy just might pay off.

11. Granted Benítez hadn't fought in eleven months, but it was a nice victory for Turner.

12. The Garden operated under a set of restrictions different from those of both Don King and Bob Arum. Don King's first co-production, under the Madison Square Garden umbrella, took place on October 27 and was a financial success (Michael Dokes took a unanimous decision over Eugene Green). However, the evening, which attracted some 16,000 fans, was marred during the last event by a shooting.

13. An Italian-American actor and retired professional boxer, Vito Antuofermo (born February 9, 1953) won the EBU light middleweight title in 1976 and the WBA, WBC and lineal middleweight titles in 1979. He turned pro in 1971 and his first battle inside the City Ring was on August 28, 1972. Fighting fifteen times in Madison Square Garden, he lost only once, to Harold Weston, Jr.

14. In March 1970, Weston, Jr., defeated Ronald Columbus for the 147-lb. open-class New York Golden Gloves welterweight championship in front of a sold-out crowd at Madison Square Garden. While in Gil Clancy's stable of pugilists, he chose a mentor in Emile Griffith. After retiring from boxing, Weston supported Clancy in the boxing department at Madison Square Garden from 1980 to 1986. He also assisted in transforming many young fighters into world champions, including Héctor Camacho, Juan La Porte and Iran Barkley.

Chapter 16

1. MSG fights dates: Durán, 6/16/83, 6/22/79, 12/8/78, 4/27/78, 11/17/72, 6/26/72, 9/13/71; Hagler, 10/19/84; Leonard, 2/9/91; Hearns—zero.

2. Fortunately the system would end in 1994.

3. Holmes was fighting while Ali, the WBA champion, was doing international exhibitions.

4. In stark contrast to Leonard was Leon Spinks. Knocked out by Gerrie Coetzee in the first round of their June 24 battle in Monte Carlo, Spinks was falling fast. At the youthful age of twenty-five, with a record of 7-2-1, Spinks, the former heavyweight champion of the world, appeared to be old news.

5. Some sources claimed it was two rights hands that did the damage.

6. Chuck Wepner finished his career with a record of 35-14-2, having fought inside Madison Square Garden twelve times (9-3).

7. An official had to flag down a passing ambulance on the street on November 23, 1979, and it reportedly took about a half hour. Classen's death was instrumental in forcing New York to reform some of their regulations.

8. It took almost a year, but the widow of Willie Classen filed a $675 million lawsuit against four NYSAC doctors and the referee involved in the fatal Garden fight on November 20, 1980.

9. Alexis Argüello would finish his career with a record of 82-8. He would do battle inside Madison Square Garden five times (4-1).

10. Speaking of bad behavior, Bobby Halpern, the former heavyweight fighter, was acquitted on January 25 of charges that he and two others had set a destructive Bronx fire a year earlier. Halpern was then returned to Westchester County Jail in Valhalla, where he had been imprisoned; his parole on another charge, involving kidnapping, robbery and assault, was revoked.

11. Later, Page would become a regular sparring partner for Mike Tyson, famously knocking down the then-undefeated world champion during a 1990 session. This event was Page's Madison Square Garden debut and his only fight inside the City Ring.

12. Although some saw the match as inevitable, Pryor never met Durán.

13. Ticket refunds for the show began on February 13. For ticket collectors, one could only wonder how many of these still exist.

14. The NABF was part of a boxing federation within the World Boxing Council (WBC). Regional federations, such as the NABF, would sanction championship bouts and crown regional champions. The first NABF title bout was between Sonny Liston and Leotis Martin on December 6, 1969.

15. On April 12, 1981, Joe Louis Barrow died of cardiac arrest in Las Vegas, Nevada. He was 66 years of age. Louis was the dominant force in boxing from 1937 until 1948, not to mention the ruler of the heavyweight class. The "Brown Bomber" was the first black heavyweight champion since Jack Johnson, who had reigned earlier in the century. When Louis had a job to do, he did it; consequently, of twenty-five title defenses by the champion, only three went the fifteen-round distance. President Ronald Reagan waived the procedural requirements for burial at Arlington National Cemetery to allow Joe Louis to be interred there. New York Governor Hugh L. Carey had been an advocate for legislation that would make ambulances and medical equipment mandatory for professional and amateur boxing matches and exhibitions in the state. The tragic death of Willie Classen provided the impetus for the bill: an ambulance was not immediately available to service the needs of Garden medical staff at the time of the boxer's injury.

16. A Puerto Rican professional boxer and entertainer, Héctor Luís Camacho Matías (May 24, 1962–November 24, 2012) was commonly known by his nickname "Macho" Camacho. Camacho competed professionally from 1980 to 2010, and was a three-weight world champion. He held the WBC super featherweight title from 1983 to 1984; the WBC lightweight title from 1985 to 1987; and the WBO junior welterweight title twice between 1989 and 1992.

17. The gloves became a requirement on January 15.

18. John Condon, the president of the Garden's boxing department, didn't know which way to turn to resolve the issue. His options included moving the Garden schedule to another state, battling with NYSAC, or forcing the issue with the fighters.

19. See: http://assembly.state.ny.us/leg/?default_fld=&bn=A3081&term=2017&Memo=Y. In July 1982, the legislature authorized a real property tax exemption for MSG. The owners of MSG had contended that the arena was operating at a loss and had threatened to relocate the Rangers hockey franchise and Knicks basketball franchises to East Rutherford, New Jersey. Under the terms of the 1982 legislation, the franchises were required to agree to continue to play their home games at MSG for ten years in order to benefit from the tax break.

20. Featherweight Juan LaPorte, who fought many times in the City Ring, defeated Mario Miranda on September 15 to grab the WBC feather crown.

21. A Jamaican professional boxer, Mike "The Bodysnatcher" McCallum (December 7, 1956) competed from 1981 to 1997. He was a three-weight world champion, having held the WBA super welterweight title from 1984 to 1988; the WBA middleweight title from 1989 to 1991; and the WBC light heavyweight title from 1994 to 1995. McCallum battled inside the City Ring seven times.

22. Not bad, considering he had substituted for Tony Ayala, the top-ranked WBA junior middleweight contender, who had recently been arrested and would later face a thirty-five year prison sentence.

23. Lewis had worked in the corners of Vito Antuofermo, Roberto Durán and Aaron Pryor.

24. See also: 746 F. Supp. 360 (1990), *Andrea Lee COLLINS, individually and as Administratrix of the Goods, Chattels and Credits which were of Billy Ray Collins, Jr., deceased and Billy Ray Collins, Sr., Plaintiffs, v. Luis RESTO, et al., Defendants*, No. 83 Civ. 5480 (RO). United States District Court, S.D. New York. September 19, 1990.

25. It was Reno's first championship fight since Jack Johnson knocked out James J. Jeffries to successfully defend the World Heavyweight Championship on July 4, 1910.

26. An American professional boxer, Raymond Michael Mancini (born March 4, 1961), best known as Ray "Boom Boom" Mancini, competed from 1979 to 1992. He held the WBA lightweight title from 1982 to 1984. Mancini inherited his distinctive nickname from his father, veteran boxer Lenny "Boom Boom" Mancini, and both father and son fought inside the City Ring. Ray Mancini's first fight in the City Ring was inside the Felt Forum on March 12, 1981. His second and final Garden duel was inside the arena on September 15, 1983.

27. The defenses were as follows: WBA Middleweight

Title (9th defense by Hagler), WBC Middleweight Title (9th defense by Hagler), and IBF Middleweight Title (4th defense by Hagler).

28. Also, in his professional debut, 1984 Olympic Games flyweight gold medalist Steve McCrory, younger brother of Milton McCrory, defeated Jeff Hanna. The four-round fight was stopped at the 0:33 mark of the fourth term.

29. As time progressed, the event was billed as "The Night of Gold," and modified to include six Americans who had won medals at the previous summer Olympics.

30. An American professional boxer, Iran "The Blade" Barkley (born May 6, 1960) competed from 1982 to 1999. He is a three-weight world champion, having held the WBC middleweight title from 1988 to 1989; the IBF super middleweight title from 1992 to 1993; and the WBA light heavyweight title in 1992. His first fight inside the City Ring was on April 26, 1985, in the Felt Forum; it was the first in nine consecutive duels between the ropes. His last Garden fight took place on January 10, 1992 inside the Paramount Theatre. He fought inside Madison Square Garden eleven times.

Chapter 17

1. In addition to Jacobs and Cayton, others had assisted in guiding the Tyson Fight machine, including promoter Jeff Levine and publicist Mike Cohen. Cus D'Amato died at Mount Sinai Hospital of pneumonia on November 4, 1985. He was 77 years of age.

2. Camacho, who hailed from Spanish Harlem, spent nearly $8,000 on tickets to give to his friends; Camacho was announced as winner and still WBC world lightweight champion by a split decision (scores of 118–111 and 115–114 for Camacho, and 114–113 for Rosario). The fight's result proved controversial; Puerto Ricans and other boxing fans who saw the fight have argued about the scoring ever since.

3. The HBO Boxing battle was the fourth time that two Puerto Ricans battled for a world boxing title.

4. The fight led NYSAC to request the resignation of three employees for perceived oversights at the end of January 1987.

5. A retired Assyrian/Syriac boxer, Mustafa Hamsho (born October 10, 1953) never won a world title, but fought some big names in his career. The Syrian southpaw defeated Wilford Scypion on June 15, 1980, and former world middleweight champion Alan Minter on June 6, 1981, before losing twice to Marvin Hagler (1981 and 1984) for the lineal middleweight titles. Between both Hagler bouts, Hamsho took victories over Curtis Parker, Bobby Czyz and Wilfred Benítez. He fought four consecutive battles inside the City Ring from May 1986 to May 1987.

6. Olajide had been under the Madison Square Garden umbrella via verbal agreement, but was thinking about signing with Don King.

7. Chris "Shamrock Express" Reid battled at light heavyweight and super middleweight.

8. An American former professional boxer, Kevin Philip Kelley (born June 29, 1967) competed from 1988 to 2009, and held the WBC featherweight title from 1993 to 1995. Nine of Kelley's first ten professional fights were inside Madison Square Garden. His first defense of the WBC Continental Americas featherweight title took place inside the Paramount Theatre on February 18, 1992. His first arena performance was a loss to Naseem Hamed on December 19, 1997. Kelley was undefeated in his first forty-one fights.

9. Some sources vary and put his record at 39–2–1.

10. Not everyone remembered him fondly. Carmen Basilio, who was pictured on the cover of *LIFE* magazine with Robinson, routinely crossed out the fighter's face whenever he autographed the periodical. "I hated the son of a bitch," he would often state. As was the case with many celebrities, when the cameras were turned on them you saw a different person than when they were turned off.

11. Not to defend the champion, but he was facing a slew of personal issues.

12. That battle saw James "Bonecrusher" Smith knock out Tim Witherspoon, the WBA world champion in the opening round.

Chapter 18

1. The silence of the City Ring increased the availability of the Madison Square Garden arena. Benefactors of the indolence included concert promoters, who were able to lure popular acts to the venue, on many key dates (weekends). During the absence of boxing, in 1993 alone those acts included Aerosmith, Mariah Carey, Eric Clapton, Neil Diamond, Steely Dan, the Grateful Dead, Janet Jackson, Elton John, Billy Joel, Madonna, Jimmy Page and Robert Plant, R.E.M., Barbra Streisand and Yes.

2. An asterisk indicates a future member of the International Boxing Hall of Fame.

3. Time Warner Sports companies (HBO and TVKO) stated that they would no longer offer multi-bout deals to boxers due to the selection of inferior opponents.

4. By the end of July, TVKO announced they were scaling back on boxing shows, from a dozen shows a year to six. This decision was ignited by poor sales of the Holyfield v. Holmes fight and a multimillion-dollar loss by Time Warner.

5. For the record, this was Barkley's eleventh and last fight inside Madison Square Garden. He fought nine consecutive battles inside the Felt Forum.

6. At the time, the Garden had not confirmed the date.

7. Bob Fitzsimmons held the title from 1897 to 1899.

8. Holyfield remained hesitant about retiring. Meanwhile, George Foreman, at forty-four years old and under a television agreement with HBO, just wanted a title fight.

9. Hospitalized on January 25 with heart trouble, the trainer was on the road to recovery. Resuming his duties by February 1, Futch just wanted to keep a close eye on his fighter.

10. To this date, every boxer, with the exception of James "Bonecrusher" Smith, who had won a heavyweight title fight in the Garden—under the stated conditions—had made it into the International Boxing Hall of Fame.

11. Many of those associated with Garden boxing felt that they were being evaluated. Was boxing still a viable Garden option?

12. The champion was nine years younger, two inches taller, one pound lighter and had a three-inch reach advantage.

13. Some sources noted the stoppage at the 2:19 mark.

14. An American professional boxer who competed from 1982 to 1997, James Walter "Buddy" McGirt was a two-weight world champion, having held the IBF junior welterweight title in 1988, and the WBC and lineal welterweight titles from 1991 to 1993. McGirt was a prolific boxer inside the City Ring. He appeared twenty-six times inside Madison Square Garden. McGirt's first City Ring battle was September 30, 1983. He fought in six consecutive fights inside the Felt Forum from September 1983 until July 1984. After ten appearances inside the Felt Forum, he fought his first arena battle on May 20, 1986. The boxer from Brentwood, New York, with his trademark left hook, was one of the Garden's most popular fighters.

15. Paramount Communications, which owned the Garden, had also been upset over allegations that fighters associated with the arena had ties to organized crime. Later, Ray Mercer was arrested and charged with sports bribery that allegedly took place during his Garden bout with Jesse Ferguson. Perhaps the Bowe versus Dokes fight was the turning point in the decision.

16. Ron Stevens was the only full-time boxing promoter left in New York. The Garden would charge between $30,000 and $40,000 to rent the Paramount.

17. Casino boxing certainly impacted demand, but state and city taxes, along with the mandatory use of thumbless gloves, didn't help the situation.

18. Eight fights were originally scheduled, but only five took place.

19. There was something terribly sad about Kevin Kelley, the only boxing champion New York City had, announcing that he would defend his WBC featherweight title on January 7, 1995, in San Antonio, Texas. Adding to the disappointment, the Queens-born "Flushing Flash" made the announcement during a prefight news conference at Jimmy's Neutral Corner, a veritable shrine to boxing.

20. The 1988 Summer Olympics were celebrated from September 17 until October 2, 1988, in Seoul, South Korea.

21. The author still recalled the day Pat Nappi, a veteran amateur and Olympic boxing coach, came into his central New York restaurant and was comparing Jones, then a teenager, to two gold medalists from 1976, Sugar Ray Leonard and Howard Davis. While it was hard to believe at the time, Nappi's ring observations were typically razor-sharp.

22. An official IOC investigation ending in 1997 found that, although the offending judges had been wined and dined by South Korean organizers, there was no evidence of corruption in the boxing events in Seoul.

23. On a positive note, Governor Pataki nominated Floyd Patterson as the new NYSAC head.

24. In a binary or digital world, the alphabet soup designations weren't working.

25. A product before his conviction, Mike Tyson was *the* product upon his release. Boxing attracts more parasites than undercooked meat. Upon his release from Indiana Youth Center Prison, the bottom feeders were there as well, kissing up to him every step of the way. The event, covered live on cable television, was nothing short of a pathetic display.

26. The Garden also announced that HBO had shown significant interest in the venue and hoped to stage monthly events.

27. Zora Hurston, *Their Eyes Were Watching God* (University of Illinois Press, 1937).

28. Boxing lore had one of Gatti's seconds tapping on his back the answers to the physician's finger-holding questions as he was being examined in his corner.

29. An Italian-Canadian professional boxer, Arturo Gatti (April 15, 1972–July 11, 2009) competed from 1991 to 2007. Nicknamed "Thunder," Gatti was known for his heart and bravery in the ring, and also carried exceptional punching power. A two-weight world champion, Gatti held the IBF junior lightweight title from 1995 to 1998, and the WBC super lightweight title from 2004 to 2005. He also participated in *The Ring* magazine's Fight of the Year a total of four times (1997, 1998, 2002, and 2003). Gatti announced his retirement on July 14, 2007, and finished his career with a ring record of 40–9, with 31 knockouts. He died on July 11, 2009, at the age of 37.

30. Just about two hundred nations (a record), all current IOC member nations, took part in the Games, comprising 10,318 athletes.

31. Lewis, the WBC's number-one contender, accepted $4 million to step aside and let Tyson fight the WBA champion Bruce Seldon on July 13, in Las Vegas. The fight was later postponed.

32. The police learned of the incident at about 10:45 P.M.

33. Before the battle, Andrew Golota had refused to participate in the event due to a contract misunderstanding: the number of rounds in the fight was not specified, as the contract called for a "ten or twelve rounder." As no official title was at stake, Golota's team presumed it would be only ten rounds. However, the *Daily News*, pushing the boundaries of definition, offered a belt to the winner. Naturally a title fight of any kind was far easier to sell than a non-title fight, so Team Bowe, to say nothing of the promoters, went with the title fight scenario, or twelve rounds. Golota, who had trained for ten rounds, would not engage until an additional monetary incentive was added to his contract.

34. ITT was already involved with the sport of boxing through its ownership of Caesars Palace hotels, resorts and casinos.

35. Spencer VP Bernard Brooks was required to resign, and Jason Harris, the son of Spencer's president, was barred permanently from association with either the fighter or the promotion firm.

36. An American professional boxer who competed from 1979 to 2003, Tim Witherspoon (born December 27, 1957) was a two-time world heavyweight champion, having held the WBC title in 1984, and the WBA title in 1986. Witherspoon was also known as a regular sparring partner for Muhammad Ali. His first appearance inside the City Ring was on December 12, 1986. Witherspoon fought inside Madison Square Garden three times.

Chapter 19

1. Just a reminder that sources often vary with regard to fight records. The Nielsen fight was held in Copenhagen.

2. In the co-feature, Bert Cooper knocked out Richie Melito, Jr., at the 1:51 mark of the opening round.

3. Christy Renea Salters, aka "The Coal Miner's Daughter," was five feet, four and a half inches tall and fought as a light middleweight. Born on June 12, 1968, she would become a pioneer in professional women's boxing. Her record entering this battle was 32-1-2.

4. The number of events being held inside the Garden continued to increase, led by both the theater and the expo center. The company reported 508 events in 1996.

5. A Puerto Rican world champion professional boxer who competed from 1979 to 1997, Edwin "Chapo" Rosario (March 15, 1963–December 1, 1997) won the lightweight championship of the world three times, as the WBC lightweight champion (1983–84), and the WBA champion (1986–87 and 1989–90). Rosario won a 4th world championship after moving up to the junior welterweight division by claiming the WBA title, holding that crown from 1991 to 1992. Larry Holmes (born November 3, 1949) competed from 1973 to 2002. He grew up in Easton, Pennsylvania, which gave birth to his boxing nickname of the "Easton Assassin." With his trademark left jab, Holmes held the WBC heavyweight title from 1978 to 1983, *The Ring* magazine and lineal heavyweight titles from 1980 to 1985, and the inaugural IBF heavyweight title from 1983 to 1985. He made 19 successful title defenses, placing him third all time, behind only Joe Louis at 25 and Wladimir Klitschko at 22. Larry Holmes made his first appearance inside the City Ring was on September 10, 1973. His third and last battle in the City Ring took place in the Theater at Madison Square Garden on July 29, 1997.

6. Mayweather's first professional bout took place on October 11, 1996, at Texas Station, North Las Vegas, Nevada, and it was against Roberto Apodaca. He would defeat Arroyo in a fifth-round TKO.

7. Floyd Mayweather, Jr., would never box in the City Ring.

8. Holyfield had been involved in four of the top five boxing pay-per-view shows ever. It should be noted that two of those events included Mike Tyson.

9. It was estimated that he did "blow-by-blow" action for over 2,000 fights.

10. The Garden Theater seated 5,200 and tickets ranged from $18 to as high as $100 (ringside). As the USA Network had abandoned its *Tuesday Night Fights* series, the TNT announcement filled an enormous void and was welcomed.

11. As a publicist and then the boxing director, Markson was associated with thousands of fights, nearly ten times that of Willie Pep, and that spoke volumes. His most famous was the 1971 extravaganza in the present Garden that pitted Muhammad Ali against Joe Frazier, both undefeated, for the heavyweight championship. In 1937, he became the head of publicity for boxing at the Garden. Harry Markson died on Tuesday, November 10, 1998, at Riverview Hospital in Red Bank, NJ. He was 92.

12. Any evidence of a criminal nature found by the State Senate Investigation Committee was turned over to the Manhattan District Attorney.

13. Originally Williams was to meet Hasim Rahman, but the fighter pulled out of the event due to a back injury.

14. HBO's boxing czar was Lou DiBella.

15. Mayweather believed he was on the same economic plateau as Oscar De La Hoya and Roy Jones, Jr.

16. See also: *United States v. Lee*, 01–1629 (3rd Cir. 2004), Court of Appeals for the Third Circuit. Filed: February 20th, 2004, Precedential Status: Precedential, Citations: None known, Docket Number: 01-1629.

17. There were no knockdowns. The verdict was swift and decisive: a unanimous decision for Lennox Lewis, who unified the title and became the first British heavyweight champion since Bob Fitzsimmons.

18. Also, on February 5, 1999, Tyson was sentenced to a year's imprisonment, fined $5,000, and ordered to serve two years' probation along with undergoing 200 hours of community service for assaulting two motorists after a traffic accident on August 31, 1998. He served nine months of that sentence. Trinidad v. De La Hoya was close, yet uneventful.

19. Eva Shain, the first woman to serve as a boxing heavyweight championship judge (Muhammad Ali versus Earnie Shavers), died on Thursday, August 19, in Englewood, New Jersey. Her husband, Frank, the longtime ring announcer, confirmed that cancer had taken her life.

20. Gatti weighed in at 9 A.M. the morning of the fight; he tipped at 149 pounds. This was one pound over weight, so all parties agreed to amend the contract.

21. The complex, officially stylized as STAPLES Center, was a multi-purpose sports arena in downtown Los Angeles. It was located next to the Los Angeles Convention Center complex along Figueroa Street.

22. Mosley earned a minimum of $15 million, while De La Hoya was guaranteed $35 million. As for the scoring: Judges Lou Filippo and Pat Russell scored the fight 116–112 and 115–113, respectively, for Mosley, whilst judge Marty Sammon had it 113–115 for De La Hoya. The fight was named *The Ring* magazine Event of the Year for 2000.

23. The welter champion was prolific and landed twice as many punches as Diaz.

24. Jones vs. Hopkins was on the undercard of Riddick Bowe's heavyweight title defense against Jesse Ferguson.

25. An undefeated Mexican professional boxer, Ricardo "El Finito" López Nava (born July 25, 1966), defended the lineal and WBC strawweight championship a record 21 times. He also won the WBA and WBO championships in the same weight class. López later won the IBF light flyweight championship and defended it twice before retiring. He was one of over a dozen elite boxing champions to retire without a loss, and his boxing skills enticed his son, flyweight prospect Alonso López, to enter the ring.

26. Competing from 1992 to 2008, Vernon Forrest (January 12, 1971–July 25, 2009) was a four-time, two-weight world champion, having held the IBF welterweight title in 2001; the unified WBC, *Ring* magazine, and lineal welterweight titles from 2002 to 2003; and the WBC super welterweight title twice, from 2007 to 2009. In 2002, Forrest was voted Fighter of the Year by *The Ring* magazine and the Boxing Writers Association of America. In 2009, Forrest was murdered after he was robbed at a gas station in the Mechanicsville neighborhood of Atlanta, Georgia.

27. McCline would lose to Klitschko, but would return to the City Ring one more time to face Chris Byrd in 2004. McCline retired in 2012 at the age of 42, leaving behind a boxing record of 41-13-3.

Chapter 20

1. The September 20 match, held in Mohegan Sun Arena, ended in a controversial win for Byrd; many people felt Oquendo had won. Toney's kayo of Holyfield came in the ninth round of their bout on October 4 in Las Vegas.

2. Johnson tore a muscle during training. Klitschko was the WBC's No. 1-rated heavyweight contender and, as fate might have it, was on the undercard, scheduled to fight Cedric Boswell.

3. This was Lewis's last fight. He announced his retirement on February 6, 2004. HBO's *World Championship Boxing* broadcast the fight and it was seen in 4.6 million homes. It was the network's highest rated fight since Oscar De la Hoya vs. Oba Carr on May 22, 1999.

4. Johnson entered the battle 34–1–1, with victories over Larry Donald and Al Cole.

5. Mayorga would turn back to the Garden in 2004, for back-to-back battles.

6. A Ukrainian politician and former professional boxer, Vitali Volodymyrovych Klitschko (born July 19, 1971) was a three-time world heavyweight champion, the second longest reigning WBC heavyweight champion of all time, and has the third longest combined world championship reign in history at 2,735 days. He turned to politics after boxing.

7. Also on the undercard: Mitchell versus Mayorga and Braithwaite versus Azille. The WBA version of the heavyweight title was given back to John Ruiz when Roy Jones, Jr., who had defeated Ruiz in March 2003, dropped back down to the light heavyweight division.

8. An American former professional boxer who competed from 1993 to 2009, Christopher Cornelius "Chris" Byrd (born August 15, 1970) was a two-time world heavyweight champion. He made three appearances inside the City Ring.

9. Ruiz's suit was believed to be the first case of one professional athlete suing another for using a performance-enhancing drug.

10. The official outcome was a majority decision (scored 114–116, 113–116, and 114–114), but it was also a controversial one. Ruiz was convinced that his jab/combination-punch technique had given him a clear victory, and many spectators agreed. He demanded that his promoter, Don King, set up an immediate rematch. Ruiz's longtime manager, Norman Stone, declared that they would also formally petition the WBA.

11. A Puerto Rican former professional boxer who competed from 2001 to 2017, Miguel Ángel Cotto Vázquez (born October 29, 1980) was a multiple-time world champion, and the first Puerto Rican boxer to win world titles in four weight classes. His first battle inside the City Ring was on June 11, 2005. After defeating Zab Judah, he would defeat Shane Mosley in the City Ring's replacement confine on November 10, 2007. Cotto was born in Providence, Rhode Island, and his family relocated to Caguas, Puerto Rico.

12. NSAC fined Judah $250,000 and had his boxing license revoked. Judah's father and trainer, Yoel Judah, was fined $100,000 and had his seconds license suspended for a year. Roger Mayweather was fined $200,000 and suspended for a year. Mayweather's cornerman was fined $50,000 and had his seconds license suspended for four months. Later, Mayweather gave up the IBF belt, which Kermit Cintron claimed on October 28 by stopping Mark Suarez in the fifth round of a bout held in West Palm Beach, Florida. On November 4, 2006, Mayweather won a one-sided 12-round decision in Las Vegas over Baldomir to gain recognition as the legitimate WBC welterweight champion.

13. The fight for the WBC super featherweight belt was held in Las Vegas on January 21, 2006.

14. An American professional boxer, Zabdiel Judah (born October 27, 1977) was a former world champion in two weight classes, having held the IBF and WBO junior welterweight titles between 2000 and 2004; the IBF junior welterweight title again in 2011; and the undisputed welterweight title in 2005, which included a reign as the lineal champion from 2005 to 2006. His first battle inside the City Ring was on October 4, 1996. After losing to Miguel Cotto, he would fight three more times (2–1) before returning to the City Ring's replacement confine on November 8, 2008.

15. Judah's trainer was Yoel Judah and his cutman was James Judah. Cotto's trainer was Evangelista Cotto and his cutman was Miguel Diaz.

Chapter 21

1. The word derived from the Latin reliquiae, meaning "remains," and a form of the Latin verb relinquere, to "leave behind, or abandon."

2. News release, Madison Square Garden, September 19, 2007, p. 1.

3. *The Ring* magazine was established in 1922. In 1954, the magazine established its own boxing Hall of Fame and inducted 155 members before it was abandoned after the 1987 inductions.

4. News release, Madison Square Garden, September 19, 2007, p. 2.

5. *Ibid.*

Bibliography

As many of the sport's early records are incomplete, sources may vary. As the City Ring answered the call to its owner, it underwent numerous alterations and may even have appeared at alternate sites. Fight card alterations were common, leading to times when some fighters may have been incorrectly identified.

Books

Andre, Sam, and Nat Fleischer. *A Pictorial History of Boxing*. New York: Bonanza, 1981.
Arnold, Peter. *All-Time Greats of Boxing*. Edison, NJ: Book Sales, 1993.
Aycock, Colleen, and Mark Scott. *Tex Rickard, Boxing's Greatest Promoter*. Jefferson, NC: McFarland, 2012.
Baker, Mark Allen. *Battling Nelson, The Durable Dane*. Jefferson, NC: McFarland, 2016.
_____. *The Fighting Times of Abe Attell*. Jefferson, NC: McFarland, 2017.
_____. *Title Town USA: Boxing in Upstate New York*. Charleston: History Press, 2010.
Brenner, Teddy, and Barney Nagler. *Only the Ring was Square*. Englewood Cliffs, NJ: Prentice-Hall, 1981.
Brooks, Ken. *Ingemar Johansson*. Jefferson, NC: McFarland, 2017.
Cavanaugh, Jack. *Tunney: Boxing's Brainiest Champ and His Upset of the Great Jack Dempsey*. New York: Ballantine, 2006.
Citro, Ralph. *Computer Boxing Update*, 7th ed. New York: Ralph Citro, 1990.
Collins, Nigel. *Boxing Babylon: Behind the Shadowy World of the Prize Ring*. New York: Carol, 1990.
Dempsey, Jack, with Barbara Piattelli Dempsey. *Dempsey*. New York: Harper & Row, 1977.
Dewey, Donald. *Ray Arcel: A Boxing Biography*. Jefferson, NC: McFarland, 2012.
Fitzgerald, F. Scott. *The Great Gatsby*. New York: Collier, 1992.
Fleischer, Nat. *50 Years at Ringside*. New York: Greenwood, 1969.
Freedman, Lew. *Joe Louis: The Life of a Heavyweight*. Jefferson, NC: McFarland, 2013.
Goldman, Herbert G., ed. *Boxing: A Worldwide Record of Bouts and Boxers*. Jefferson, NC: McFarland, 2012.
_____. *The Ring Record Book and Boxing Encyclopedia*. New York: Ring, 1985.
Golesworthy, Maurice. *Encyclopedia of Boxing*. London: Robert Hale, 1988.
Hassan, John. *1998 ESPN Information Please Sports Almanac*. New York: Warner, 1997.
Heinz, W.C. *The Fireside Book of Boxing*. New York: Simon & Schuster, 1961.
Kahn, Roger. *A Flame of Pure Fire*. New York: Harcourt Brace, 1999.
Lang, Arne. *Prize-Fighting: An American History*. Jefferson, NC: McFarland, 2008.
Levy, Alan H. *Floyd Patterson: A Boxer and a Gentleman*. Jefferson, NC: McFarland, 2008.
Linder, Doveed. *Ringside*. Jefferson, NC: McFarland, 2016.
Lindsay, Andrew. *Boxing in Black and White*. Jefferson, NC: McFarland, 2004.
Loubet, Nat, ed. *The 1979 Ring Boxing Encyclopedia and Record Book*. New York: The Ring Book Shop, 1979.
McNeil, William F. *The Rise of Mike Tyson, Heavyweight*. Jefferson, NC: McFarland, 2014.
Mullan, Harry. *The Great Book of Boxing*. New York: Crescent, 1987.
Nagler, Barney. *James Norris and the Decline of Boxing*. Indianapolis: Bobbs Merrill, 1964.
Oates, Joyce Carol. *On Boxing*. Garden City, NY: Dolphin/Doubleday, 1987.
Ritter, Lawrence S. *East Side West Side: Tales of New York Sporting Life, 1910–1960*. New York: Total Sports, 1998.
Roberts, James B., and Alexander G. Skutt. *The Boxing Register*. Ithaca: McBooks, 2002.
Roberts, Randy. *Jack Dempsey: The Manassa Mauler*. Baton Rouge: Louisiana State University Press, 1979.
Ryan, Joe. *Heavyweight Boxing in the 1970s*. Jefferson, NC: McFarland, 2013.
Silver, Mike. *The Arc of Boxing*. Jefferson, NC: McFarland, 2014.
Sugar, Bert Randolph. *Boxing's Greatest Fighters*. Guilford: Lyons Press, 2006.
_____. *The Ultimate Book of Boxing Lists*. Philadelphia: Running Press, 2010.
Trager, James. *The New York Chronology*. New York: HarperResource, 2003.

Archival Sources

Associated Press
International Boxing Hall of Fame, Canastota, New York
The Library of Congress
United Press International

Blog Entries

allthebestfights.com
boxing.com/blog
boxing-social.com
boxing247.com
boxinginsider.com
boxingnews24.com
boxingscene.com
britishboxers.co.uk
fightnews.com
insidehboboxing.com
irish-boxing.com
proboxing-fans.com
reddit.com/r/Boxing
ringtv.com
roundbyroundboxing.com
saddoboxing.com
secondsout.com
titleboxing.com/news
wbaboxing.com
worldboxingnews.net

Internet Sources

badlefthook.com
boxrec.com
britannica.com
cyberboxingzone.com
espn.com
history.com
ibhof.com
imdb.com
wikipedia.org
YouTube.com

Magazines

Boxing Monthly
Boxing News
KO Magazine
The Ring
Sports Illustrated
Weekly Boxing World

Newspapers

Albuquerque Tribune
Alexandria Gazette
Baltimore News-American
Birmingham Post-Herald
Bisbee Daily Review
Boston Courier
Boston Evening Transcript
Boston Post
Bridgeport Evening Farmer
Brooklyn Eagle
Brooklyn Times-Union
Buffalo Courier-Express
Butte Daily Bulletin
Carson City Daily Appeal
Chicago Press and Tribune
Cincinnati Daily Star
City Sun
Clearwater Sun
Cleveland News
Commercial & Financial Chronicle
Daily Compass
Daily Gate City and Constitution-Democrat
Dallas Times Herald
Denver Post
El Paso Herald
Evansville Courier & Press
Evening Capital News
Evening Statesman
Evening World
Hartford Times
Helena Independent
Houston Post
National Republican
New York Daily Mirror
New York Herald Tribune
New York Journal-American
New York Sun
New York Times
New York Tribune
New York World Journal Tribune
New York World-Telegram
Newark Evening News
Pacific Commercial Advertiser
Philadelphia Journal
Pittsburgh Press
Powder River County Examiner
Record-Union
Richmond Palladium and Sun-Telegram
Rocky Mountain News
Syracuse Herald-Journal
Topeka State Journal
USA Today
Washington Star
Washington Times
West Virginian

Index

Numbers in ***bold italics*** indicate pages with illustrations

Abdullaev, Muhammadqodir 270
Abrams, Georgie 81–82, 101, 104
Addie, Johnny 112–113, 118
Agosta, Joe 95
Agosto, Pedro
Ahumada, Jorge 187, 189
Aidala, Arthur 112, 179–182
Aiken, Virgil 139
Akinwande, Henry 252
Alexander, Bobby "Wildman" 206
Alfaro, Manuel 143
Ali, Laila 256, 266; versus Jacqui Frazier-Lyde 261
Ali, Muhammad 163, ***164***, 165–167, 173, 175–177, 179–188, 190, 194–196, 199, 203, 206–207, 225, 244; biography 167–168; court cases 174, 178–179; The Thrilla in Manilla 189; *see also* Clay, Cassius
Alvarez, Rosendo 262
Ambers, Lou (Luigi Giuseppe d'Ambrosio) 56–57, 60, 62, 64, 66, ***67***, 68, 73, 75, 77, 83, 109
Anastasia, Albert 139, 191
Anaya, Romeo 185
Anderson, Dewey 59
Andrade, Cisco 142
Andrews, Al 124
Andrews, Paul 131
Angott, Sammy 89, 91
Anifowoshe, Akleem 233
Anthony, Tony 144
Antuofermo, Vito 184–185, 188, 196, 199–200, 204–206, 299n13
Apostoli, Freddie 70
Arcel, Ray 182, 213
Archer, Freddie 104
Archer, Jimmy 138, 156
Archer, Joey 135, 149, 159, 161, 228; biography 156
Archibald, Joey 86, 109
Argüello, Alexis ***194***–196, 200, 206, 210, 213, 299n9
Arizmendi, Baby 64
Armstrong, Gene "Ace" 148, 154
Armstrong, Henry (Henry Melody Jackson, Jr.) 64–66, 68, 70, 73, 75–77, 79–81, 90, 94, 145, 225, 227
Armstrong, Terry 229
Arnold, Billy 95–96

Arroyo, Hector 252
Artis, Jerome 196
Artis, John 224
Arum, Bob 165, 177, 215
Attell, Abe 20
Augustus, Emanuel 262
Austin, Tim 236
Ayala, Mike 206

Backus, Billy ***277***
Baer, Jacob "Buddy" 78–79, 85, 99
Baer, Max 45–46, 48, 53–54, 56–58, 66, 72, 76, 80
Bahama, Yama 138
Baker, Bob 128
Baksi, Joe 93–94, 105
Baldomir, Carlos Manuel 271
Baltazar, Tony 215
Banks, Kelcie 240
Banks, Sonny 151, 168
Banovic, Joe 44
Barbetta, Lou 74
Barkley, Iran 219, 225, 229, 234, 236, 301n30
Barlund, Gunnar 70
Barnum, Phineas T. 11, 22, 25, 35, 39
Barone, Joseph "Pep" 191
Barone, Nick 116
Barrera, Marco Antonio 262, 266, 271, ***275***
Barrett, Jack 139
Barrios, Miguel 134–135, 138
Barto, Tommy 128
Bartolo, Sal 98, 101
Basilio, Carmen 114, 126, ***129***, 130–132, 135, 137–138, 141, 144, 147, 150, 163–164, 227, 275
Basora, Jose 85
Bass, Benny 38, 87
Bassett, Percy 128
Bassey, Hogan "Kid" 144
Batista, Danilo 196
Battalino, Christopher "Bat" 45, 47–48
Bazzano, Tommy 124
Beacon Theater 229
Beau, Jimmy 113–114, 120
Beauhuld, Billy 74
Becerra, Joe 144
Bell, Harry 140
Bell, Robert "Bobby" 131

Bell, Tommy 100, 104–105
Bello, Billy 157–158
Belloise, Mike 64
Belloise, Steve 78, 83, 104
Beltram, Willie 109
Benitez, Frankie 195, 198
Benítez, Wilfred ***191***, 193, 195–196, 199–200, 202–203, 206–208
Bennett, Harold 238
Bennett, Michael 259
Benton, George 159, 224
Benvenuti, Nino 166, 170, 175, 178
Berbick, Trevor 221–222
Berg, Jack 45, 50, 182
Berger, Maxie 104
Berl, Al 137
Berle, Milton 169
Berlenbach, Paul 29–31, 35, 37, 114
Berrios, Kenny 259
Besmanoff, Billy 141
Bettina, Melio 54, 71, 104
Bianco, Roman 172–173
Biggs, Tyrell 216–217
Bimstein, Whitey 76, 159
Birkie, Hans 53
Bivins, Jimmy 98
Black, Julian 61
Black Diamond Glove Tournament 59
Blackburn, Jack 37, 61, 79
Blair, Frank 65
Blake, George 47
Blake, Robin 215
Blunt, Eddie 59, 65
Boardman, Larry 133
Bobick, Duane 194
Bolden, Nate 85
Bonavena, Oscar "Ringo" 160–161, 164–165, 167, 173, 177
Booze, Tyrone 218
Bos, Johnny 256
Bostice, David 257
Botha, Frans 257
Bowe, Riddick 231, 235–238, 241, 245–248, 252
Boza-Edwards, Cornelius 215
Braddock, James J. 4, 35, 38, 43, 53–58, 60, ***63***, 64, 69, 71, 182
Bradley, Lonnie 238
Brady, William A. 15
Brannon, Bryant 248–249
Bratton, Johnny 118, 120

Index

Breeze, Johnny 113
Breland, Mark 215–**216**, 217, 219
Brennan, Bill 27
Brenner, Teddy 142, 151, 165, 181, 184–185, 187, 199, 202
Brescia, Jorge 63
Briggs, Shannon 242, 263
Brion, Cesar 109
Briscoe, Bennie 184, 188, 196, 199
Britt, Jimmy 23
Brock, Calvin 270
Brooks, Monroe 200
Broughton, Jack 8
Brouillard, Lou 51, 55
Brown, Freddie 159
Brown, Glenwood 225
Brown, Jimmy 70
Brown, John 253
Brown, Joseph 135, 150, 296*n*20
Brown, Panama Al 38
Brown, Roger 223
Brown, Simon 226, 233, 236
Brown, William "Billy" (Dominick Mordini) 139
Bruno, Frank 243, 267
Bucceroni, Dan 117, 120
Buchanan, Ken 177, 181–182, 184, 203
Buckley, F. Mac 211
Bugner, Joe 185, 189
Bumpus, Jeff 218
Buonvino, Gino 107
Burford, Ernest 224
Burley, Charley 98
Burman, Clarence "Red" 83, 85
Burns, Johnny 96, 104, 108
Burns, Tommy (Noah Brusso) 20
Burton, Richard
Busso, Johnny 140–141
Byarm, Lionel 217
Byars, Walter 138
Byrd, Antoine 240
Byrd, Chris 236, 261, 264, 267–268, 270, 304*n*8

Cabanela, Fernando 196
Cabrera, Danilo 224
Calhoun, Rory 138, 143, 162, 297*n*14
Camacho, Héctor, Jr. 258
Camacho, Héctor "Macho" 209–211, 213, 221, 247–249
Campas, Yory Boy 266
Campolo, Victorio 48
Canady, Lorenzo 226
Canastota, New York 1, 3, 82, 126, 129, 137, 144, 261, 275–279
Canizales, Orlando 226, 243
Canzoneri, Tony 31, 33, 36, 38–39, 45, 47, 52–53, 56–57, 60, 62, 73, 75, 87
Capo, David 205
Carbajal, Michael 238–239
Carbo, Paul John "Frankie" 62, 139–140, 144, 147, 153, 190–191
Cardell, Vic 114, 130
Carey, Hugh L. 190
Carey, William F. 41–42

Carnera, Primo 51–54, 58, 60, 149
Carpentier, Georges 25
Carter, Jimmy 101, 114, 127
Carter, Rubin "Hurricane" 154, 159, 164, 224
Casale, Guy 198
casino economics 5, 225, 229, 236, 238–239
Cassiani, Roque 251
Castellani, Rocky 109, 135, 138
Castellano, Tony 196
Castillio, Adolpho 238
Castillio, Chucho 178, 181
Castillo, Ruben 218
Castro, Jorge 239
Cauthen, Terrance 245
Cavanagh, Billy 76–77
Cayton, Bill 221
Cerdan, Marcel 101–102, 146–147
Certo, Al 216–217, 226
Cervantes, Antonio 191, 202, 228
Cesario, Johnny 109
Chacon, Bobby 188, 213, 215
Chambers, John Graham 9
champions: (1967) 165; (1991) 232–233
Charles, Ezzard 104–105, 113–114, 116, 119, 125–126, 128, 131, 166, 182
Charleston, Matthew 246
Charnley, Dave 140, 150
Charpentier, Patrick 253
Chávez, Julio César 5, **218**, 221, 224–226, 230, 232–233, 237–238, 242, 246
Checketts, Dave 242
Chestnut, Ike 139, 141
Chocolate, Kid (Eligio Sardinias Montalvo) 38, 45, 47, 50, 52–54, 65
Chong, Ralph 70
Christenberry, Robert K. 116–117, 120
Christie, Agatha 274
Churchill, Winston S. 250
Chuvalo, George 141, 161, 167, 174–175, 178
City Ring *see* Madison Square Garden Ring
Clancy, Gil 150, 202, 209
Clark, Howard 59
Classen, Willie "Macho" 204–206
Clay, Cassius 1, 4, 145, 148, 154–156, 159–161, **164**, 167–168, 174, 176, 179, 180; City Ring debut 151; *see also* Ali, Muhammad
Clay, Von 150
Clay-Bey, Lawrence 245
Cobb, Randall "Tex" 208
Cochrane, Freddie "Red" 83, 88, 92, 96, 100
Coetzee, Gerrie 215
Cohen, Alan N. 187, 189
Cokes, Curtis 154, 175, 178
Colan, Johnny 167
Cole, Al "Ice" 242, 263
Coley, Derrell 256
Collins, Billy "Irish," Jr. 213–214

Collins, Kathleen 248
Colonello, Italo 65
Comiskey, Patrick 74
Compo, Eddie 118
Conn, Billy 70–71, 74, 78–80, 82, 87, 99–100, 122
Conn, Mark 115, 171–172, 177
Connecticut casinos: Foxwoods 239; Mohegan Sun 263, 304*n*1
Cooke, Jack Kent 178–181
Cooney, Gerald "Gerry" 190, 196, 198, 200, **205**, 206–210
Cooper, Henry 161, 168
Corbett, James J. 14–17, 58
Corbett, Young III 70
Corea, Feliciano 246
Corrales, Diego 262
Corri, Pietro 42
Cortez, Joe 219, 225, 245, **276**
Costa, Carmelo "Chubby" 131, 134, 138
Costello, Billy (William Donald Castiglioni) 206
Costello, Frank 191
Cotto, Miguel 270–271, **276**, 304*n*11; last City Ring battle 271–273
Cotton, Charlie 139
Crabtree, Bobby 228
Craig, Dante 259
Crawford, Mickey 141
Cregan, Johnny 87
Crosby, Bing 169
Cruz, Angel 210–211
Cruz, Leonardo 202
Cuevas, Pepino 193
Curry, Bruce 196, 199
Curry, Donald 219, 222, 224
Czyz, Bobby 245

Da Cruz, Francisco Tomas 224
D'Amato, Cus 160, 220, 222
D'Ambrosio, Jerry 93
Dauthuille, Laurent 113
Davey, Chuck 118
Davilla, Roberto 174
Davis, Aaron "Superman" 228–229, 238
Davis, Al "Bummy" 68, 70, 73–74, 77, 83, 92–94, 96, 104
Davis, Howard, Jr. 190, 194, 205, 211, 226
Davis, Johnny 99
Davis, Teddy "Red Top" 128, 131
DeCola, Tony 138
De Foe, Johnny 65
De Grasse, Pete 45
de Jesús, Esteban 183, 188; death 228
DeJohn, Joey 108
DeJohn, Mike 141, 148
De La Hoya, Oscar 231, 236, 238–239, 240–242, 246, 251, 253–254, 256, 258, 260, 262, 265–266, 268, 270
Delaney, Jack 29–31, 36–38
deLeon, Manuel 227
Del Genio, Leonard 62, 65

Della, Petey 194
Del Valle, Lou 252
DeMarco, Anthony "Tony" 130, 132, 134–135, **275**
DeMarco, Paddy 101, 105, 107, 117, 127
Dempsey, William Harrison "Jack" 4–5, 21, **23**, 24–29, 31–32, 34–40, 46, 50, 53–54, 56–57, 61, 70, 79, 108, 113, 147, 170, 178, 190, 204, 215, 274
DePaula, Frank 171–172; mysterious death 173–174
DeShong, Andrea 248
Devere, Bob 27
Diaz, Antonio 258
Diaz, David 245
DiBase, Tony 138
DiBella, Lou 259–260
Dickson, Blaine 210
DiVeronica, Dick 144, **277**
DiVodi, Andrew 33
Dix, Madison 47
Dixon, George 69
Dokes, Michael 215, 223, 225–226, 229–230, 235–237, 252
Donald, Larry 246
Dong Kyun Yum 202
Donovan, Art 42, 46, 52, 54–55, 59, 65, 67–68, 71, 73, 76, 78–80, 93, 98
Dorfman, Jack 42
Dorsey, Troy 234
Douglas, Buster 229, 251, 255
Doyle, Benny 160
Doyle, Jimmy (James J. Delaney) 98, 102, 293n13
Dozier, Malik 208
Dublinsky, Harry 56
Dudas, Steve 62, 74
Duk Koo Kim 212
Duke, Johnny 86
Dundee, Angelo 176, 179–181, 202, **276**
Dundee, Chris 83
Dundee, Johnny 28, 33
Dundee, Vince 33, 36, 45–46, 48, 59, 70
Dunphy, Don 150, 163, 252
Dupas, Ralph 151
Durán, Roberto 1, 5, 181–184, 188–189, 199–203, 207, 213, 215, 228–229, 232, 246, 252
Durando, Ernie 122, 138
Durango, Tony "Kid" 184
duration champions 89
Durelle, Yvon 141
Duva, Dan 217, 239
Duva, Lou 218, 247–248
Dylan, Bob 224

Earp, Wyatt 17
Ebbets Field 17
Echevarria, Joe 77, 84, 227
Egan, Edward P.F. 116
Eisenhower, Dwight D. 132
Eleta, Carlos 182
Elliott, Christy 193

Elliott, Jimmy 11
Ellis, Jimmy 166–167, 173, 176, 184
Ellis, Romallis 240
Elorde, Gabriel "Falsh" 135, 163, 165
Enberg, Dick 196
Ennis, Jack 60
Epperson, Lee 126
Erdei, Zsolt 268
Erne, Frank 19
Escalera, Alfredo 200, 210
Esch, Eric "Butterbean" 242, 251
Escobar, Sixto 62
Esposito, Mike 33
Ettore, Al 63
Evangelista, Alfredo 196, 200
Evans, Billy 44

Fallen, Darren 259
Famechon, Ray 114
Farber, Mickey 74
Farnsworth, Wilton "Bill" 69
Farr, Tommy 64–65
Feldman, Lew 45, 48, 50
Felix, Barney 141
Feliz, Fernely 248
Felt, Irving 142, 187
Felt Forum opening 170–171
Felton, Lester 118
Ferguson, Charles 95
Ferguson, Vince 143
Fernandez, Antonio 95
Fernández, Florentino 143, 154, 160
Fernandez, Ignacio 42
Fernandez, Jorge 150
Fernandez, Jose 185, 195
Fernandez, Vilomar 188
Fichique, Kid 143
Fields, Jackie 62
Figueroa, Ruben 175
Finch, Bruce 214
Finkel, Shelly 218
Finnegan, Chris 183
Fiore, Carmine 118, 122, 126, 130
Firpo, Luis Ángel 27–28, 79
Fisher, Jimmy 135
Fitzsimmons, Robert **16**, 17, 236, 265
Flanagan, Glen 114
Flaubert, Gustave 231
Flores, Victor 113
Flowers, Tiger 31, 33
Floyd, Calrence 148
Flynn, Dan "Porky" 27
Flynn, Jim "Fireman" 26–27
Flynn, Leo P. 27
Foley, Zora 154, 161–162, 165–166, 177
Fontanna, Larry 96
Forbes, Eddie 36, 54
Forbes, Frank 115
Foreman, George 175, 178, 181, 184–188, 222, 224, 239, 241, 255, 263
Forgotten Rounds 33, 35, 38–39, 45–46, 47–48, 50, 53, 55, 59–60, 65, 70, 74, 77, 83–84, 87–88, 91,
93–94, 96, 100–101, 103–104, 107, 109, 113–114, 116–117, 120, 122, 127–128, 130–131, 134–135, 138, 140–141, 144, 148, 150, 153–154, 159, 178, 181, 196, 199–200, 251, 262, 268, 269–270
Forrest, Vernon 250, 255, 261–264, 266, 303n26
Foster, Bob 154, 170, **171**, 173, 183, 185, 187
Foster, George 228
Foster, Mac 178, 229
Foster, Todd 240
Foster, Vince 109
Fourie, Pierre 185
Fox, Billy 103, 105, 107, 146–147
Francis, Kid 38
Franconeri, Frank 88
Frank, Raul 261
Franklin, Jeff 229
Franklin, Matthew 196
Frayne, Ed 69
Frazer, Alfonso 183
Frazier, Jacqui 261
Frazier, Joe 164–**165**, 167, 170, 171, 173–177, 179–187, 195, 199, 237, 261; The Thrilla in Manilla 189
Frazier, Marvis **216**
Frazier, Ricky 251
Frias, Arturo 213
Friday Night Fights 136, 145–146, 158, 162, 253, 296n1
Friedkin, Bernie "Schoolboy" 68
Fuentes, Ramon 134
Fugazy, Humbert J. 41
Fullam, Frank 72, 92, 95, 103
Fuller, Sammy (Sabino Ferullo) 50–51, 56
Fullmer, Don 138, 149–151, 156, **275**
Fullmer, Gene 131–133, **135**–136, 139, 142, 144, 154, 162–163, 227; biography 137–138
Fullmer, Jay 138
Fumerelle, Rocky 150
Fusari, Charley 96, 104, 109, 112
Futch, Eddie 237, **276**; The Thrilla in Manilla 189

Gainer, Al 55
Gainer, Derek "Smoke" 252
Gainford, George 119
Galento, Domenico "Two Ton" Antonio **72**, 73, 76
Galíndez, Víctor 189, 191
Galvan, Martin 229
Gamache, Joey 256
Gannon, Joe 127
Gans, Joe 19–20, 69
Garafola, Gary 173–174
Garcia, Ceferino 62, 70, 74, 78
Garcia, Julio 198
Garcia, Nieves 252
Garcia, Ruby 84
Garza, Loreto 229
Gatti, Arturo 242–244, 246, 249, 251, 258, 263–264, 269, 302n19; weigh-in controversy 256–257

Gavilan, Kid (Gerardo Gonzalez) 101, **106**–107, 109–110, 114–115, 117, 127, 131, 147, 164, 227
Gelormino, Gino 227
Genovese, Gabriel 140
Giambra, Joey 134
Giardello, Joey (Carmine O. Tilelli) **121**, 122, 124, 128, 162, 164
Gibran, Kahlil 176
Gibson, Billy 34
Gibson, Truman, Jr. 147; list of believed controlled fighters 147
Gilmore, Patrick S. 11
Giosa, Eddie 109
Giovanelli, Patsy 96
Girgrah, Isra 251
Giuliani, Sammy 124
Gleason's Gym 17
Glick, Joe 33, 36, 43, 45, 62
Godih, Lahouari 148
Godoy, Arturo 76
Goins, Ed 255
Goldberg, Benny 98
Goldberg, Marvin 161
Golden Gloves 33, 54, 71–72, 75, 77, 82, 84, 93, 107, 127, 141, 156, 160, 168, 174, 190, 192, 206, 210, 215–216, 235
Goldman, Charlie 127
Goldstein, Ruby 43, 100, 103, 116–117, 119, 121, 125, 151, 153, 228
Golota, Andrew 231, 245–248, 267, **275**
Gomes, Harold 141
Gómez, Tommy 101
Gómez, Wilfredo 202, 210, 213
Gonzales, Tex 134
González, Jorge Luis 245–246
Gonzalez, Jose 156
González, Julio César 262, 268
Gonzalez, Manuel 163
Gonzalez, Mario 226
Gonzalez, Paul 215
Gooding, Gladys 98
Goodman, Bobby 238
Goodman, Jack 65
Goss, Sammy 185
Gould, Kenneth 240
Graham, Billy 105, 115, 122, 124, 129–131
Graham, Bushy (Angelo Geraci) 62
Grant, Bertram 139
Grant, Michael 242, 255, 257, 263
Graves, Jackie 98
Graziano, Rocky (Yhomas Rocco Barbella) 93–94, 97–98, 100–102, 109, 112, 114, 119, 227, 263; biography 95–96
Graziano, Tony **277**
Greaves, Wilfrid 138, 142, 162
Greb, Harry 5, 26, 32–33
Greco, Johnny 91, 94, 100
Green, Harold 93–95, 292n32
Green, Julio César 251
Green, Mitch "Blood" 221
Greene, Graham 41

Griffin, Corn 55
Griffin, Montel 246
Griffith, Emile 141, 143, 146–148, 150–155, 157, 163–166, 170, 175, 181–182, 188, 193, 196–197, 205
Griffiths, Gerald "Tuffy" 38
Grillo, Armadeo 44
Gross, Reggie 221
Grove, Calvin 226
Grove, Izzy (Eddie Poplick) 42–43
Guardado, Albert 245
Guerrero, Ray Chavez 195
Guido, Al 94
Guittierrez, Miguel 259
Gutierrez, Lupe 229
Gwin, Rudy 134–135
Gwinn, Donald 219

Haezel, Francis J. 142
Hagler, Marvelous Marvin 194, 201, **204**, 206, 214, 216–217, 219, 222–224, 260
Hairston, Gene 116
Hakkar, Morrade 265
Halimi, Alphonse 144
Hall, Richard 258
Halpern, Bobby 198
Hamas, Steve 55
Hamed, Prince Naseem 251, 255, 262
Hamia, Cherif 134
Hamilton, Gene 160
Hammond, Col. John S. 41
Hammond, Ned 7
Hamsho, Mustafa 216, 222–223, 301ch17n5
Hank, Henry 148, 154
Harada, Fighting 165, 173
Harding, Eric 258
Harmon, Derrick 262
Harrington, Stan 148
Harris, Maurice 255, 261
Harris, Percy 240
Harris, Ronnie 194
Harris, Roy 160
Harris, Wilbur Maurice 250
Hart, Garnet "Sugar" 138
Hart, Marvin 20
Harvey, Charley 78
Harvey, Len 46, 48
Hatcher, Gene 229
Hatton, Ricky 251
Haugen, Greg 229
Hearns, Tommy 201, 203, 207–208, 210, 219, 222–225, 232, 234
Heeney, Tom 36–37, 46
Helfand, Julius 131, 139
Hembrick, Anthony 240
Hemingway, Ernest 264
Hernandez, Carlos 252
Hicks, Lou 160
Hidalgo, Dario 172–173
Hidalgo, Juan 209
Hide, Herbie 246
Hill, Harry 12–13
Hill, Virgil 216
Hilton, Matthew 221
Hindenburg 61

Hinnant, Clarence 141
Hitler, Adolf 61
Hogan, Frank 139
Holiday, Philip 258
Hollis, Charles 227
Holmes, Keith 260
Holmes, Larry 5, 198, 200, 203, 206–208, 210, 214–215, 219, 221, 224–225, 235, 239, 250–251, 271, 303n5
Holyfield, Evander 5, 216–217, 222, 224, 226, 229–230, 232–233, 235–236, 238–239, 243, **245**–246, 252–254, 256–257, 264, 267, 270
Honeyghan, Lloyd 222
Hope, Bob 169
Hope, Maurice 208
Hopkins, Bernard 240, 250, 259–260, 262, 265–266, 268–270
Houk, Craig 246
Howard, Louis 216
Huertas, Benny 181
Huffaker, Marcel 238
Humez, Charles 133–134, 138
Humphreys, Joe 31, 34, 53–54
Hunsaker, Tunney 148, 168
Hunter, Billy 144, 148
Hutchinson, Andrew 259
Hutchinson, Joe 258
Hyer, Tom 8

Ichinose, Sad Sam 148
Impellittiere, Ray 63
Ingle, Paul 257
International Boxing Clubs (IBC) 109, 112, 117–120, 123–125, 127, 129, 132–133, 136–137, 139–142, 147
Isaac, Curtis 226
Ivy, Bobby 86

Jack, Beau 88–91, 93–94, 98, 100, 263, **275**
Jackson, Jesse 201
Jackson, John David 239
Jackson, Julian 235
Jackson, Phil 239
Jaco, Dave 220
Jacobs, Jim 221
Jacobs, Joe 42, 46, 50
Jacobs, Mike 56, 58–61, 63–64, 66, 68–69, 75–76, 79, 82–83, 85, 87, 92, 98, 101–104, 108–109, 122, 184; death 122
Jakubowski, Eric 257
Janiro, Tony 94, 104, 112, 147
Jannazzo, Izzy 62
Jeffries, James J. 17, 19–20
Jenkins, Johnny 148
Jenkins, Lew 74–77, 83
Jimenez, Nestor Carlos 202
Jofre, Eder 150, 154, 165
Johansson, Ingemar 143 143–144, 148–149
Johnson, Arthur 240
Johnson, Austin 208
Johnson, Billy 96

Index

Johnson, Dave "Big Foot" 206
Johnson, Glen 268–269
Johnson, Harold 125, 128, 131, 149, 150
Johnson, Jack 20, 24
Johnson, Kirk 264–265, 267
Johnson, Larry 44–45
Johnson, Marvin 196, 206
Johnston, Charley 106
Johnston, James J. 48, 54, 56, 59, 63, 184
Jones, Calvin 242
Jones, Danny 156
Jones, Doug 141, 143–144, 148, 150, 154–155, 161, 168, 170
Jones, Junior 229, 235–236, 238, *243*, 248–249, 251, 257–258
Jones, Nate 245
Jones, Ralph "Tiger" 120, 131, 134, 138
Jones, Robert Tyre "Bobby" 90
Jones, Roy, Jr. 234–236, 239–242, 248–250, 252, 258, 260, 262, 264–267
Jones, William "Gorilla" 42–43
Joppy, William 251–252, 260–261, 265, **276**
Jordan, Don 141, 146, 153
Joyce, Willie 94–95, 98
Juarez, Rocky 271
Judah, Zab 269; last City Ring battle 271–273, 304n14

Kalule, Ayub 209
Kane, Kevin "Kip" 219
Kansas, Rocky 37
Kaplan, Louis "Kid" 47, 62
Kaplan, Phil 38
Kates, Richie 191
Kearns, Jack 119, 147
Kellem, Roland 154
Kelley, Kevin 226, 229, 234, 236, 238–239, 251–252, 271, 301ch17n8
Kelly, Wayne 244, 247–248
Kemaci, Cemal 195
Kennedy, John F. 145, 155
Kennedy, Robert F. 169
Kenny, Jack 104
Kensett, George 7
Kenty, Hilmer 210
Kerwin, Gale 138
Kessler, Harry 118
Kettles, Art 184
Kidd, Terry Lee 208
Kimery, Dewey 65
King, Arthur 109
King, Don 187–188, 199, 202, 212, 215, 221, 254, 260
King, Martin Luther, Jr. 167, 169
Klem, Bill 44
Klick, Frankie 62
Klitschko, Vitali 264–266, 268–**269**, 304n6
Klitschko, Wladimir 257–258, 263, 270–271
Knoetze, Kallie 201–202
Koch, George 87

Krieger, Solly 47, 60, 65
Krumpe, Jack 215
Kushner, Cedric 263

La Barba, Fidel 45, 47, 62
Labarbara, Antone "Tony" 159
LaBua, Jackie 138
LaFalgio, George 113
Laguer, Victor 215
Laguna, Ismael 167, 172–173, 181
Lalonde, Donny "The Golden Boy" 223
Lamar, Henry 44
LaMotta, Giacobbe "Jake" 85–86, **88**, 89, 95–96, 98, 103–105, 114, 117, 120, 146–147, 163, 206, 227
LaMotta, Joey 96
Lampkin, Ray 189, 228
Lane, Garing 239
Lane, Ken 140, 143–144
Langlois, Pierre 124
Larkin, Tippy 73–74, 77, 88, 93, 104
LaRocco, George 36
Las Vegas migration 146, 219
Laskey, Art 55, 57
LaStarza, Roland 104, 107, 109–112, 120–121, 123, 127
Latzo, Pete 38, 45
Lausse, Eduardo 127, 131
Lawless, Bucky 45
Layne, Rex 113, 116–117
LeDoux, Scott 198, 208
Lee, Bruce 220
Leija, Jesse James 241–242, 256, 258
Léon, Genaro 236
Leonard, Benny 25, 51, 92
Leonard, Ray "Sugar" 5, 190, 197, 201–**202**, 205–207, 209–210, 214–215, 223–224, 230–233; biography 203–204; only MSG appearance 231–232
Leslie, Jock 106
Lesnevich, Gus 54, 84, 91, 98, 101–102, 104, 107, 110, 119
Levinsky, Battling 27, 47–48, 55
Levy, Lionel 121
Lewis, Butch 221
Lewis, Carlos "Panama" 213–214
Lewis, John Henry 55, 71
Lewis, Lennox **235**, 236, 238–239, 243, 245, 252–258, 261, 263–266, 268
Licata, Tony 189
Light, Billy 47
Limón, Rafael "Bazooka" 213
Lincoln, Amos 173
Lindbergh, Charles A. 33–34
Lindstrom, Freddy 44
Lipton, Ron 245
Liston, Sonny 144, 153, 156, 159–160, 164, 168, 173, 191
Lobianco, Johnny 183, 196
Locatelli, Cleto 53, 62
Lockridge, Rocky 226
Logan, George 145
Logart, Isaac 131, 134, 138–139, 150

Lomeli, Louie 229
Lomski, Leo 36
London, Jack 20
London Prize Ring Rules 8
Lopez, Danny 188, 206
López, Juan Antonio 202
Lopez, Raphael 211
López, Ricardo 251, 262, 303n25
Lopez, Tony 226, 230, 233
Loughran, Tommy 35, 36, 43, 47–48
Louis, Joe 56, 58, 60–61, 63–64, 66–67, 69–71, 73–76, 78–80, **81**, 82–85, 88, 92, 98–99, 101–105, 107–109, 113, 114, 116, 119, 122, 131, 187, 237, 300n15
Loy, Louie "Golden" 211
Lubbers, Rudi 185
Lyle, Ron 189, 208
Lynch, Vernon 154

Machen, Eddie 146, 151, 161
Machiavelli, Niccolo 98
Machon, Max 68
Madison Square 10
Madison Square Garden I 10–13
Madison Square Garden II **15**, 14–28
Madison Square Garden III 29–169; closing 169; event mix 35
Madison Square Garden IV 150, 158–159, 169–273; boxing department kayoed 238; opening 169–170
Madison Square Garden Bowl (Long Island City Bowl) 18, 49, 54, 55, 57–58, 64, 66
Madison Square Garden Centennial 203–204
Madison Square Garden Ring (City Ring), New York **277–278**; birth 29; components 278–279; debut 30–31; extension 47; firsts 30; lighting 50; post lights 75; ring adjustments (see Appendix II); ropes 156, 213; rounds 156, 212–213; storage area 275; training facility 167
Magnolia, Lou 44
Maldonado, Iggy 134
Maldonado, G.G. 198
Malignaggi, Paul 271
Maloney, Frank 239
Maloney, Jim 34
Mamby, Saoul 206, 225–226
Mancini, Ray 212–214, **275**, 300n26
Mandell, Sammy 37–38, 45
Manfredy, Angel 253
Manfro, Joey 93
Mann, Nathan 70, 78
Mantilla, Miguel 202
Marcel, Ernesto 183
Marciano, Rocky (Rocco F. Marchegiano) 4–5, 109, 111–112, 116–117, 120–123, 125, 130, 135, 170, 214, 274, 280; biography 126–127

Marcune, Pat 121
Marino, Marty 74, 83
Markson, Harry 105, 139, 142, 146, 165, 177, 183–184
Marotta, Eddie 113
Marquart, Billy 74
Marshall, Lloyd 98
Martin, Christy 248, 251–252, 266, **276**
Martin, Danny 104
Martin, Frankie "Chief Crazy Horse" 83
Martin, Leotis 167
Martin, Teddy 140
Martinez, Mario "Azabache" 218
Martinez, Miguel 157
Martinez, Vince 122, 139
Marullo, Tony 36
Maskaev, Oleg 248, 270, 274
Mason, Gary 267
Mathis, Buster 165, 170
Mathis, Buster, Jr. 241, 248
Matteoni, Dario 252
Matthews, Harry 116–117
Matthews, Len 144, 148
Matthews, Walter "Matty" 19
Mauriello, Tami 79, 83–85, 87, 88, 91, 93–94, 98, 101, 104, 293n20
Maxim, Joey (Giuseppe A. Berardinelli) 117, **119**–120, 125, 127, 143, 227
Maynard, Andrew 234
Mayorga, Ricardo 266, 268, 270
Mayweather, Floyd, Jr. 244, 250, 252, 255, 262, 269, 271–272
Mayweather, Roger 218, 271
McArdle, Tom 38, 41, 64
McAuliffe, Jack 16
McAvoy, Jock 60
McCall, Oliver 239, 241
McCallum, Mike 213, 224, 249, 300n21
McCline, Jameel 263, 267
McClure, Wilbert "Skeeter" 154, 158
McCoy, Young Kid 84
McCrory, Milton 219
McCrory, Steve 215
McDermott, Jimmy 171–172
McDowell, Lyle 242
McGirt, James "Buddy" 215, 217, 219, 222–224, **226**–227, 229, 232–233, 235–238, 302n14
McGovern, Terry 19, 23, 69
McGraw, Phil 37
McGrew, Darren 227
McGuigan, Barry 219
McIntire, Bobby 86
McKay, Jim 197
McKim, Mead & White 13, 21
McKinney, Kennedy 240, 251
McLarnin, Jimmy 5, 37–38, 43, 45, 47, 50, 54–57, 61–63, 75
McLaughlin, James P. 24
McMahon, Jess 37–38, 289ch4n7
McMurty, Pat 141
McNair, Jimmy 143
McNeeley, Peter 241

McNeeley, Tom, Jr. 141, 145, 198
McPartland, Billy 36, 38
McQuade, Sam 54
McTigue, Mike 31, 35–36
McVey, Jack 38
Mead, Margaret 155
Mead, Pete 108–109
Meade, Eddie 64
Medina, Manuel 263, 271
Meehan, Willie 27, 35
Melendez, David 173
Mercado, Bernardo 196, 198
Mercante, Arthur 138, 141, 144, 159, 172, 178–182, 183, 217, 258, **276**
Mercante, Arthur, Jr. 223, 225, 261, 265; last City Ring battle 271–273
Mercer, Ray 240, 245, 252, **275**
Merchant, Larry 196, **276**
Methot, Leo 96
Miceli, Joe 114, 120, 141
Mildenberger, Karl 167
Miller, Art 174
Miller, Ray 115, 119
Millett, Terron 263
Mims, Holly 224
Minaya, Juan 225
Minelli, Livio 118
Mitchell, Brian 233
Mitchell, Clinton 260
Miteff, Alex 139, 146
Molina, John John 258
Molineaux, Tom 71
Molnar, Gene 74
Monroe, Willie 204, 214
Monte, Joe 38, 42
Montes, Fernando 229
Montgomery, Bob 82–83, 89, 91–94, 98, 101, 104
Monzón, Carlos 178, 181–183, 189–190, 262
Moore, Archie (Archibald Lee Wright) 5, 98, 117, **123**, 125, 128–130, 135, 149, 151, 280
Moore, Davey 1, 144, 147, 157, 213
Moorer, Michael 239
Morales, Eduardo 253, 258
Morales, Érik 269, 271
Moran, Frank 24, 69
Morel, Eric 245, 251
Morgan, Kevin 211
Morgan, K.O. (Andrea Esposito) 33
Morgan, Tod (Albert Pilkingon) 36
Morris, Carl 27
Morrison, Tommy 229, 242–243
Mosley, Shane 250, 253, 257–258, 262–263, 266, 268–269
Moyer, Denny 141, 148, 152, 154, 227
Moyer, Phil 154
Mudgett, Clyde 198
Mueller, Peter 130
Mugabi, John 222–223, 230
Muhammad, Eddie Mustafa 218–219

Muhammad, Elijah 165
Muhammad, Herbert 165, 194
Muhammad, Matthew Saad 206
Muller, Hans 47
Muniz, Armando 189, 196
Murphy, Bob 113–114, 116–117
Muscato, Phil 98

Nápoles, José 175, 178, 189, 277
Nardico, Danny 117
Narvaez, Frank 154, 163
Navarro, José 259
Nazario, Juan 230
Negron, Carmelo 206
Nelson, Azumah 212–213, 235
Nelson, Oscar "Battling" 19–20, 69
Nesbit, Evelyn (Mrs. H.K. Shaw) 21
Neusel, Walter 55
New York City 17–18
New York State Joint Legislative Committee on Boxing 153
Newman, Randy 226
Newman, Rock 239, 247–248
Nielsen, Brian 250
Nieves, Peter 236, 238
Ninas, Arturo 248
Nixon, Mike 196
Nolan, Billy 23
Nonella, Andy 75
Noonan, Gregory F. 123
Norris, James D. 109–110, 119, 123, 125, 128, 135–137, 139, 142, 147, 182, 184, 294n18
Norris, Terry 230, 232–233
Norton, Ken 184–185, 188, 190, 194, 196, 200, 205, 207–**208**, 209–210
Nova, Lou 70, 72, 79–80, 88

Obelmejias, Fulgencio 223
Ocasio, Ossie 224
O'Grady, Sean 194–195, 210, 213
Olajide, Michael "The Silk" 223, 225
Olin, Bob 55, 71
Olivera, Tony 98
Oliveras, Rubén 175, 178, 182
Olson, Carl "Bobo" 119–121, 123, 133, 163
Olympics 160, 164–165, 168, 204, 218, 234–236, 244, 259, 270; 1984 boxing team 215–216; 1988 boxing team 240; 1996 boxing team 244–245; 2000 boxing team 259
Oma, Lee 94, 98, 116, 166
O'Melia, Brian 193
O'Neill, Bob 206
Oquendo, Angelo 171
Oquendo, Fres 264, 267
Ortega, Gaspar 128, **133**–135, 141–143, 146, 148, 151, 157, 159
Ortiz, Carlos 131, 141–144, 150, 165, 167; biography 140
Ortiz, Manuel 91, 98
Ortiz, Ruby 228
Otto, Young 96
Overlin, Ken 78–79, 83
Owens, Frank 223

Pacho, Bobby 62, 65
Pacquiao, Manny 266, 269, 271
Paduano, Donato 177
Páez, Jorge 226
Pagan, Pete 198
Page, Greg 206, 260
Page, Jerry 216
Palermo, Blinky 114, 147, 153, 191, 294n6
Palomino, Carlos 191, 193, 196, 202–203, 206
Panamanian division dominance 183
Papp, László 160
Paramount Theater opening 234
Paret, Benny 143, 147–148, 150, 155, 164; tragic death 152–153
Park Si-Hun 240
Parker, Jim 120
Parkey, Ricky 224
Pastor, Bob (Robert E. Pasternak) 54, 62–63, 78, 87
Pastrano, Willie 131, 162
Patterson, Floyd 4, 127–128, 135, 138, 143–144, 148–150, 153, 159–161, 167, 183, 190, 221, 223, 280
Patterson, Jackie 98
Patterson, Tracy Harris 223, 226, 242
Payne, Cecil 53
Payne, Jack 38
Pazienza, Vinny (Vinny Paz) 240
Pedroza, Eusebio 219
Pelkey, Arthur 27
Pellone, Tony 96, 104, 107, 109
Pena, Bobby 148
Pep, Willie (Guglielmo Papaleo) 1, 5, 84, **86**, 87–89, 91, 94, 96, 98, 101, 105–106, 108, 110, 112–113, 115–117, 120 121, 123–124, 131, 152, 170
Perez, Gino 214
Perez, Lulu 123–124, 128
Pérez, Pascual 135
Pérez, Raúl 120
Perez, Tony 212
Perlata, Joey 104
Perry, Aaron 93
Persol, Johnny 165–166, 171
Peter, Samuel 274
Petrolle, Billy 45, 47–48, 62
Phelan, Brig. Gen. John J. 54
Piccirillo, Michele 262
Pimental, Joe 59
Pinder, Enrique 183
Pinter, Lupe 213
Pinto, Kelson 270
Pires, Luis 181
Polite, Charley 208
Poll, Jesus 238
Porter, K.P. 223
Postaway, Hank 78
Powell, Wayne 260
Pratchett, Dwight 218
Prater, Tom 205
Price, Andy 195, 206
Priest, Al "Red" 103, 109
Pryor, Aaron 207, 213
Puller, Tim 248

Qawi, Dwight Muhammad 222, 224
Quarry, Jerry 167, 174–175, 177–178, 184–185, 187, 195
Quarry, Mike 175, 185, 198
Quartey, Ike 251
Quinones, Nestor 214
Quintana, Carlos 55, 62
Quiroga, Robert 233

Raging Bull 206
Raheem, Zahir 245
Rahman, Hasim 261, **266**–268
Rainone, Vinny 211–212
Ramírez, José Luis 221, 225, 229
Ramos, Cheto 221
Ran, Eddie 47
Randall, Ricky 240
Randolph, Leo 190, 205
Rangel, Eddie 235
Ranzany, Pete 206, 213
Ratford, Doug 105
Ravelo, Jerson 259
Ray, Johnny 70
Recht, Bill 179–182
Reeves, Jimmy 85
Reid, Al 69, 74
Reid, Chris 223
Reid, David 245, 255
Reif, Morris 98
Renault, Jack 27
Resto, Jose 211
Resto, Luis 213–214
Reynolds, Bernie 120
Richards, Pat 109
Rickard, George Lewis "Tex" 4, **18**, 19–21, 22–29, 31–38, 41–42, 58, 60, 69–70, 122, 150, 184; death 39–40
Riggio, Steve 95
Rinaldi, Giulio 149
Rindone, Joe 127
ring riots 77, 115, 163, 172–173, 188, 247
ring rules 8–9
Ringling, John 40
Risko, Eddie "Babe" 59–60, 70
Risko, Johnny 35–37, 42
Rivera, Wilce 74
Rivera, Wilfredo 258
Rizzo, Phil 128
Roberts, Danny 131, 140
Robinson, "Sugar" Ray (Walker Smith, Jr.) 5, 72,75, 77, 83, 87, **88**, 89–90, 96, 98, 100–102, 104, 115, 117, 119–121, 127, 129, 133, 135–139, 147, 154–156, 275, 285; adversaries of note and death 227–228; biography 84; first MSG feature 81; last MSG feature 151–152; retirement ceremony 163–164
Rocky 197
Rodak, Leo 62
Rodriguez, Juan F. 196
Rodriguez, Luis 147–148, 153–154, 156–159, 172–173, 175
Rodriguez, Mario 259

Rodriguez, Wilson 243–244
Rogers, Nat 87, 101, 108
Rojas, Refugio 209, 221
Rolden, Juan 224
Rollo, Pero 150
Romero, Orlando 214
Rone, Bradley 242
Roof Garden Murder 20–21
Rooney, Jimmy 113
Roosevelt, Franklin 51, 75, 78
Rosario, Edwin "Chapo" 209–210, 221, 224–226, 230, 251, 303n5
Rose, Lionel 173, 175
Rose, Mitchell 242
Rosenberg, Phil 163
Rosenbloom, Maxie "Slapsi" 38, 43–44, 46, 53, 55
Rosi, Paolo 140, 150, 154
Ross, Barney (Beryl David Rosofsky) 52–57, 62, 66, 142, 152, 182
Rossman, Mike 196
round adjustment 212–213
Routis, André 38–39
Rowan, Joey 131
Roxborough, John 61
Rubicini, Tommy 124
Ruddock, Donovan "Razor" 230
Ruffin, Bobby 91, 94
Ruiz, John 257, 265, 267, 269–270
Runyon, Damon 69
Russell, Roger 196
Ruth, George H. "Babe" 44, 227
Ryan, Dickie 251
Ryan, Johnny 107
Ryan, Paddy 11–13
Ryan, Tommy 19
Ryff, Frankie 133, 142

Saddler, Joe "Sandy" 96, 105–108, 112–113, 115–117, 120, 128, **131**, 135, 138
Salazar, Juan Pablo 238
Saldivar, Vicente 168
Salim, Farid 154, 159
Salo, Bruno 44
Sanchez, Jose "Cocoa" 194
Sánchez, Salvador 210, 212–213
Santana, Luis 229
Santarpi, Joe 206, 237
Santiago, Eduardo 188
Santiago, Marcial 209
Santos, Daniel 251
Santos, Wilson 248
Satterfield, Bob 116
Savarese, Lou 242, 248, 255
Savold, Lee 91, 107, 114, 119
Saxon, Eddie 59
Saxton, Johnny 107, 114, 118, 120, 127, 135
Scaff, Sammy 219
Scalfaro, Joey 38
Scalzo, Petey 74, 114
Schaff, Ernie 45–46, 48, 51–52
Schmeling, Max 4, 38, 42–44, 46–47, 49–50, 56, **60**, 61, 63–64, 66–68, 70, 83, 190, 201
Scholz, Gustav 124
Schopenhauer, Arthur 56

Schreck, Mike 20
Schulz, Axel 241
Schwartz, Arthur 112, 115
Schwartz, Rollie 190
Scott, Charley 143, 151
Scott, Phil 37, 44
Scypion, Wilford 204–205
Seabrooks, Kelvin 226
Seales, Ray 194
Sekyra, Joe 42
Seldon, Bruce 241, 243, 245
Senate Antitrust Investigation 146–147
Serrano, Sammy 211
Servo, Marty 81, 88, 100–101, 109, 112
Shade, Dave 27
Shain, Eva 196
Shank, Ruben "Cowboy" 102–103
Shannon, Robert 216
Shans, Cleo 91
Shapiro, Max 74, 81
Sharkey, Jack (Joseph Paul Zukauskas) 4, 34, 36–38, 40–44, 46, 48–50, *51*, 52, 63, 190
Sharkey, Jack, Jr. (Joseph Cervati) 70
Sharkey, William "Bill" 198, 201
Shavers, Ernie 184, 195–196, 200
Shaw, Harry K. 21
Shaw, Joe 172–173
Shaw, William "Billy" 38
Shor, Bernard "Toots" 193
Shuler, James 222
Siegel, Bugsy 191
Simon, Abe 85
Simpkins, Anthony 259
Sims, Eddie 63
Sinegal, John 223
Singer, Al 38, 42, 45, 48
Sirutis, Yustin 65
Slade, Jimmy 128
Slattery, Jimmy 35–36, 46
Smallwood, Hardy 134
Smith, Al 19
Smith, Ed "Gunboat" 26–27, 49
Smith, James "Bonecrusher" 222, 230, 236–237
Smith, Kevin 198
Smoger, Steve 262, 268
Snipes, Renaldo 210
Soose, Billy 79, 81, *82*, 83–84, 99
Sorrentino, Greg 198
Sosa, Merqui 227, 241–242, 246
Soto, Angelo 159
Soto, Pedro 193, 196, 199
Spallotta, Fernando 138
Speigal, Tommy 90
Spencer, Thad 167
Spinks, Cory 266, 269, 271
Spinks, Leon 190, 197, 199, 219, **275**
Spinks, Michael 190, 197, 205, 215, 218–219, 221, 224–225
Spoldi, Aldo 62
Squires, Johnny 38
Stanton, Larry 200
Starling, Marlon "Magic Man" **209**–212

Steele, Freddie 182
Steele, Richard 271
Stephaney, Greg 210
Steward, Emanuel 254, 267, 270, **276**
Stewart, Alex 226, 229–230
Stillman's Gym 70, 95, 298*ch*13*n*8
Stinson, Marv 199
Stolz, Allie 74, 83, 88, 93, 98, 101
Stracey, John 189, 191, 193
Strauss, Eduard 14
Strauss, Sol 102
Stribling, Young (William L. Stribling, Jr.) 36, 38, 41, 47
Stokes, Andrew
Stubbs, Reybon 134
Sugar, Bert **276**
Sulaimán, José 236
Sullivan, John L. *11*–13, 15–19, 58
Sullivan, Yankee 7–8
Summerhays, Gary 196
Supreme Court Decision 142

Tapia, Johnny 252, 263
Tarver, Antonio 245, 267–269, **276**
Tate, Bill 138
Tate, Frank 216, 234
Tate, John 199
Tate, Thomas 240
Taylor, Arnold 185
Taylor, Bud 45, 62
Taylor, Jermain 259, 269
Taylor, Meldrick 216–217, 226, 230, 233
Tei Ken, Joe 55
Telesco, David 258
television 80, 117–118, 136–137, 139, 143, 146, 150, 152, 154, 157, 165, 185–186, 196–197, 205, 209, 217, 238, 249, 252–253, 272; closed circuit (CCTV) 149, 177, 188–189, 210; color 124, 163; contracts 255; NYC 159; pay-for-view 173, 233–235
Terranova, Phil 96, 98
Terrell, Ernie 159, 161, 164–165, 167, 171
Terris, Danny 31
Terris, Sid 28, 38
Tessier, Andre 143
Thomas, Harry 70
Thompson, Federico 147, 153
Thornton, Tony 240
thumbless gloves 210–211
Tibbs, Tommy 144
Tiger, Dick (Richard Ihetu) 121, 143–144, 154, 162, 164–165, 171–172, 175, 228
Tillis, James "Quick" 216, 221
Tillman, Henry 216, 224, 230
Tilston, William 11
Tinley, Mike 219
Tomasello, Joe "Rocky" 128
Toney, James 235, 240, 264, **265**, 269
Toro, Pete 178
Torres, José "Chegüi" **160**–162, 175
Toweel, Willie 144

Townsend, Billy 53
Trammell, Jack 65
Trice, Tyrone 226
Trinidad, Felix "Tito" 251, 253–254, 256, **260**–262, 268–269
Tripp, Earl 190
Truman, Harry S. 95, 97
Trump, Donald J. 189, 225
Tua, David 257
Tubbs, Tony 222
Tucker, Tommy 78
Tucker, Tony 236, 238, 267
Tunney, Gene 4, **26**, 27, 29, 32–38, 40, 42–44, 137, 170, 190, 204
Turner, Don 257
Turner, Gil 131–132, 135, 138, 295*n*2
Turner, Johnny 198
Turpin, Randy 115, 120–123, 163, 228
Tyson, Michael "Mike" 5, 216, 219–**220**, 229–230, 235, 239, 241, 243, 245, 251, 257, 267, 280; arrest 232–233; prison release 240; youngest heavyweight champion 221–225

Usai, Giancarlo 205
Uzcudon, Paulino 35, 37, 43, 48, 50, 59

Vaca, Jorge 234, 240
Valdez, Adrian 259
Valdéz, Niño 128
Valdéz, Rodrigo 188
Valentine, Louis 72
Valuev, Nikolai 269–270
Vanderbilt, Cornelius **9**–10
Vanderbilt, William Kissam 11–12
Van Horn, Darrin 234
Vargas, Fernando 245, 260, 262
Varner, Claude 47
Vasquez, David 195
Vazquez, Wilfredo 251
Vega, Luis 204
Vejar, Chico 114, 117–118, 120–122, 129, 131
Venturi, Enrico 65, 145
Vera, Angel Herrera 218
Villa, Pancho 61
Villareal, Neto 154
Villemain, Robert 109, 117
Vingo, Carmine 111, 127
Vinson, Clarance 259
Viruet, Adolfo 200
Viscusi, Lou 105
Viserto, Andy 114, 118

Walcott, Jersey Joe (Arnold Cream) 101, 103–105, 113, 117, 119
Walheim, Donald 175
Walker, James J. 31, 40–41, 50; law 25
Walker, Mickey 46, 48, **49**, 50, 53
Walker, Moses 141
Walker, William "Billy" 96
Wallace, Coley 107, 128
Wallman, Herman "Hymie the Mink" 139, 296*n*15; stable of fighters 147

Walsh, Chris 259
Ward, Arch 192
Ward, Micky 262–264
Ward, Moses 138
Warhol, Andy 169
Warren, Earl 129
Warren, Frankie 226, 229
Waters, Troy 251
Watson, Jack 104, 112
Watt, Jim 210
Watts, Bobby 214
Weaver, Mike 203, 208, 216, 230
Webb, Jimmy 78
Weil, Armand "Al" 64, 75, 109, 126
Welling, Joe 25
Wells, Nick 198
Wells, Rhoshii 245
Welsh, Freddie 25
Wepner, Chuck 161, 173, 189, 205, **275**
Werblin, David A. "Sonny" 196, 199, 202, 215
Weston, Herald, Jr. 193, 195, 200, 210–211, 299n14
Whitaker, Lance 263
Whitaker, Pernell 5, 216–218, 229, 232–233, 236–238, 253–254
White, Jimmy 139

White, Stanford 14, 21
Willard, Jess 24, 27, 40, 69
Williams, Carl 210
Williams, Cleveland 144, 151
Williams, Dwight 217
Williams, Holman 98
Williams, Ike 94–95, 107, 109, 114, 130
Williams, Jeremy 255
Williams, Johnny 107
Williams, Ricardo, Jr. 259
Willis, Karl 246
Wills, Harry 29, 32, 40
Wilson, Malcolm 187
Wilson, Tug (Joseph Collins) 12
Winstone, Howard 168
Wirtz, Arthur 110, 119, 123, 137, 142, 294n18
Wise, Willy 258
Witherspoon, Tim 222, 237, 242, 245, 249, 302n36
Wooden, John 201
Woolf, Virginia 29
women's first professional match 248
Womer, Mutt 83
Woods, Clinton 268
Woods, Walter 65, 74

Wright, Chalky 69, 86–87, 98
Wright, Ted 154
Wright, Winky 268–269, **276**

Yankee Stadium 17, 32, 34, 37, 40–41, 43–45, 51, 58, 61, 64, 66, 72–73, 76, 80, 99, 100–101, 105, 109, 112–113, 119, 125–126, 129–130, 137, 143–144, 190, 254, 281
Yarosz, Teddy 70
Yirov, Vassily 251
Young, Jimmy 196, 208
Young, Paddy 113, 116, 122
Young, Terry 105, 107, 109, 118

Zalazar, Victor 156
Zale, Anthony (Anthony Florian Zaleski) 54, 79, 81–82, 84, 87, 91, 98–102, 182, 263
Zamora, Alfonso 196
Zarate, Carlos 196, 202
Zengaras, Geroge 83, 86, 90
Zimmer, Ken 242
Zivic, Fritzie 70, 76–77, 80–81, 83–85, 88, 91–92, 96, 227
Zulueta, Orlando 139
Zurita, Juan 64

www.ingramcontent.com/pod-product-compliance
Ingram Content Group UK Ltd.
Pitfield, Milton Keynes, MK11 3LW, UK
UKHW051850210426
5322IPUK00025B/650